TRANSLINGUISTICS

Translinguistics represents a powerful alternative to conventional paradigms of language such as bilingualism and code-switching, which assume the compartmentalization of different 'languages' into fixed and arbitrary boundaries. Translinguistics more accurately reflects the fluid use of linguistic and semiotic resources in diverse communities.

This ground-breaking volume showcases work from leading as well as emerging scholars in sociolinguistics and other language-oriented disciplines and collectively explores and aims to reconcile the distinction between 'innovation' and 'ordinariness' in translinguistics. Features of this book include:

- 18 chapters from 28 scholars, representing a range of academic disciplines and institutions from 11 countries around the world;
- research on understudied communities and geographic contexts, including those of Latin America, South Asia, and Central Asia;
- several chapters devoted to the diversity of communication in digital contexts.

Edited by two of the most innovative scholars in the field, *Translinguistics: Negotiating Innovation and Ordinariness* is essential reading for scholars and students interested in the question of multilingualism across a variety of subject areas.

Jerry Won Lee is an Associate Professor at the University of California, Irvine, USA.

Sender Dovchin is a Senior Research Fellow in the School of Education at Curtin University, Australia.

TRANSLINGUISTICS

Negotiating Innovation and Ordinariness

Edited by Jerry Won Lee and Sender Dovchin

Routledge
Taylor & Francis Group

LONDON AND NEW YORK

First published 2020
by Routledge
2 Park Square, Milton Park, Abingdon, Oxon OX14 4RN

and by Routledge
52 Vanderbilt Avenue, New York, NY 10017

Routledge is an imprint of the Taylor & Francis Group, an informa business

British Library Cataloguing-in-Publication Data
A catalogue record for this book is available from the British Library

Library of Congress Cataloging-in-Publication Data
Names: Lee, Jerry Won, editor. | Dovchin, Sender, editor.
Title: Translinguistics: negotiating innovation and ordinariness /
edited by Jerry Won Lee and Sender Dovchin.
Description: London; New York, NY: Routledge, 2019. |
Includes bibliographical references and index.
Identifiers: LCCN 2019028085 (print) | LCCN 2019028086 (ebook)
Subjects: LCSH: Multilingualism—Social aspects.
Classification: LCC P115.45 .T73 2019 (print) | LCC P115.45 (ebook) |
DDC 306.44/6—dc23
LC record available at https://lccn.loc.gov/2019028085
LC ebook record available at https://lccn.loc.gov/2019028086

ISBN: 978-1-138-32632-3 (hbk)
ISBN: 978-1-138-32633-0 (pbk)
ISBN: 978-0-429-44991-8 (ebk)

Typeset in Bembo
by codeMantra

CONTENTS

List of contributors   *viii*
Acknowledgements   *xii*

Introduction: negotiating innovation and ordinariness   1
Jerry Won Lee and Sender Dovchin

PART I
Translinguistics, space, and time   **7**

1 The mundanity of metrolingual practices   9
   Alastair Pennycook and Emi Otsuji

2 The ordinary semiotic landscape of an unordinary place:
   spatiotemporal disjunctures in Incheon's Chinatown   24
   Jerry Won Lee and Jackie Jia Lou

3 A language socialization account of translinguistic mudes   37
   Anna Ghimenton and Kathleen C. Riley

4 The ordinarization of translinguistic diversity in a
   'bilingual' city   49
   Claudio Scarvaglieri

5 Ordinary difference, extraordinary dispositions: sustaining
multilingualism in the writing classroom 61
Sara P. Alvarez and Eunjeong Lee

PART II
The in/visibility of translinguistics 73

6 Formatting online actions: #justsaying on Twitter 75
Jan Blommaert

7 The ordinariness of translinguistics in Indigenous Australia 90
Jill Vaughan

8 *Hablar portuñol é como respirar*: translanguaging and the
descent into the ordinary 104
Daniel N. Silva and Adriana Carvalho Lopes

9 Translanguaging as a pedagogical resource in
Italian primary schools: making visible the ordinariness of
multilingualism 115
Andrea Scibetta and Valentina Carbonara

10 Reimagining bilingualism in late modern Puerto
Rico: the 'ordinariness' of English language use among
Latino adolescents 130
Katherine Morales Lugo

11 The ordinariness of dialect translinguistics in an internally
diverse global-city diasporic community 146
Amelia Tseng

PART III
Translinguistics for whom? 161

12 The everyday politics of translingualism as transgressive
practice 163
Sender Dovchin and Suresh Canagarajah

13 Tranßcripting: playful subversion with Chinese characters 179
Li Wei and Zhu Hua

14 Transmultilingualism: a remix on translingual
communication 194
Shanleigh Roux and Quentin Williams

15 'Bad hombres', 'aloha snackbar', and 'le cuck': mock
translanguaging and the production of whiteness 206
Catherine Tebaldi

16 Invisible and ubiquitous: translinguistic practices in
metapragmatic discussions in an online English learning
community 217
Rayoung Song

17 On doing 'being ordinary': everyday acts of speakers' rights
in polylingual families in Ukraine 228
Alla V. Tovares

18 Ordinary English among Muslim communities in South
and Central Asia 241
Brook Bolander and Shaila Sultana

Index 255

CONTRIBUTORS

Sara P. Alvarez is an Assistant Professor in the Department of English at Queens College, City University of New York (CUNY), and 2018–2020 Cultivating New Voices (CNV) Fellow at the National Council of Teachers of English (NCTE). Sara's research focuses on the intersections and frictions between language, immigration, and race.

Jan Blommaert is a Professor of Language, Culture and Globalization and the Director of the Babylon Center at Tilburg University, the Netherlands. He also holds appointments at Ghent University and the University of the Western Cape. His work focuses on the effects of globalization in the online–offline nexus.

Brook Bolander is a Lecturer in Linguistics in the School of Languages, Literatures, Cultures and Linguistics at Monash University and an Honorary Assistant Professor at The University of Hong Kong. Her work focuses on language and transnationalism and digital discourse, with recent publications appearing in *Language in Society*, *Language Policy*, and *International Journal of the Sociology of Language*.

Suresh Canagarajah is the Edwin Erle Sparks Professor of Applied Linguistics, English, and Asian Studies at Penn State University. His forthcoming book is *Transnational Literacy Autobiographies as Translingual Writing* (Routledge, 2020).

Valentina Carbonara is a Postdoctoral Fellow at the University for Foreigners of Siena in Italy. She has experience in teaching in bilingual contexts as well as teacher education. Her research interests focus on early language education, bilingualism, and translanguaging.

Sender Dovchin is a Senior Research Fellow at the School of Education, Curtin University. She is also a Discovery Early Career Research Fellow of the

Australian Research Council. Her research interests are the sociolinguistics of globalization and the linguistic injustice among vulnerable youth groups worldwide. Her most recent books are *Language, Media and Globalization in the Periphery* (2018) by Routledge and *Popular Culture, Voice, and Linguistic Diversity: Young Adults On- and Offline* (2017) by Palgrave-Macmillan, co-authored with Alastair Pennycook and Shaila Sultana.

Anna Ghimenton is an Associate Professor at the Université Lumière Lyon 2 and conducts research at the *Dynamique du Langage* Centre, UMR 5596 (France). Her research interests concern bilingual development, social cognition, interaction, and socialization within the Romance context (Italy and France). Her work has been published in *International Journal of Bilingualism, Journal of Language Contact,* and *Linguistics.*

Eunjeong Lee is an Assistant Professor of English at Queens College, City University of New York. Her research interests include multilingual literacy practices, critical approaches to language and literacy learning and pedagogy, and language ideologies. Her work has appeared in *Journal of Multicultural Discourses, Crossing Divides,* and *Korean Englishes in Transnational Contexts.*

Jerry Won Lee is an Associate Professor at the University of California, Irvine. His publications include *The Politics of Translingualism: After Englishes* (Routledge, 2018).

Li Wei is the Chair of Applied Linguistics and Director of the UCL Centre for Applied Linguistics at University College London, UK. His research interests cover different aspects of bilingualism and multilingualism. He is a Fellow of Academy of Social Sciences, UK.

Adriana Carvalho Lopes is a professor of Applied Linguistics, Sociolinguistics and Language and Education at the Federal Rural University of Rio de Janeiro (UFRRJ) and at the Federal University of Rio de Janeiro (UFRJ). Her research interests concern language and education, African diaspora, translanguaging, and the relationship between language, politics, and education.

Jackie Jia Lou is a Lecturer in Sociolinguistics at Birkbeck College, University of London. Her research focuses on language, discourse, and social interaction in transnational and urban spaces. Her publications include *The Linguistic Landscape of Chinatown: A Sociolinguistic Ethnography* (Multilingual Matters, 2016).

Katherine Morales Lugo is a visiting professor of Sociolinguistics, Applied Linguistics, and English Language Education at the University of Puerto Rico, Mayagüez. Her research interests concern stylistic variation in relation to ideologies of language, social identities, class, and educational inequalities in bilingual contexts.

Emi Otsuji is a senior lecturer in International Studies and Education at the University of Technology Sydney and a visiting research scholar at the Institute of Asian Cultural Studies at International Christian University (ICU), Tokyo. She is currently working on a book project with Dr. Shinji Sato on the ecological approach to welfare linguistics and language education.

Alastair Pennycook is a Distinguished Professor of Language, Society and Education at the University of Technology Sydney and the author most recently, with Sinfree Makoni, of *Innovations and Challenges in Applied Linguistics from the Global South* (Routledge).

Kathleen C. Riley teaches anthropology at Rutgers University and has conducted research on language socialization, language ideologies, multilingualism, and foodways in French Polynesia, France, Vermont, Montreal, and New York City. She has published work in *Language and Communication* and *Journal of Linguistic Anthropology*, co-edited issues of *Anthropologie et Sociétés* and *Semiotic Review*, and co-authored *Food and Language: Discourses and Foodways across Cultures*.

Shanleigh Roux is a PhD candidate in the Linguistics Department at the University of the Western Cape. Her research interests include linguistic landscapes, virtual linguistic landscapes, and gender.

Claudio Scarvaglieri is an Assistant Professor at the Department for Translation, Interpreting and Communication at the University of Ghent. His research areas include societal multilingualism, language ideologies, and institutional communication.

Andrea Scibetta completed his PhD in Linguistics and Second Language Acquisition at the University for Foreigners of Siena (Italy) in 2017. He is currently a postdoctoral fellow at the University for Foreigners of Siena and has experience in Chinese language teaching and cultural mediation. His scientific activity mainly concerns pragmatics, second language acquisition, Chinese, and translanguaging as a pedagogy in multilingual schools.

Daniel N. Silva is a professor of Sociolinguistics, Pragmatics and Sociolinguistics at the Federal University of Santa Catarina (UFSC) and Federal University of Rio de Janeiro (UFRJ), Brazil. His research interests include mobility, circulation of discourses, violence in language, and hope. His edited volume, *Language and Violence: Pragmatic Perspectives*, was published in 2017 (John Benjamins Publishing).

Rayoung Song is a PhD candidate at the University of Massachusetts, Amherst. Her research explores informal language learning in online contexts as well as the relationships between identity and ideologies in multilingual settings.

Shaila Sultana is a Professor in the Department of English Language, Institute of Modern Languages, University of Dhaka, Bangladesh. Her recent publications include chapters in *Critical Inquiries in the Studies of Sociolinguistics of Globalization* (Multilingual Matters) and *Language and Culture on the Margins: Global/Local Interactions* (Routledge).

Catherine Tebaldi is a PhD candidate at the University of Massachusetts, Amherst. Her dissertation explores teachers' engagement with right-wing media and white identity politics.

Alla V. Tovares is an Associate Professor in the Department of English at Howard University in Washington, DC. Her current research focuses on language ideologies and digital communication. She is the co-author of *How to Write about the Media Today*; her recent articles have appeared in *World Englishes*, *Discourse & Society*, and *Multilingua*.

Amelia Tseng is an Assistant Professor of Linguistics and Spanish in World Languages and Cultures at American University and holds a Research Associate appointment at the Smithsonian Center for Folklife and Cultural Heritage. Her work focuses on language and identity in multilingual immigrant communities. Her recent work has appeared in *Text & Talk,* the *Routledge Handbook of Spanish in the Global City*, and the *Routledge Handbook of Migration and Language* (shortlisted for the British Association for Applied Linguistics 2018 Book Prize).

Jill Vaughan is a postdoctoral fellow with the Research Unit for Indigenous Language at the University of Melbourne, Australia. Her work in sociolinguistics and linguistic anthropology is concerned with multilingualism, contact, and variation in Indigenous languages of northern Australia, as well as language practices in the context of the Irish diaspora.

Quentin Williams is a Senior Lecturer in the Linguistics Department at the University of the Western Cape and a Research Fellow at the Centre for Multilingualism and Diversities Research (CMDR). He is currently writing a book on *Youth Multilingualism*.

Zhu Hua is a Professor of Educational Linguistics, School of Education, University of Birmingham and a Fellow of the Academy of Social Sciences, UK. Her main research interests span multilingual and intercultural communication and child language. Among her recent publications are *Exploring Intercultural Communication: Language in Action* (2019 Routledge, 2nd edition) and a special issue on multilingual, multisensory, and multimodal repertoires in corner shops, streets, and markets (*Social Semiotics* with Emi Otsuji and Alastair Pennycook).

ACKNOWLEDGEMENTS

We would first like to thank Danuta Gabrys and Eva Vetter, editors of the *International Journal of Multilingualism*, for the opportunity to guest-edit a special issue of their journal on 'the ordinariness of translinguistics'. Six of the chapters in this volume derive from that special issue (see Permissions). We also would like to thank our team of contributors for producing such excellent work for that special issue and for this present volume. We thank the anonymous reviewers for the effort and expertise that they have contributed, without which it would be impossible to maintain the high standards demanded by peer-reviewed books. Further, we would like to thank Allison Dziuba for her indispensable editorial work along the way, and Cheryth Dai for her help with editing the figures throughout the book. Finally, we would like to thank Angeline Hernandez for her help editing the cover image, representing a visualization of the simultaneity of that which is both ordinary and not.

This work was made possible by funding from the University of California, Irvine Humanities Commons, in particular, the Individual Research Grant and the Faculty Publication Support Grant—thank you so much to Julia Lupton and Amanda Swain for your ongoing support. This work was also supported by the Australian Research Council (ARC) [grant number DE180100118] and the Japan Society for the Promotion of Science [grant number 17K13504].

Permissions

Six of the chapters in this volume represent edited versions of the following articles, which initially appeared as part of a special issue of the *International Journal of Multilingualism* on 'the ordinariness of translinguistics', guest-edited by Sender Dovchin and Jerry Won Lee:

1. Blommaert, J. (2019). Formatting online actions: #justsaying on Twitter. *International Journal of Multilingualism*, *16*(2), 112–126.

2. Canagarajah, S. & Dovchin, S. (2019). The everyday politics of translingualism as a resistant practice. *International Journal of Multilingualism, 16*(2), 127–144.
3. Li Wei & Zhu Hua. (2019). Tranßcripting: Playful subversion with Chinese characters. *International Journal of Multilingualism, 16*(2), 145–161.
4. Bolander, B. & Sultana, S. (2019). Ordinary English amongst Muslim communities in South and Central Asia. *International Journal of Multilingualism, 16*(2), 162–174.
5. Pennycook, A. & Otsuji, E. (2019). Mundane metrolingualism. *International Journal of Multilingualism, 16*(2), 175–186.
6. Lee, J. W. & Lou, J. J. (2019). The ordinary semiotic landscape of an unordinary place. Spatiotemporal disjunctures in Incheon's Chinatown. *International Journal of Multilingualism, 16*(2), 187–203.

Reprinted by permission of the publisher, Taylor & Francis Ltd, www.tandfonline.com.

INTRODUCTION

Negotiating innovation and ordinariness

Jerry Won Lee and Sender Dovchin

Translinguistics reflects an orientation in sociolinguistics that foregrounds three realities:

1. boundaries between 'languages' are the result of ideological invention and sedimentation;
2. such boundaries do not unilaterally guide communication in everyday contexts; and
3. communication itself is not limited to 'language' insofar as interlocutors draw on a range of semiotic and spatial repertoires.

Translinguistics has been discussed in the form of 'new' concepts such as translingual practice (Canagarajah, 2013), translanguaging (Li Wei, 2018), transidioma (Jacquemet, 2005), polylingualism (Jørgensen & Møller, 2014), truncated multilingualism (Blommaert, 2010), metrolingualism (Pennycook & Otsuji, 2015), transglossia (Sultana, Dovchin, & Pennycook, 2015), and linguascapes (Dovchin, 2018). However, there is simultaneously nothing 'new' about translinguistics. For instance, that individuals in diverse contexts draw on resources from multiple languages to the extent that the very notion of 'language' is put into crisis is not a remarkable observation for those familiar with such communicative realities.

The practice of reframing 'ordinary' phenomena as 'innovative' and through terminology that is 'innovative' reflects, at first glance, the pervasive and long-standing problem of intellectual fetishism. In Said's (1979) classic *Orientalism*, western writers are critiqued for their practice of discursively constructing the 'Orient' as a place that is chronically distant, foreign, exotic, and overall fascinating. Not dissimilar to how Orientalist writers find themselves drawn to the appeal of seeking and encountering a 'visionary alternative' (Said, 1979, p. 185), the translinguistic turn in sociolinguistics suggests that scholars of language too oftentimes find themselves seeking what might be called a 'linguistic alternative'.

In some strands of scholarship within translinguistics, we are bearing witness to a fetishization of translinguistics, celebrating and privileging the creativity of such 'innovative' language practices despite the simultaneous insistence that they are indeed 'quite normal' (Blommaert, 2013), 'unremarkable' (Pennycook & Otsuji, 2015), 'ordinary' (Dovchin, 2018), 'basic' (Androutsopoulos, 2007), 'everyday' (Leppänen et al., 2009), and by no means a 'new' phenomenon (Canagarajah, 2013; see also Khubchandani, 1997; Makoni, 2002; May, 2014; Sugiharto, 2015). This 'turn' in sociolinguistics, then, demands that we ask ourselves what would scholarship look like if, instead of seeking out and documenting exotic social phenomenon and cultural practices, we reflected more thoroughly on the fundamental assumptions driving our tendency to construct something as *not ordinary* in the first place? And further, why is that which has always been 'ordinary' dependent on 'innovative' terminology in order to be legible and recognized as legitimate in its own right (Lee, 2017)?

Translinguistics is a reminder that the very desire or need to remark on a particular social phenomenon, including a sociolinguistic phenomenon, derives from the evaluation or presumption of it as 'unordinary'. Deleuze's (1986) conceptualization of 'any-space-whatever' is useful in our collective effort to make sense of the exaltation of the 'ordinary' into the status of the 'unordinary'. As Abbas (2008) describes, 'any-space-whatever is the polar opposite of an actualized "state of things", which is always framed in terms of spatiotemporal-psychic coordinates that we tacitly understand. By contrast, any-space-whatever involves a series of deframings' (p. 245). Abbas (2008) offers an illustration of any-space-whatever through the opening sequence of Wong Kar Wai's film *Chungking Express*, which features the unusual strategy of presenting a 'skyline of nondescript rooftops on nondescript residential buildings' instead of a more conventional 'establishment shot' with recognizable landmarks of the setting, Hong Kong (p. 245). Paek (2016) offers a complementary understanding of the interdependency of actuality (the 'state of things') and representation (e.g., through framings and deframings). Through an analysis of paintings of street signage in Seoul, it is argued that attention to seemingly minor details such as the size and alignment of text can lead to productive inquiry into the 'tension between the ordinary and extraordinary' (Paek, 2016, p. 232). By examining paintings of the Seoul cityscape by French artist Manoël Pillard, Paek (2016) argues that the artistic rendition of something mundane such as street signage, which is familiar and ordinary to most Koreans, is able to be viewed 'anew with wonder and curiosity' (p. 234). In short, a given 'state of things' is always subject to representational contingency, which is itself understood at the moment of encounter with a 'different' representation of an otherwise familiar object or phenomenon.

Insofar as any-space-whatever enables us to make sense of how a 'nondescript' representation is achievable through the strategy of 'deframing', it simultaneously allows us to recognize how the 'ordinary' becomes reframed as 'unordinary' through the representational politics of sociolinguistic inquiry. To reiterate, there is nothing inherently 'innovative' about translinguistics. Instead, sedimented understandings of the boundaries, both horizontal (what are the boundaries between one language and another?) and vertical (what are the capacities of language? Or what constitutes language or not in the first place?), of language predicate the characterization of translinguistics as 'innovative'.

This volume is based on the premise that the analytic potential of translinguistics can be enhanced by accounting for the simultaneities of innovation (e.g., the 'creativity' of code-meshing) and ordinariness. In other words, how can something such as a given linguistic practice or phenomenon be constructed by the researcher as 'innovative' (frequently as a euphemism for peculiar, exotic, eccentric, unconventional, or strange) but understood simultaneously by the research subject as everyday, quotidian, basic, mundane, unremarkable, banal, and, quite simply, *ordinary*?

This book is divided into three parts: (1) Translinguistics, space, and time; (2) The in/visibility of translinguistics; and (3) Translinguistics for whom? The chapters in Part I seek to examine how translinguistics is practiced not only across space but in tandem with space, resulting in unexpected reconfigurations of public space. These chapters focus on contexts as diverse as a Bangladeshi-run mixed-goods store in Tokyo (Pennycook & Otsuji); the Chinatown in Incheon, South Korea (Lee & Lou); French-and-Italian-speaking immigrant families in France, and French-and-English-speaking youth in Montréal, Canada (Ghimenton & Riley); the 'bilingual' city of Biel/Bienne, Switzerland (Scarvaglieri); and classroom contexts in New York, Kentucky, and Texas (Alvarez & Lee). They seek to understand the interrelationships between translinguistics and time, especially in the context of the differentiation between innovation and ordinariness.

In Part II, 'The in/visibility of translinguistics', the authors collectively ask the following: How is translinguistics rendered as ordinary in different contexts? Chapters focus on hashtags in social media discourse (Blommaert); Indigenous language practices in Maningrida, Australia (Vaughan); along with language ideologies as they pertain to speakers of Portuñol across Brazil and Uruguay (Silva & Lopes); multilingual immigrant youth in Italy (Scibetta & Carbonara); bilingual youth in Puerto Rico (Morales); and the Spanish-speaking Latino community of Washington, DC (Tseng). The chapters enable us to understand the ways in which ordinariness is rendered not only visible, as innovation, but also as invisible, along with the ideological ramifications of such renderings.

Part III is guided by the overarching question of 'Translinguistics for whom'? The chapters include inquiries into translingual practice among youth in Mongolia and Japan (Canagarajah & Dovchin); the hybridization of Chinese characters with diverse scriptal and semiotic systems (Li Wei & Zhu Hua); digital 'transmultilingual' practice in South Africa (Roux & Williams); the appropriation of translinguistics by the US far-right in digital contexts (Tebaldi); metapragmatic reflections on online translingual practice among Koreans (Song) and on polylanguaging in Ukraine (Tovares); and English practices among Muslim communities in South and Central Asia (Bolander & Sultana). The chapters in this section invite us to consider the following: Who practices translinguistics? For whom is it innovative, and for whom is it ordinary? What are the political outcomes of translinguistics? Who is, or is not, allowed to practice translinguistics as a result of various political or ideological factors?

The 18 chapters in this volume remind us that, as scholars tasked with uncovering 'new' information, whether 'new' language practices or new interpretations of familiar phenomena, we are faced with something of a paradox. We are left with the challenge of reconciling the scholarly imperative to investigate that which is 'unique' or 'noteworthy' when the object or phenomenon of inquiry is anything but, yet imagined as such through an etic, institutional locus. Put differently, how does one inquire into the sociolinguistics of globalization in tandem with the recognition that translinguistics is inevitably an inquiry into the sociolinguistics of the *ordinary*?

The authors attempt to answer some of these questions by engaging directly with various conceptual dimensions of ordinariness and innovation in translinguistics. This being said, this volume does not presume to offer a panacea to the human tendency to fetishize 'difference', which is, arguably, itself an 'ordinary' phenomenon, nor does it hope to present a definitive approach to foregrounding the question of ordinariness in the context of sociolinguistic plurality and diversity. We offer, nonetheless and less ambitiously, some potential ways forward to a critical understanding of the ordinariness of translinguistics (Dovchin & Lee, 2019).

References

Abbas, A. (2008). Faking globalization. In A. Huyssen (Ed.), *Other cities, other worlds: Urban imaginaries in a globalizing age* (pp. 243–266). Durham, NC: Duke University Press.

Androutsopoulos, J. (2007). Bilingualism in the mass media and on the Internet. In M. Heller (Ed.), *Bilingualism: A social approach* (pp. 207–232). Basingstoke, UK: Palgrave Macmillan.

Blommaert, J. (2010). *The sociolinguistics of globalization*. Cambridge, UK: Cambridge University Press.

Blommaert, J. (2013). *Ethnography, superdiversity and linguistic landscapes: Chronicles of complexity*. Bristol, UK: Multilingual Matters.

Canagarajah, S. (2013). *Translingual practice: Global Englishes and cosmopolitan relations*. London, UK: Routledge.

Deleuze, G. (1986). *Cinema I: The movement-image*. Trans. H. Tomlinson & B. Habberjam. Minneapolis: University of Minnesota Press.

Dovchin, S. (2018). *Language, media and globalization in the periphery*. New York, NY: Routledge.

Dovchin, S., & Lee J. W. (2019). Introduction to special issue: 'The ordinariness of Translinguistics'. *International Journal of Multilingualism, 16*(2), 105–111.

Jacquemet, M. (2005). Transidiomatic practices: Language and power in the age of globalization. *Language & Communication, 25*(3), 257–277.

Jørgensen, J. N., & Møller, J. S. (2014). Polylingualism and languaging. In C. Leung & B. V. Street (Eds.), *The Routledge companion to English studies* (pp. 67–83). London, UK: Routledge.

Khubchandani, L. M. (1997). *Revisualizing boundaries: A plurilingual ethos.* Thousand Oaks, CA: Sage.

Lee, J. W. (2017). *The politics of translingualism: After Englishes.* New York, NY: Routledge.

Leppänen, S., Pitkänen-Huhta, A., Piirainen Marsh, A., Nikula, T., & Peuronen, S. (2009). Young people's translocal new media uses: A multiperspective analysis of language choice and heteroglossia. *Journal of Computer-Mediated Communication, 14*(4), 1080–1107.

Li Wei. (2018). Translanguaging as a practical theory of language. *Applied Linguistics, 39*(1), 9–30.

Makoni, S. (2002). From misinvention to disinvention: An approach to multilingualism. In S. Makoni, G. Smitherman, A. F. Ball, & A. K. Spears (Eds.), *Black linguistics: Language, society, and politics in Africa and the Americas* (pp. 132–153). London, UK: Routledge.

May, S. (2014). Introducing the 'multilingual turn'. In S. May (Ed.), *The multilingual turn: Implications for SLA, TESOL, and bilingual education* (pp. 1–7). London, UK: Routledge.

Paek, S. (2016). Asian city as affective space: Commercial signs and mood in the paintings of Manoël Pillard. *Verge: Studies in Global Asias, 2*(1), 222–249.

Pennycook, A., & Otsuji, E. (2015). *Metrolingualism: Language in the city.* London, UK: Routledge.

Said, E. (1979). *Orientalism.* New York, NY: Vintage.

Sugiharto, S. (2015). The multilingual turn in applied linguistics? A perspective from the periphery. *International Journal of Applied Linguistics, 25*(3), 414–421.

Sultana, S., Dovchin, S., & Pennycook, A. (2015). Transglossic language practices of young adults in Bangladesh and Mongolia. *International Journal of Multilingualism, 12*(1), 93–108.

PART I

Translinguistics, space, and time

1

THE MUNDANITY OF METROLINGUAL PRACTICES

Alastair Pennycook and Emi Otsuji

Introduction

This chapter addresses two particular aspects of spatiotemporal entanglements: everydayness and simultaneity. This is in part a response to the challenge posed by the editors of this volume to readdress questions of ordinariness and diversity. This is also a response to Kramsch's (2018) warning that the contemporary focus on space that has emerged in translingual metaphors and ideas such as *spatial repertoires* (Canagarajah, 2018; Pennycook & Otsuji, 2014, 2015a) runs the danger of omitting time, history, and subjectivity from our understanding: 'in any trans-perspective on language theories and practices, a post-structuralist focus on Space must be supplemented by a post-modern concern with Time' (Kramsch, 2018, p. 114). It is to bring time and space—everydayness and worldliness—together and to show how time and space are entangled in everyday simultaneous activities that we have here adopted the term *mundane metrolingualism*, drawing, on the one hand, on our prior work on metrolingualism (Otsuji & Pennycook, 2010; Pennycook & Otsuji, 2015a) and, on the other, a focus on ordinariness. Alongside its slightly negative implications—not just ordinary but also tedious, prosaic, and repetitive—the term *mundane* carries (via its historical connections to contemporary *le monde*) a sense of worldliness, or terrestrial and material relations. It is these two senses that we wish to convey here: the quotidian and the worldly. *Worldliness* itself has been used (Pennycook, 1994; Said, 1983) to steer a path between notions of language as an idealized abstract system disconnected from its surroundings, and a materialist view of language that reduces it to circumstantial determinations. For us the challenge was how to describe everyday urban multilingualism as part of the fabric of ordinary lives in the city.

A focus on the 'ordinariness of diversity' derives from Higgins[1] and Coen's (2000) argument that what humans have in common are differences: 'diversity is the given reality of human social action' (p. 15). From 'the drag queens, who sought tolerance for their lifestyles' to the *discapacitados* (disabled) 'who were seeking new opportunities', their 'expressions of agency and transgression were geared to the very specific details of their everyday lives … They wanted people to know how ordinary they were, at least in their own context' (Higgins & Coen, 2000, p. 18). Wessendorf (2014) makes a related point in her study of Hackney, London, arguing that 'visible differences along ethnic, racial and religious lines do not matter in the daily doings of a super-diverse neighbourhood' and 'these differences have become commonplace' (p. 173). By proposing notions such as *corner-shop cosmopolitanism, banal cosmopolitanism, pragmatic-being-together*, or *unpanicked multiculturalism*, Noble (2009) similarly draws attention to the ordinariness of diversity in everyday life.

The notion of the ordinariness of diversity, therefore, is important from several standpoints: it is a political statement that insists that in order for there to be a 'world in which the ordinariness of diversity is the "normative" reality, the vast inequalities in the material wealth' of the world must be challenged and changed (Higgins & Coen, 2000, p. 276). Ethnographic praxis, from this point of view, is about understanding how difference is lived in particular contexts, and how that difference can be changed from marginalized practice only by addressing broader forms of social and economic inequality. It is also an epistemological statement aimed at the narrow and normative understandings of life on which much of the social sciences have been based: the ways in which linguistic diversity has been understood, for example, has been premised on assumptions of normative homogeneity derived from particular class, educational, and ethnic backgrounds. It is also a statement about human experience: difference—social, cultural, sexual, economic, racial—rather than commonality is the core experience of human life; diversity is not exotic or something that others have, but key to all experience.

The political and the epistemological come together in many related ways of considering the ordinariness of diversity. The cluster of terms that have been variously used to address these concerns—everyday, unremarkable, mundane, grassroots, from below—all seek to raise similar questions, though from slightly different perspectives. An emphasis on the everyday, as Semi et al. (2009) note, directs attention toward 'the situated character of social relations and practices' as a 'set of ordinary, banal, constitutive, incorporated practices' (p. 69). The idea of practices invokes repeated social and linguistic activities (Pennycook, 2010) as well as the ways in which social activity is organized and embodied (Bourdieu, 1977). As de Certeau (1984) argued in *The practice of everyday life*, 'everyday practices, "ways of operating" or doing things' should no longer 'appear as merely the obscure background of social activity' but rather should be seen as a key to understanding social and cultural relations (p. xi). This is not, he insists, a return to the individual, but a focus on how everyday practices such as walking, talking, reading, writing, dwelling, or cooking are organized. Similarly, Schatzki (2002) points to the key understanding that social life is 'plied by a range of such practices as negotiation practices, political practices, cooking practices, banking practices, recreation practices, religious practices, and educational practices' (p. 70). For Wise and Velayutham (2009), everyday multiculturalism is understood as 'a grounded approach to looking at the *everyday practice* and lived experience of diversity in specific situations and spaces of encounter' (p. 3).

A focus on the everyday is by no means, therefore, a celebration of everydayness; any critical project—and this is evidently part of Bourdieu's focus on *habitus*—also involves a critical analysis of the ways in which social structure is not just an abstract structuring of inequality but a lived and embodied experience of social difference. Everyday diversity is not only, therefore, concerned with temporal dimensions as part of repeated everyday practice but also with the non-elite world of struggle for recognition. The notion 'from below', for example, has been used in various domains, including linguistic landscapes (Coupland, 2010) to distinguish between official, state-sanctioned signage (from above) and signs put up by ordinary people (from below). Although the above/below distinction is a considerably simplified approach to social order, it draws attention to every-day or ordinary linguistic practices that are often different from, if not overtly in opposition to, state-sanctioned language policies. This framing has also been used to distinguish between 'English from above'—'the promotion of English by the hegemonic culture for purposes of "international communication"'—and 'English from below'—'the informal—active or passive—use of English as an expression of subcultural identity and style' (Preisler, 1999, p. 259). The distinction further occurs in work that attempts to capture the difference between the dominant and homogenizing forces of globalization 'from above' and globalization 'from below', which is 'structured by flows of people, goods, information, and capital among different production centres and marketplaces which, in turn, are the nodes of the non-hegemonic world-system' (Ribeiro, 2012, p. 223).

This focus is echoed in work on *grassroots* language and literacy. Khubchandani (1983) draws our attention to the distinction between officially regulated and described modes of plurilingualism (*mandatory bilingualism*) as they occur in educational and legislative frameworks and the ordinary plurilingualism of everyday language use (*grassroots* pluralism). Mohanty (2013) maintains this distinction between 'grassroots multilingualism'—the use of 'multiple languages in daily life transactions' (p. 307)—and the language policies of Indian education. Blommaert's (2008) *grassroots literacy* is similarly concerned with 'writing performed by people who are not fully inserted into elite economies of information, language and literacy' (p. 7). These terms all draw attention to everyday social practices compared to mandated, regulated, and standardized visions (Pennycook, 2016). This is about the material, the ordinary, and the tangible. It is also about the counter-hegemonic, about resistance, struggle for recognition, and opposition to dominant or normative indications of language.

All these terms—grassroots, from below, everyday, ordinary—draw attention to repeated social practices that are frequently not in accordance with, and often in opposition to, the sanctioned, top-down, hegemonic world of normative action and beliefs. Drawing on prior work (Pennycook, 2007) that developed the notion of *worldliness* in relation to Mignolo's (2000) understanding of *mundialización/ mondialisation* (as opposed to *globalización/globalisation*) as 'local histories *in* which global histories are enacted or where they have to be adapted, adopted, transformed, and rearticulated' (p. 278), we here take up the notion of *mundanity* to emphasize local contexts of everyday diversity. This is akin to Santos' (2018) understanding of 'bottom-up subaltern cosmopolitanism' with its focus on decolonization and 'intercultural translation' (p. 8). Our own interests in the everyday entanglements of language, people, place, and objects have, thus, brought us to the notion of *mundane metrolingualism* as a way of dealing with the ordinary assemblages of people, objects, and linguistic resources in a Bangladeshi-owned corner store in Tokyo.

Comings and goings in *Isuramu Yokochō*

The Bangladeshi-owned corner shop we focus on in this chapter is located in *Isuramu Yokochō* (Islamic alley) in *Hyakunin-chō* in Shinjuku (Tokyo). As we have argued elsewhere (Pennycook & Otsuji, 2017), Bangladeshi-run stores in different parts of the world may contain similar goods, from imported riverine fish, spice, and rice to locally grown (and slightly different) vegetables (onions and bitter melon), as well as items such as phone and SIM cards. Yet, when these objects encounter the variable affordances of these different shops, they enter into new and momentary sets of relationships that we call *semiotic assemblages* (Pennycook, 2017; Pennycook & Otsuji, 2017). The notion of assemblages as 'ad hoc groupings of diverse elements, of vibrant materials of all sorts' (Bennett, 2010, p. 23) allows for an understanding of how different trajectories of people, semiotic resources, and objects meet at particular moments and places. To this understanding of the vibrancy of matter, the importance of things (goat meat, phone and SIM cards, Henna hair coloring products), and the significance of place as the geographical context for the entanglement of physical, social, and economic processes, we can then reintroduce our interest in the key question of ordinary diversity.

Varis (2017) challenges the idea of diversity based on a normative reaction to the unexpected and proposes making diversity a default position in order to 'un-exoticise at least some of what is considered institutionally as "unusual"' (p. 37). While at first glance the focus on an 'unusual' shop in Tokyo may appear to exoticize diversity, our interest by contrast is in the ordinariness of the available and sedimented human and non-human resources (linguistic, material, sensory, and other semiotic resources that make up the spatial repertoire) that have emerged from the repeated practices related to this particular place. Everydayness we therefore see in spatiotemporal terms formed by a 'set of ordinary, banal, constitutive, incorporated practices' (Semi et al., 2009, p. 69). For customers, *halal* matters, familiar foods such as plain *paratha* (flatbread) and *shaki* (cow stomach) matter, the price matters, and the location matters (especially being on the next block from the local mosque). These are crucial elements for their ordinary lives and activities. While such linguistic and multimodal landscapes, smellscapes (Pennycook & Otsuji, 2015b) or activities occurring in the shop might generally be seen as foreign, unfamiliar, and exotic from certain Japanese or other viewpoints, they are not unusual from the viewpoint of diversity from below, from the everyday perspectives of the participants.

People who shop here are both diverse (in terms of linguistic and ethnic backgrounds) and dispersed (traveling from different parts of Tokyo to stock up on food and various products). The produce, shops, and more generally *Isuramu Yokochō* (and beyond) invite diverse multilingual and multisensory engagements and experiences—not only different ways of speaking but also different people, different clothes, different smells, and different goods. Thus, for example, as a tall, bearded male customer of Pakistani background—wearing a blue woolen hat— who is shopping with his Thai wife (they shop here regularly every fortnight), chats with *Shachō* (the shop owner) in English, Japanese, and Urdu while they are packing a large suitcase (it is quite common for regular customers to arrive with various kinds of wheeled bags to accommodate a variety of goods) with frozen chicken from Brazil, plain paratha (flatbread), canned mackerel, frozen sausages, and other produce (see Figure 1.1). *Shachō* asks in Urdu 'Lahore mein saare aadmi aise tall figure hota hai? (are all the men in Lahore this tall?)'. A Nigerian man, newly married to a Japanese woman, lists his purchases in Yoruba (*iyan*, pounded yam; *shaki*, cow stomach; *ponmo*, cow skin), Hausa (*garri*, cassava flour), and

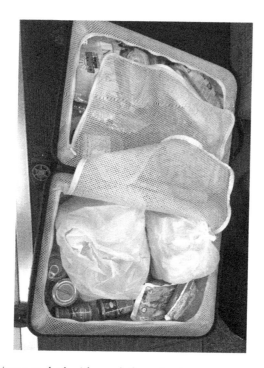

FIGURE 1.1 A suitcase packed with goods from the shop.

English (semolina powder, hard chicken, and skin-off frozen goat meat; the latter a compromise for his Japanese wife who does not like the strong smell of the skin).

For others who come to the shop, this is not just an ordinary or regular day's shopping: for the Japanese woman with two small children who lives in the neighborhood but reports 'Kankō gatera nozoite mitan desu (I checked this place out as an excursion)', seeking ingredients for her curry (ghee, coconuts, dried curry leaves, and frozen green peppers) from a handwritten shopping list, or the Italian-speaking Swiss/Korean couple (recently relocated from Switzerland to Tokyo) checking out certain goods on their way back from their shopping trip to the neighboring Korean precinct, this has been a rather novel experience, though the shop assistants have seen these multilingual, multipurposed excursions many times before. When the cooking ingredients purchased at the shop are not part of their common kitchen repertoires and the visit to the shop is not part of their routinized activities (though might become so), their activities nonetheless become part of the ordinary diversity of the shop. For others, however, there is nothing much out of the ordinary here as they seek out goods that to them are ordinary (though harder to find in Tokyo). We need, therefore, to account for multiple levels and perceptions of diversity as different types of people (along class, ethnic, and gendered lines) interact in this space. Diversity and ordinariness are diversely perceived.

The particular aspect of these everyday interactions that we draw attention to in this chapter is the expanded and interlocking spatiotemporal dimension produced by the use of mobile technologies within the daily activities of shopping, with an emphasis particularly on the simultaneity of entangled activities. The recent proliferation of digital technologies, particularly mobile phones, has meant that a different type of spatiotemporal entanglement has become part of our everyday life (Pink et al., 2018; Pink & Leder Mackley, 2013). Besides being a sales product neatly displayed in the glass showcase behind the cash counter, the presence of mobile phones is conspicuous in the shop: they are used for shopping lists, as a source of music and videos (through headphones), for timekeeping, and as a communicative or information-gathering tool. They also enable people to connect with other social spaces. Table 1.1 is an example of how simultaneous activities occur across space and time and how work, home, leisure, and play become entangled in new ways.

It is early evening during Ramadan and two shop assistants (SA1 and SA2) and the shop manager are taking turns to attend to customers, who are coming in waves. Two customers of Bangladeshi background are in the shop: a regular customer (RC) and a newcomer (NC). Before the excerpt, SA1 has been answering the RC's questions about SIM cards while simultaneously browsing his mobile phone to find the live stream match between Bangladesh and New Zealand at the 2017 International Cricket Council Champions Trophy in England and Wales. It is only after RC leaves and the other customer (NC) takes his position at the counter that SA1 manages to connect to the live stream site. SA1 ushers NC to the cash register side of the counter (from the other end of the counter near the

FIGURE 1.2 Fixing the mobile phone by the counter.

glass case where SIM cards and mobile phones are stored) and sets the mobile phone above the cash register at eye level (see Figure 1.2). He takes a plastic bag from the wall behind him (without looking, he knows exactly where to stretch his arm to reach them) and packs the noodles without raising his eyes from the phone screen (Figure 1.3).

There are ways in which some of this is not, strictly speaking, everyday activity: SA1's white *taqiyah* (cap) is for him a sign of Ramadan (he does not normally wear one otherwise); there are fewer customers than usual before dusk during the holy month; it is NC's first visit to the shop; and the Champions Trophy is only held every four years. The sounds of motorbikes from the front street, however, the frozen chicken on sale, spice smells, a mundane exchange over the price of chicken, as well as SA1's Bangla slang are very much part of the everyday life of this store, while other aspects (particularly those linked to Ramadan) are part of a longer cycle of ordinary activity. In their study of the entangled everyday relationships between the world of mobile media, people, and spaces associated with work and play, Pink et al. (2018) argue that the boundaries between work and home have become less conspicuous, resulting in a shift from sites of 'compartmentalization' to 'entanglement'.

Like one of the participants in their study 'weav(ing) in and out of work/ leisure/relaxation' (p. 35), SA1 provides carefree (slang) commentary as if watching the cricket game in a more private space, cursing the weather and the players, insulting the location (Wales) as 'shuorer bacha' (son of a pig) and 'baaler desh' (pubic hair country) in line 1, while simultaneously carrying out his usual task as a shop assistant, packing products, and serving a customer 'on

TABLE 1.1 Interaction in a Bangladeshi shop in Shinjuku (Tokyo)

SA1: Shop assistant 1; SA2: Shop assistant 2; NC: New customer; Plain: Bangla; *Italics: Japanese* (translation in brackets).

1. SA1: naa ... oije brishti shuru hoya gese ... khela shuru na hoite brishti hoya shuru hoya gese ... shuorer baccha ei baaler desh a khela falaise.
(noo ... see it has already started raining ... it has started raining even before the match started ... son of a pig. they have set the match in a bloody country like this[a]

2. NC: [laughs]

3. SA1: tirish run diya laise ... koi over e? (they have already given away thirty runs ... in how many overs?)
[SA1 takes the plastic bag. Sound of a message on the shared shop mobile phone. Figure 1.3]

4. SA1: chaeer over e. chaeer-choi chobbish__shaitaish ball e tirish run koira falaise
(in 4 overs. 4 times 6, 24 ... they have already scored 30 runs in 27 balls)
[NC looking toward the freezer: Figure 1.4]
[SA2 calling out *irasshaimase* (welcome) to attract customers outside the entrance]

5. NC: eita ki boro pack gula nai na? (you don't have the bigger packets, do you?)
[throughout the interaction, together with the English narration from the cricket game, SA2's voice calling *irasshaimase*, the rustling sounds of plastic bags, sounds of incoming text messages on another shop phone, and motor bikes on the street out front can be heard.]

6. SA1: na. (no.)

7. NC: murgi. Ak keji: ... khola? (Chicken ... 1 kg ... open ones?)

8. SA1: ak keji tinsho.ponchas. (1 kg is 350)

9. NC: tinta na charta? (three or four?{chicken})

10. SA1: nods
[NC hand gesture signaling confusion: Figure 1.5]

11. SA1: charta noisho ... charta noisho ... (four pieces are 900)
[SA1 shakes his head]

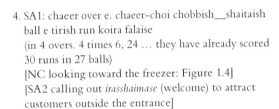

12. SA1: tinta noisho. akta share tinsho. (three of them are 900 in total {3 pcs chicken} and one is 350)

[English narration (Indian accent) from the cricket game: … 'finished a game yesterday, had a meeting delayed, up at 5:30 this morning on the M4 {motorway from London to Cardiff} … maybe once the game goes though we'll see more of the reactions to the after effect…']

[NC takes his mobile phone out and checks the time: Figure 1.6]
[SA1 sits and adjusts the position of the mobile phone]
[sound of text message on the shared mobile phone]
[NC takes the wallet out and passes a bank note to SA1 after finding out that he does not have enough change]

13. SA1: [talking to himself about cricket] Mashrafee … baro run khaya laiche … choi … chaeer … egaro run khaya laise … sha:la shuorer baccha. (Mashrafee {a Bangladeshi cricketer} has wasted big runs … six … four … eleven runs have been wasted … stupid idiot)

---

a In Turns 1 and 13, a literal translation of 'baal' would be 'pubic hair'. In Turn 1 it has been translated as 'bloody' and as 'stupid' in line 13 where it is used with 'shala' (brother-in-law), which can also mean stupid.

the side'. While NC is undoubtedly amused by SA1's derogatory remarks and gives a small laugh in line 2, NC is still in a shopping frame of mind, looking in the direction of the freezer where sales-of-the-day products—frozen chicken—are stored, and makes inquiries about the product and its price. Still gazing at the mobile phone, SA1 answers NC's inquiries halfheartedly, causing confusion by not providing the information about the price of three or four chicken pieces (line 9), which is then corrected incorrectly in line 11 'charta noisho… charta noisho…(four pieces are 900)' and then again correctly after shaking his head 'tinta noisho. Akta share tinsho. (three of them are 900 in total and one is three fifty)'. Giving up on the idea of purchasing chicken, NC checks the time on his mobile phone and takes out his wallet to pay, while SA1 continues his derogatory commentary.

In their paper on interactions in a 'Polish Shop' in London, Zhu Hua, Li Wei, and Lyons (2017) describe a similar interaction between the shop assistant, who is looking at her mobile phone, and a customer, in terms of a 'face-to-face communicative zone at the counter and the other digital communicative zone to which the mobile serves as a gateway' (p. 426). Drawing on these insights, we prefer to look at this not in terms of two interlocking communicative zones but rather as one semiotic assemblage. This interaction brings together watching cricket (a common activity even if this particular tournament is held only every four years) with serving a customer (who is new to the shop), a 'live' stream (where the mediatized action actually occurs a few seconds after the original) and a live interaction (which is delayed by the cricket), a rainy early morning in Cardiff and a warm evening in Tokyo, discussion of a drive down the M4, and a motorbike passing in the street. The mobile phone that enables this is not simply a medium of entertainment, but part of the process by which people entangle the lines between work and pleasure and 'make everyday environments in ongoing ways at the interface between work and home' (Pink et al., 2018, p. 34). This process of making everyday environments by bringing time and space—everydayness and worldliness—together is part of what we call *mundane metrolingualism*. These spatiotemporal entanglements are the everyday assemblages made possible by mobile technologies as chicken, noodles, and talk about prices come together with commentary, cricket, and metacommentary.

Mobile assemblages of concurrent space

The next excerpt also shows how a mobile phone not only allows for but is also a part of everyday spatiotemporal entanglements or 'throwntogetherness' (Massey, 1994) where 'a here-and-now (itself drawing on a history and a geography of thens and theres)' and 'human and nonhuman' are negotiated (p. 140). In this second excerpt, a customer (C) is looking to buy a particular type of dried fish (and other products), using his mobile phone to check on the suitability of the product. The excerpt in Table 1.2 starts when SA1 urges SA2 to bring another type of dried, smoked fish from the back of the shop (two other types of dried fish, one from Japan and the other from Africa, had already been rejected so this time he tries smoked fish).

In this excerpt we see an early evening assemblage of people (a customer of West African background, Bangladeshi shop assistants) and objects (mobile phones, fish, plastic bags, frozen goat meat), an expanded spatial repertoire made possible by the use of the mobile phone, various sensory effects (sounds, smells), and the particular linguistic resources made possible by the simultaneity of these everyday activities. Following SA1's instruction, when SA2 brought C a package of dried, smoked fish, C was at first hopeful that he had found the right fish: '*on dirait ça, c'est ce qu'il vient de me montrer là* (it seems like it, that's what he has just shown me)'. He takes and sends a photo but it turns out this is not the right fish. Parallel to C's endeavor, SA1 shows him all the possible fish he could think of (including Japanese semi-dried *Sukimi tara*, a type of cod) and SA2 goes back and forth between the counter and the back corner where the dried fish is stocked.

TABLE 1.2 Interaction in a Bangladeshi shop in Shinjuku (Tokyo)

SA1: Shop assistant 1, a younger brosther; SA2: Shop assistant 2, an older brother; C: Customer; SA3: a shop assistant; Bangla: **Bold**; English: Plain; French: *Italics*; unknown: ***Bold Italics*** (translation in brackets)

1. C: ah no. not this one. she said not this one
   [C returns the fish]
   [SA1 makes a phone call from his mobile phone on speaker mode to SA3]

2. SA1 to SA2: **oije boroda lon taile.** smoked fish **boroda den.** (give that big one in that case. give me the bigger smoked fish.) **oije boroda ano. boroda ano.** (bring the big one. bring the big one.)

3. C: *allo.* **OK**. [to the phone and keeps the line on hold]
   [SA1's call was picked up by SA3]

4. SA3: hello:
   SA1 [to the phone]: **ak case american___ loya ahen toh.** (bring one case of American___)

5. SA3: **a: achha** (okay)
   [SA1 finishes the phone conversation]
   SA1 to C: may be this one better not small fish.
   [SA2 brings the dried smoked fish, SA1 points to the fish: Figure 1.7]

6. C: [goes back to the phone] *ah? allo? il faut regarder ton portable. On dirait ça, c'est ce qu'il vient de me montrer là. attends je prends un photo. je vais t'envoyer.* don't worry. ***da da da da.*** (hello? you have to look at your phone. it seems like it, that's what he has just shown me. hang on I'll take a photo. I'll send it to you. don't worry da da da da da).
   [C takes a photo of the smoked fish: Figure 1.8]

7. C: [into phone: Figure 1.9] *qu'est-ce qu'il a fait, hein? ... il faut regarder.* [unclear] *en haut.* (What did he do, eh? you have to look. [unclear] at the top)
   [waiting for his partner's response]

8. C: *allo? c'est pas ça? ah.* **OK.** (Hello? It's not that? Oh, OK.)
   [SA1 turns around and takes plastic bags from the wall behind him]

9. C: not this one [to SA1] [laughs] no not this one

10. SA1: [pointing behind customer] easy to [the rustling sounds from opening the plastic bag which overlaps with the word here] dry fish.
    [C looks behind]

11. C: [to SA2] No. not this one. [to phone] **OK.** *je suis désolé alors. désolé.* **bye.** (Ok. well then I'm sorry. sorry.)
    [C finishes the phone call and removes the ear phones: Figure 1.10]
    [SA1 continues packing three packs of skin-on frozen goat meat and semolina powder]

There are considerable resources—linguistic, artefactual, spatial, technological, personal—at play here as they try to find a suitable fish. Meanwhile, in a parallel space, C's interlocutor remains connected to the shop while C talks with shop assistants, takes a photo (Figure 1.10), and waits for SA2 to bring the 'Smoked fish **boroda den** (bigger smoked fish)'.

Compared to the excerpt in Table 1.1, the mobile phone plays an important though very different spatiotemporal role in this assemblage. Thurlow and Mroczek (2011) point to 'a certain materiality to communication technologies' (p. xxiv) as 'prosthetic extensions of people's everyday lives' (p. xxv). This is in line with the argument we have made elsewhere about spatial repertoires (Pennycook & Otsuji 2014), distributed agency, and assembling artifacts (Pennycook & Otsuji 2017). From this point of view, mobile devices are more than mediating devices: it is not only that 'everyday relations and worlds are mediated' by digital mobile media (Pink et al., 2018, p. 27) but rather that they become players in the production of simultaneous and everyday spatial repertoires. Technologies are indeed 'embedded in complex ways into the banal practices of everyday life' (Thurlow & Mroczek, 2011, pp. xxiv–xxv), and thus become part of the dynamics of the production of an assemblage. Understanding these interactions in terms of concurrent assemblages helps to foreground the ways that the fish (various smoked and dried options), the phones (connecting people in different ways), and the French linguistic resources (to verify the fish) create a particular dynamic alongside other common aspects of this spatial repertoire.

Conclusion: Mundane metrolingualism

Mundane metrolingualism suggests that ordinariness emerges from the repeated and sedimented practices of humans and non-human actors (material objects) involved in the sets of activities related to particular places. Mundane metrolingualism, therefore, offers an epistemological shift in understanding diversity by thinking in terms of local assemblages or entanglements rather than diversity premised on either normative, demographic accounts of human diversity or more interactive accounts of superdiversity. Everyday mundane diversity is a multilingual, multimodal, and multisensory spatial entanglement, a worldliness of material relations that may be tied to a particular place but also happening simultaneously in different spaces. By focusing in this account on assembling artifacts (Pennycook & Otsuji, 2017) as much as languages or people, we have been trying to open up an alternative way of thinking that focuses not so much on language use in particular contexts—as if languages preexist their instantiation in particular places, transported to and fro by mobile language containers (people)—but rather on the ways in which particular assemblages of objects, linguistic resources, and places come together.

By focusing on two particular spatiotemporal themes, everydayness and simultaneity, we have sought to shed light on the ways in which different activities, conversations, and artifacts may be brought together through mobile technologies. Thus, a cricket game in Cardiff watched on a mobile device in a shop in Tokyo, or a conversation (in French) between a customer and another person about the right kind of fish to buy, point to the ways that simultaneous activities are entangled in the ordinary practices of the everyday. This has particular implications for how we understand assemblages and the role of mobile devices. For us, they are not so much mediating devices as part of the dynamics of an assemblage, expanding the possibilities of concurrent spatial repertoires.

Note

1 Part of our interest in Higgins and Coen's argument also derived from one of us [AP] being taken round Oaxaca in Mexico by the late Michael Higgins, introducing the ordinary people he worked with and explaining how diversity worked on the streets, in bars, in communities on the outskirts. This is where Michael lived and did his work as part of an *ethnographic praxis* that sought to understand and change the lives of the 'urban poor, *discapacitados*, transvestites' (2000, p. 17) and other marginalized communities in the city.

References

Bennett, J. (2010). *Vibrant matter: A political ecology of things.* Durham, NC: Duke University Press.

Blommaert, J. (2008). *Grassroots literacy: Writing, identity and voice in Central Africa.* London, UK: Routledge.

Bourdieu, P. (1977). *Outline of a theory of practice. (Esquisse d'une théorie de la pratique* (1972))* Cambridge, UK: Cambridge University Press.

Canagarajah, A. S. (2018). Translingual practice as spatial repertoires: Expanding the paradigm beyond structuralist orientations. *Applied Linguistics, 39*(1), 31–54.

Coupland, N. (2010). Welsh linguistic landscapes 'from above' and 'from below'. In A. Jaworski & C. Thurlow (Eds.), *Semiotic landscapes: Language, image, space* (pp. 77–101). London, UK: Continuum.

De Certeau, M. (1984). *The practice of everyday life* (S. Rendall, Trans.). Berkeley: University of California Press.

Higgins, M., & Coen, T. (2000). *Streets, bedrooms and patios: The ordinariness of diversity in urban Oaxaca: Ethnographic portraits of the urban poor, transvestites, discapacitados, and other popular cultures.* Austin: University of Texas Press.

Khubchandani, L. (1983). *Plural languages, plural cultures: Communication, identity and socio-political change in contemporary India.* Honolulu: University of Hawai'i Press.

Kramsch, C. (2018). Trans-spatial utopias. *Applied Linguistics, 39*(1), 108–115.

Massey, D. (1994). *Space, place and gender.* Cambridge, UK: Polity Press.

Mignolo, W. D. (2000). *Local histories/global designs: Coloniality, subaltern knowledges, and border thinking.* Princeton, NJ: Princeton University Press.

Mohanty, A. (2013). Multilingual education in India: Overcoming the language barrier and the burden of the double divide. In P. Siemund, I. Gogolin, M. Schulz, & J. Davydova (Eds.), *Multilingualism and language diversity in urban areas: Acquisition, identities, space, education* (pp. 305–326). Amsterdam, The Netherlands: John Benjamins.

Noble, G. (2009). Everyday cosmopolitanism and the labour of intercultural community. In A. Wise & S. Velayutham (Eds.), *Everyday multiculturalism* (pp. 46–65). Basingstoke, UK: Palgrave Macmillan.

Otsuji, E., & Pennycook, A. (2010). Metrolingualism: Fixity, fluidity and language in flux. *International Journal of Multilingualism, 7*(3), 240–254.

Pennycook, A. (1994). *The cultural politics of English as an international language.* Harlow, UK: Longman.

Pennycook, A. (2007). *Global Englishes and transcultural flows.* London, UK: Routledge.

Pennycook, A. (2010). *Language as a local practice.* London, UK: Routledge.

Pennycook, A. (2016). Language policy and local practices. In O. García & N. Flores (Eds.), *The Oxford handbook of language and society* (pp. 125–140). Oxford, UK: Oxford University Press.

Pennycook, A. (2017). Translanguaging and semiotic assemblages. *International Journal of Multilingualism, 14*(3), 269–282.

Pennycook, A., & Otsuji, E. (2014). Metrolingual multitasking and spatial repertoires: 'Pizza mo two minutes coming'. *Journal of Sociolinguistics, 18*(2), 161–184.

Pennycook, A., & Otsuji, E. (2015a). *Metrolingualism: Language in the city.* London, UK: Routledge.

Pennycook, A., & Otsuji, E (2015b). Making Scents of the Landscape. *Linguistic Landscape, 1*(3), 191–212.

Pennycook, A. & Otsuji, E. (2017). Fish, phone cards and semiotic assemblages in two Bangladeshi shops in Sydney and Tokyo. *Social Semiotics, 27*(4), 434–450.

Pink, S., Hjorth, L., Horst, H., Nettheim, J., & Bell, G. (2018). Digital work and play: Mobile technologies and new ways of feeling at home. *European Journal of Cultural Studies, 21*(1), 26–38.

Pink, S. & Leder Mackley, K. (2013). Saturated and situated: Rethinking media in everyday life. *Media, Culture & Society, 35*(6), 677–691.

Preisler, B. (1999). Functions and forms of English in a European EFL country. In T. Bex & R. Watts (Eds.), *Standard English: The widening debate* (pp. 239–267). London, UK: Routledge.

Ribeiro, G. L. (2012). Conclusion: Globalization from below and the non-hegemonic world-system. In G. Mathews, G. L. Ribeiro, & C. A. Vega (Eds.), *Globalization from below: The world's other economy* (pp. 221–235), London, UK: Routledge.

Said, E. (1983). *The world, the text and the critic.* Cambridge, MA: Harvard University Press.

Santos, B. de S. (2018). *The end of the cognitive empire: The coming of age of epistemologies of the South.* Durham, NC: Duke University Press.

Semi, G., Colombo, E., Camozzi, I., & Frisina, A. (2009). Practices of difference: Analysing multiculturalism in everyday life. In A. Wise & S. Velayutham (Eds.), *Everyday multiculturalism* (pp. 66–84). Houndmills, UK: Palgrave Macmillan.

Schatzki, T. R. (2002). *The site of the social: A philosophical account of the constitution of social life and change.* University Park: The Pennsylvania State University Press.

Thurlow, C., & Mroczek, K. (2011). Introduction: Fresh perspectives on new media sociolinguistics. In C. Thurlow & K. Mroczek (Eds.), *Digital discourse: Language in the new media* (pp. xix–xliv). Oxford, UK: Oxford University Press.

Varis, P. (2017). Superdiverse times and places: Media, mobility, conjunctures and structures of feeling. In K. Arnaut, M. Sif Karrebæk, M. Spotti, & J. Blommaert (Eds.), *Engaging superdiversity: Recombining spaces, times and language practices* (pp. 25–46). Bristol, UK: Multilingual Matters.

Wessendorf, S. (2014). *Commonplace diversity: Social relations in a super-diverse context*. London, UK: Palgrave Macmillan.

Wise, A., & Velayutham, S. (Eds.). (2009). *Everyday multiculturalism*. Houndmills, UK: Palgrave Macmillan.

Zhu Hua, Li Wei, & Lyons, A. (2017). Polish shop(ping) as Translanguaging Space. *Social Semiotics, 27*(4), 411–433.

2

THE ORDINARY SEMIOTIC LANDSCAPE OF AN UNORDINARY PLACE

Spatiotemporal disjunctures in Incheon's Chinatown

Jerry Won Lee and Jackie Jia Lou

Introduction

The city of Incheon in Korea was established in 1883 as a trade port with China and thrived as a Chinese settlement until the 1960s. Following the Asian financial crisis in the 1990s, resulting in Korea's International Monetary Fund (IMF) bailout in 1997 (Kim, 2000), the investment in and development of 'new' Chinatowns were pursued as one means to promote economic growth in Korea and across Asia (Eom, 2017). The 'old' Chinatown of Incheon, in Jung-gu (Jung District), was not viewed as a viable option for capital investment, and, according to transnational developers, was ideal for only 'small shops and restaurants' whose economy would center on 'low-paid workers and petty merchants' because of its hilly geography and limited space (Eom, 2017, pp. 707–708). In 2002, in the space of the 'old' Chinatown in Jung-gu, the local government established the country's first official Chinatown in an effort to create a tourist destination. In 2005, a 'new' Chinatown was developed in Song-do in the nearby Yeonsu-gu of Incheon, with tax incentives designed to attract overseas investors (Eom, 2017). Neither the 'old' nor 'new' are actually populated by a significant percentage of Chinese residents, and other regions, such as Garibong-dong of the Guro-gu of Seoul, have higher concentrations of Chinese Koreans (Lee, 2009). Despite the absence of a Chinese residential population, the reinvention of the 'old' Chinatown in Incheon relies heavily on buildings, facades, and signage—in other words, material, semiotic, and linguistic resources that characterize Chinatowns around the world. It is marked as distinctively non-Korean yet shaped linguistically and culturally by the larger Korean context around it.

On the surface, this Chinatown appears 'unordinary': it is marked as conspicuously 'different' from the rest of Korea, and thus 'unordinary' to local Koreans. Further, the concept of a 'Chinatown' does not exist in China proper, and as such, it is potentially 'unordinary' to Chinese who visit Korea. Because of the conspicuousness of its linguistic, visual, and architectural features, it is an 'unordinary' experience more universally, which is not dependent on a particular cultural background or geopolitical vantage point. However, by examining the semiotic landscape of Incheon Chinatown more closely using the geosemiotic framework (Scollon & Scollon, 2003), we demonstrate the dialogical relationship between the spectacular and the banal, for the play between these two enables the production of a 'Chinatown' to begin with. In this framework, Chinatown is viewed as a geosemiotic aggregate composed of visual semiotics (e.g., signage and facade), place semiotics (e.g., architecture and layout), and interaction order (e.g., communicative practices in place). In each of these aspects, we examine how 'ordinary' material and semiotic resources become 'unordinary'. This study of 'translingual ordinariness' also allows us to reflect on the broader conditions under which 'language' and 'nation' can be rendered legible in the first place.

Translinguistics, semiotic landscape, and the legibility of nation

Translinguistics can be understood as an orientation to language and communication that recognizes the fluidity of linguistic boundaries (Canagarajah, 2013, 2018; Dovchin, 2017; García, 2009; García & Li, 2014; Jacquemet, 2005, 2013; Jørgensen, 2008; Jørgensen & Møller, 2014; Lee, 2018; Li, 2011; Pennycook, 2007, 2010; Pennycook & Otsuji, 2015; Sultana, Dovchin, & Pennycook, 2015). Bauman and Briggs's (2003) description of the 'metadiscursive regimes of language' was a critical precursor to translinguistic thought. The authors respond to Chakrabarty's (2000) call to 'provincialise Europe' by reminding readers that various conceptual categories of human communication, along with their derivative hierarchies, are inventions of Eurocentric thought, including European philology. Developing this line of inquiry, Makoni and Pennycook (2005) call for a 'disinvention' of language as such, moving away from ostensibly fixed categories between one language and another in order to 'reconstitute' them otherwise. Indeed, in the analysis below, we will explore how the assumed transposability between Korean and other 'languages' was put into crisis by the need to create separate linguistic and national categories in the project of reinventing Chinatown.

Translinguistics reflects a paradigm of communication that understands 'linguistic' communication as complementary to a range of 'non-linguistic' resources, including semiotic and material resources present in the same space as languages themselves. Pennycook (2010) and Pennycook and Otsuji (2015) foreground the role of language in the production of social space, while Li (2011), in his description of 'translanguaging space', emphasizes the conduciveness of space to particular kinds of language resources. In short, translinguistics situates the analysis of the functions and capacities of 'language' within a wide range of 'spatial repertoires' (Canagarajah, 2013, 2018).

Translinguistics' spatial orientation connects to research on semiotic landscapes, which Jaworski and Thurlow define as 'any (public) space with visible inscription made through deliberate human intervention and meaning making' (2010, p. 2). In acknowledging the potential for a translinguistic approach to analyzing the semiotic landscape, we do not merely wish to foreground the types of translingual practice in public space. Instead, analogous to how translinguistic inquiry can call into question the assumed unordinariness of translingual practice itself, we contend that this approach can lead to a productive inquiry into the conditions by which not only linguistic 'difference' but also semiotic and material 'differences' are utilized as resources for place-making.

The translingual landscape of Incheon Chinatown provides an opportunity to understand how nationness comes to be rendered legible in 'unexpected places' (Heller, 2007; Pennycook, 2012). This focus on 'nationness' foregrounds Bhabha's (1994) theorization of nation as 'narrative strategy' that 'produces a continual slippage of categories, like sexuality, class affiliation, territorial paranoia, or "cultural difference" in the act of writing the nation' (p. 201). Bhabha continues that despite the inherent instability and impossibility of 'nation' as a reliable cultural category, it is discursively reproduced and sustained through various acts of narration such as literary works. For instance, an author can deploy a protagonist who allegorizes the nation or can provide incidental juxtapositions to another nation, which in turn produces 'national' categories such as 'America' or 'China' (p. 201). The latter strategy is especially relevant to our understanding of the legibility of Chineseness in Incheon Chinatown, for Chineseness is always necessarily in contention with the broader sociocultural milieu of 'Korea'. Koreanness operates through inconspicuous or 'banal' (Billig, 1995) means within Korea, except in designated tourist traps, such as Itaewon or Insadong, which are characterized by an 'unbanality', or excess, of Koreanness (Lee, 2017). Likewise, as we will demonstrate, the linguistic, semiotic, and spatial features of Incheon's Chinatown create an unordinary place by juxtaposing a spectacular display of Chineseness with the quotidian manifestation of a globalized Korea.

Through the geosemiotic lens

We adopt a geosemiotic framework (Scollon & Scollon, 2003) in our analysis of Incheon Chinatown. Geosemiotics refers to 'the study of the social meaning of the material placement of signs and discourses and of our actions in the material world' (p. 2), in which the meaning of a place is conceptualized as a dialogical interaction among three main semiotic systems: place semiotics, visual semiotics, and interaction order.

Scollon and Scollon coin *place semiotics* in order to connect the studies of micro-level social interaction and language use with research on social space. It is concerned with the meaning system of spatial organization and includes a typology of spaces according to their uses, for example, frontstage versus backstage, private versus public, display space versus passage space. We also include here five sensory spaces as defined by Hall (1966). Inversely defined as 'the huge aggregation of semiotic systems which are not located in the persons of the social actors or in the framed artifacts of visual semiotics' (Scollon & Scollon, 2003, p. 8), *place semiotics* underscores the importance of space not simply as the context of language use but also as a semiotic vehicle itself.

Visual semiotics are defined as 'the ways in which pictures (signs, images, graphics, texts, photographs, paintings, and all of the other combinations of these and others) are produced as meaningful wholes for visual interpretation' (Scollon & Scollon, 2003, p. 8). In our analysis, this also includes other visual characteristics of signs, such as code preference, inscription, and emplacement, moved from place semiotics in Scollon and Scollon's original framework (see pp. 20–21) because these characteristics are intrinsic to the visual display of language.

Interaction order is a term Scollon and Scollon (2003) borrowed from Goffman (1959) but also expanded to include any analytical tools concerned with 'the current, ongoing, ratified (but also contested and denied) set of social relationships we take up and try to maintain with the other people who are in our presence' (p. 16). As Scollon and Scollon remind us, it is important to recognize *interaction orders* also as semiotic signs, which 'give off' (Goffman, 1959) social information about social actors. Scollon and Scollon include the five types of perceptual spaces developed by Hall (1966), which in our analysis will be moved under *place semiotics*, the first component. A modified outline of geosemiotics and its component systems is presented in Table 2.1 (see Lou, 2014, 2016a, 2017 for other applications of this modified geosemiotic framework).

TABLE 2.1 Modified outline of geosemiotics based on Scollon and Scollon (2003, pp. 20–21)

Geosemiotics		
Interaction order	*Visual semiotics*	*Place semiotics*
1. Interpersonal distance (intimate, personal, social, public) 2. Personal front (appearance, behavior) 3. Units of interaction order (single, with, file or procession, queue, contact, service encounter, conversational encounter, meeting, people-processing encounter (interview, screening, examination), platform event, celebrative occasion)	1. Pictures (represented participants modality, composition, interactive participants) 2. Material aspects of visual semiotics [moved from place semiotics] (code preference, inscription, emplacement)	1. Perceptual spaces [moved from *interaction order*] (visual, auditory, olfactory, thermal, haptic) 2. Use spaces (frontage or public (exhibit/display, passage, special use, secure), backstage or private, regulatory spaces (vehicle traffic, pedestrian traffic, public notice), commercial space (e.g., holiday market), transgressive space (e.g., homeless hangouts))

We examine each of the three aspects forming the geosemiotic aggregate of Incheon Chinatown and discuss how the interaction among them transforms a historical ethnic enclave into a tourist destination, reinforcing linguistic, cultural, and national boundaries. While each of the following sections focuses on one of the three dimensions, we would like to emphasize that they are followed as a heuristic guide as intended by Scollon and Scollon (2003) and inevitably overlap across the analytical categories.

Juxtaposing the unordinary and ordinary: place semiotics in Chinatown

One of the most prominent features of any Chinatown, whether in San Francisco, Yokohama, or London, is the main archway, or *paifang*. Combining influences from ancient Indian and Chinese vernacular architecture, *paifangs* may have originated in the Zhou Dynasty, about 2,000 years ago, and mainly served memorial functions in China until the late 19th century, with the inscriptions often extolling moral virtues, commending achievements, or offering prayers (Wang & Duan, 2016). A *paifang* decidedly symbolizes traditional Chinese architecture, and new *paifangs* have rarely been built in China since the end of 19th century. However, their construction has continued in Chinatowns around the world. Funding for such projects often comes from both local municipal governments and Chinese governments at respective levels. The Friendship Archway in Washington, DC was a joint venture between Washington, DC and Beijing, the capital cities of two superpowers in the 1980s. The archway in Incheon was built in 2000, with funding from the Chinese city of Weiha, as part of the Incheon government's efforts to revitalize this historic area (Eom, 2017).

Incheon Chinatown features four archways, the main one at the South entrance, one each on the West and East entrances, and another to the North, serving as the entrance to Jayu Park, a park that features serene walking trails for visitors. The main archway for the South entrance is an extravagant design with four pillars, creating a primary entryway of about 6.5 meters wide and two peripheral entryways of approximately 3 meters wide each (Figure 2.1). It features three full pagoda-style eaves and two half-eaves. Each full eave features the 12 Chinese zodiac animals, while each of the half-eaves features 6 animals. The archway is approximately 11 meters tall and 16 meters wide. The golden inscription in the central banner reads 'China Street', presented in the traditional reading path from right to left and written in Traditional Chinese characters, completed with the signature of the calligrapher, again a feature of entrances into traditional Chinese houses. This modern traditional *paifang*, thus, exemplifies what Hobsbawm (1983) calls 'invented traditions', which foreground the role of state ideologues and functionaries in the manufacturing of heritage for the purposes of facilitating nationalist sentiment and ideological allegiance. It commemorates the nation rather than its subjects (albeit under a different nation then), who migrated from their country to settle in Korea more than a 100 years prior (Kim, 2004).

FIGURE 2.1   Main archway at the south entrance of Incheon Chinatown in 2016.

Comparing photographs of the archway from 2016 to the one from 2015 provides an even starker juxtaposition. The photograph taken in June 2015 (an archived image from Google Maps) shows the archway in its bare concrete state, with only the Chinese characters painted in red lacquer (Figure 2.2). Blommaert (2013) emphasizes the importance of attending to the semiotic landscape not only as a series of achronic, static artifacts but as chronicling semiosis across time. In our case, such an approach is made possible by not only knowledge of the recent construction date (the year 2000) of the archway but also the availability of a photograph from 2015, which is in turn juxtaposed with the image taken during field research in 2016. This miniature 'knowledge archive' (Blommaert & Dong, 2010) enables us to document the invention of tradition through not merely the production of the archway but also its subsequent ornamentation into a monument of excess, or 'unbanality' (Lee, 2017; Lou, 2016b). This possibility was enabled by the serendipitous timing of the field research, which allowed us to document the invention of tradition-in-progress, as it were, through the image of workers painting the buildings to the left of the archway with red in an effort to reinforce Chineseness (Figure 2.3). A notable feature of this China-town is the excessive use of red, a color typically associated with Chinese culture (Scollon & Scollon, 2003). If the 'invention' of nation is made possible through the invention of tradition, as argued by Hobsbawm (1983), then the use of red is one such effort to resemiotize the space as 'traditionally' Chinese. It is, of course, not to suggest that there is anything inherently Chinese about the color red. Our point is that red indexes Chineseness in Incheon through its excessive

FIGURE 2.2 Main archway at the south entrance of Incheon Chinatown in 2015 as captured in Google Maps.

FIGURE 2.3 Workers painting buildings with red accents in 2016.

and conspicuous usage in an effort to resemiotize, or indeed 'invent', the space as 'authentically' Chinese, an effort which is premised on the possibility of an 'authentic' Chineseness outside of or prior to its *narration*.

The *paifangs* also demarcate the Chinatown as a space of 'difference'. Along with tourist maps near the arches, they serve to foreclose undesignated and un-intended use of the Chinatown. Chinatown is then turned into 'exhibit-display spaces' and 'passage spaces', per Scollon and Scollon's (2003) place semiotics.

They direct visitors to enter Chinatown and, upon exiting, visitors are informed of their egress or their 'return' to Korea. The maps not only serve to facilitate navigation but also to differentiate the space semiotically as a discrete space of Chineseness by, for example, visually contrasting the architectural styles of ornate Chinese tiled roofs inside Chinatown with modern buildings, such as the police station located just outside it.

Intriguingly, within the borders of Chinatown, as delineated by the *pai-fangs*, we found diverse uses of space. The incongruity is most noticeable in the Fairy Tale Town, an area in Chinatown in which the buildings are decorated with Japanese anime characters in pastel colors, invoking a childish space, similar to the Disneyland discussed by Baudrillard (1994), a simulacrum of Los Angeles's everyday consumerist life. But here, the Fairy Tale Town has no apparent connection to Chinatown at all. Instead it reminds us of indoor children's playgrounds and video game arcades that are common scenes in many East Asian cities—in other words, it is a rather 'ordinary' space in the globalized urban landscape. As de Certeau (1984) argues, despite top-down efforts by institutional apparatuses to assign names to social space, the nominal value of such designations is reimagined bottom-up by everyday users of the space. The seemingly incongruent Fairy Tale Town could be seen as one such unexpected spatial practice, contradicting the officially intended 'Chineseness' of the space. At the same time, this ordinary space for children's play holds up a mirror to the simulacrum of Chinatown, reminding us that the unordinary space itself is a sign of a place and time that exists only in moments of discursive imagination.

Re-indexing Chinese as the Other: the visual semiotics of translingualism

We now turn our attention toward how the 'tension between the ordinary and extraordinary' (Paek, 2016, p. 232) plays out in the visual semiotics of Chinatown's linguistic landscape, paying particular attention to the 'emplacement' (Scollon & Scollon, 2003), the physical location, and the material means of multilingual display.

While in our visual survey the frequency of Chinese in the linguistic landscape is lower than that of Korean, wherever it occurs it appears significantly more prominent both visually and materially. The restaurant signs in the Chinatown frequently feature Chinese names in much larger size than Korean or English words. On one sign, the high contrast between the red background and yellow or white font colors also affords a greater salience, even when viewed from a distance. Both of the main buildings in front of the viewer repeat the restaurant names three times on the top, middle, and ground floors. One could suggest that the Chinese serve a more symbolic function, while the Korean a pragmatic one, as can be seen in the much smaller yellow road sign to the right of the same building. We would like to suggest a more spatial reading of this dichotomy by situating it not only in the spatial context of Incheon Chinatown but also in the history of language ideologies and policies in Korea more broadly.

Chinatown in Incheon is situated in a very different linguistic ecology from other Chinatowns, especially those in the English-speaking world. Prior to the invention of Hangeul in the 14th century CE, Koreans did not have their own script and relied exclusively on the Chinese writing system. Today, while the use of Chinese characters and loanwords from other languages (especially Japanese and English) is quite common, there is an active movement toward language 'purification', attempting to ban the use of loanwords and even Chinese characters. Curiously, Hangeul was not actively promoted as a national script until the 20th century in the years during and immediately following colonial occupation by the Japanese (Jung, 2012; Suh, 2013). In other words, the use of Chinese to signify Chineseness, such as in the case of Chinatown, is a relatively recent phenomenon, involving a gradual re-indexing of both languages to two distinctive geopolitical identities. Meanwhile, the use of English has come to index modernity and cosmopolitanism (Lee, J. S., 2006; Park & Abelmann, 2004), especially in the context of South Korea.

This history of shifting language ideologies and policies informs our visual semiotic analysis of the three 'languages' in the linguistic landscape of Incheon Chinatown. Drawing on the concept of 'emplacement' (Scollon & Scollon, 2003), we can observe that the visual prominence of each language varies across unordinary and ordinary spaces. The Chinese inscription '中華街 (Chinese Street)', for example, is only found on the main archway, whereas the less spectacular side arches are inscribed in Korean and English, where even the Korean words for Chinatown '차이나타운' are in fact a transliteration of 'Chinatown' in English. Banners for events and exhibitions are written almost exclusively in Korean, while English dominates the signs for ostensibly modern global establishments, such as cafés and convenience stores. The mapping of different languages onto respective spatial domains within Chinatown both physically and symbolically re-indexes Chinese as the Other, simultaneously erasing its role from the linguistic history of Korea and reinforcing contemporary Korean nationness by linking it with the hybrid use of Hangeul script and English words.

Scaling ordinariness: the performance of interaction orders

While some history is erased, other histories are made more visible for the purpose of inventing tradition. Rather curiously, what has come to symbolize everyday life in Incheon Chinatown is *jajangmyeon*, a noodle dish with black bean sauce. A primary attraction is the Jajangmyeon Museum, at the site of the original Gonghwachun restaurant, which opened in 1905 and was the first in Korea that served the now globally popular noodle dish. A bowl of jajangmyeon was considered an expensive dish until the 1960s when the Korean government, after investigating the consumer price index, mandated lower prices, which made the dish more accessible to a wider consumer base. Today, jajangmyeon is considered a central part of Korean food culture and 'closely related with Korean identity'

(Yang, 2005, p. 75). Unsurprisingly, this ordinary noodle dish is monumentalized in Incheon Chinatown, as it serves to accentuate Koreanness while maintaining a historical connection to Chinese immigration.

In the Jajangmyeon Museum, visitors encounter artifacts from the turn of the century, such as woks in which jajangmyeon was made. Life-sized plaster sculptures of human figures (e.g., cooks, hawkers, and customers) are placed along with objects and photographs to recreate the everyday contexts in which the noodle was made, sold, delivered, or consumed. Visitors can even enter the scene by sharing a table with the plaster models permanently suspended in the action of enjoying the noodle. The re-enactments of these scenes not only provide photo ops for the visitors but they also turn ordinary interaction orders (e.g., sharing a table with strangers in a noodle restaurant) into a spectacle and turn the 'use space' of the restaurant into a 'display space' or 'performance space'.

Another feature is a display of packages of 56 different instant jajangmyeon brands. The display documents the cultural influence of jajangmyeon as an everyday phenomenon in Korea, easily accessible within minutes and at a very low price. However, in the same way that translinguistics demands a reconsideration of sedimented social 'realities', the emplacement of the instant jajangmyeon at the Jajangmyeon Museum, a space designated to celebrate the history of jajangmyeon and its quotidian iterations through instant jajangmyeon, calls one to recognize the larger context of its history. Instant jajangmyeon is consumed without much thought to its origins. However, because it is encountered in a museum, a space that, at least ostensibly, maintains historical fact, it is especially curious to recognize that instant noodles are themselves a Japanese invention (JIFIA, n.d.). Our purpose, to be sure, is not to arbitrarily valorize 'authenticity' for its own sake (Ku, 2014). We are not merely trying to point out that instant jajangmyeon is indebted to Japanese culinary entrepreneurship. Instead, we underscore the impossibility of celebrating innovation in food culture, and perhaps innovation more generally, through the rubric of 'nation'. It is a reminder of the challenges of constructing the historical contributions of a particular 'national imaginary', and, most significantly, a reminder that it is in an exceptional space, such as Chinatown, that we are most likely to encounter such narratives of 'national' history, embedded within the historical narrative of transnational immigration.

Conclusions

Our initial analysis of Incheon Chinatown's semiotic landscape approached it as a space of visually conspicuous translingual excess, a linguistic and cultural spectacle, which is characteristic of Chinatowns worldwide as a 'ritual place' (Lou, 2016a). However, by applying Scollon and Scollon's (2003) geosemiotic framework to examine more closely its place semiotics, visual semiotics, and interaction order, we have reached a paradox in our conclusion—that is, the unordinariness of Chinatown itself is mutually constituted by ordinary architecture, signs, languages, and objects.

The social semiotic strategies that constitute this Chinatown can be understood through the heuristic of scale (Blommaert, 2010; Carr & Lempert, 2016): the discursive strategy by which objects and phenomena are described and conceptualized in relation to other interscalar objects or phenomena. Significantly, scalar work is by no means ideologically neutral and can be used for persuasive purposes (Carr & Lempert, 2016). We deploy the heuristic of scale to make sense of various paradoxes in the geosemiotic aggregate of Incheon Chinatown. Most obviously, it problematizes the consolidation of Chineseness to one 'Chinatown' or even particular elements that are ostensibly representative of China, such as the color red. This practice of down-scaling, for the purposes of representational facility, raises the question of what elements of the ordinary, everyday lives of Chinese migrants in Korea have invariably been neglected, or perhaps need to be neglected, through the very attempt to represent Chineseness in Chinatown through merely conspicuous means.

Incheon's Chinatown demonstrates the semiotic and material production of 'unordinariness' through 'ordinariness'. It is a translingual space constituted by a constellation of both discrete and fluid resources from Chinese, Korean, and English. The juxtaposition of the old (e.g., historic buildings and relics) and the new (e.g., modern establishments, such as cafés and convenience stores) and of the 'local' (Korean), the 'foreign' (Chinese), and the 'global' (English) results in a spatiotemporal disjuncture that asks what roles touristic and Orientalist gazes play in the shaping of nationness, and, in particular, 'Korean' and 'Chinese' nationness by recreating the history and the space of transnational migration. These collective spatiotemporal disjunctures reveal unexpected but nonetheless crucial intersections among language, semiotics, and nationness. A space like this Chinatown offers insights into how boundaries between 'languages' and between 'nations' were resurrected through linguistic, visual, and material means in the service of place-making.

References

Baudrillard, J. (1994). *Simulacra and simulation*. Ann Arbor: University of Michigan Press.

Bauman, R., & Briggs, C. L. (2003). *Voices of modernity: Language ideologies and the politics of inequality*. Cambridge, UK: Cambridge University Press.

Bhabha, H. K. (1994). *The location of culture*. London, UK: Routledge.

Billig, M. (1995). *Banal nationalism*. London, UK: Sage.

Blommaert, J. (2010). *The sociolinguistics of globalization*. Cambridge, UK: Cambridge University Press.

Blommaert, J. (2013). *Ethnography, superdiversity and linguistic landscapes: Chronicles of complexity*. Bristol, UK: Multilingual Matters.

Blommaert, J., & Dong, J. (2010). *Ethnographic fieldwork: A beginner's guide*. Bristol, UK: Multilingual Matters.

Canagarajah, S. (2013). *Translingual practice: Global Englishes and cosmopolitan relations*. London, UK: Routledge.

Canagarajah, S. (2018). Translingual practice as spatial repertoires: Expanding the paradigm beyond structuralist orientations. *Applied Linguistics, 39*(1), 31–54.

Carr, E. S., & Lempert, M. (Eds.). (2016). *Scale: Discourse and dimensions of social life*. Berkeley: University of California Press.

Chakrabarty, D. (2000). *Provincializing Europe*. Princeton, NJ: Princeton University Press.

de Certeau, M. (1984). *The practice of everyday life*. Berkeley: University of California Press.

Dovchin, S. (2017). The ordinariness of youth linguascapes in Mongolia. *International Journal of Multilingualism, 14*(2), 144–159.

Eom, S. (2017). Traveling Chinatowns: Mobility of urban forms in Asia in circulation. *Positions: East Asia Cultures Critique, 25*(4), 693–716.

García, O. (2009). *Bilingual education in the 21st century: A global perspective*. Oxford, UK: Wiley-Blackwell.

García, O., & Li Wei. (2014). *Translanguaging: Language, bilingualism, and education*. Basingstoke, UK: Palgrave Macmillan.

Goffman, E. (1959). *The presentation of self in everyday life*. New York, NY: Doubleday.

Hall, E. T. (1966). *The hidden dimension*. New York, NY: Doubleday.

Heller, M. (2007). The future of 'bilingualism'. In M. Heller (Ed.), *Bilingualism: A social approach* (pp. 340–345). Basingstoke, UK: Palgrave Macmillan.

Hobsbawm, E. (1983). Introduction: Inventing tradition. In E. Hobsbawm & T. Ranger (Eds.), *The invention of tradition* (pp. 1–14). Cambridge, UK: Cambridge University Press.

Jacquemet, M. (2005). Transidiomatic practices: Language and power in the age of globalization. *Language & Communication, 25*(3), 257–277.

Jacquemet, M. (2013). Transidioma and asylum: Gumperz's legacy in intercultural institutional talk. *Journal of Linguistic Anthropology, 23*(3), 199–212.

Japan Instant Food Industry Association. (n.d.). *The birth of instant noodles*. Retrieved from http://www.instantramen.or.jp/history/origin.html

Jaworski, A., & Thurlow, C. (Eds.). (2010). *Semiotic landscapes: Language, image, space*. London, UK: Bloomsbury.

Jørgensen, J. N. (2008). Polylingual languaging around and among children and adolescents. *International Journal of Multilingualism, 5*(3), 161–176.

Jørgensen, J. N., & Møller, J. S. (2014). Polylingualism and languaging. In C. Leung & B. V. Street (Eds.), *The Routledge companion to English studies* (pp. 67–83). London, UK: Routledge.

Jung, J. (2012). Haebang hu urimal doro chatgi undongui naeyonggwa seonggwa [The recovery campaign of our mother tongue after Korean liberation]. *Hangeul [Korean Language], 296*, 151–196.

Kim, K. (2004). Chinese in Korea. In M. Ember, C. R. Ember, & I. A. Skoggard (Eds.), *Encyclopedia of diasporas: Immigrant and refugee cultures around the world* (pp. 688–697). New York, NY: Springer.

Kim, S. S. (2000). Korea and globalization (segyehwa): A framework for analysis. In S. S. Kim (Ed.), *Korea's globalization* (pp. 1–28). Cambridge, UK: Cambridge University Press.

Ku, R. J. (2014). *Dubious gastronomy: The cultural politics of eating Asian in the USA*. Honolulu: University of Hawai'i Press.

Lee, J. S. (2006). Linguistic constructions of modernity: English mixing in Korean television commercials. *Language in Society, 35*(1), 59–91.

Lee, J. W. (2017). Semioscapes, unbanality, and the reinvention of nationness: Global Korea as nation-space. *Verge: Studies in Global Asias, 3*(1), 107–136.

Lee, J. W. (2018). *The politics of translingualism: After Englishes*. New York, NY: Routledge.

Lee, Y. (2009). Migration, migrants, and contested ethno-nationalism in Korea. *Critical Asian Studies, 41*(3), 363–380.

Li Wei. (2011). Moment analysis and translanguaging space: Discursive construction of identities by multilingual Chinese youth in Britain. *Journal of Pragmatics*, *43*, 1222–1235.

Lou, J. J. (2014). Locating the power of place in space: A geosemiotic approach to context. In J. Flowerdew (Ed.), *Discourse in context* (pp. 205–223). London, UK: Bloomsbury.

Lou, J. J. (2016a). *The linguistic landscape of Chinatown: A sociolinguistic ethnography*. Bristol, UK: Multilingual Matters.

Lou, J. J. (2016b). Shop sign as monument. *Linguistic Landscape*, *2*(3), 211–222.

Lou, J. J. (2017). Spaces of consumption and senses of place: A geosemiotic analysis of three markets in Hong Kong. *Social Semiotics*, *27*(4), 513–531.

Makoni, S., & Pennycook, A. (2005). Disinventing and (re)constituting languages. *Critical Inquiry in Language Studies*, *2*(2), 137–156.

Paek, S. (2016). Asian city as affective space: Commercial signs and mood in the paintings of Manoël Pillard. *Verge: Studies in Global Asias*, *2*(1), 222–249.

Park, S. J., & Abelmann, N. (2004). Class and cosmopolitan striving: Mothers' management of English education in South Korea. *Anthropological Quarterly*, *77*(4), 645–672.

Pennycook, A. (2007). *Global Englishes and transcultural flows*. London, UK: Routledge.

Pennycook, A. (2010). *Language as a local practice*. London, UK: Routledge.

Pennycook, A. (2012). *Language and mobility: Unexpected places*. Clevedon, UK: Multilingual Matters.

Pennycook, A., & Otsuji, E. (2015). *Metrolingualism: Language in the city*. London, UK: Routledge.

Scollon, R., & Scollon, S. W. (2003). *Discourses in place: Language in the material world*. London, UK: Routledge.

Suh, S. (2013). *Treacherous translation: Culture, nationalism, and colonialism in Korea and Japan from the 1910s to the 1960s*. Berkeley: University of California Press.

Sultana, S., Dovchin, S., & Pennycook, A. (2015). Transglossic language practices of young adults in Bangladesh and Mongolia. *International Journal of Multilingualism*, *12*(1), 93–108.

Wang, Y., & Duan, Y. (2016). A study on the classification and value of Ming Dynasty paifang in China: A case study of paifang in Jinxi County. *Journal of Asian Architecture and Building Engineering*, *15*(2), 147–154.

Yang, Y. (2005). Jajangmyeon and junggukjip: The changing position and meaning of Chinese food and Chinese restaurants in Korean society. *Korea Journal*, *45*(2), 60–88.

3

A LANGUAGE SOCIALIZATION ACCOUNT OF TRANSLINGUISTIC MUDES

Anna Ghimenton and Kathleen C. Riley

Introduction

The language socialization paradigm was formulated to understand how individuals acquire cultural knowledge, practices, and identities through specific social interactions (Duranti, Ochs, & Schieffelin, 2011; Ochs & Schieffelin, 1984). Given that language socialization is enacted at the intersection of language use and language ideology (Riley, 2011), this paradigm elucidates local ideologies as they are constructed, negotiated, and reinforced through individuals' specific social engagements, and how these impact individuals' translinguistic practices and related identities. As a lifelong process, language socialization is an apt prism for illuminating the continuity and discontinuity of individuals' interactional dispositions across cultural communities, life stages, and social settings. Thus, the ethnographic study of language socialization allows researchers to 'follow' individuals' movements through various geographic and symbolic spaces, examining the social situations they confront, the linguistic resources they acquire, and the heteroglossic strategies they exploit in these spaces.

We use Bakhtin's (1981) term *heteroglossic* to refer to the everyday lamination of linguistic forms from distinctive linguistic systems—whether languages, dialects, speech genres, or quoted voices—within specific socio-spatio-temporal settings; by contrast, we reserve *translinguistic* to refer to speakers' transitions across and transforming commitments to various linguistic systems and dialogic identities. We adopt the term *mudes*, proposed by Pujolar and Gonzàlez (2013; see also Lamarre, Lamarre, & Lefranc, 2015), to explore how individuals' habitus (Bourdieu, 1979), ideologies, and identities are socialized as they traverse key junctures in life where symbolic and economic power are interlaced in contemporary society: schooling, working, and parenting (Gonzàlez, Pujolar, Font, & Martínez, 2009). Mudes are, thus, the moments when social subjectivities are expressed and transformed through heteroglossic practices (Pujolar & Puigdevall, 2015). The interconnectedness of language and social life is made manifest by how language repertoires (re)configure and are (re)configured by the social developments within an individual's translinguistic trajectory.

As social groups are the loci for the establishment of norms via ordinary practices (Sacks, 1985), they provide the contexts within which vectors of innovation and change are unleashed. Authoritative voices (Bakhtin, Holquist, & Emerson, 1986) and established structures of normalcy have an impact on—threatening, constraining, or supporting—individuals' agency and the extent to which new and creative practices emerge and are accommodated in a group. Multilingual speakers' heteroglossic practices, translinguistic ideologies, and dialogic identities (Bakhtin, 1981; Hill & Hill, 1986) challenge structures of normalcy in various ways.

In this chapter, we present data collected through participant observation, interviews, and natural discourse in two contrasting contexts in order to identify some of the relationships between the language ideologies and socializing practices of the communities and the individuals who emerge from these contexts, probing some of the discursive exchanges through which linguistic resources, values, and dispositions are acquired in ways that forge mudes, that is, socio-spatio-temporal junctures of translinguistic change in a speaker's life. Comparing several heteroglossic engagements in two multilingual contexts, we illustrate how new discourse practices and ideologies, institutions and actors, can emerge similarly out of ordinary practices even in distinct sociocultural and political economic contexts. The overarching aim is to demonstrate how mobile and multilingual social actors are not only shaped by but also shape the conditions (practices, institutions, and ideologies) of their own socialization.

Fields, settings, and data collection

Data were collected in French-and-Italian-speaking immigrant families in France and French-and-English-speaking youth in Montréal, Canada. In the first context, developmental and language socialization data were collected between 2013 and 2015, consisting of French-Italian interactions recorded during family dinners and interview data with the caregivers in three upper-class Italian families having recently moved to France (Grenoble and Paris). The children's ages range between two and six. The second set of data was collected in Montréal between 2004 and 2007, and contextualized by background research and ethnographic observations in Montréal. Situated, semi-structured interviews were conducted in relevant domestic and public settings, focusing on the language socialization biographies of the participants (19- to 40-year-old multilinguals), and then transcribed and analyzed for their heteroglossic practices.

Because speakers are socialized by their movements among variable settings, a useful approach to analyzing data is to identify and compare the socio-spatial settings, the spatio-temporal movements between settings, and the socio-temporal developments of multilingual individuals within and across these settings, thus identifying important junctures of change (mudes). To accomplish this, we employed three main methods to provide multiple perspectives on the heteroglossic socialization trajectories: ethnographic participant observation, semi-structured and situated interviews, and recorded and analyzed socialization discourse.

Participant observation

Everyday socializing interactions were collected and/or contextualized by ethnographic research, especially participant observation. This classic anthropological method allows researchers to identify and conceptualize (a) the locally salient micro settings (spatial, temporal, and social) in which these interactions occur; (b) participants' spatio-temporal movements between social settings, as well as the praxes through which they enact symbolic interplay indexing these settings; and (c) the macro contexts (including language ideologies and regimes) shaped by the political–economic and ideological forces at work in that place and time in history.

Semi-structured, situated interviews

Semi-structured and situated interviews (i.e., open-ended yet guided conversations within socially relevant settings) enable researchers to elicit participants' narratives and self-reports about their behaviors and beliefs concerning language, society, caregiving, personal development, etc. From multiple interviews with caregivers, we can extrapolate patterns concerning the macro context—that is, the influential settings, events, and forces that affect individuals' acquisition of and commitment to various linguistic resources and strategies over historical and developmental time. Conducting interviews with participants about their own language socialization histories can provide insight into the processes by which they developed their language ideologies and practices over the course of their lives, their significant moments of change (i.e., mudes), and their present-day interactional and socializing practices through which praxes are reproduced or transformed. Moreover, these semi-naturalistic discourse data can also allow for the pragmatic and metapragmatic analyses of individuals' actual language practices, the ideologies shaping these, and the ways these emerge in real-time socializing discourses.

Socialization discourse analysis

Socialization discourse analysis requires the longitudinal recording and ethnographic transcription of socializing interactions, focusing on the routine practices of socio-spatial settings and socio-temporal events. These data allow us to analyze how specific language ideologies, practices, and identities are socialized and developed by individuals as they move physically and symbolically within and between a range of socio-spatial contexts, and as they transform socio-temporally over the course of a few weeks or a lifetime. In the first study, we were able to investigate the socializing interactions within and across two socio-spatial settings (home and school), allowing for a comparative analysis of the socio-temporal impact of these settings over developmental time. These intercontextual data take the form of either narrated moments or semiotic re-enactments from other settings, and the socializing interactions effect in real time the individuals' translinguistic mudes or socio-spatio-temporal junctures of transformation. By contrast, in the second study the socializing contexts and developmental mudes were only referentially discussed rather than captured in real time.

Two ethnographic stories

These two ethnographic stories account for the historical settings, some heteroglossic socialization practices, and some translinguistic mudes in the lifespans of several individuals. By analyzing some specific discourse data, we focus on the connections between the micro and macro socio-spatio-temporal contexts, and how the heteroglossic practices observed reflect and create new contexts of socialization. We present the analyses following a chronological perspective, representing the lifespan dimension, moving from interactions between children and caregivers to contexts where the participants are themselves older and can speak to their own translinguistic trajectories.

Immigrant France

The three upper-class families in this corpus are Italian professionals who moved to France for career purposes. Although technically immigrants, these families manifest an 'elite bilingualism' (Hélot, 2006) that is different from the stigmatized bilingualism developed by those who are not welcomed—socially, politically, or economically—by the host country. Elite bilingualism is commonly viewed as an asset, while immigrant bilingualism is seen as resistance or even a threat to the host community's ideals and principles of social unity. Yet, despite their relative privilege, even elite immigrants may experience linguistic vulnerability, living as they do in a country defined by a long history of linguistic nationalism (Riley, 2011).

All families have children attending French monolingual kindergartens or schools. Both the parents and children bring French words from the outer social sphere into the domestic sphere without losing their dominant Italian practices (Ghimenton & Costa, 2016). See, for example, how *sage* (well-behaved) is used in the extract in Table 3.1.[1]

Words like *sage* and *très calme* have an indexical function: they point to the French world yet creatively bridge two distinctive socio-spatial socialization settings: French-school and Italian-home. In addition, French words embedded in essentially Italian conversations are semantically and culturally specific. For instance, during one dinner, the French term *sage* was used by parents talking about their children's behavior during the day. When asking the child 'Sei stato

TABLE 3.1 At home, a family dinnertime interaction with mother, father, and child discussing the child's day at school

1.	Mother:	Sei stato bravo oggi vero? *(You well-behaved today, weren't you?)*
2.	Child:	Sì *(Yes)*
3.	Father:	Sei stato molto **sage** sei molto sei molto bravo (*You were very **well-behaved**, you are very good?*)
4.	Mother:	**Très calme** [mi ha detto] (***Very calm**, she told me*)
5.	Father:	[Ubbidiente] *(Obedient)*
6.	Child:	**Qui c'est qui a tapé sur mon verre**? (***Who tapped on my glass?***)
7.	Father:	Toi *(you)* (Mother points to her son)
8.	Father:	Senti ma *(Listen)*
9.	Child:	**Non c'est pas moi** (*No it's not me*)
10.	Father:	La maestra, che ha detto la maestra, sei stato bravo, hai fatto i compiti? (*What did your teacher say, were you good, did you do your homework?*)
11.	Child:	Sì *(Yes)*

sage oggi? Sei stato bravo oggi vero?' (turn 3), the father initiates an ordinary Italian dinnertime conversation with elements from a typical French school setting, *sage*, and then immediately and translinguistically reformulates with the Italian term *bravo*. While these two terms contain the same referential information, their side-by-side performance enacts different connotations of the two types of good behavior considered compliant with the rules and expectations of these two cultural–national communities. *Sage* refers to the rational and social constraints the dominant French society (in particular in institutional contexts) imposes on behavior while Italian *bravo* is a term which is semantically less specific as it can refer to behavior but also to skillfulness. Importing French terms such as *sage* followed immediately by the Italian translation recontextualizes and embraces terms instilled in one space of socialization to serve another one, thereby furthering the child's development of a bilingual–bicultural metapragmatic awareness of how to speak and act in each setting. The speakers' practices—children's and adults'—ingeniously index what the world is and simultaneously create and co-construct it, defining and redefining their conditions of socialization.

In another dinnertime example, a two-year-old boy in a Parisian Italian family asked his mother whether at home they had a *goûter* ('tea-time snack'). The *goûter* is a daily French sweet snack eaten by children after school. As the interaction unfolds, the mother responded that at their home there was none, but he would find a *goûter* in pre-school (Table 3.2).

In an ordinary dinnertime conversation, parents and child interactively define what a *goûter* is, meaning it consists of sweet (and not salty) foods. Both parents are clear that this can happen in the French-school space (turn 6) but not in their home, while acknowledging that such treats are available at his grandparents' place (turns 8, 11). The child 'tests the limits' of what can cross the public–private divide via a single word—what it contains referentially and what it can do performatively.

TABLE 3.2 At home, a family dinnertime interaction between mother, father, and child having a discussion focused on food and snacks

1.	Child:	Il **gouter** c'è? (*Is there a* **snack***?*)
2.	Mother:	Qua? (*Here?*)
3.	Child:	Il **gouter** c'è? (*Is there a* **snack***?*)
4.	Mother:	Non c'è il **goûter** a casa nostra Luigi (*No, there isn't a* **snack** *at home Luigi*)
5.	Child:	All'asilo? (*In preschool?*)
6.	Mother/Father:	All'asilo sì (*In preschool yes*)
7.	Child:	E a casa di nonna Betta? (*And at grandmother Betta's place*)
8.	Father:	Probabilmente sì (*Probably so*)
9.	Child:	E a casa di babbo? (*At daddy's place?*)
10.	Father:	È la tua (*It's yours*)
11.	Mother:	Vabbé che la nonna Lisa ne ha di **goûter** c'ha tutto quel che vuoi (*Well at grandmother Lisa's there are all sorts of* **snacks***, whatever you want*)
12.	Child:	Ha tantissime **goûter**? (*She has lots of* **snacks***?*)
13.	Mother:	Ha tutti quelli che vuoi (*Whatever kinds you want*)
14.	Child:	Si (*yes*)
15.	Mother:	Gelati, yogurt, di tutto (*Ice-cream, yogurt, anything*)
16.	Father:	Pizza (*Pizza*)
17.	Child:	No!
18.	Father:	Tortellini
19.	Child:	No!
20.	Father:	Prosciutto, formaggio, salmone (*Ham, cheese, salmon*)
21.	Child:	No!

These are only two examples of how, in dinnertime conversations, both children and parents exploit their heteroglossic resources to define and acknowledge their translinguistic conditions and contexts of language socialization. These intercontextual socializing practices potentially impact children's developmental paths in that they (re)create spaces for the long-term construction and transformation of both their language repertoires and their identities.

Montréal

The multilingual practices of young adults in Montréal reflect the forces that have over the past 300 years shaped this region of North America. Used as one of the original encampments for French explorers and missionaries in the early 17th century, the island served as the French colony's key port until 1760, when it was surrendered to Britain and transformed over the next two centuries into the primary economic hub of Canada. The *Révolution tranquille* of the 1960s, implementation of *Loi 101*,[2] and several fiery referendums over Québécois independence led to the exodus of many anglophones and the transfer of economic prominence to Toronto. Nonetheless, Montréal has emerged as a linguistically and culturally diverse and cosmopolitan city due to the established population of *Québécois de souche*, continued presence of many monied anglophones, and an ever-increasing influx of anglo-, franco-, and allophone (i.e., neither anglo- nor francophone) immigrants from around the world and other Canadian provinces. As a result, many of the young participants in the study tended to be multilinguals who had traveled much in one way or another (Das, 2016). For this chapter, we focus on two adults in their 20s, A and R, who move fluently and playfully between French and English, in ways that index the significant socio-spatio-temporal moves in their lives while actively constructing new settings and stances with their code-switching (see Riley, 2013 for more details about these interactions and other study participants).

A is a chef, who switches frequently between Québécois French (QF) and English in the interview situated in his home kitchen in Montréal as he tells stories of his culinary training in France. In the extract in Table 3.3,[3] he uses QF to point metaphorically and emotionally to the time and place where he was socialized into his various kitchen roles. For instance, he switches in turn

TABLE 3.3 At home in A's kitchen, with cousin/researcher C and American researcher K discussing his culinary apprenticeship in France and how a Japanese chef taught him to clean fish

1.	A:	*okay. I'll do it huh the way you want. so then you do it one time two times. the way he wants … and then you're cleaning his fish for all time. so he has. less job to do. but since he has less job to do and you have MORE … you sorta distance yourself from the whole. okay. I'm no longer scrubbing the floor aspect … cause. this guy needs me … he NEEDS me … so he's gonna make sure that somebody else is doing the BULLSHIT work that I'm supposed to be doing.* **les jobs PLATTES. les jobs CHIANTS. le MEnage. nanana … pis moi j'nettoie pas ça …** *(the dull jobs. the boring jobs. the CLEANing, yuk … then me I won't clean that) okay. and then you do his fish for him. you do his fish for him.[and then he'll like okay.*
2.	C:	*[so you had a higher status*
3.	A:	*well now okay. start doing this like this and we tie this like this starts explaining stuff to you as you go along. and for him I was* **Yakuza**.[JAP] *cause I had tattoos. which XX* **Yakuza**…[JAP]
4.	K:	*yakuzo. is what*
5.	A:	*is the mafia in Japan. and they all have tattoo. so we could XX* **Yakuza**[JAP] *he called me* **Yakuza**[JAP].
6.	K:	*ahah ahah okay … so he called you yakuzo. uhuh*
7.	A:	*and everybody else called me* **québec**.
8.	K:	*okay. and you spoke french with everybody*
9.	A:	*uh. yeah … who did I speak English with. there was one. somebody spoke English there … can't remember who.*
10.	K:	*did you. miss your English part. you were happy. being. totally. in French, did you*
11.	A:	*NO-***on**. *I was fine. I was fine in French … it was fine. I mean I spoke like a Quebeker. so… a* **serpillière je savais pas c'est quoi. une serpillière … c'est une moppe. une moppe c'est une serpillière** *(a mop [FF] I didn't know what it was. a mop [FF] … it's a mop [QF]. a mop [QF] is a mop [FF])*

1 to emphasize his displeasure at being assigned menial labor in the kitchen by immediately translating *BULLSHIT work* into QF as *les jobs PLATTES. les jobs CHIANTS. le MEnage. nanana* (the DULL jobs, the BORING jobs, the CLEANing, yuk). Not only does this switch emphasize his disgust it also highlights his success in finding a way out of such tasks: *pis moi j'nettoie pas ça* (so then me I don't clean that). That is, by acquiring skills and making himself essential to the Japanese chef, he has secured, as his cousin names it in turn 2, his *higher status* as a fish-cleaner instead of a floor-cleaner.[4] Additionally, he switches from English to QF in turn 11 to discuss, again metaphorically and somewhat emotionally, how he was socialized in France to replace the QF term for 'mop' *moppe* (one of many QF borrowings from English) with the FF term for 'mop' *serpillière*: *so … a serpillière je savais pas c'est quoi. une serpillière. c'est une moppe. une moppe c'est une serpillière* (mop [FF] I didn't know what was a mop [FF]. It's a mop [QF], a mop [QF] is a mop [FF]).

A also uses switching to negotiate his identity. In turn 7, he dialogically switches to French to quote how his colleagues in France called him *québec* in an apparently joking fashion. Calling someone by the name of the province they hail from, especially in a professional kitchen where homosocial name-calling is common, clearly has some performative force in the moment that we can only guess at from this remove. By contrast, in turn 11, he uses English to dialogically claim his identity as a *Quebecker* (this is the English term for a citizen of Québec), an identity that only became apparent to him as a result of his contrastive interaction with his culturally French culinary colleagues. Not only does he self-identify as an anglophone Quebecker because he is in the middle of speaking English at this moment in Montréal he also appears to be distancing himself somewhat from the French attribution. In effect, the tension between these two labels—the French one that indexically constructed his identity in the French kitchen and the self-performing label reclaimed here in his own Montréal kitchen—says a lot about the translinguistic mudes or slippages A experienced in his movements between kitchens in Montréal and France. His code-switching here seems to index not only his evolving mastery of these various linguistic varieties plus the mixed code known as Franglais but also his dialogic identification with the translinguistic Montréal identity that has emerged out of the *Révolution tranquille, Loi 101*, and failed referendums for Québec's national independence.

As an interesting contrast, R is a musician/performer who grew up in a small francophone community in Saskatchewan where her adolescent friends code-switched frequently and fluently. Her heteroglossic narratives in her Montréal kitchen (Table 3.4) actively reflect and indexically contribute to the ongoing performative production of her dialogic identity.

In contrast with A, R's discursive switches rarely indicate any sort of metaphoric connection to a sociocultural French versus English identity or setting; they serve instead a rhetorical strategy. Her code-switches instigate a shift in perspectival footing or stance as she expresses an emotion or opinion about someone or something she is describing. For instance, in turn 6 R uses French to explain

TABLE 3.4 At home in R's kitchen with three friends: R, P, and S (the researcher) as R reveals that two mutual friends are breaking up

1.	S:	*geez how long have they been together*
2.	R:	*fifteen years*
3.	P:	*yeah*
4.	S:	*oh fuck*
5.	R:	*yeah* **mais i est super pas conte:nt en campagne ... mais genre i voulait un chien. pis D__ i dit non. pis le i était comme ben. peut-être qu'on peut habiter XX. pis i dit non be. be.** (but he's not super ha:ppy in the country ... but like he wanted a dog. then D___ he said no. then he was like to him well. maybe we can live XX. then he says no wel. wel.) *it's like we-ll you can't always. just say no to everything that I want*
6.	P:	*well maybe D__'s not happy as well.* **c'est comme** (it's like)
7.	R:	**be:n D___ euh:. c'est u:n. moi j'aime bien D__.** (we:ll D___ uh: he's a:. I like D__.) *I really like [him he's a really great guy*
8.	P:	*[NO NO he's a nice guy I mean*
9.	R:	*but* **i est difficile.** (he's difficult) *for sure ...* **i est vraiment. TRÈS. particulier** (he's really. VERY. special)
10.	P:	**a:h no:n mais ça me fait de la peine** (a:h no: but that hurts)
11.	R:	**ben c'est sûr là** (well that's for certain)

some sensible reasons why their friends are splitting up and finally provides her most intimate take on the situation (turns 8, 10), that in fact one friend in the couple is a bit difficult, in fact is *particulier*. This term, for which there is no good English translation, indicates the speaker's disaffiliation from someone based on some specific grounds that will go unspecified but are presumed to be visible to others.

Our interpretation of the differences in A's and R's heteroglossic practices have to do with the socio-spatio-temporal contexts of their translinguistic mudes. R's dialogic identity emerged during her heteroglossic upbringing in Saskatchewan, such that now her code-switching practices are aimed at rhetorically framing the present interaction. By contrast, A went back and forth in his life between Québécois and Quebecker before discovering something closer to a more dialogic identity while in France; thus, his heteroglossic practices during the interview carry the metaphoric stamp of those mudes. Nonetheless, both speakers are clearly invested in a heteroglossic style that speaks to the complexities of the sociopolitical context into which they were born and their translinguistic trajectories through it.

Discussion/Conclusion

Despite the social, political, and economic differences in these two macro contexts, the processes and consequences of individuals' translinguistic socialization reveal remarkable similarities and interesting contrasts. In both field sites, individuals (from infancy to adulthood) receive substantial input from two or more languages, both within and beyond the home, as well as ideological input about the socially marked meanings of these languages. Speakers move between monolingual and multilingual spaces throughout a lifetime, juggling varying degrees of individual and societal pressure regarding appropriate and/or creative language usage as a means to integrate and/or stand out within social groups and settings. Consequently, these multilingual speakers use everyday practices to index (reflecting and creating) present and potential social and linguistic realities.

The heteroglossic interactions observed would appear disorderly by 'purist' standards and yet are all sensibly and semiotically rooted in the geographic and social mobility of these speakers (Auzanneau, Bento, & Leclère, 2016). That is, heteroglossic utterances are the traces of the translinguistic mudes wherein individuals have acquired communicative resources and social commitments as a result of socializing engagements at home, school, and work. The commonality and coherence of these engagements lie precisely in the everyday socio-temporal movements of individual speakers within and across these interactionally defined spaces of socialization—from kitchen tables to workplaces—over the course of a lifetime. Indeed, the interculturality of the spaces the individuals cross is not only a powerful steering force for their performances but also for their heightened awareness of the transformative power of their translinguistic stances. Sometimes their linguistic choices match the prevailing norms, while at other times their social identifications are translated into playful practices that trespass ethnic, regional, and class boundaries, challenging the established structures. Heteroglossic practices become powerful dialogic means for expanding the pragmatic potential of speakers' practices.

The power of linguistic varieties with international capital such as FF can be imported into immigrant homes in France and complexly colonized regions such as Montréal and metapragmatically reframed as relative rather than absolute. Implicit in the examples of *sage* and *goûter* in the Italian family's home and *serpillière* in the Québec chef's kitchen is the understanding that the socialized and socializing individuals could master the power code without bowing to its dominance. We also see in the Italian-French situations how personal mobility can transform the power of a single code (Italian); in this immigrant context, the children are socialized to associate the power of the code with their parents' class status despite the new socio-spatio-temporal setting. Finally, a core element underlying the heteroglossic practices in both contexts is a quest for 'authenticity' (i.e., the socio-spatio-temporal link to what is genuinely and uniquely 'ours') that goes beyond the expected code choices linked to age, class, gender, or ethnicity. During Italian family dinners, French words encode a social reality that becomes integrated into a new 'authenticity'; similarly, Montréal FF words, such as *particulier*, can best express the translinguistic realities the individuals have perceived and experienced and the dialogic identities they are forging as a consequence. Authenticity in both cases is expressed through the trespassing of criteria of normalcy through these heteroglossic practices. The latter are the dialectal resources that multilingual speakers can exploit to perform their realities, as they have lived and interpreted them via their translinguistic mudes.

Language ideologies linking value to linguistic forms and competencies assume different interpretations when translated into different socialization practices and socio-spatio-temporal engagements. Consequently, understandings of social identities and their translinguistic voicings can undergo radical transformations at various mudes in an individual's life trajectory. Having acquired heteroglossic competency, the multilingual actors in our corpora, irrespective of their social or cultural backgrounds, now play with power structures and their own dialogic identities through their innovative practices. They ingeniously perform these as a challenge to normalcy and everyday praxis, while their everyday performances may yet 'normalize' and legitimize their heteroglossic practices and translinguistic stances.

Notes

1 In Tables 3.1 and 3.2, Italian is in plain script, French appears in bold, and the translations appear in italics. Stretches of overlapped discourse are marked by square brackets.
2 Canada's Constitution Act of 1867 provided official protection to both English and French languages; Québec made French the official language of the province in 1974; but it was Loi 101 of 1977, requiring that new immigrants be educated in French, that has been most effective at maintaining the language.
3 Tables 3.3 and 3.4 follow these conventions: italics = English utterances; bold italics = QF utterances; (plain script) = translation of QF utterances; [= overlap; periods = pauses; : = vowel lengthening; CAPS = louder volume; small letters = softer volume.
4 His use of the loanword jobs may speak not only to its full incorporation into both QF and FF at this moment but also to its salience as an index of French youths' general rebellion against Ancien Régime purism, the professional French kitchen being a key context where the tensions between French chauvinism and globalization are confronted.

References

Auzanneau, M., Bento, M. & Leclère, M. (2016). Introduction. In M. Auzanneau, M. Bento, & M. Leclère (Eds.), *Espaces, mobilités et éducation plurilingues* (pp. i–viii). Paris, France: Éditions Archives contemporaines.

Bakhtin, M. M. (1981). *The dialogic imagination: Four essays*. Ed. M. Holquist. Trans. C. Emerson & M. Holquist. Austin: University of Texas Press.

Bakhtin, M. M., Holquist, M., & Emerson, C. (1986). *Speech genres and other late essays* (1st ed.). Austin: University of Texas Press.

Bourdieu, P. (1979). *La Distinction: Critique sociale du jugement*. Paris, France: Les Editions de Minuit.

Das, S. N. (2016). *Linguistic rivalries: Tamil migrants and Anglo-Franco conflicts*. Oxford, UK: Oxford University Press.

Duranti, A., Ochs, E., & Schieffelin, B. B. (Eds.) (2011). *Handbook of language socialization*. Malden, MA: Blackwell.

Ghimenton, A., & Costa, L. (2016). Code-switching et socialisation plurilingue au sein de trois familles italophones en France. In M. Langner & V. Jovanovic (Eds.), *Facetten der Mehrsprachigkeit. Reflets du plurilinguisme* (pp. 97–117). Oxford, UK : Peter Lang.

Gonzàlez, I., Pujolar, J., Font, A., & Martínez, R. (2009). *Entre la identitat i el pragmatisme linguístic. Usos i percepcions linguístiques dels joves catalans a principis de segle.* Research report. Generalitat de Catalunya.

Hélot, C. (2006). De la notion d'écart à la notion de continuum. Comment analyser le caractère inégalitaire du bilinguisme en contexte scolaire? In Dans C. Hélot, E. Hoffmann & M.-L. Scheidhauer (Eds.), *Écarts de langue, écarts de culture. A l'école de l'Autre* (pp. 185–206). Frankfort, KY: Peter Lang.

Hill, J. H., & Hill, K. C. (1986). *Speaking Mexicano: Dynamics of syncretic language in Central Mexico.* Tucson: University of Arizona Press.

Lamarre, P., Lamarre, S., & Lefranc, M. (2015). *La socialisation langagière comme processus dynamique. Suivi d'une cohorte de jeunes plurilingues intégrant le marché du travail.* Québec, Canada: Conseil supérieur de la langue française du Québec.

Ochs, E., & Schieffelin, B. B. (1984). Language acquisition and socialization: Three developmental stories and their implications. In R. A. Schweder & R. A. Le Vine (Eds.), *Culture theory: Essays on mind, self and emotion* (pp. 276–320). Cambridge, UK: Cambridge University Press.

Pujolar, J., & Gonzàlez, I. (2013). Linguistic 'mudes' and the de-ethnicization of language choice in Catalonia. *International Journal of Bilingual Education and Bilingualism, 16*(2), 138–152.

Pujolar, J., & Puigdevall, M. (2015). Linguistic mudes: How to become a new speaker in Catalonia. *International Journal of the Sociology of Language, 2015*(231), 167–187.

Riley, K. C. (2011). Language socialization and language ideologies. In A. Duranti, E. Ochs, and B. B. Schieffelin (Eds.), *Handbook of language socialization* (pp. 493–514). Malden, MA: Blackwell.

Riley, K. C. (2013). L'idéologie hétéroglossique et l'identité dialogique à Montréal. In C. Trimaille & J.-M. Eloy (Eds.), *Idéologies linguistiques et discriminations* (pp. 59–83). Paris, France: Harmattan.

Sacks, H. (1985). On doing 'being ordinary'. In J. Maxwell Atkinson (Ed.), *Structures of social action* (pp. 413–429). Cambridge, UK: Cambridge University Press.

4

THE ORDINARIZATION OF TRANSLINGUISTIC DIVERSITY IN A 'BILINGUAL' CITY

Claudio Scarvaglieri

Introduction

The concept of the ordinariness of translinguistic diversity (Dovchin, 2017; Dovchin & Lee, 2019) captures the fact that, for many language users, combining linguistic resources from different language systems is 'normal' (Blommaert, 2013, p. 14) and 'basic practice' (Androutsopoulos, 2007, p. 208). This chapter describes the differences in the ordinariness of communicative practice in an officially bilingual German-French city in Switzerland and argues that these different degrees of ordinariness are societally produced through a process I call *ordinarization*. In the following, I first discuss the concept of ordinariness in relation to Foucault's *normalisation* (Foucault, 1976). I then introduce Biel/Bienne, the city where processes of linguistic ordinarization were studied. Based on data from ethnography and the linguistic landscape (LL), I show which activity types are perceived as ordinary in Biel/Bienne. In the second analytic step, I show that these perceptions are societally produced through language policy and language ideologies expressed in public discourse. I, thus, conclude that ordinariness should not be understood as a natural trait of certain activity types, but as a product of social processes that lead to the ordinarization of these activity types.

Ordinariness and *normalisation*

The concept of 'normal' or 'normality' was first used in scientific discourse in the 18th century. Based on statistical and biological work, scholars like August Comte and Francis Galton started to distinguish between those parts of a certain sum of objects (defined in biological, demographic, or anthropological terms) that represented the average or the 'normal' parts of the group investigated, and those parts that constituted the periphery or margins of that group

(Link, 2009). While it originally served as a scientific tool to identify structures of the groups investigated, the normality concept was quickly transferred to various domains of everyday and institutionalized life. One of the first applications was the production of uniforms for Prussian soldiers based on four different types of 'normal' body shapes and sizes (Krause, 1965, pp. 39–43). Based on the identification of 'the normal body', instead of tailoring clothes individually for each person, it became possible to produce clothing for soldiers more efficiently. Of course, this also meant that 'less normal' body types either had difficulty fitting into a uniform or were more readily rejected for military service. Another early example was the establishment of the so-called 'normal schools', first in Austria and then in France, that regulated and unified the education of teachers, thereby producing what could be called the 'normal teacher', with a certain, pre-defined set of competences and knowledge items (Link, 2009, pp. 179–180). These schools were, thus, the first step in the creation of a centralized education system that enabled representatives of the nation-state to control what knowledge was produced and transferred not only in higher education but also in the emerging primary school system. Normalizing teacher education, thus, meant gaining control over the knowledge system of the population (cf. Foucault, 1976).[1]

As these examples show, the concept of normality is connected to societal power (Foucault, 1995): those who control what kinds of knowledge, character traits, physical traits, or kinds of behavior are perceived as 'normal' also control, among other things, the production and evaluation of knowledge, the selection of individuals for certain positions, and the sanctioning and regulation of behavior. Following Foucault, the social process of *normalisation* (Foucault, 1976, p. 138), therefore, has far-reaching effects in disciplining and standardizing behavior since what is perceived as 'normal' will be more accepted and more positively sanctioned than what is seen as less normal or deviant.

In this vein, the concept of ordinariness (Dovchin, 2017) invites researchers to change their perspective on translinguistic diversity and describe the use of linguistic resources from different language systems by the same speaker(s) not as something extraordinary that should be celebrated, but as ordinary, everyday practice that is just as normal as the use of linguistic resources from only one language system. 'Normalizing' multilingual language practice in this way, by pointing out its ordinariness, can, therefore, contribute to a different societal perspective on translinguistic diversity and to more accepting attitudes toward activity types that cross traditional linguistic boundaries.

Describing, as this volume does, the ordinariness and unremarkability of translinguistic diversity can, thus, support the societal acceptance of such diversity. However, as the brief discussion of the normality concept shows, neither the concept of ordinariness nor the fact that it is ascribed to certain objects and not others should be understood as natural. Instead, I argue that it is possible and necessary to describe and understand the processes that lead to differing ascriptions of ordinariness, and that these processes are related to societal hierarchies and boundaries. Similar to the *normalisation* of body types and knowledge items, the ordinarization of specific communicative activity types establishes the possibilities of control and incentivizes certain types of behavior while discouraging others.

In this chapter, I conceive of a linguistic activity type as 'ordinary' if language users treat it as an unremarkable part of everyday life. I illustrate this point by investigating the processes of ordinarizing linguistic behavior in a social space in which, based on its history and demographic structure, a high degree of ordinary linguistic diversity would be expected.

Biel/Bienne: a 'bilingual' city

The city of Biel (its German name) or Bienne (its French name) is the largest officially bilingual municipality in Switzerland. According to the city's official statistics, 55% of its population is German-speaking, 39% is French-speaking, and 36% uses a first language other than German or French (Stadt Biel, 2016). The city is, thus, characterized by an 'autochthonous' German-French bilingualism that has existed since the mid-19th century, when for economic reasons the city attracted large numbers of francophone horologists who quickly formed a '*colonie française*' (Werlen, 2005, p. 7), and by a high degree of 'allochthonous' linguistic diversity, which has emerged in recent decades as a result of immigration. As such, Biel/Bienne presents a rather unique case of translinguistic diversity: in contrast to most Western cities, there exists not only a high degree of migratory multilingualism but also an officially recognized societal bilingualism. Research has investigated whether this sociolinguistic situation has given rise to a special 'Biel Model' of communication in which the person who starts the conversation 'determines a common language, which is subsequently used by both participants' (Elmiger, 2015, p. 41). This model supposedly contrasts with a 'Swiss Model' in which each person uses their own language and passively understands the other.[2] Questions remain as to whether speakers in practice actually draw such sharp distinctions between different ways of communicating, or whether proposing a specific 'Biel Model' is more a result of the city's 'bilingualism ideology' (Scarvaglieri, 2018) emanating into academic research. Nevertheless, the fact that a specific model of intercultural communication in Biel/Bienne is discussed by Swiss linguists (see also Werlen, 2005) points toward a general potential for the establishment of new and innovative forms of communicating across ethnic and cultural groups.

Because of Biel/Bienne's diverse demographic constituency and its long history of communication across cultures and languages, it might be expected that its translinguistic diversity is managed in specific ways, and that such diversity is generally perceived as ordinary and unremarkable. After a short account of the methods used, I first describe which communicative activity types are perceived as ordinary in Biel/Bienne. I then show how this ordinariness is produced through language policy and media discourse.

Methods

Linguistic diversity in Biel/Bienne was investigated by a research team combining methods from ethnography (cf. Heller, Pietikäinen, & Pujolar, 2018), linguistic landscaping (cf. Blommaert, 2013; Scarvaglieri et al., 2013), and discourse analysis (cf. Wodak & Meyer, 2009). We studied the use of different languages in public and semi-public spaces (urban places, streets, playgrounds, train stations) and institutions (shops, hairdressers), observing communication, taking fieldnotes, and recording specific conversations over 160 hours. Combining ethnography and linguistic landscaping (as demonstrated in Blommaert, 2013), we observed the shaping of public space via written language by photographing and analyzing public signage in the city center (overall, 1,251 signs were documented and categorized). Taking the influence of language policies into account, data on political decisions about language were collected and official actors' comments, such as those of the city's mayor, on language questions were analyzed. As language is an important topic of public discourse in Biel/Bienne, the way language issues were covered in the media was also investigated.

Ordinariness of language practice in Biel/Bienne

Language policy and public space

Biel/Bienne follows a distinct bilingualism policy: all official documents, forms, regulations, and announcements are in both German and French. Citizens have the right to address the administration in one of the two languages and they must receive a response in the language they choose. In public spaces, this bilingualism policy is made visible as well: all signs within what Kallen (2010, p. 43) has called the 'civic frame', that is, signage by the authorities, are in German and French. On these 'top-down' signs, German is always to the left or on top of French (see Figure 4.1 for an example). Thus, German will be the language seen or read first, which indicates a clear language hierarchy, related to the fact that the majority of the city's inhabitants are German-speaking. Hence, although the city's language policy treats the two languages as equal, it also indexes differences in status by literally putting one language above the other. Overall, however, the official

FIGURE 4.1 Bilingual sign of Biel/Bienne's public library.

policy concerning language in the public expresses very clearly that the use of German and French alongside each other is not only the *ordinary* but also the most *appropriate* way of communicating in public.

Language practice in the public

In Biel/Bienne, language policy influences the language use of private actors rather indirectly. Although shop owners are required by federal regulations to announce products and services in one of the national languages (German, French, Italian, and Rheto-Romanic), these regulations are loosely enforced and do not preclude the use of other languages alongside the national languages. Therefore, if we focus on 'bottom-up' signs, that is, signs produced by companies, households, or individuals, we find a more diverse mosaic of language use. As indicated in Figure 4.2, similar to official signs, German and French are the two most visible languages on bottom-up signs. Contrary to the civic frame, however, there is a clear distinction between the two official languages, with German being used on 41% of signs and French on 29%. There is also a high presence of English (23%), while other languages are much less visible.

Both official languages are well represented in the city center: a person walking through the major shopping streets would probably not notice a predominance of one over the other. This finding suggests that language users accept the use of both German and French as common and ordinary, and that they engage in this bilingual activity in a manner similar to municipal signs. At the same time, the numbers show that more (a difference of 12 percentage points) signs appear in German than in French. Focusing on individual instances of language use in the LL, in the following, I will show that language use in the LL follows a pattern and that the two 'interior' languages, while ordinarily used together, serve different communicative purposes. Their different communicative usage explains the quantitative difference between German and French and gives the first hint at processes of linguistic ordinarization.

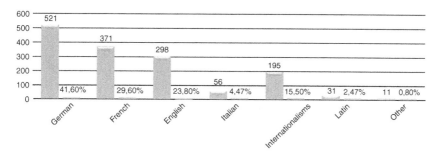

FIGURE 4.2   A numerical perspective on the linguistic landscape in Biel/Bienne (Bahnhofstrasse, Nidaugasse).

FIGURE 4.3 Infinitiv, a home-décor store in Biel/Bienne.

The home-décor store *infinitiv* illustrates this pattern (Figure 4.3; for other examples see Scarvaglieri, 2018; Scarvaglieri & Pappenhagen, 2018). Its name combines Latin and French (*la boutique*) and it advertises its services and goods on windows in German and French. The store also presents its business hours bilingually and uses a monolingual French sign to inform passersby that it is closed (*Ferme*[3]). There is also the English slogan 'painting the past', but above this on the door is a handwritten monolingual German sign stating that the store is closed this Friday and will be open again on Saturday. Actions like naming and advertising, which in a very general way create a framework for interaction (by informing the reader about the store and its products), are bilingual. Meanwhile, an action that presents specific information about the concrete possibilities of accessing the store and interacting with its owners is rendered in German only.

Statistical data supports this finding: the share of French is much higher for actions like naming or advertising than for informing or prohibiting, which are predominantly in German. Language users use the two languages for different things and ascribe different communicative values to them. French is used to frame the context in a general way as bilingual and to demonstrate appreciation of the francophone language group. German, in contrast, is used for complex, non-standardized actions that often carry considerable communicative weight, as an inability to understand them will impede interaction between the author and the reader (in Figure 4.3, not understanding the monolingual German sign will make it difficult for potential customers to know when the store is open again, whereas not understanding the bilingual signs would clearly entail less consequences). Language users, thus, employ German as the main language for communication, whereas French serves primarily as a symbol of the city's bilingualism, and to a much lesser extent, to conduct specific complex communicative tasks.

Even though French apparently carries less communicative value, language users continue to use it to an extent almost matching that of German. They use French alongside German as often as possible and take on additional costs to have signs translated or a second lettering affixed to their store's windows. Thereby, they take a stance (Spitzmüller, 2013) expressing that they value the city's official bilingualism and aim to display it as often as possible, despite the limited communicative importance of French. Language users, thus, position themselves (Spitzmüller, 2013) as appreciating the officially promoted activity type of using German and French alongside each other and make clear that they see this as normal. Other activity types, like using English as a lingua franca, relying on German alone, or employing one of the languages of immigration, are less common and used only for specific communicative purposes.

Language practice in the LL, thus, shows that language users judge the activity type of German and French alongside each other as the standardized or ordinary way of conducting interaction in public spaces. Ethnographic data reveals a similar pattern in less public spaces.

Language practice in institutions

As mentioned, communication in retail stores, supermarkets, and hairdressers was observed. The Art Coiffure hairdresser was one of our main places of observation, and it presents a particularly striking case. Approaching the hairdresser's from the outside, one notices a French name, English advertisements for styling products, and hip-hop concerts and business hours in German and French. The hairdresser's LL, thus, mirrors the description above, with German, French, and English all used on publicly visible signs. Inside, however, French is not used, as neither the owner nor his often-changing employees speak the language. The occasional francophone customer is served in (standard) German, with some English sprinkled in, if necessary. Standard German is, thus, an important language at the hairdresser's, as it is used for communication between different linguistic and ethnic groups. This distinguishes the language use at Art Coiffure from common practice in German-speaking Switzerland, where a Swiss dialect of German is usually the medium of oral communication, while standard German is generally used only in writing (concerning this 'diglossia', see e.g., Flubacher, 2014, pp. 69–70; Elmiger, 2015, pp. 45–46). The reason for the deviation from common Swiss-German practice is that the hairdresser's owner and his employees immigrated to Switzerland from Kosovo and learned German as a foreign language. They, therefore, have only passive knowledge of the dialect, as usually only the standard is taught in language courses. Because many of the customers also come from Kosovo or other Albanian-speaking countries (Macedonia, Albania), Albanian is the language used most in the store. The hairdresser's not only serves as a place where men (there is almost no female clientele) get their hair cut but also as a meeting point for the Albanian-speaking community, where people come to chat with the owner and to meet friends or relatives.

From the outside, however, this is not visible: passersby will have no inkling of the place's main linguistic characteristic, as there is no sign in Albanian. Instead, they must know this already: they have to be part of the community, an insider, to get inside and make use of the communitarian (Ehlich, 2007, p. 30) value that the place offers to their language community (cf. Scarvaglieri, 2018).

In this hairdresser's French is, thus, made visible in line with the city's official bilingualism. However, for oral communication with customers or business representatives, French is not used. Communicative practice shows that German suffices (the owner supported this by stating in an interview that they 'get by with German'). As in the LL of Biel/Bienne, German is used as an important language for specific communicative purposes that allows interaction across different language groups. Albanian, a language of immigration, is not made visible, which again mirrors our observations from the LL, even though the language is very important for oral communication and defines the hairdresser's as a place where Albanian-speaking persons meet.

Language practice, thus, shows that language users treat the use of German and French together as *the* ordinary activity type in public settings and apply it as often as possible. At the same time, it is evident that this is not so for purely communicative reasons, as language practice in itself indicates that German alone often suffices in Biel/Bienne. Instead, it seems that there are factors beyond understanding and being understood that influence language use and contribute to the ordinariness of the bilingual activity type. These factors become more visible when we investigate language policies and discourse about language in the media.

Ordinarizing language use: language policy and media discourse

Earlier, I described the bilingualism policy that authorities follow when using language in the public. Language policy in Biel/Bienne is, however, not restricted to the language use of official bodies but also comprises measures designed to influence the linguistic behavior of 'ordinary people' and companies. Together with the Canton of Berne and the federal government, the city finances the Forum for the Bilingualism foundation (*Forum für die Zweisprachigkeit/Forum du bilinguisme*), whose purpose is to support the city's official bilingualism. It carries out various programs to promote bilingualism and awards a bilingualism label to companies and institutions that are deemed to deal with the two official languages in an appropriate way. In 2012 and 2013, the forum ran a campaign in support of a bilingual LL that used posters, press releases, and public presentations urging language users (mainly businesses) to 'Live the Bilingualism'.

The campaign was critical of the fact that only 20% of publicly visible posters were in French (it is not clear how this figure was obtained) and that 'some nationally operating corporations revert to English ads or ads with no text at all' (press release by the Forum from 11/29/2012) instead of using German and French. In a press release, the forum mentioned that visitors traveling through the city perceived Biel/Bienne as German rather than bilingual and urged businesses to use both German and French in public communication. The campaign was supported by the city's mayor and the local chamber of commerce; the urge to use more French in public, thus, had the official backing of major local authorities.

The campaign clearly constituted an attempt to influence language choice in public by invoking certain positive language attitudes (Lasagabaster, 2004; Ziegler, Schmitz, & Uslucan, 2018) regarding the city's established linguistic constituency. It was based on the recognition that, for communicative reasons alone, language users do not make French as visible as desired, and therefore need to be nudged toward equal use of both languages. To convince them of this, the campaign referred, inter alia, to the city's image and its perception by others.

The campaign, thus, represents an instance of *ordinarization* of language use: the activity type of using German and French together in public is framed as the most appropriate, socially desirable way to communicate in public. Other ways of communicating are either not mentioned at all (immigrant languages) or explicitly criticized as inappropriate and unfitting (use of English, no languages). We see that language practice in Biel/Bienne is not the natural product of actants' communicative and cooperative needs, but that it is being influenced by powerful social actors who frame certain activity types as desirable and strive to make them ordinary, to *ordinarize* them, while rejecting others as inappropriate. Similar to the examples discussed in relation to the normality concept, ordinarizing certain activity types at the same time means characterizing other activities (English as lingua franca, German only, communication without language) as not normal and therefore inappropriate. As our observations of language practice have shown, language users follow the call for equal representation of both languages as much as possible and only stray from this in specific situations, when linguistic, financial, or temporal resources for translation are not available, even though in practice French carries a reduced communicative value.

The bilingualism ideology that is brokered by the Forum for bilingualism and that governs the city's language policy is also visible in media discourse on language in Biel/Bienne. In general, media discourse focuses on the city's two official languages and portrays bilingualism positively, as a precious social and economic resource (e.g. Chabloz, 2013; Wäber, 2016). Problems and threats to the city's bilingualism are also very present in the discourse, as illustrated by a radio feature that ran on SRF 4, a German-language public radio broadcaster.[4] The feature expresses a general concern about the city's sociolinguistic situation and starts with the question 'What continues to hold the city together—together for now'? It investigates threats to the city's bilingualism, identifying as the main problem the dominance of the German-speaking majority. Beneath this general threat, the feature names specific problems, particularly the fact that the local 'hospital's emergency doctor speaks High German only',[5] and that 'multi-culti, with over 100 languages', has 'upstaged bilingualism'. The use of English as a lingua franca in Biel/Bienne is referred to as 'the nightmare of any true Bieler'. The radio program, thus, makes it clear that using German and French is not only the normal or ordinary, but the preferable linguistic activity type in Biel/Bienne. The discussion of threats to the city's bilingualism portrays the use of German and French as a social norm that is supposedly in danger and needs to be protected through language users' sustained employment of both languages. The list of specific problems mentioned in the feature reveals that using languages other than German or French (like 'High German', English or one of the more than 100 'multi-culti languages' of immigration) is not perceived as ordinary, but as potentially threatening the city's unique sociolinguistic character.

As the Forum for the Bilingualism's campaign also demonstrated, the brief examination of media discourse reveals that language practice does not emerge naturally out of the need to use language for interindividual cooperation. Instead, the examples discussed indicate strong influences on language use: based on language attitudes and ideologies (Blommaert, 2006; Heller, 2007), different activity types are evaluated against each other in public discourse, with the use of German and French clearly marked as the most appropriate. What at first sight seems ordinary and normal—the use of German and French alongside each other—is the result of processes of ordinarization: processes that evaluate ways of using language and clearly identify one particular way as the most normal and most desirable. The constant use of this activity type, especially in public settings, results in the impression of ordinariness, whereas the processes that guide and ordinarize such language use are much less visible.

Discussion

From an empirical perspective, this chapter has attempted to demonstrate two things: first, the use of German and French in public settings in Biel/Bienne is *the ordinary way* of communicating; and second, this ordinariness is not simply the natural result of users fulfilling cooperation needs, but that it is societally produced. The observation that language users, while making both languages visible to a similar degree, rely mostly on German for complex communicative tasks hinted at factors other than cooperative needs as influencing language use and resulting in an almost equal public representation of both languages, despite their different communicative values. Investigating language policy and discourse in the mass media, I have indeed been able to identify such factors that push for a greater use of French in public and, thereby, contribute to the ordinarization of a specific language practice. What at first sight seems a natural and ordinary way to communicate in a 'bilingual' city is actually the result of processes that evaluate certain activity types as desirable and thus ordinarize them, while ignoring other activity types or expressly marking them as inappropriate and unordinary.

I, therefore, suggest that, while the concept of the ordinariness of translinguistics in general seems to entail strong normalizing effects regarding linguistic diversity, the process that leads to the ordinarization of certain activity types needs to be considered as well. This not only allows us to reconstruct how ordinarization occurs but also shines an analytical light on those activities that fall by the wayside, that is, are perceived as unordinary or extraordinary. Often these activity types are 'erased' from public visibility by the effects of language ideologies (Irvine & Gal, 2000, p. 38). Investigating ordinarization, therefore, allows us to better understand the ideological processes that influence social structure and social behavior in ways that remain largely unnoticed by ordinary, everyday perspectives on social interaction.

Acknowledgements

This work has been made possible through financial support by the Swiss National Science Foundation, Project PZ00P1_161248.

Notes

1 This process of establishing control was a gradual one and was influenced and restricted by other types of knowledge that were more difficult to control (like fairy tales, myths, common sense, and other types of folk knowledge).
2 This model is more aptly termed 'receptive multilingualism' or 'Lingua Receptiva' (Rehbein, ten Thije & Verschik, 2012) and found in numerous contexts outside of Switzerland (see e.g. ten Thije & Zeevaert, 2007).
3 *Ferme* in French means 'farm'. The correct form for 'closed' would be *Fermé*.
4 https://www.srf.ch/play/radio/srf-4-news-spezial/audio/zweisprachiges-biel-tout-va-bien?id=3814f876-fa41-4880-a237-96072cc6ca45&station=69e8ac16-4327-4af4-b873-fd5cd6e895a7 (checked January 26th 2019).
5 In this context, 'High German' (*Hochdeutsch*) indicates that the person is a German national who speaks neither a Swiss German dialect nor French. 'High German' here serves as a cipher for 'foreigner from Germany'.

References

Androutsopoulos, J. (2007). Bilingualism in the mass media and on the Internet. In M. Heller (Ed.), *Bilingualism: A social approach* (pp. 207–230). Basingstoke, UK: Palgrave Macmillan.

Blommaert, J. (2006). Language ideology. In K. Brown (Ed.), *Encyclopedia of language & linguistics, volume 6: Sociolinguistics* (2nd ed., pp. 510–522). Oxford, UK: Elsevier.

Blommaert, J. (2013). *Ethnography, superdiversity and linguistic landscapes: Chronicles of complexity.* Bristol, UK: Multilingual Matters.

Chabloz, R. (2013). "Sich gegenseitig bereichern"/ "S'enrichir, pas s'aplaventrir". *Biel Bienne* 5/22/2013: 3.

Dovchin, S. (2017). The ordinariness of youth linguascapes in Mongolia. *International Journal of Multilingualism, 14*(2), 144–159.

Dovchin, S., & Lee, J. W. (2019). Introduction to special issue: The ordinariness of translinguistics. *International Journal of Multilingualism, 16*(2), 105–111.

Ehlich, K. (2007). Thrifty monolingualism and luxuriating plurilingualism? In F. Coulmas (Ed.), *Language regimes in transformation* (pp. 19–32). Berlin, Germany: de Gruyter.

Elmiger, D. (2015). Equal status, but unequal perceptions: Language conflict in the bilingual city of Biel/Bienne. *International Journal of the Sociology of Language, 235,* 33–52.

Flubacher, M.-C. (2014). *Integration durch Sprache - die Sprache der Integration.* Göttingen, Germany: V&R.

Foucault, M. (1976). *La volonté de savoir*. Paris, France: Gallimard.

Foucault, M. (1995). Discipline and punish. New York, NY: Vintage.

Heller, M. (2007). Bilingualism as ideology and practice. In M. Heller (Ed.), *Bilingualism: a social approach* (pp. 1–22). Basingstoke, UK: Palgrave Macmillan.

Heller, M., Pietikäinen, S., & Pujolar, J. (2018). *Critical sociolinguistic research methods: Studying language issues that matter*. London, UK: Routledge.

Irvine, J., & Gal, S. (2000). Language ideology and linguistic differentiation. In P. V. Kroskrity (Ed.), *Regimes of language: Ideologies, polities, and identities* (pp. 35–84). Santa Fe, NM: School of American Research.

Kallen, J. (2010). Changing landscapes: Language, space and policy in the Dublin linguistic landscape. In A. Jaworski & C. Thurlow (Eds.), *Semiotic landscapes: Language, image, space* (pp. 41–58). London, UK: Continuum.

Krause, G. (1965). *Altpreußische Uniformfertigung als Vorstufe der Bekleidungsindustrie*. Hamburg, Germany: Schulz.

Lasagabaster, D. (2004). Attitude / Einstellung. In U. Ammon, N. Dittmar, K. J. Mattheier, & P. Trudgill (Eds.), *Sociolinguistics: An international handbook of the science of language and society* (Vol. 3.1, pp. 399–405). Berlin, Germany and New York, NY: de Gruyter.

Link, J. (2009). *Versuch über den Normalismus: Wie Normalität produziert wird* (4th ed.). Göttingen, Germany: V&R.

Rehbein, J., ten Thije, J. D., & Verschik, A. (2012). Lingua receptiva (LaRa) – Remarks on the quintessence of receptive multilingualism. *International Journal of Bilingualism, 16*, 248–264.

Scarvaglieri, C. (2018). Spracheinstellungen und Sprachideologien im "zweisprachigen" Biel/ Bienne. In K. Roth, K. Schramm, & J. Spitzmüller (Eds.), *Phänomen, mehrsprachigkeit: Einstellungen, ideologien, positionierungspraktiken* (pp. 169–188). Duisburg, Germany: Universitätsverlag Rhein-Ruhr.

Scarvaglieri, C., & Pappenhagen, R. (2018). Sprachliche praxis und spracheinstellungen in mehrsprachigen Grenzräumen: Fallstudien in Biel/Bienne (CH) und Ústí nad Labem (CZ). In S. Schiedermair (Ed.), *Deutsch als fremd- und zweitsprache und kulturwissenschaft* (pp. 108–132). München, Germany: Iudicium.

Scarvaglieri, C., Redder, A., Pappenhagen, R., & Brehmer, B. (2013). Capturing diversity: Linguistic land- and soundscaping in urban areas. In J. Duarte & I. Gogolin (Eds.), *Linguistic superdiversity in urban areas: Research approaches* (pp. 45–73). Amsterdam, Netherlands: Benjamins.

Spitzmüller, J. (2013). Metapragmatik, indexikalität, soziale registrierung. *Zeitschrift für diskursforschung, 1*(3), 263–287.

Stadt, B. (2016). *Biel/Bienne. Statistisches fact sheet*. Biel, Switzerland: Stadt Biel.

ten Thije, Jan D., & Zeevaert, Ludger (Eds.) (2007). *Receptive multilingualism*. Amsterdam, Netherlands: Benjamins.

Wäber, I. (2016). Vergraulte Romands. *Biel Bienne* 8/10/2016: 2.

Werlen, I. (2005). Biel/Bienne – Leben in einer zweisprachigen Stadt. *Bulletin Suisse De Linguistique Appliquée, 82*, 5–16.

Wodak, R., & Meyer, M. (Eds.) (2009). *Methods of critical discourse analysis*. Los Angeles, CA: SAGE.

Ziegler, E., Schmitz, U., & Uslucan, H. H. (2018). Attitudes toward visual multilingualism in the linguistic landscape of the Ruhr Area. In M. Pütz & N. Mundt (Eds.), *Expanding the linguistic landscape: Linguistic diversity, multimodality and the use of space as a semiotic resource* (pp. 264–299). Bristol, UK: Multilingual Matters.

5

ORDINARY DIFFERENCE, EXTRAORDINARY DISPOSITIONS

Sustaining multilingualism in the writing classroom

Sara P. Alvarez and Eunjeong Lee

Introduction

In the last two decades, sociolinguists have shown that contemporary language use characterized by globalization, accelerated mobility, and complexity cannot be productively explained with the assumptions of homogeneity, fixity, and stability (Blommaert & Rampton, 2011; Pennycook & Otsuji, 2015). Simultaneously, these scholars have also argued that the dynamic character of language practice should not be treated outside of its quotidian context. As Dovchin and Lee (2019) have recently argued, a 'necessary condition of "linguistic paradox" is its "regularity"' (p. 105). Home to at least 138 named languages, as well as its ethnically, racially, and economically diverse speakers, Queensborough, NY exemplifies such dynamicity and complexity of language pluralism in its everyday linguistic landscape (Iyer, 2015, p. 67; *The Newest New Yorkers*, 2013). In Queens, older and newer immigrant and non-immigrant communities group, and regroup, showing that what was 'new' and 'different' before is another everyday formation of cultural and linguistic pluralism (Lee, 2015, p. 298).

City University of New York (CUNY) campuses, specifically Queens College, a Hispanic-Serving Institution (HSI) where we are situated, also reflect these nuanced and plural differences—to the extent that Parmegiani (2014) contends that linguistic and cultural pluralism is an everyday occurrence for most of the transnational students at CUNY. Indeed, at Queens College (2018), approximately 71.2% of undergraduate students identified as part of an ethnic, racial, and/or culturally named community, with 37.1% of students identifying as part of a historically underrepresented group. Additionally, 34.1% of students marked a territory outside the United States as their place of birth, with the majority of them identifying as Chinese-born. As of 2015, 70% of the students enrolled in the First-Year Writing program reported speaking 62 different languages beyond English in their everyday practice (Wan, 2018).

These diverse student populations bring rich and complex language practices, as well as ample schooling experiences, to the writing classroom (Brooks, 2017; Corcoran, 2017; Suárez-Orozco, Suárez-Orozco, & Todorova, 2008). Yet, students at CUNY continue to face multiple struggles and barriers both tied to the long-standing English-only, monolingual ideology of US education and the stigma attached to students labeled or identified as multilingual, in particular, in the writing classroom (Alvarez, 2018). Highlighting this irony, Hall (2014) argues that when it comes to schooling, culturally and linguistically diverse students 'are part of the class, but they are not yet part of the course, part of the curriculum' (p. 43). Certainly, Hall is not the only one to have called attention to this issue of ideology and praxis in responding to cultural and linguistic pluralism in the classroom, as paradigmatic and pedagogical changes that value these practices and students' multilingual identities have also received necessary attention (Lin, 2013; Paris & Alim, 2017).

In this chapter, we argue that while multilingualism in most late modern societies can be an ordinary everyday occurrence, as it is for Queens College students, its cultivation and sustainability in educational settings require 'extraordinary' multilingual-oriented dispositions, specifically educators' material and dispositional labor. In other words, if translanguaging as theorized in García's *Bilingualism in the 21st century* (2009), is to see each and every student's embodied language practice as accessing a continuum of languaging, we ought to approach each multilingual interaction and site with critical care for how students and teachers are rhetorically attuned to multilingual practices (Lorimer Leonard, 2014). This chapter draws on a collaborative teacher narrative of navigating multilingual practices in the college writing classrooms. As writing instructors with specialized training in applied linguistics and urban and bilingual education, we reflect on how our dispositional and pedagogical labor is emergent and attuned to sustaining students' multilingual practices and historicities. We particularly focus on the 'extraordinary' labor and expertise that needs to be brought to spaces where 'multilingualism is the mainstream', but not grounded in the instructional approach (Hall, 2014).

Labor in teaching linguistically and culturally diverse students

With changing linguistic landscapes, scholars have emphasized the need to better understand how language pluralism and difference intersect and shape students' everyday lives, and accordingly, how we can better address the rich practices of linguistically and culturally diverse students. Proponents of culturally sustaining pedagogies (Paris & Alim, 2014) have called on educators to reorient their stance to the 'democratic project of schooling'. Alim and Paris (2017) critique the assimilationist stance of asset-based pedagogy in schools where students' linguistic and cultural difference only matters to the extent that it helps them to acquire a white gazed form of 'academic' English. From this perspective, they argue, matters of 'access' and 'equity' are reframed away from the 'white gaze', which views and treats students of color and their language and cultural practices as deficient, different, and in-need of approximation to the white gaze (p. 3). Instead, schools should be 'a site for *sustaining* the cultural ways of being of communities of color rather than eradicating them' while also helping students to develop a critical eye toward their own linguistic and cultural practices (p. 2, emphasis added). Expanding on this argument, Flores and Rosa (2015) pose that a person's linguistic performance is always evaluated on the backdrop of their assumed racial identity. Writing classrooms are then generally interpreted as spaces for students to 'master' a discourse that is derivative of the monolingual white gaze.

Moving away from this monolingual ideology and English-only bias, translingualism forwards the view that language difference and multilingualism is our communicative norm, rather than deviation (Canagarajah & Dovchin, 2019). Translingualism emphasizes the nature of language as heterogeneous, fluid, and emergent. Working toward similar goals, and arguing for translanguaging, García (2009) poses that multilinguals '*make sense of their bilingual world*' by drawing on one holistic languaging repertoire, across different named languages and modalities as well as different material means developed throughout their own languaging histories and practices (p. 45; emphasis in the original). With this reconceptualization of language and literacy, scholars have called for a translingual-oriented teaching of writing, by which '[t]he possibility of writer error is reserved as an interpretation of last resort' (Horner, Lu, Royster, & Trimbur, 2011, p. 304).

Understanding how language pluralism and our students' *doing* of language functions in their writing requires us to be 'rhetorically attuned' to language differences and literate activities that our students bring into our own classrooms (Horner, 2018; Lorimer Leonard, 2014). This rhetorical attunement is an emergent practice that is directly tied to work and labor, as Gallagher and Noonan (2017) argue:

> Translingualism is not … an accomplishment or a status. It is instead an orientation to language difference and the reading, writing, and teaching practices that emerge from that orientation. We cannot claim to *be* translingual; we can only learn to practice translingualism.
>
> *(pp. 175–176, emphasis original)*

These series of calls for *doing* of translingualism have generated fruitful discussions on pedagogy and programmatic reforms predominantly centered on students' emergent and situated language practices (Horner & Tetreault, 2017; Lee & Jenks, 2016). However, as E. Lee and Canagarajah (forthcoming) note, teachers' own dispositions can influence their everyday multilingual interactions with their students, including their pedagogical labor. And such dispositions are constitutive of language ideologies, undergirding one's recognition of language difference as 'ordinary' or 'unordinary'.

As briefly discussed earlier, linguistic and cultural pluralism are the social reality of CUNY and specifically Queens College campuses. Yet, even with the prevalence of plurality, hybridity, and fluidity of language and literacy practices, our metropolitan space is not free from the imposition of a dominant monolingual ideology; after all, this is the very place that contributed to the construction and development of the field of basic writing, which largely emerged from the perspective that public university students in the city of New York (in particular, students of color) needed 'English' and English writing 'remediation' (Otte & Mlynarczyk, 2010; Trimbur, 2016). As we write, we feel the friction between such multilingual reality and strong monolingual orientation—so much so that even including non-alphabetic characters on our business cards became something Eunjeong had to negotiate in detail, and our students still bring stories of how writing instructors continue to perceive their writing as 'unreadable', 'unclear', or 'not understandable'.

Here, we make a note of the fact that this inequitable schooling with a dominant English-only (as monolithically and monolingually conceived) orientation, too, is part of our students' everyday lived experiences. And as we have written before, it is also a part of our own ethnic and ethnicized writing instructor experiences (Alvarez et al., 2017). The very co-presence and friction between translinguality and the English-only ideology make all the more important the efforts to not only recognize such linguistic context but also reflect the reality in our pedagogy in a sustainable manner. To that end, we offer our reflection of two experiences as language users, educators, and researchers with particular identities and positionalities that ultimately led us to a series of reattunements and pedagogical labor.

In these two narratives, we, Eunjeong and Sara, show the ways in which we extend our own multilingual practices into the writing classroom, and are constantly looking to better understand the educational linguistic landscapes we work in. In discussing these narratives, we hope to show how we come to take on a stance and disposition toward multilingualism across the different sites of writing classrooms.

Learning and unlearning 'normal' difference: Eunjeong

'Why would he always call your name /ʒʊəng/? It's not French. Like, my name too. It's Andrea, not Andréa in Spanish'. My friend Andrea, an immigrant of Maori heritage from New Zealand, pointed out how our names were often pronounced differently. There I was in Lubbock, a small town in West Texas where my difference was visible on and off campus. Through my efforts to negotiate with being racialized, I acquired a range of variations of my name, from /ʒʊən/ to /junʦⁱʰʌn/ to /unʤɔŋ/ sometimes with an added stress on /un/. And just like with my names, I learned to hear and recognize differences as I moved across different places.

As an English major and a writing instructor, I was supposed to 'master' 'The English', the language that my fellow literature and cultural studies colleagues and professors spoke that I didn't ever think will ever become mine. Living with the deficient gaze toward my own English while trying to hide it was the norm that I couldn't overcome. While in that position, I worked as an online grader, and I never knew whose paper I was grading. This was supposed to be a 'fair' system to students. I hid behind this 'fair' system, working hard to be a faceless reader and emulate the English that was never mine. Any mistakes I made, I attributed to my own English.

I quickly realized that my new 'normal' scene can flip its face so easily—even within the same campus, and so does what it means to bring a form of difference. I started working in the Applied Linguistics program where a majority of graduate students spoke English as their additional language. I slowly realized the deficiency I carried myself was also shared among my students. I tried to 'unlearn' my obsession with mastery of English. Instead, I tried to read and listen to students away from my internalized white gaze, while trying to make transparent the 'standardized English' and the ideology underneath it for my students.

Five years later, when I thought I had a better understanding of what my 'normal' teaching looks like and includes, I started teaching in Monterey, California. Many of my students at this HSI grew up speaking varying degrees of Spanishes, African American Englishes, Mandarin, Cantonese, and Urdu at home, while navigating the monolingual space of the English-only ideology in school. Because of this rich set of linguistic practices, I told myself that I needed to better understand what works in this new setting. I adopted readings by authors with similar linguistic and cultural backgrounds to my students, which generated insightful and critical discussions on their schooling experiences and 'fake' and 'superficial' diversity in Monterey.

One day, my students wrote a response based on their reading of Joanne Kilgour Dowdy's (2002) 'Ovuh Dyuh'. Their responses forced me to see how I, who grew up in a seemingly monolingual and monocultural country, failed to recognize the complexity in my students' experiences with race, language, and ethnicity. One student wrote, 'I never reveal to anyone that I am of Mexican heritage because I look whiter, and I don't speak fluent Spanish. They almost immediately ask me, "so you speak Spanish?" and I have to feel guilty about that'. Another student stated,

> I noticed that a lot of American friends correct my English, but I was perplexed because that's how I spoke Singaporean English growing up. And of course, they assume I'm Chinese, because I look like one [and therefore think that] I need to speak American English.

After all these years, I continue to learn and unlearn my assumptions about language difference—more so as now at Queens College, my students and I engage in semester-long inquiries about our own positionality and embodied experiences and our relationships with language, race, ethnicity, and writing. I still don't have a ready-made answer to 'what works in the multilingual classroom'? And I don't think I ever will. But what became crucial in my praxis throughout the years is this: only when I put the onus on myself and my institutional position, not my students, to better read their history and practice as a writer, can I see the rich complexity behind their different meaning makings.

One classroom activity, different instructor dispositions: Sara

As a Latina educator, with over 10 years of experience teaching in secondary and post-secondary urban and rural settings, one of my most vivid teaching memories dates back to when I first taught first-year writing at a flagship school in Kentucky. Despite all the anticipated changes for someone coming from a large metropolitan space in the Northeast to a small city within the culture of a college town, the change I remember most was relating my bi-national and ethnic background to my first-year writing students. Growing up in Queens I always described myself as 'Colombian'. This description went without offering much more explanation about my multilingual upbringing in what many consider the heart of New York City. I realized, however, that navigating these identity vectors with students was an important practice of linguistic and cultural pluralism.

During the third week of classes, I shared with students that they would have an opportunity to interview me. I had designed this activity for students to gain practice with interviews and experience how interviews mediate power and personal information. I was impressed by how excited and invested students were in this task. Working in teams, my Southern students asked questions like, 'Are you married'? 'What religion are you'? 'Do you like basketball'? I didn't answer all of their questions, and sometimes I deflected answering to redirect the narrative they constructed about me. I found that students' questions, too, offered me great insight about their context and social lives, but it was one of my least conscientious responses that generated the most commotion and confusion in the classroom.

> 'What do you miss the most about New York—besides your family'?
> 'The food; Colombian food', I said.

My response seemed to throw students in a loop, as I watched teams reorganize their questions and reconstruct what Colombian meant in relation to my identity. From this moment on, many of my students' questions ruminated around and about identity and language. 'How come I sounded and acted so much like a New Yorker'? Some students even offered examples of what they had identified and observed as my New York attitude: eating while walking, dressing in dark colors, and timing activities. Students also asked about how I had learned English, and could I speak, read, and write in other languages. Their inquiries were genuinely curious and revealed much about the dominant linguistic and cultural context of the space, by which English was a dominant language and most of my students identified as white with no ethnic affiliation. Though, in retrospect, my initial response was also situated in my own upbringing in Queens, where languages and ethnicities collide easily with Americanisms. But even this experience is limited to the time in which I experienced Queens and my positionality and disposition as an educator.

Fast forward 6 years, I'm teaching first-year writing at Queens College (CUNY), and I find that for my students this same interview activity yields similar interest differently. And, once again, I find myself reattuning my disposition. Students in Queens find my Colombian-Americanness and my immigrant roots identifiable with their own experiences. They tell me this explicitly, but I also see this in the many questions students ask about my parents. 'How do your parents deal with English', they ask. Students want to know if I've experienced anything like what we read in class from Martínez's (2016) 'Academia Love Me Back'.

Yet, students also question the ideology that language is directly tied to ethnicity and place of birth. My Asian Latina students, who often mediate Cantonese, Mandarin and Caribbean Spanishes in the classroom ask, 'Anything else besides Colombian'? I've also often pondered about this because of my own research with immigrant communities and how the often-constructed linearity between language, writing practice, nationality, and ethnicity is a lot more complex and particular to each of the people I've spoken with. In fact, this has become one of the aspects of writing instruction that has become most apparent to me throughout the years, the demand for complex ways of understanding how multilingualism, race, immigration, and writing instruction connect to one another, and can (and do) yield specific dispositions in writing instruction.

Instructor reattunement in the writing classroom

Our experiences of attunement and redispositioning across the writing classrooms signal how we have learned to treat our ethnic identities, writing instructor expertise, and multilingual orientation as an emergent practice that requires extraordinary care and educator labor. We have come to consciously think about how our own loci of enunciation (Mignolo, 2002) are viewed against various language practices, including those that undergird colonial and Western hegemonic discourses dominant in academia. The different socializations we embody, and dispositions fostered through such processes, provide us a lens through which we see and can sometimes fail to see.

At the same time, reflecting on these experiences allows us to see that while Pennycook's (2010, p. 51) argument that 'language creativity is about sameness that is also difference' can hold in every writing classroom, the ways in which instructors navigate, enrich, and sustain multilingualism require different forms of work. Specifically, foregrounding linguistic and cultural pluralism in the classroom demands consistent and evolving reattunements toward different multilingual spaces. Here, we want to note that we are treating multilingualism as a practice that all students navigate in their everyday literacies and is not limited to their racialized positioning.

For Eunjeong, moving between Englishes on paper in a supposedly 'fair' system, these differences became normality but also interpreted against the monolithic 'Standardized English' she herself was read against. Additionally, teaching writing to students that were institutionally categorized as English as a Second Language (ESL) students in Texas and then working with students deemed as multilingual in California challenged Eunjeong to think about the different complex relationships that her students had formed with Englishes as well as her own relationship with Englishes.

For Sara, attuning herself to the questions her students asked of her, as a person who embodied difference in Kentucky, helped her reposition the ways in which she offered and understood her own positionality. Moreover, conducting this very same activity in a supposedly local 'multilingual' setting helped her realize how her students also understood their friction against an English-only orientation. For example, her students in Queens were more likely to focus on the complexities of raciolinguistics in writing and how English-only affected their family and community dynamics.

This type of reattunement and dispositioning is the kind of extraordinary writing instructor labor we argue for. While some calls for multilingual-oriented classrooms have often been contended as 'an everything goes' and 'all is creativity', our own experiences show that this type of orientation requires expertise, reflexivity, and lending of our own dispositions to sustain students' rich practices. In this way, we identify three specific aspects of our practice of reattunement: (1) Sustain and enrich our students' multilingual practices by prioritizing them in writing tasks and activities; (2) Closely examine how students both *respond to* and *labor with* classroom tasks and activities; (3) Focus our reading of students' alphabetic-based writing on what we see their writing conveying and making sense of, as opposed to what we have been trained to read as 'variation' or 'difference'.

In forwarding these practices of reattunement, we are also specifically thinking about what these forms of labor entail for our own involvement in the 'democratic project of schooling' (Paris & Alim, 2014). As Flores (2016) rightfully argues, schooling spaces, especially in the context of writing, 'in their own way seek to monitor and control the language practices of language-minoritized students' (p. 2). In this sense, working to sustain the 'ordinary difference' of multilingualism means working against the dominant monolingual ideologies that create marginalizing experiences for all students, but especially language-minoritized students who are also often confronted with unequal social experiences, spaces, and opportunities (Jemmott, 2019). In our own multilingual context at Queens College, in which, as noted earlier, most of our students have confronted the institutional surveillance and policing of their own language practices, we feel a greater demand to labor against the superimposition of English-only ideology. For language-minoritized students, the expansion of their language and literacy practices moves beyond cultural and material capital; it is also about the community and family ties that are part of their embodied experiences as bilinguals. For this reason, in our role as writing instructors, we see this labor reattunement as one that is also tied to critically caring for our students' growth and overall being.

These dispositional practices influenced our assignments and curricula design, guiding us to particularly focus on opportunities for students to engage with language plurality and difference. For example, in our multilingual mini-ethnography project, our students interviewed other individuals they viewed as multilingual and learned about their language and literacy practices. Many students interviewed their family members or friends in languages they felt 'experienced with'. Surprisingly, many students reported about how this experience had given an opportunity to talk to their interviewee about a topic that they never had a chance to before in a language other than English for a school project. Additionally, as students ultimately reported verbatim quotes from the interviewee along with their own analysis and interpretation, it provided them a chance to think about their role in representing the knowledge and language practices of the communities they feel belonging with. Through these assignments, our students engaged in an inquiry project while also enriching their 'everyday' multilingual practices. Doing so has also helped us further understand the complexity behind our students' languaging history and practices.

Conclusion

If contemporary global and digital contexts demand that people negotiate a variety of possible and often competing communicative practices, educators and writing instructors are then at a prime place for sustaining and enriching students' multilingual practices. However, because of the dominant monolingual orientation of educational settings and writing communication—in particular—addressing and enriching a multilingual classroom requires rhetorically attuned multilingual-oriented instructor dispositions.

To dismantle the monolingual ideology and sustain our students' multilingual practices at the center of our classroom, we need to reconceptualize not only what legitimate language is but also what legitimate labor includes beyond our traditional understanding of what a teacher should know and be able to do toward what end. Finally, the labor of attuning and reattuning ourselves to difference may not be always visible as we notice, understand, and interpret difference, and such practice needs to be also made visible to students as a crucial way to engage with multiple differences. The series of labor we describe will help us not only imagine but materialize a multilingual-oriented educational space that encourages students to see the languaging practices between school and home not as separate but as one dynamic continuum.

References

Alim, H. S., & Paris, D. (Eds.) (2017). What is culturally sustaining pedagogy and why does it matter? In D. Paris & H. S. Alim (Eds.), *Culturally sustaining pedagogies: Teaching and learning for justice in a changing world* (pp. 1–21). New York, NY: Teachers College Press.

Alvarez, S. P. (2018). Multilingual writers in college contexts. *Journal of Adolescent & Adult Literacy, 62*(3), 342–345.

Alvarez, S. P., Canagarajah, A. S., Lee, E., Lee, J.W., & Rabbi, S. (2017). Translingual practice, ethnic identity, and voice in writing. In B. Horner & L. Tetreault (Eds.), *Crossing divides: Exploring translingual writing pedagogies and programs* (pp. 20–31). Logan: Utah State University Press.

Blommaert, J., & Rampton, B. (2011). Language and superdiversity. *Diversity, 12*(2). UNESCO. Retrieved from www.unesco.org/shs/diversities/vol13/issue2/art1

Brooks, D. M. (2017). How and when did you learn your languages?: Bilingual students' linguistic experiences and literacy instruction. *Journal of Adolescent & Adult Literacy, 60*(4), 383–393.

Canagarajah, A. S., & Dovchin, S. (2019). The everyday politics of translingualism as a resistant practice. *International Journal of Multilingualism, 16*(2), 127–144.

Corcoran, L. (2017). 'Languaging 101': Translingual practices for translingual realities of the SEEK composition classroom. *Journal of Basic Writing, 36*(2), 54–77.

CUNY Total Enrollment by Race/Ethnicity and College. (2017). [Graph illustration Total Senior Colleges, Fall 2017]. Retrieved from https://www.cuny.edu/irdata-book/rpts2_AY_current/ENRL_0015_RACE_TOT_PCT.rpt.pdf

Dovchin, S., & Lee J. W. (2019). Introduction to special issue: 'The ordinariness of Translinguistics'. *International Journal of Multilingualism, 16*(2), 105–111.

Dowdy, J. K. (2002). Ovuh dyuh. In L. Delpit & J. K. Dowdy (Eds.), *The skin that we speak: Thoughts on language and culture in the classroom* (pp. 3–14). New York, NY: The New Press.

Flores, N. (2016). Combatting marginalized spaces in education through language architecture. *Perspectives on Urban Education, 13*(1), 1–3.

Flores, N., & Rosa, J. (2015). Undoing appropriateness: Raciolinguistic ideologies and language diversity in education. *Harvard Educational Review, 85*(2), 149–301.

Gallagher, C., & Noonan, M. (2017). Becoming global: Learning to 'do' translingualism. In B. Horner & L. Tetreault (Eds.), *Crossing divides: Exploring translingual writing pedagogies and programs* (pp. 161–180). Logan: Utah State University Press.

García, O. (2009). *Bilingual education in the 21st century: A global perspective.* Oxford, UK: Wiley-Blackwell.

Hall, J. (2014). Multilinguality is the mainstream. In B. Horner & K. Kopelson (Eds.), *Reworking English in rhetoric and composition* (pp. 31–48). Carbondale: Southern Illinois University Press.

Horner, B. (2018). Knowledge as social practice. Making futures matter, *Watson Conference*, Kentucky, conference presentation.

Horner, B., Lu, M., Royster, J. J., & Trimbur, J. (2011). Language differences in writing: Toward a translingual approach. *College English, 73*(3), 299–317.

Horner, B., & Tetreault, L. (Eds.). (2017). *Crossing divides: Exploring translingual writing pedagogies and programs.* Logan: Utah State University Press.

Iyer, D. (2015). *We too sing America: South Asian, Arab, Muslim, and Sikh immigrants shape our multiracial future.* New York, NY: The New Press.

Jemmott, E. (2019). The implicit punishment of daring to go to college when poor. *New York Times.* Retrieved from https://www.nytimes.com/2019/03/28/opinion/college-admissions.html?fbclid=IwAR3uLGWgWJjU_W47wSDBCCKHPeiQq-_3K_CTy2FqszWTmsfYssxBW8L9GWo

Lee, E. (2015). *The making of Asian America: A history.* New York, NY: Simon & Schuster Paperbacks.

Lee, E., & Canagarajah, A. S. (forthcoming). Beyond native and nonnative: Translingual dispositions for more inclusive theorization of language teacher identity. *Journal of Language, Identity, and Education.*

Lee, J. W., & Jenks, C. (2016). Doing translingual dispositions: Considerations from a US–Hong Kong partnership. *College Composition and Communication, 68*(2), 317–344.

Lin, A. (2013). Toward paradigmatic change in TESOL methodologies: Building plurilingual pedagogies from the ground up. *TESOL Quarterly, 47*(3), 521–545.

Lorimer Leonard, R. (2014). Multilingual writing as rhetorical attunement. *College English, 76*(3), 227–247.

Martínez, T. (2016). Academia, love me back. *WordPress-Tiffany Martínez: A Journal*, 27. Retrieved from https://vivatiffany.wordpress.com/2016/10/27/academia-love-me-back/

Mignolo, W. D. (2002). The geopolitics of knowledge and the colonial difference. *The South Atlantic Quarterly, 101*(1), 57–96.

The Newest New Yorkers. (2013). Chapter 3: Immigrant settlement patterns in New York City. *NYC City Planning and Mapping.* Retrieved from https://www1.nyc.gov/assets/planning/download/pdf/data-maps/nyc-population/nny2013/chapter3.pdf

Otte, G., & Mlynarczyk, R. W. (2010). *Basic writing.* West Lafayette, IN: Parlor Press and The WAC Clearinghouse.

Paris, D., & Alim, H. S. (2014). What are we seeking to sustain through culturally sustaining pedagogy? A loving critique forward. *Harvard Educational Review, 84*(1), 85–100.

Parmegiani, A. (2014). Bridging literacy practices through storytelling, translanguaging, and an ethnographic partnership: A case study of Dominican students at the Bronx community college. *Journal of Basic Writing, 33*(1), 23–51.

Pennycook, A. (2010). *Language as a local practice.* London, UK: Routledge.

Pennycook, A., & Otsuji, E. (2015). *Metrolingualism: Language in the city.* New York, NY: Routledge.

Queens College Enrolled Student Profile. (2018). [Graph illustration Queens College Fall 2018]. Institutional Effectiveness. Retrieved from https://www.qc.cuny.edu/about/research/Pages/CP-Enrolled%20Student%20Profile.aspx

Suárez-Orozco, C., Suárez-Orozco, M. M., & Todorova, I. (2008). *Learning a new land: Immigrant students in American society.* Boston, MA: The Belknap Press of Harvard University Press.

Trimbur, J. (2016). Translingualism and close reading. *College English, 78*(3), 219–227.

Wan, A. J. (2018). Reports on multilingual writing projects. [unpublished report]. Queens College, CUNY. New York, NY.

PART II

The in/visibility of translinguistics

6

FORMATTING ONLINE ACTIONS

#justsaying on Twitter

Jan Blommaert

Translingualism in the online–offline nexus

Three substantive claims underlie the argument in this chapter. *One*: in considering the contemporary forms of translingualism one can neither avoid online sites of scripted interaction as loci of research nor the online–offline nexus as an area of phenomenal innovation. *Two*: approaching such online forms of translingual interaction can benefit substantially from a radically action-centered approach, rather than from an approach privileging participants and their identity features, or privileging the linguistic/semiotic resources deployed in translingual events. And *three*: addressing online forms of translingual interaction from this perspective can reveal the core features of contemporary social life and serve as a sound basis for constructing innovative social theory.

Of the three claims, the first one is by now widely shared (see e.g. Chapter 13). There is an increasing awareness among students of language in society that the online social world has by now become an integrated part of the sociolinguistic economies of societies worldwide, and that the zone in which we situate our investigations should now best be defined as the online–offline nexus, with phenomena from the online world interacting with those of the offline world and vice versa. There are specific rescaling and chronotopic features of online communication, where interaction is, as a rule not an exception, no longer tied to physical co-presence and effectively shared timespace; and where interactions, as a rule not an exception, include translocal and transtemporal rhizomatic uptake (cf. boyd, 2014; Tagg, Seargeant & Brown, 2017). There are also the outspokenly multimodal default characteristics of online communication. Taken together, it is evident that online communication must be the locus of intense translingualism. My first claim gestures toward the theme of this collection: the online–offline nexus must turn translingualism into the *rule*, the normal, ordinary, and unremarkable sociolinguistic state of affairs.

The two other claims might demand somewhat more attention. The second claim—an action-centered perspective on online interaction—is grounded in (but transcends) a serious methodological problem complicating research: the indeterminacy of participant identities online. Given the widespread use of aliases and avatars on, for instance, social media platforms, nothing can be taken for granted regarding who exactly is involved in interactions. Whether we are interacting with a man or woman, a young or an old person, a local or non-local one, someone communicating in his/her 'native' or 'first' language: none of this can be conclusively established (cf. Li & Blommaert, 2017). This straightforward feature of online interactions destabilizes much of what we grew accustomed to in social studies, including sociolinguistic research. It makes us aware that our sociological imagination is strongly hinged on the self-evident transparency of who people are, the communities they are members of, and the languages that characterize them ethnolinguistically and sociolinguistically. The sociological sample—one of the key inventions of 20th-century social science—cannot be reliably drawn from online data.

Thus, we find ourselves in a research situation in which little can be said a priori about participants and resources involved in social action. The action itself, however, can be observed and examined, and my second claim is to put the analysis of actions central in online–offline nexus research as a firm empirical basis for theory construction (cf. Szabla & Blommaert, 2018). My third claim tags onto that: it is by looking at actions, and at how such actions effectively *produce* participants and resources,[1] that we can get a glimpse of elementary patterns of social behavior through interaction—an opportunity for retheorizing our field. The target of this chapter is to empirically demonstrate that.

I shall do so by looking at a common feature of online interaction: the use of hashtags, in this case on Twitter. The point I am seeking to make is that hashtags, as an entirely new feature in interaction interfering with established ones into a translingual whole, can be shown to be subject to rather clear and strict functions and norms of deployment. In Garfinkel's (2002) terms, they can be shown to involve *formatted actions* with a high degree of normative recognizability, turning them into transparent framing devices in Twitter interactions.

Hashtags and translingualism

If we see translingualism (*pace* the editors of this issue) as the fluid movement between and across languages or—more broadly—semiotic systems, hashtags definitely can serve as prime instances of translingualism. As a feature of social media scripted discourse, the construction '# + word(s)' is a 21st-century innovation. Surely the sign '#' itself was used before the advent of social media: it was, for instance, a symbol on dial phones and was widely used elsewhere as a graphic symbol indicating numbers or, in old-school proofreading practices, indicating a blank space to be inserted in the text. But as we shall see, the social media use of hashtags cannot be seen as an extension of those previous forms of usage. When social media emerged, the hashtag was a free-floating resource that could be functionally redetermined and redeployed in a renewed sociolinguistic system. The fact that the symbol was not tied to a particular language or graphic system such as English or Cyrillic script made it, like the '@' sign, a polyvalent and user-friendly resource, capable of becoming part of global social media discursive repertoires—a process I called 'supervernacularization' (Blommaert, 2012).[2] This means that such symbols can be incorporated—by translanguaging actions—in a nearly unlimited range of language-specific expressions while retaining similar or identical functions.

While the use of hashtags has by now become a standard feature of several social media applications (think of Facebook and Instagram), its usage is most strongly embedded in Twitter. Hashtags there tie together and construct topical units: within the strict confines of message length on Twitter, Hashtags enable users to connect their individual tweets to large thematically linked bodies of tweets and add specific orientations to specific tweets within that larger body (cf Wikström, 2014). In that sense—but I shall qualify this in a moment—their function, broadly taken, is *contextualization*: individual tweets can be offered to audiences as understandable within the topical universe specified by the hashtag. Thus, the '#MeToo' hashtag (one of the most trending hashtags since the 2017 Harvey Weinstein scandal) ties together millions of individual tweets, produced in a variety of languages around the world, within the topical universe of gender-related sexual misconduct and abuse. As a consequence, within Twitter analytics, hashtags are used to define what is 'trending' or 'viral', and other forms of big data mining on social media likewise use hashtags as analytical tools for modeling topics and tracking participant engagement and involvement (e.g., Blaszka et al., 2012; Wang et al., 2016).

There is some work on what is called hashtag activism (e.g. Bonilla & Rosa, 2015; Jackson, 2016; Mendes, Ringrose & Keller, 2018; Tremayne, 2014), but qualitative sociolinguistic or discourse-analytic work focused on hashtags remains quite rare (but see e.g. Wikström, 2014; Zappavigna, 2012). In a recent study, De Cock and Pizarro Pedraza (2018) show how the hashtag '#*jesuis* + *X*' (as in '#jesuisCharlie') functionally shifts from expressing solidarity with the victims of the terrorist attack on the Charlie Hebdo editorial offices in Paris, 2015, to expressing cynicism and critique about hypocrisy when such forms of solidarity are being withheld from the victims of similar attacks elsewhere (as in '#jesuisIstanbul, anyone?'), or jocular and non-sensical uses as in '#jesuis Cafard' ('I am a hangover'). Observe that the corpus used in De Cock and Pizarro Pedraza's study was multilingual, and that the 'French' origins of '#*jesuis* + *X*' did not impede fluency of usage across language boundaries—the hashtag operates translingually.

We can draw a simple but fundamental insight from De Cock and Pizarro Pedraza's study: the functions of hashtags are unstable, changeable, and dynamically productive. The same hashtag can be functionally reordered and redeployed whenever the topical field of the hashtag changes (or can be seen to be changing).

In the analysis of De Cock and Pizarro Pedraza, '*#jesuis* + *X*' shifts from an emblematic sign of (emotional and political) alignment to one of disalignment and even distancing. This shift in function—and the resulting plurality of functions—instantiate *mature enregisterment* in that different, but related, interactional stances are available to users; the hashtag '*#jesuis* + *X*' has become a lexicalized but elastic signifier enabling and marking a variety of forms of footing within a connected thematic domain (c.f., Agha, 2005). It is, to adopt Goffman's (1975) terms now, a *framing device*, enregistered as such within a globally circulating and, of course, translingual, social media supervernacular. De Cock and Pizarro Pedraza call the functions they described for the #jesuis + X hashtag 'pragmatic'. As framing devices, however, hashtags are *metapragmatic* as well, they are interactionally established elements of voicing (Agha, 2005). And the latter takes us to the core of my argument.

Functions of hashtags are interactionally established and should not be seen as simply the activation of latent and stable meaning potential. Seen from an action perspective, the different forms of footing enabled by a hashtag such as '#jesuis + X' represent the different forms of communicative action within what Goffman (1975) called a 'realm'—a 'meaningful universe sustained by the activity' (p. 46). At first glance, the difference between this formulation and the prior ones centering on contextualization, (dis)alignment, and enregisterment seems minimal; in fact, the shift is quite substantial. We now move away from an analytical perspective focused on participants and resources (as in De Cock and Pizarro Pedraza's analysis) to one in which concrete actions are central and seen as points from which both the participants' roles and the values of the resources used in interaction *emerge* (c.f., Cicourel, 1973; Garfinkel, 2002; Goodwin & Goodwin, 1992, 2004). Enregisterment, from this action perspective, does not only stand for the formation of registers-as-resources but also as the emerging of *formats for communicative action*, in which such formats also include the ratification of participants and the concrete mode of effective deployment of semiotic resources. Formats are framed patterns of social action, and I believe I stay very close to what Goffman suggested when I define framing as exactly that: the ordering of interactional conduct in ways that valuate both the roles of participants and the actual resources deployed in interaction between them.

#justsaying as action: basics

I will now illustrate this by means of examples of the interactional deployment of the hashtag *#justsaying*. This hashtag—manifestly English in origin—is widely used on Twitter (also in variants such as #JustSayin, #justsayingg), as well as in non-English messages.[3] And contrary to many other hashtags, it is *not* a topical marker but an explicitly metapragmatic one. The expression 'just saying', in offline vernacular interaction, often indexes consistency in viewpoint and factual certainty in the face of counterargument (Craig & Sanusi, 2000). Let us take a look at what can be done with it on Twitter and concentrate on the types of action it can contribute to. In what follows, I shall use examples of #justsaying deployed in Dutch-language tweets from Belgium and the Netherlands, followed by approximate English translations. Note that there is no Dutch equivalent to #justsaying used on Twitter: it is a fully enregistered (translingual) element in 'Dutch' Twitter discourse.

I must first identify some basic actions performed and performable by means of #justsaying.

Standalone act

A first observation is that #justsaying is very often used for a *standalone communicative act*: a tweet which is not part of a Twitter 'thread' (a series of interactionally connected tweets) but which appears as an individual statement, as in the following:

> Na weken alleen maar foto's over de warmte worden alle media nu overspoeld met foto's en filmpjes met regen, donder en bliksem. #justsaying
>
> Replies: 2; Retweets: 0; Likes: 4

Those are standalone communicative acts, but evidently they are not without contextualization cues. In this tweet from early August 2018, which says 'After weeks of only pictures about the heat, all media are now swamped with pictures and videos with rain, thunder, and lightning', the timing is the cue, as the author refers to the end of the heatwave that swept over Western Europe during that period. Contextualization can also take a more explicit shape as when authors use topical hashtags tying their standalone statement into larger thematic lines, as in the following tweet:

> Tip voor #fgov ... voer de legerdienst terug in zodat onze kinderen zich kunnen verweren tegen de agresseive #islam in ons #europa. Kwestie van tijd dat onze #democratie verdedigd moet worden #manumilitari #justsaying (suggestion for #fgov ... reinstate national service to enable our children to defend themselves against the aggressive #islam in our #europe. Matter of time before our #democracy has to be defended #manumilitari[4] #justsaying)
>
> Replies: 3; Retweets: 12; Likes: 32

In the above instance, we see that the standalone statement has an indirectly called-out and identified addressee, the Belgian Government, hashtagged as #fgov. Specific addressees can, of course, be directly called out through the use of the standard symbol '@', and tweets by default have the author's followers as audiences. Thus, a standalone communicative act does not equal a decontextualized act nor an act that doesn't invite uptake from addressees. On social media, standalone communicative acts are *interactional* by definition, for the congregation of one's Twitter followers (or a section thereof) will see the tweet on their timelines anyway, and they respond by means of 'likes', 'retweets', or 'comments', as we can see in examples 1 and 2. I shall return to this point of addressee responses in greater detail below and underscore its importance.

The main point here is: such standalone tweets are, thus, *framed* in Goffman's sense. They engage with existing 'realms' and select participants. And what they do within such meaningful units and in relation to ratified participants is to signal a particular footing: a self-initiated, detached, factual but critical, sometimes implicitly offensive statement not directly prompted by the statements of others and often proposed as the start of a series of responsive acts by addressees. They trigger and flag from within a recognizable universe of meaningful acts (the registers we use on Twitter and the communities we use them with) a specific *format of action* involving particular forms of 'congregational work', the work we do to make sense of social actions and establish them as social facts (Garfinkel, 2002, p. 245). We can paraphrase the format as: 'here I am with my opinion, which I state in a critical, sober and detached way unprompted by others, and which I offer to you for interactional uptake'.

Let me stress this point once more: standalone acts such as those that are not *isolated* or *non-interactional* are fully social acts performed in a collective of participants who know how to make sense of #justsaying action formats and their concrete contextualized instances. They merely *initiate* such action formats, and, in that sense, provide an initial definition of their main ordering parameters.

Sidetracking and reframing

When #justsaying is interactionally deployed in a thread, we see partly different things. What remains stable is the sober, confident, and detached footing we encountered in standalone instances. But very different formats of action are triggered and flagged by it. And before we engage with these formats of action, I must return to a particularly important feature of the examples that will follow: the duality of addressees. In a thread, an author responds directly to previous tweets and to those identifiable participants involved in those previous tweets. But the individual response tweet also attracts responses from other addressees: the likes and (sometimes) retweets and comments from participants not directly operating within that specific thread. Consider the following example, which is a tweet in response to two other users:

> Ik zeg niet date r iets mis is met grote boeren. Stip alleen aan dat 200 koeien peanuts is vergeleken met de aantallen in Canada. Geen aanval. Geen oordeel. #JustSaying (I'm not saying that something is wrong with large farms. Just pointing out that 200 cows are peanuts compared to the numbers in Canada. No attack. No judgment. #JustSaying)[5]

> Replies: 0; Retweets: 1; Likes: 2

While the author directly responds to two other participants (@X and @Y), her tweet receives a retweet and two likes from different Twitter users. This is important, for we see *two separate lines of congregational work* here: one line performed between the author and her two called-out and identified interlocutors, the authors of previous tweets; another line performed between the author and addressees not involved in the thread but responding, very much in the way described for standalone acts, to the author's specific tweet. Two frames co-occur here, and this is important for our understanding of what follows.

A format of action frequently triggered and flagged by #justsaying on Twitter threads is 'sidetracking', or more precisely, *opening a second line of framing*. In the following series of tweets, the thematic universe of the thread is disrupted by the introduction of another one, initiated on the same detached and sober footing as the standalone cases I discussed above:

> **Participant 1:** Kan iemand even @X vragen of ze mij kan ontblokken? (Can anyone ask @X whether she can unblock me?)
>
> Replies: 7; Retweets: 0; Likes: 2
>
> **Participant 2 (responding to participant 1):** Ik ook....heb volgens mij nooit op haar gereageerd....raar wijf. (Me too....I don't think I ever reacted against her ....strange bitch.)
>
> Replies: 1; Retweets: 0; Likes: 1
>
> **Participant 3 (responding to participants 1, 2):** Vrouwen 'wijf' noemen lijkt mij op zich dan wel weer aanleiding voor een block. #justsaying (Calling women 'bitch' seems to me to be cause for blocking. #justsaying)
>
> Replies: 1; Retweets: 0; Likes: 1
>
> **Participant 2 (responding to participant 3):** Rare madammeke wel ok? (Strange madam ok then?)
>
> Replies: 0; Retweets: 0; Likes: 0

The topic launched by participant 1 is not uncommon among active Twitter users: a complaint about being blocked by someone, @X, articulated here as an appeal to others to help being unblocked by @X. The direct response to this comes from participant 2, who endorses what participant 1 says by expanding the case: he, too, was blocked by @X, apparently for no good reason. In this response, participant 2 uses the term 'bitch' ('wijf'), and this leads to the #justsaying reframing action by participant 3. From the actual case proposed by participant 1 as the topic of the thread, participant 3 shifts to an entirely different one related to the use of derogatory and sexist terminology within the moral framework of 'proper' Twitter usage. The shift, thus, is more than just topical: it reorders the entire normative pattern of interaction. Participant 2 immediately responds defensively by offering an alternative, only slightly less derogatory term. A new frame has been introduced and a new format of action—from collaborative work on one topic to oppositional work on another—has been started.

In opening a second line of framing, the participation framework is also redefined. In the above example, participant 1 is sidelined as soon as the #justsaying remark is made, and the direct interaction in the thread is reordered: it becomes a direct engagement of participant 3 with participant 2, and what started as a one-to-all thread becomes a one-on-one thread. A new line of action is generated by the #justsaying statement.

#justsaying as complex reframing

We have come to understand some of the basic actions in which #justsaying is used. Now look at the following example, an interaction started by the Mayor of Antwerp (participant 1 in the transcript) tweeting from his holiday site in Poland about the Gay Pride held in his town that day:[6]

Participant 1: Ik ben nog in Polen, maar ik wens alle deelnemers in A een geweldige Pride. [Rainbow Flag Emoji] Veilig en vrij, daar draait het om vandaag. [Victory Hand Emoji] (I'm still in Poland but I wish all the participants in Antwerp a great Pride. [Rainbow Flag Emoji] Being yourself safely and freely, that's what matters today. [Victory Hand Emoji])

Replies: 65; Retweets: 91; Likes: 752

Participant 2: Ik vind het cultureel promoten van buitennormaal sexueel gedrag, niet bepaald iets voor een conservative partij.
   Niks tegen holebi's en wel iets tegen hun bashers, maar ook tegen reklame (I find the cultural promotion of extra-natural behavior not suited for a conservative party. I have nothing agains LGBTs, have something against their bashers, but also against publicity)

Replies: 4; Retweets: 0; Likes: 4

Participant 2: Van mij krijgt ieder zijn vrijheid, maar promotie voor tegennatuurlijke handelingen vind ik er dik over (I grant everyone their freedom, but I find the promotion of counternatural acts entirely unacceptable)

Replies: 7; Retweets: 0; Likes: 1

Participant 3: Laten we dan ook reclame voor vliegreizen verbieden. Mensen die vliegen is ook tegennatuurlijk. Om maar 1 voorbeeld te geven. Maar ik geef er met plezier nog enkele indien gewenst. #Just Saying #WearWithPride #antwerppride #KortzichtigeMensen (Let's also prohibit publicity for traveling by plane then. People flying is a counternatural thing as well. To give just 1 example. But I'll happily provide more examples if you wish. #justsaying #WearWithPride #antwerppride #NarrowmindedPeople)

Replies: 1; Retweets: 1; Likes: 8

His tweet is meant as a public, one-to-all statement, and it has the expected effects: it goes viral with hundreds of 'likes' and a large number of retweets. Apart from these forms of response, the tweet also develops into a thread: the Mayor gets several 'comments' from participants addressed by his tweet. The Mayor's public salute to the Antwerp Pride (interestingly, without any topical hashtags) is critically commented on in two turns by participant 2, someone who clearly aligns himself with the right-wing conservative forces opposing the Pride. Observe that participant 2 addresses the Mayor in his responses and comments on the topic initiated by the Mayor. He stays within the frame of the initial activity, and his comments receive a number of likes as well as comments. The #justsaying comment by participant 3 is of particular interest, for it opens a new line of framing and reorders the participation framework. The Mayor is eliminated as a relevant direct addressee and the frame he started is dismissed, as the #justsaying statement by participant 3 is targeting the anti-LGBT turns made by participant 2. In addition, participant 3 connects his tweet explicitly with the Antwerp Pride by means of a string of topical hashtags. The tweet is shifted to another universe of meaning and another audience.

Like in the previous 'blocking' example above, the shift in participation framework is effective: participant 3 gets a reply from participant 2 after his #justsaying statement:

> **Participant 2:** Er zijin wel minder mensen die kotsen als ze een vlieg-tuig zien, dan mensen die misselijk worden bij het zien van homoseksuel praktijken. (There are less people throwing up when they see a plane, than people feeling sick when they see homosexual acts.)
>
> Replies: 3; Retweets: 0; Likes: 1

> **Participant 3:** Omdat het hen goed uitkomt. De reden maakt da teen boodschap mag gedeeld worden. Dat is pas zum kotsen. Zegt veel over de mensen. Maar verhuis gerust naar Rusland als het u zo stoort. (Because it suits them well. The reason ensures that a message can be shared. Now that is zum kotsen (sic, literally 'to make you barf'). Tells a lot about people. But feel free to move to Russia if it annoys you that much.)

A new format of action has been started: an escalating, one-on-one fight between both participants, on the issue of what does or doesn't constitute 'counternatural' conduct.

But there is more. The topical hashtags in participant 3's tweet caused a larger shift in audience and universe of meaning, and so we get different lines of congregational work here. While participant 3 enters into an argument with participant 2, his #justsaying statement gets eight 'likes' and a retweet from Twitter users not otherwise active in this thread. So, parallel to the one-on-one thread developing within a one-to-all interaction started by the Mayor, another one-to-all thread emerges, inviting very different forms of response.

We see the full complexity here of the actions involved in reframing, and we can represent them graphically (Figure 6.1). On Twitter, what we see is a thread opened by the Mayor's one-to-all tweet which triggers collective as well as individual responses, all of it within the frame initiated by the tweet (Frame 1 in Figure 6.1). The thread, therefore, is a unit of action, but a composite and unstable one.[7] Why? Because the #justsaying comment by participant 3 shapes, within the thread as a unit of action, a different frame (Frame 2 in Figure 6.1). In Frame 2, we also see collective as well as individual responses—we see the same genres of action, in other words—but they are performed in a frame shaped by the #justsaying statement by participant 3. This frame is only indirectly related to Frame 1, and it draws participant 2—who reacted initially within Frame 1 to the Mayor's tweet—into a different role and position, with a different interlocutor and with (partly) different audiences, on a different topic. The reframing of the actions means that they are thoroughly *reformatted*: while, formally, the participants in Frames 1 and 2 appear to do very similar things, the difference in frame turns their actions into very different kinds of normatively judged congregational work, creating different social facts.

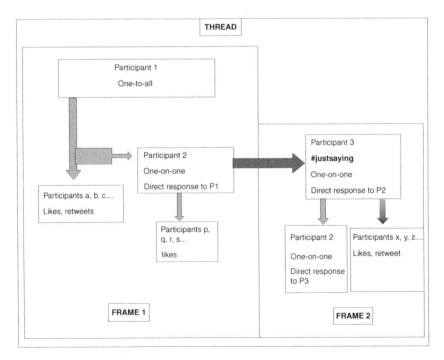

FIGURE 6.1 Graphical representation of reframing on Twitter.

What we see in these examples is how the hashtag #justsaying appears to 'open up' a seemingly unified and straightforward activity (the Twitter thread) to different forms of social action invoking, and thus proleptically scripting, different modes of participation and different modes of uptake, appraisal, and evaluation. It interjects, so to speak, entirely different formats of action into a Goffmanian 'realm', enabling the shaping of very different 'meaningful universes sustained by the activity'. As a framing device, #justsaying is, thus, more than a pragmatic-and-metapragmatic tool. It is something that proleptically signals various allowable modes of conduct and various forms of ratified participation and congregational work in social activities that appear, from a distance, simple and unified.

Hashtags and translingualism revisited

The latter remark takes us to fundamental issues in methodology. Many years ago, Goodwin and Goodwin (1992) told us that 'there are great analytical gains to be made by looking very closely at how particular activities are organized' (p. 96). They made that point in a paper that demonstrated that what is usually perceived as one activity—a 'conversation', for instance—actually contains, and is constructed out of, a dense and complex web of distinct smaller actions, all of which have important contextualizing dimensions and many of which reorder the patterns of roles and normative scripts assumed by the participants. About participants, the Goodwins (2004) later also observed that the frequent use of generalizing category labels such as 'speaker' and 'addressee' again obscure important differences and shifts in the actual actions performed by participants in social interaction. One is not always an 'addressee' *in the same way* during a speech by a 'speaker', for instance: sometimes one is a distant addressee, at other moments an involved one; one's response behavior can be cool and detached at times and deeply engaged and emotional at others, positively sanctioning specific parts of the talk and negatively sanctioning others.

The appeal launched (and continuously reiterated) by the Goodwins was for *precision in analyzing social action* as a key methodological requirement for discourse analysis, something they shared with the likes of Garfinkel, Cicourel, and Goffman, and something that motivated my efforts in this chapter. I tried to demonstrate that the interactional deployment of the hashtag #justsaying involved multiple and complexly related forms of social action, including the profound reframing of activities in such ways that morphologically similar actions (e.g., 'likes' or comments) are formatted differently—they are part of different modes of making sense of what goes on.

The complexity of such discursive work, performed by means of a hashtag productive across the boundaries of conventionally established languages, to me demonstrates advanced forms of enregisterment and, by extension, of communicative competence (cf., Agha, 2005, 2007). This implies—it *always* implies—advanced forms of socialization, for enregisterment rests on the indexical recognizability of specific semiotic forms within a community of users who have acquired sufficient knowledge of the normative codes that provide what Goffman (1975) called 'a foundation for form' (p. 41). Translated into the discourse of translingualism, the complexity of discursive work performed by means of #justsaying demonstrates how translingual forms of this type have acquired a 'foundation', in Goffman's terms, and operate as enregistered, 'normal' features of semiotic repertoires within a community of users. Such users are able to recognize #justsaying (even across language boundaries) as indexing a shift in interactional conduct, introducing a different frame and allowing different forms of footing in what might follow. Translingual practice of this kind is an established social fact; in line with the theme of this volume, it is mundane, banal, and unremarkable, despite its complexity of function and use.

But recall the compelling appeal by the Goodwins: we must be precise here. The rules for such translingual practices as were reported here are not generic, they are *specific* to concrete chronotopically configured situations of social media communication: interactions on Twitter. The community of users, likewise, is ratified as competent in the use of such forms of discursive practice only within that area of social life—the valuation of their competence cannot be generalized or extrapolated without elaborate empirical argument. And so the translingual practice I have described here is a *niched* social fact, part (but only part) of the communicative economies of large numbers of people occasionally entering that niche.

The niche is new: at the outset of this chapter I insisted that the use of hashtags in the way described here is a 21st-century innovation, an expansion and complication of existing communicative economies. This is why I find it exceedingly interesting, for novelty means that people have to *learn* rules that are not explicitly codified yet; they have to actually engage in the practices and perform the congregational work required for an emerging code of adequate performance to acquire a sense of what works and what doesn't. They cannot draw on existing sets of norms of usage. My analysis of #justsaying has, I believe, shown that the use of hashtags cannot be seen as an extension and continuation of prior forms of usage of the symbol '#'—the symbol is used in ways that are specific to the social media niche that emerged in the last couple of decades, and the rules for its deployment are, thus, developed through congregational work performed by people who had no pre-existing script for its usage. As mentioned before, the value of semiotic resources (such as the hashtag) and the identities of its users (as competent members of a community of users) emerge out of the actions performed.

In that sense and from that methodological perspective, the use of hashtags directs our attention to the fundamental aspects of the organization of social life, of meaning making, of interaction, and of language. There is room now for a theorization of translingualism in which, rather than the creative bricolage of cross-linguistic resources, we focus on complex and niched social actions in which participants try to observe social structure through their involvement in situations requiring normatively ratified practice—I'm paraphrasing Cicourel (1973) here—in emerging and flexible communities populating these niches of the online–offline nexus. It is a move that David Parkin (2016) nicely summarized as 'from multilingual classification to translingual ontology', in which the translingual nature of communicative action is an entirely normalized point of departure, a default and mundane given upon which innovative insights can be built.

Acknowledgements: I dedicate this chapter to the memory of Charles Goodwin, a source of inspiration and an engaging interlocutor for several decades, who sadly passed away while I was developing the analysis reported here. This chapter is part of a project I call 'Online with Garfinkel', in which I explore the potential of action-centered analyses of online–offline communication. A precursor of the project is Blommaert (2018). I am grateful to Piia Varis and Barbara De Cock for helpful feedback on a draft version of this text.

Notes

1 See Herbert Blumer's famous formulation: '(…) social interaction is a process that *forms* human conduct instead of being merely a means or a setting for the expression or release of human conduct' (Blumer, 1969, p. 8).
2 The point that the widespread availability of online technologies has reshaped the sociolinguistic system is missed by some critics of notions, such as translanguaging, who point to the prior existence of formally similar or identical forms of language and/ or script to argue that there is nothing 'new' happening. In such critiques, Hymes' (1996) important warning is disregarded: that the study of language is not merely a study of the *linguistic* system—the formal aspects of language, say—but also, and even more importantly, the study of the *sociolinguistic* system in which language forms are being distributed, functionally allocated, and deployed in concrete social circumstances. The arrival of the Internet has caused a worldwide change in the sociolinguistic system, provoking enormous amounts of sociolinguistically new phenomena. And even if such phenomena have *linguistic* precursors, they do not have any *sociolinguistic* ones. See Blommaert (2018) for a discussion.
3 I collected a small corpus of #justsaying examples from my own Twitter account between March and August 2018 (N=186) and found the hashtag incorporated into English, Dutch, Danish, Spanish, Hindi, Bulgarian, and Arabic tweets. Hashtags are also (and increasingly) used offline in marches and other forms of public demonstrations, as well as in advertisements.
4 'fgov' is the Twitter name of the Belgian Federal Government; 'manu militari' means 'by the use of military force'. The author of this tweet is a former MP for a Flemish extreme right-wing party.
5 One can note the explicit description of the footing for #justsaying statements here: 'No attack. No judgment. #JustSaying'.
6 The Mayor is a controversial, very outspoken right-wing politician. The 'victory' icon he posts at the end of his tweet is a campaign emblem of his party, and the phrase 'being yourself safely' is a direct reference to the Mayor's re-election program.
7 In Szabla and Blommaert (2018) we analyzed a long discussion on Facebook and called the entire discussion (composed of the update, comments, and subcomments) the 'main action'. In a more traditional sociolinguistic vocabulary, one can also see the overall unit of action the 'event'.

References

Agha, A. (2005) Voice, footing, enregisterment. *Journal of Linguistic Anthropology, 15*(1), 38–59.

Agha, A. (2007) *Language and social relations.* Cambridge, UK: Cambridge University Press.

Blaszka, M., Burch, L., Frederick, E., Clavio, G., & Walsh, P. (2012). #Worldseries: An empirical examination of a Twitter hashtag during a major sporting event. *International Journal of Sport Communication, 5*(4), 435–453.

Blommaert, J. (2012). Supervernaculars and their dialects. *Dutch Journal of Applied Linguistics, 1*(1), 1–14.

Blommaert, J. (2018). *Durkheim and the Internet: On sociolinguistics and the sociological imagination.* London, UK: Bloomsbury.

Blumer, H. (1969). *Symbolic interactionism: Perspective and method.* Berkeley: University of California Press.

Bonilla, Y., & Rosa, J. (2015). #Ferguson: Digital protest, hashtag ethnography and the racial politics of social media in the United States. *American Ethnologist, 42*(1), 4–17.

boyd, d. (2014). *It's complicated: The social life of networked teens.* New Haven, CT: Yale University Press.

Cicourel, A. (1973). *Cognitive sociology: Language and meaning in social interaction.* Harmondsworth, UK: Penguin Education

Craig, R., & Sanusi, A. (2000). 'I'm just saying...': Discourse markers as standpoint continuity. *Argumentation, 14*(4), 425–445.

De Cock, B., & Pizarro Pedraza, A. (2018). From expressing solidarity to mocking on Twitter: Pragmatic functions of hashtags starting with #jesuis across languages. *Language in Society, 47*(2), 197–217.

Garfinkel, H. (2002). *Ethnomethodology's program: Working out Durkheim's aphorism.* Lanham, UK: Rowman & Littlefield.

Goffman, E. (1975 [1974]). *Frame analysis: An essay on the organization of experience.* Harmondsworth, UK: Penguin.

Goodwin, C., & Harness Goodwin, M. (1992). Context, activity and participation. In P. Auer & A. DiLuzio (Eds.), *The contextualization of language* (pp. 77–99). Amsterdam, Netherlands: John Benjamins.

Goodwin, C., & Harness Goodwin, M. (2004). Participation. In A. Duranti (Ed.), *A companion to linguistic anthropology* (pp. 222–44). Malden, UK: Blackwell.

Hymes, D. (1996). *Ethnography, linguistics, narrative inequality: Toward an understanding of voice.* London, UK: Taylor & Francis.

Jackson, S. J. (2016). (Re)imagining intersectional democracy from black feminis to hashtag activism. *Women's Studies in Communication, 39*(4), 375–379.

Li, K., & Blommaert, J. (2017). The care of the selfie: Ludic chronotopes of *Baifumei* in online China. *Tilburg Papers in Culture Studies,* paper 197. Retrieved from https://www.tilburguniversity.edu/upload/9e59d9c2-fe63-4ed0-9e80-16148f872229_TPCS_197_Li-Blommaert.pdf

Mendes, K., Ringrose, J., & Keller, J. (2018). #MeToo and the promise and pitfalls of challenging rape culture through digital activism. *European Journal of Women's Studies, 25*(2), 236–246.

Parkin, D. (2016). From multilingual classification to translingual ontology: A turning point. In Arnaut, K., Blommaert, J., Rampton, B., & Spotti, M. (Eds.), *Language and superdiversity* (pp. 71–88). New York, NY: Routledge.

Szabla, M., & Blommaert, J. (2018). Does context really collapse in social media interaction? *Applied Linguistics Review* (In press).

Tagg, C., Seargeant, P., & Brown, A. (2017). *Taking offence on social media: Conviviality and communication on Facebook*. London, UK: Palgrave Pivot.

Tremayne, M. (2014). Anatomy of protest in the digital era: A network analysis of *Twitter* and occupy wall street. *Social Movement Studies, 13*(1), 110–126.

Wang, Y., Liu, J., Huang, Y., & Feng, X. (2016). Using hashtag graph-based topic model to connect semantically related words without co-occurrence in microblogs. *IEEE Transactions on Knowledge and Data Engineering, 28*(7), 1919–1933.

Wikström, P. (2014). #srynotfunny: Communicative functions of hashtags on Twitter. *SKY Journal of Linguistics, 27*, 127–152.

Zappavigna, Michele (2012) *Discourse of Twitter and social media: How we use language to create affiliation on the Web*. London, UK: Continuum.

7

THE ORDINARINESS OF TRANSLINGUISTICS IN INDIGENOUS AUSTRALIA

Jill Vaughan

Introduction

Recent debates within the sociolinguistics of multilingualism have highlighted the challenges posed by new complexities in the semiotic space of 'superdiversity' (Blommaert, 2013), where linguistic repertoires cannot be neatly partitioned according to socially or politically constructed language boundaries (Otheguy, García, & Reid, 2015). The methodological and descriptive toolbox of social scientists has, thus, been found wanting, and new terms and approaches have been proffered and tested to better represent the apparent complexities of this new 'turn'.

It has been noted, however, that discourses framing these processes as 'new' tend to focus on the City and the West. Indeed, languages and societies at the 'periphery' (Pietikäinen & Kelly-Holmes, 2013) have long been sidelined by hegemonic discourses within linguistics and multilingualism studies due to the sheer volume of work on major world languages in urban and western contexts. This new turn, in particular, reveals an 'unreflexive ethnocentrism' in western sociolinguistics (May, 2016, pp. 12–13), and risks erasing diversities that have long been acknowledged as commonplace in other—for example, Indigenous—settings. As Silverstein (2015, p. 7) frames it, 'such phenomena that have emerged in the investigation of peripheral local language communities have now gone mainstream at the metropole'.

This chapter explores multilingual practices within the context of Indigenous northern Australia through a translingual lens and considers major discourses produced by academia, local institutions, and local communities that have framed thinking on this topic. I consider the nature of communication in Indigenous Australian communities in historical and contemporary perspective, focusing on how speakers draw on high levels of local linguistic diversity and how they recruit language in socio-indexical practice. Drawing on ethnographic and language documentation data from Arnhem Land (Australia), I highlight that translingual practices born of diversity (and superdiversity) are neither new nor extraordinary and that the supposed 'new complexities' of globalization have significant reflexes in the 'peripheries' of its reach.

This chapter, therefore, contributes to the emerging body of work on the 'ordinariness of translinguistics' (Dovchin & Lee, 2019) and 'the ordinariness of diversity' (Pennycook, 2007, p. 93) in communities around the world. This work has been driven by a desire to normalize the kinds of language practices comprising diverse linguistic resources and which transgress established linguistic boundaries—practices that have been unnecessarily treated as remarkable or even eccentric. The discussion here aligns with work on the translinguistics of 'peripheral' communities, especially work in Africa and Asia (e.g. Makoni & Makoni, 2009 on Ghana and South Africa; Lee & Lou, 2019 on South Korea; Bolander & Sultana, 2019; Dovchin, 2017, 2018; Pennycook & Otsuji, 2019, and Sultana, Dovchin, & Pennycook, 2015 on Mongolia, Bangladesh, Pakistan, and Tajikistan). This work has exemplified the ways in which observable translingual practices are crucially situated within intersections between diverse local sociolinguistic affordances and transnational linguistic resources. This chapter responds in particular to Piller's (2016) critique that sociolinguistic scholarship on multilingualism has focused largely on local languages in relation to English, and indeed few translinguistics studies consider relations between languages that are not major world languages (Canagarajah & Dovchin, 2019 is a notable exception). The data presented here centralizes the dynamics between several Australian Indigenous languages, as well as English, with a view to making a small contribution to redressing this balance. Finally, it is hoped that work on translingual practices in northern Australia will contribute to understandings of the richness and diversity of contemporary Indigenous communicative repertoires, with vital implications for language maintenance and multilingual education.

Conceptual framework: languaging at the 'periphery'

This chapter draws on two key conceptual frames. The first, translinguistics, enables the analysis to move beyond named language categories to reveal the emergent dynamics of situated communication. Translinguistics helps 'release histories and understandings' (García & Li Wei, 2014, p. 21) that may be veiled by colonial agendas, western discourses, and local language ideologies. This is especially important in work on the translinguistics of global 'peripheries'—the chapter's second conceptual frame. Languages and communities at the edges of the reach of globalization have too often been absent or overlooked in the development of linguistic theories and methodologies. The 'centre'/'core' versus 'periphery' metaphor here refers to how political and economic power and social influence have been understood to circulate on both a global scale and within societies, with the urban West imagined as a central base of power in opposition to groups on the margins who do not wield great power within these structures. This opposition is destabilized to an extent by more recent work on migration, mobility, and transnational networks (e.g. Blunt, 2007; Sassen, 1998), which demonstrates that reality is not so neat but rather that communities are complex and shifting and that boundaries may be fluid. This work has revealed the 'core' versus 'periphery' metaphor to ultimately be a discursive construct, and even a performative notion, in the 21st century; nevertheless, it is a construct that operates within historically and culturally situated spaces and has great power to shape contemporary practices and systems (Pietikäinen & Kelly-Holmes, 2013). These dynamics have inevitable implications for language.

Despite the focuses of some earlier scholarship (such as Americanist work on pre-contact language ecologies (e.g. Boas, 1940), more recent work under the umbrella of bi/multilingualism has taken a somewhat narrow view in modeling how non-monolingual repertoires are deployed in practice (e.g. Fishman's (1967) influential 'domain-separation' model). A western/urban bias has been particularly strong in recently dominant discourses within the 'trans-super-poly-metro' turn (Pennycook, 2016). Yet, humanity has a long (if not always well-documented) history of non-polyglossic, 'meshed', translingual communicative practices, which draw on multiple named languages but which do not conform to monolingual or indeed established 'orderly' multilingual ideologies. While the archetypal 'village' (as opposed to the 'city') has been popularly imagined as linguistically homogenous, in reality small, remote communities may be sites of great diversity and connectedness (Canagarajah, 2013, p. 37; Vaughan & Singer, 2018). This is true of the pre-modern west, before linguistic and cultural homogeneity were recruited as tools of the nation-state capitalist enterprise (Heller, 2013), as well as of various contemporary 'peripheral' communities largely ignored in recent dominant discourses. While the historical picture is not always readily retrievable, elements of earlier cultural and linguistic systems may be pieced together by consulting diverse early sources (e.g. oral histories, scholarly and governmental writing) and inferring—with caution—from certain modern practices and ideologies. Communicative practices of the translingual type may be observed as perfectly 'ordinary' within the rich body of work on highly diverse and multilingual Indigenous communities around the globe. This includes work in Africa (Lüpke, 2017), India (Gumperz & Wilson, 1971), South America (Epps, forthcoming), Australia (Singer & Harris, 2016), and Melanesia (Francois, 2012), to name but a few examples.

In the following sections, I add further support to the argument that key principles within translinguistics apply readily, and may indeed be enriched by, communicative contexts at the peripheries of globalization, in this case in the Arnhem Land region of northern Australia. Specific examples are drawn from naturalistic interactional data, interviews, and in-depth ethnographic work based primarily in ongoing fieldwork and research collaborations in Maningrida since 2014.

Language, land, and culture in Arnhem Land

Modern-day Australia is home to a diverse and rapidly evolving language ecology. The continent's traditional Indigenous languages are spoken alongside more recent arrivals—like English and other migrant languages—and a range of contact varieties, most of which have developed since British invasion in 1788. At that time, some 700 named language varieties were in use across the region. The devastating effects of colonization have dramatically altered the linguistic landscape, however, and now fewer than 20 of these are still subject to intergenerational transfer (McConvell, Marmion, & McNicol, 2005), located mostly across the north and in the center of Australia. Speaker communities in the region are small by global standards, and it appears that even languages with just a few dozen speakers have been maintained for many generations (Green, 2003).

On Australia's north-central coast, at the mouth of the Liverpool River, Maningrida community serves as a regional 'hub' for the Indigenous-owned region, Arnhem Land. Maningrida is home to some 2,500 people and boasts dramatic coastal scenery, world-renowned bark and sculptural artists, skilled weavers and textile printers, and unique local wildlife. The region is distinguished by a highly diverse language ecology, with dozens of socially and linguistically recognized languages from several distinct language families. Local estimates vary, but typically between 12 and 16 languages are named in the local space, most with further named sub-lects which may be understood to be distinct languages. Local linguistic repertoires typically take in elements of several traditional languages as well as localized Englishes, often Kriol (an English-lexified creole spoken across northern Australia), and a local alternate sign language system. Texts and talk in Maningrida are rarely monolingual, and the semiotic work of communication transcends individual languages simply placed in sequence. Indeed, it is likely that separating messages into distinct systems in attempting to interpret them may even (in some contexts at least) undermine their meaning. Instead, following Enfield (2009, p. 6) 'when encountering multiple signs which are presented together, [we should] take them as one'.

While it seems that seasonal mobility has long played an important role in socio-cultural and economic life in Indigenous Australian societies, widening social spheres and new trajectories of mobility serving the contemporary life projects of Indigenous Australians[1] have had significant ramifications for language maintenance and loss, the make-up of linguistic repertoires, and the deployment of linguistic variation. This mobility further contributes to the fluidity of language group boundaries, and yet traditional languages in Indigenous Australia are ideologized by their speakers as inherently bounded—primordially connected to particular tracts of land, which are the eternal homeland of that linguistic variety and its people (Merlan, 1981). These connections between language and land have genuine effects in lived experience. Individuals are understood to own a certain language by virtue of their clan membership, and they inherit language affiliations through kinship structures, with the individual's father's language (the patrilect) primary. Further languages are connected to through extended kinship.

These connections exert a strong influence on expectations around individuals' code use, and they project code boundaries into the linguistic field that are attended to, and reproduced in, discourse to various extents depending on a host of factors, such as domain, speaker role, audience, and genre. 'Appropriate' code use is sometimes socially policed. For example, young people may be chastised for using the 'wrong' language or dialectal variants, and individuals may be laughed at for 'trying' to speak a language not theirs (despite it being within their linguistic repertoire). The school library has a bilingual reader entitled *A Drunk Got His Languages Mixed*, and on a number of occasions I have heard comments that people speak certain other languages only when drunk; this suggests to me that crossing socially salient linguistic boundaries can be viewed as transgressive when the codes are not seen to be the ideologically 'appropriate' ones for the speaker. And yet, as we will see, speakers frequently use languages that are *not* their established patrilect.

'Doing difference together': examples of language use from Arnhem Land

In this section, I provide five examples to illustrate the kinds of (trans)languaging practices that are commonplace in daily communication in the Maningrida region. These examples are drawn from interactions in public and semi-private domains observed during my own visits in recent years and the recordings of other linguists working in the region. Most speakers featured here are senior community members and participants in two recent sociolinguistic documentation projects focusing on the Burarra language and multilingualism in Maningrida. Details of individual participants are provided in each case. Speakers were consulted where possible after the recordings to gain a clearer understanding of the intended meanings of their interactional moves. In these examples, the codes are differentiated using underlining and italics where needed, with the associated language name listed underneath or to the side. This is to aid the reader's navigation of the examples but is not necessarily a claim about the speaker's intended use or meaning.

The first extract is from a re-enactment of the Stations of the Cross by a local church group as part of celebrations for Good Friday. Some 50 church members paraded across the community performing the roles of Jesus and the crowd accompanying him to his crucifixion. Communication here was broadcast, rather than targeted toward individual interlocutors. The speaker, SR, is a senior man from the Djinang language group (eastern Arnhem Land). He is a Djinang language and culture teacher at the local school and a key member of the Burnawarra Elders Dispute Resolution Group (Table 7.1).

TABLE 7.1 Extract from the Stations of the Cross re-enactment

Yaw, lim-buɲi-ban Jesus, lim-buɲi-ban Jesus! Nguburr-bu barra nguburr-bu barra!						
yes	1PL-hit-TF	1PL-hit-TF	12A-hit	FUT	12A-hit	FUT
DJINANG			BURARRA			

'We're hitting Jesus, we're hitting Jesus! We'll hit (him), we'll hit (him)'!

(SR: 20150403-Good_Friday: 11:31–11:36)

SR uses features from two recognized languages from different language families: Djinang and Burarra. Djinang is his 'main' language, his patrilect, but he also feels some ownership of Burarra as his grandmother's language and he uses it very often in his daily interactions. During the re-enactment, SR's speech shifts constantly between the two languages (and sometimes also draws on English and a third Indigenous language), typically in the way illustrated here with a few clauses in one language, then a few in the other. In discussions after the event, he talked about how he wanted to incorporate both languages in his performance for two reasons: they were both important for him personally, being languages of his kin; and their use would maximize the number of people who would understand what he was saying (Interview, 30 July 2015, Maningrida, Australia). Other participants in the re-enactment largely used their own 'main' Indigenous languages (seven named Indigenous languages were identified by participants in the interaction) and also drew on English features—as is typical of the church domain in Maningrida. This example demonstrates the notion core to translinguistics that meaning in performance transcends the individual languages that can be identified. While the same information is conveyed in each utterance here (i.e. that 'we', the crowd, are hitting/going to hit Jesus), the repetition is not redundant; instead, it is 'one coordinated and meaningful performance' (Li Wei, 2011, p. 2) positioning SR, for example, as both Djinang and Burarra and as a recognized senior man and a leader in this context and beyond it.

The following two examples are taken from more private interactions among family and friends seated outside homes. The speaker in Table 7.2, CB is an elder from the Ndjébbana language group, the language of the land where Maningrida sits. Table 7.3 features PM, a Gun-nartpa man and a former teaching assistant, at his home, Gochan Jiny-jirra outstation south-east of Maningrida.

TABLE 7.2 Extract from a conversation among four women

And	an-guna an-nga	jay	barra-ngúddjeya 'babbúya'?		
	I-PROX I-what	ATT	IA-say	ironwood	
ENGLISH	BURARRA		NDJÉBBANA		

'And what's that, hey, that they (Burarra people) say for "ironwood"'?

(CB: 20151029-ABLA_CB: 08:38–08:44)

In Table 7.2, CB is sitting with three other women: Burarra woman DJ, Na-kara woman RN, and an English speaker (the author). We had been discussing local child-rearing practices, and CB had been predominantly using her main language, Ndjébbana, and drawing on some English features. In this utterance, however, she also draws on Burarra resources, in part to address her question to Burarra-speaker DJ (and possibly also RN) toward whom she directs her gaze, and perhaps also in response to a topic shift. She finishes her question by drawing again on Ndjébbana resources, in part to make explicit the Ndjébbana word she wants to translate (*babbúya* 'ironwood'). DJ takes the following turn and responds in Burarra (*'Jarlawurra? Ngardichala?'* ('Leaves? Ironwood?')). The use of Burarra features here was not strictly 'necessary', as DJ and RN would have understood had she asked in Ndjébbana, but CB draws on her 'mobile resources' (Blommaert, 2010, p. 49) to step out of her previous explanations, to engage with the group in a new way, and to draw DJ into a direct interaction.

In Table 7.3, PM is sitting with family from two different language groups. In this exchange, he speaks Gun-nartpa, but he uses the word for 'fish' from Djambarrpuyngu, a language of eastern Arnhem Land, in deference to the language of his sister-in-law to whom he is culturally expected to perform respect. Both *guya* and *ana-ganyja* are in fact flexible, heteroglossic resources that can be interpreted as belonging to multiple recognized languages or dialects in the region. In this instance, the speaker is able to make locally situated meaning readily interpretable to those present, but these features can be used to construct meaning in other ways in other local contexts, giving rise to 'multiple meanings and readings of forms' (Bailey, 2007, p. 267).

Table 7.4 is an extract from an extended, largely monologic, narrative spoken by CW, an Ilgar man from north-western Arnhem Land, and recorded by linguist Nicholas Evans in 1999 (Evans, 2010, pp. 284–286). This extract is highly performative, as in Table 7.1, but it represents a distinct genre of retelling traditional ancestor stories handed down orally through generations. Ilgar, Garig, Marrku, and Kunwinjku are all traditional languages of Western Arnhem Land, from two or three distinct language families (opinions vary on this point). Marrku, and especially Ilgar, were particularly important languages for CW's social identity. Note that none of these are actually the language that CW used most of the time (Iwaidja).

TABLE 7.3 Extract from conversation among family members

Guya	*ana-ganyja.*
fish	3l.to-take-rls
DJAMBARRPUYNGU	GUN-NARTPA
'She brought a fish'.	

(Fieldnotes 2017, M. Carew)

TABLE 7.4 Extract from narrative (Evans, 2010)

malayaka yimalkbany The Rainbow Serpent appeared	ILGAR/GARIG
ara raka, rak'ambij He went along there, that Rainbow Serpent	ILGAR/GARIG
well, Marrku, Marrku, people he said, not people, only one man Well, in Marrku, Marrku, people he said, not people, only one man	ENGLISH
one man he said	
'Iyi, muku ngurnu, ngurnu minyiwu ngurnu jang. 'Well, someone has struck a sacred place (*jang*)—a sacred place	MARRKU
jang miyiwuwu he struck the jang way over there	MARRKU
muku makalany ngurnu marruyaj that Rainbow appeared there	MARRKU
imin kilim, he kill that ah, antbed or something, stone' he hit it, he hit a termite mound or something, a stone' [...]	ENGLISH
binbum kundjak, birriyakminy rowk nawu bininj the dangerous thing had killed them (long ago), and they all died, those people	KUNWINJKU
birriyakminy rowk they all perished	KUNWINJKU
yeah yildirrindirri raka yes, it's really dangerous	ILGAR/GARIG
kayirrk rakabara yiwardudban so now they leave it alone	ILGAR/GARIG
yiwardudban yiyaldi they leave it be [...]	ILGAR/GARIG

In this narrative, each language is drawn on strategically and in a locally situated manner to play a relatively distinct role: Ilgar/Garig is used for narrator statements and to voice one of the characters; Marrku is used for another character from the island which is that language's homeland; English and Kunwinjku are used for clarification, translation, and framing (and possibly to some degree in deference to the linguist audience). In this extract, drawing on features from each code contributes something additional and specific, but taken together 'as one', these produce something that transcends the individual languages, creating a united and highly expressive performance.

In this final example, we return to Maningrida, to a school assembly where a new book is being launched. RD, a Gun-nartpa speaker—a former teacher-linguist at the school—is addressing the gathered school children and

TABLE 7.5 Extract from school assembly

Yaw, good afternoon. It took many years before, for gun-anngiya. [MC] jina-bona 1999, collecting the stories. Gu-manga janguny, gu-gutuwurra gu-manga from elders, aburr-ngaypa tribe, Gun-nartpa people. Collecting jiny-ni stories, pictures mu-manga. Then big break jiny-ninya. Big break jiny-ninya because we lost our elder, and nipa arrburrwa michpa land owner. Mun-guna in this photo gipa a-jinyjirra front–'Gun-ngaypa Rrawa'. And most of these book photos mu-werrangga aburr-yorrpuna, they've gone they've passed away from our families.

Yes, good afternoon. It took many years for this. [MC] came in 1999, collecting stories. She collected stories, gathered and collected them from elders, my tribe—Gun-nartpa people. She collected stories, and took pictures. Then she had a big break. She had a big break because we lost our elder, he was our land owner. That's his photo on the front–'My Country'. And most of these book photos are of other people who passed away. They're gone, they passed away from our families.

(RD: 20150325-GN_launch: 01:29–03:16)

community members, and she is describing her experience with the process of compiling the book (Table 7.5).

RD is drawing features from her main language, Gun-nartpa—a dialect of Burarra—and from English. The kind of translanguaging evidenced here is quite different from the examples presented above: features from each named language are freely mixed within the clause level right through the text, un-like in Tables 7.1 and (most of) 7.4, where each clause is in a single language, and unlike in Tables 7.2 and 7.3, where the introduction of features from an-other code defines a single moment within the larger text. While mixing prac-tices in Maningrida are highly diverse and constantly emergent, this points to a major distinction observable in these practices. Mixing between Indigenous languages appears to be much more constrained, less widely attested, and often has a readily identifiable motive. Mixing with English, however, is much less grammatically and socially restricted. In certain 'hybrid' spaces—spaces shaped by the interaction of diverse groups, institutions, and ways of speaking—mixing between English and Burarra (the most widely spoken Indigenous language in Maningrida) has emerged as what Makoni & Pennycook (2012, p. 447) refer to as a 'multilingua franca', whereby mixed and varied language use is the default and communication draws on a 'multilayered chain' of features, which is not fixed but adapts or 'relocalizes' to situations as they arise (Vaughan, 2018). It seems likely that this distinction has to do with the regimenting power of ideologies about language, where Indigenous language use is socially 'policed' to a much greater extent, and in a more culturally embedded way, than the use of English is.

Each example presented in this section reveals how individual communicators draw on their diverse linguistic repertoires to express their own distinct social and cultural positionalities, as well as to take advantage of the distinct affor-dances of different audiences, local domains, and communities of practice. These examples also point to a broader theme in the semiotics of cultural life in Arnhem

Land: that of 'difference' as a cultural priority that is expected to be performed in certain contexts in various prescribed ways. This may mean recruiting features from across different recognized languages within an individual's repertoire but it can also shape the manipulation of variation within languages (e.g. Bininj Kunwok's *Kun-dangwok* system of clanlectal variation (Garde, 2008)). This cultural priority is not unique to linguistic practice; in Brown (2016, p. 9), Mawng songman James Gulamuwu speaks of being 'different together' in discussing musical practice in Arnhem Land, whereby there is 'conscious differentiation [...] that occurs "together" in a shared ceremonial social space and within a unified musical framework'. I draw on this phrase but frame it as an ongoing process, and so we might consider this notion to be 'doing difference together'.

Discussion and conclusion: between innovation and ordinariness

Language practices in Arnhem Land have been demonstrated to be fundamentally characterized by diversity, flexibility, fluidity, and the depth and nuance of linguistic repertoires. These are all descriptors that have been eagerly attached to translingual practices in the globalized urban West and claimed as the exclusive and extraordinary product of recent migrations, media forms, and market pressures. Such practices are shown, then, to be in many ways perfectly ordinary and unremarkable, and certainly the stuff of everyday communication historically and in contemporary times at the 'peripheries' of globalization's reach. These findings align strongly with work on languaging at other global peripheries, in particular, Dovchin's work in Mongolia (e.g. 2017, 2018).

Practices like these are made to seem 'extraordinary' or aberrant through the lens of dominant monolingual and 'orderly' multilingual ideologies espoused and produced, for example, by institutional regimes. But it is worth noting that certain translingual practices may also be viewed as non-standard within *local* ideologies produced by longstanding cultural systems. Ideological policing of this kind is readily observable in the Maningrida space in commentary about mixing practices that recruit English features—which are frequently negatively evaluated in the community—but also about the mixing of different Indigenous languages, behavior that may be seen as transgressing the 'patrilect' priority or even as drunken behavior. Indeed, there is a tension between ideologies that prescribe particular ways of 'doing difference' in Maningrida (e.g. using one's patrilect or 'appropriate' clanlectal variants) and the reality of the everyday meaning-making practices that recruit these 'mobile resources' in ever emergent ways and in response to changing ecological affordances.

While the language practices described in this chapter are demonstrably shaped by longstanding cultural practices and priorities within the Arnhem Land regional system, this is not to say that there is nothing 'new' about them. At the community level, the language ecology has been crucially altered through the actions and goals of community institutions (e.g. the local school's trilingual program), the increasing presence of media and electronic devices, the many facets of the broader colonial project, and the ever-encroaching reach of globalization—these changes have led to the promotion of English and particular local languages such as Burarra (Vaughan, 2018). While Arnhem Land may be imagined and positioned as 'peripheral', individuals communicate within an increasingly globally connected community and continually wield new linguistic tools for meaning-making. In Arnhem Land, as in the globalized urban West, 'difference' is ordinary and ex-pected. The challenge, then, is to adjust our critical gaze so difference and diversity are acknowledged as commonplace yet constituting a core focus—'the crucial da-tum' (Evans & Levinson, 2009, p. 429) for the study of language practices.

Acknowledgements

Sincere thanks to Maningrida community and to the anonymous reviewers. This work was funded by the Endangered Languages Documentation Pro-ject (C.I. Jill Vaughan, grant IPF0256), the ARC Centre of Excellence for the Dynamics of Language (C.I. Felicity Meakins, University of Queensland, grant CE140100041), the Linguistic Complexity in the Individual and Society project (C.I. Terje Lohndal) at the Norwegian University for Science and Technology, and a University of Melbourne Early Career Researcher Grant (C.I. Jill Vaughan).

Abbreviations

1	First person exclusive
12	First person inclusive
3	Third person
A	Augmented number (alternative to 'plural', used in categories where 'unit augmented' and 'augmented' oppositions exist)
ATT	Attention getter
FUT	Future
I	Noun class (male)
PL	Plural
PROX	Proximal demonstrative
RLS	Realis
TF	Temporal focus
TO	Towards deictic centre

Note

1 Circular mobility between sites for cultural, economic, and social reasons has long been a part of life in remote northern Australia. However contemporary social lives and movements – the 'hyper-mobility essential to modern living' (Altman & Hinkson, 2007, p. 199) – have engendered changing interactions with ancestral lands with many Indigenous Australians now circulating between large urban communi-ties, regional hubs, and remote outstation communities.

References

Altman, J., & Hinkson, M. (2007). Mobility and modernity in Arnhem Land: The social universe of Kuninjku trucks. *Journal of Material Culture, 12*(2), 181–203.

Bailey, B. (2007). Heteroglossia and boundaries. In M. Heller (Ed.), *Bilingualism: A social approach* (pp. 257–274). Basingstoke, UK: Palgrave Macmillan.

Blommaert, J. (2010). *The sociolinguistics of globalization.* Cambridge, UK: Cambridge University Press.

Blommaert, J. (2013). *Ethnography, superdiversity and linguistic landscapes: Chronicles of complexity.* Bristol, UK: Multilingual Matters.

Blunt, A. (2007). Cultural geographies of migration: Mobility, transnationality and diaspora. *Progress in Human Geography, 31*(5), 684–694.

Boas, F. (1940). *Race, language, and culture.* New York, NY: Macmillan.

Bolander, B., & Sultana, S. (2019). Ordinary English amongst Muslim communities in South and Central Asia. *International Journal of Multilingualism, 16*(2), 162–174.

Brown, R. (2016). *Following footsteps: The kun-borrk/manyardi song tradition and its role in western Arnhem Land society.* PhD thesis: University of Sydney.

Canagarajah, S. (2013). *Translingual practice: Global Englishes and cosmopolitan relations.* London, UK: Routledge.

Canagarajah, S., & Dovchin, S. (2019). The everyday politics of translingualism as a resistant practice. *International Journal of Multilingualism, 16*(2), 127–144.

Dovchin, S. (2017). The ordinariness of youth linguascapes in Mongolia. *International Journal of Multilingualism, 14*(2), 144–159.

Dovchin, S. (2018). *Language, media and globalization in the periphery: The linguascapes of popular music in Mongolia.* New York, NY: Routledge.

Dovchin, S., & Lee, J. W. (2019). Introduction to special issue: 'The ordinariness of translinguistics.' *International Journal of Multilingualism, 16*(2), 105–111.

Enfield, N. (2009). *The anatomy of meaning: Speech, gesture and composite utterances.* Cambridge, UK: Cambridge University Press.

Epps, P. (Forthcoming). Amazonian linguistic diversity and its sociocultural correlates. In M. Crevels & P. Muysken (Eds.), *Language dispersal, diversification, and contact: A global perspective.* Oxford: Oxford University Press.

Evans, N. (2010). A tale of many tongues: Polyglot narrative in North Australian oral traditions. In B. J. Baker, I. Mushin, M. Harvey, & R. Gardner (Eds.), *Indigenous language and social identity: papers in honour of Michael Walsh* (pp. 275–295). Canberra, Australia: Pacific Linguistics.

Evans, N., & Levinson, S. C. (2009). The myth of language universals: Language diversity and its importance for cognitive science. *Behavioral and Brain Sciences, 32*(05), 429.

Fishman, J. A. (1967). Bilingualism with and without diglossia; diglossia with and without bilingualism. *Journal of Social Issues, 23*(2), 29–38.

Francois, A. (2012). The dynamics of linguistic diversity: Egalitarian multilingualism and power imbalance among northern Vanuatu languages. *International Journal of the Sociology of Language, 214*, 85–110.

Garde, M. (2008). Kun-dangwok: 'clan lects' and Ausbau in western Arnhem Land. *International Journal of the Sociology of Language, 191*, 141–169.

Green, R. (2003). Gurr-goni, a minority language in a multilingual community: Surviving into the 21st century. In J. Blythe & R. McKenna Brown (Eds.), *Maintaining the links: Language, identity and the land* (pp. 127–134). Bath, UK: Foundation for Endangered Languages.

Gumperz, J. J., & Wilson, R. (1971). Convergence and creolization: A case from the Indo-Aryan/Dravidian border in India. In D. Hymes (Ed.), *Pidginization and creolization of languages* (pp. 151–167). Cambridge, UK: Cambridge University Press.

Heller, M. (2013). Repositioning the multilingual periphery. In S. Pietikainen & H. Kelly-Holmes (Eds.), *Multilingualism and the periphery* (pp. 17–34). Oxford, UK; New York, NY: Oxford University Press.

Lee, J. W., & Lou, J. J. (2019). The ordinary semiotic landscape of an unordinary place: Spatiotemporal disjunctures in Incheon's Chinatown. *International Journal of Multilingualism, 16*(2), 187–203.

Li Wei. (2011). Moment analysis and translanguaging space: Discursive construction of identities by multilingual Chinese youth in Britain. *Journal of Pragmatics, 43*(5), 1222–1235.

Lüpke, F. (2017) African(ist) perspectives on vitality: Fluidity, small speaker numbers and adaptive multilingualism make vibrant ecologies. *Language* 93(4): e275–e279.

Otheguy, R., García, O., & Reid, W. (2015). Clarifying translanguaging and deconstructing named languages: A perspective from linguistics. *Applied Linguistics Review, 6*(3): 281–307.

Makoni, B., & Makoni, S. (2009). Multilingual discourses on wheels and public English in Africa. In J. Maybin & J. Swann (Eds), *The Routledge companion to English language studies* (pp. 258–270). London, UK; New York, NY: Routledge.

Makoni, S., & Pennycook, A. (2012). Disinventing multilingualism: From monological multilingualism to multilingua francas. *The Routledge handbook of multilingualism* (pp. 439–472). London, UK: Routledge.

May, S. (2016). *Linguistic superdiversity as a 'new' theoretical framework: Panacea or nostrum?* Presentation at MOSAIC, Birmingham University (3 February 2016). Retrieved from http://www.birmingham.ac.uk/generic/tlang/documents/linguistic-superdiversity-as-a-new-theoretical-framework.pdf

McConvell, P., Marmion, D., & McNicol, S. (2005). *National indigenous languages survey report*. Canberra: Australian Institute of Aboriginal and Torres Strait Islander Studies.

Merlan, F. (1981). Land, language and social identity in Aboriginal Australia. *Mankind, 13*, 133–148.

Pennycook, A. (2007). *Global Englishes and transcultural flows*. London, UK: Routledge.

Pennycook, A. (2016). Mobile times, mobile terms: The trans-super-poly-metro movement. In N. Coupland (Ed.), *Sociolinguistics* (pp. 201–216). Cambridge, UK: Cambridge University Press.

Pennycook, A., & Otsuji, E. (2019). Mundane metrolingualism. *International Journal of Multilingualism, 16*(2), 175–186.

Pietikäinen, S., & Kelly-Holmes, H. (2013). Multilingualism and the periphery. In S. Pietikäinen & H. Kelly-Holmes (Eds.), *Multilingualism and the periphery* (pp. 1–16). Oxford, UK: Oxford University Press.

Piller, I. (2016). *Linguistic diversity and social justice: An introduction to applied sociolinguistics*. Oxford, UK: Oxford University Press.

Sassen, S. 1998. *Globalization and its discontents*. New York, NY: The New Press.

Silverstein, M. (2015). How language communities intersect: Is 'superdiversity' an incremental or transformative condition? *Language & Communication, 44*, 7–18.

Singer, R., & Harris, S. (2016). What practices and ideologies support small-scale multilingualism? A case study of Warruwi Community, northern Australia. *International Journal of the Sociology of Language, 241*, 163–208.

Sultana, S., Dovchin, S., & Pennycook, A. (2015). Transglossic language practices of young adults in Bangladesh and Mongolia. *International Journal of Multilingualism, 12*(1), 93–108.

Vaughan, J. (2018). Translanguaging and hybrid spaces: Boundaries and beyond in north central Arnhem Land. In G. Mazzaferro (Ed.), *Translanguaging as everyday practice* (pp. 125–148). Cham, Switzerland: Springer.

Vaughan, J., & Singer, R. (2018). Indigenous multilingualisms past and present. *Language & Communication, 62*, 83–90.

8

HABLAR PORTUÑOL É COMO RESPIRAR

Translanguaging and the descent into the ordinary

Daniel N. Silva and Adriana Carvalho Lopes

Introduction

This chapter draws from our fieldwork in situations of multilingual diversity that are contradictorily positioned in official, power-laden discourses as monolingual and linguistically uniform. Empirically, we have been examining scenarios like the Brazilian and Uruguayan teaching of 'mother tongues' (as the teaching of Portuguese and Spanish is commonly referred to in these countries), and engaging with teachers, students, and policymakers, as well as reading historical and contemporary documents, to investigate how monolingualism has been invented in these contexts. Here, we will engage with Fabian Severo, a Uruguayan writer and teacher of Spanish born in Artigas, one of the seven Departments in the northern Uruguayan border with Brazil. Canonical sociolinguistic scholarship has characterized the translingual practices spoken in this region of intense physical and symbolic crossing and blending as 'a dialect that is the result of local Spanish-Portuguese contact' (Canale, 2015, p. 19), technically coined by Elizaincín and Behares (1981) as Dialectos Portugueses del Uruguay (DPU). Like other people from this region, Severo, however, prefers the term 'Portuñol' for communicative practices in his hometown, a translingual recombination of Portuguese and Spanish he has deployed in writing poems (Severo, 2010, 2013) and a novel (Severo, 2015). Based on an interview with Severo vis-à-vis our reading of the literature about linguistic diversity in the region, we propose a twofold argument with regard to the ordinariness of translinguistic practices.

First, we argue that although Uruguay is a multilingual and diverse country—Uruguayan Spanish, Uruguayan Portuguese, and Uruguayan Sign Language are recognized as the three *lenguas maternas* by the *Ley General de Educación* of 2008—a *de facto* standard language (Spanish) has buttressed the invention of the country as a nation-state with a uniform public culture. Thus, even if Uruguay is multiethnic, multilingual, and superdiverse, and even if a great deal of everyday linguistic practices, following ethnographic and empirical inspection, may be characterized as constituted by the mingling of diverse repertoires, registers, resources, and often languages (see Dovchin, 2017), a linguistic ideology of monoglot standard language tends to adjust the lenses that speakers rely on to look at language. The 'ordinary', thus, tends to be talked about and perceived as uniform and monolingual. In fact, this 'culture of monoglot standard', as Silverstein (1996) dubbed the language-ideological work of linguistic uniformization in centralized plurilingual societies such as the United States, is as true for Uruguay (Behares & Brovetto, 2008; Hamel, 2004) as for Brazil (Cavalcanti & Maher, 2018; Lopes & Silva, 2018). As indexical phenomena, these monoglot frames are deeply rooted in racial imaginations pervading these social landscapes. Although the imbrications between race and nationality are different in Brazil and Uruguay, both countries have promoted narratives of white nationality.[1] As we will discuss, the monoglot framing of the situation of multilingualism on the border between Brazil and Uruguay, as well as the accompanying racial and class aspirations, work as a hegemonic force attempting to efface the diversity of the ordinary.

Second, we argue that this ideological construction of the ordinary as linguistically, racially, and socially homogenous in Uruguay and Brazil is being constantly challenged. Our ethnographic site is an instance of translingual confrontations to linguistic and cultural homogeneity. During the 2017 Conference of the Latin American Association of Sociologists, we both sat down with Fabian Severo at the cafeteria in the Casa do Brasil, a cultural center in Montevideo. Although the interview had been planned, a stance of informality and solidarity—arising from our shared interest in minority communities—shaped the conversation that unfolded in Spanish, Portuguese, and the transidiomatic recombination (Jacquemet, 2016) of both. Bruno Coutinho and Marcus Dominguez, who also were in town for the conference, joined us. Thus, the very situation of interview—involving transidioma, multiple parties with varied interests, digital technologies, and the affordances and predicaments of a busy cafeteria—was an ecological niche that may be characterized as an environment of translingual dispositions (Lee & Jenks, 2016), that is, a location where one finds a 'general openness to plurality and difference in the ways people use language' (p. 317).

Hence, we will examine a metapragmatic discourse about Portuñol produced in a context of transidiomatic and diverse sociality. Severo's gesture toward interactively producing a translingual ordinariness, projected by him as disputing its value and validity with ideals of default monolingualism, indicates that the ordinary itself is not transparent. A scalar operation (Carr & Lempert, 2016) is at stake in this metadiscursive stance. In line with Ordinary Language Philosophy, we claim that Severo's *descent* into the ordinary repositioned his very attention to, and attitudes toward, the ordinary as a diverse one. Severo, thus, scales the importance of Portuñol *down* to the ordinary, as opposed to an *upper* ideal of standard Portuguese or Spanish. As Austin, Wittgenstein, and Silverstein have variously argued, the descent from language as a spiritual medium to the ordinariness of embodied everyday language use turns out to be simultaneously a movement from denotation down to performance, from a flat and static view of variation to a moving image of hierarchic ordering of resources, from expressivity to politics.

In what follows, we first present Fabian Severo's main argument about the ordinariness of translanguaging and describe the situation of linguistic diversity in the northern border of Uruguay. Next, we discuss the 'culture of monoglot standard' in Uruguay (and Brazil), and then, inspired by Severo, we critique the main foundations of this culture. Finally, we conclude by re-examining two directions that Severo's descent into the ordinary may lead us to.

Fabian Severo: translanguaging is like breathing

Fabian Severo teaches Spanish language and literature in Atlantida, a city located some 50 km from Uruguay's capital city, Montevideo. He was born in a region of intense mobility of people between Brazil and Uruguay: Artigas, in the northern border with Brazil. His growing up in a region where people ordinarily make use of communicative resources constituted by the mingling of Spanish and Portuguese, which do not fit into the boundaries of what official discourses idealize as delimiting the two national standard languages, provided him with a critical perspective on the efficacy of the translinguistic resources known as Portunõl—as well as on the symbolic and material limitations imposed on those who speak it.

In our conversation, Severo placed emphasis on the ordinariness of speaking Portuñol in the border region. In his words, people in his hometown blend Portuguese and Spanish 'naturally'. It is as ordinary as 'breathing'. Yet, early in his primary education, he realized that the mixed communicative forms available to him were sorted out in school: 'I soon realized that things were separated in school. [I soon realized that] there were words from here and words from there when they started correcting me. "No, here you can't say this"'. Thus, in Bakhtinian terms, Severo's experience as a speaker of (and as a fiction writer in) Potuñol is marked by the tension between the heteroglossic—that is, non-unified and stratified—character of his everyday translanguaging and the 'normative-centralizing system of a unitary language' (Bakhtin, 1981, p. 272), epitomized by the school as a gatekeeping institution.

Severo's writing and metapragmatic discourse are an interesting critique of the monolingual frames in Brazil and Uruguay. They are also very iconic of the political movement down to the ordinary that we spell out in the conclusion. Now we shall outline the scenario of linguistic diversity on the border between Uruguay and Brazil.

Bortolini, Garcez, and Schlatter (2015) wrote a critical sociolinguistic account of the linguistic complexity in the Departments of Northern Uruguay. They explain that this region has been often described in the literature as 'characterized by Spanish-Portuguese diglossia' (p. 164). A view of languages as homogenous, circumscribed entities has long dominated linguistic studies dealing with this scenario. Thus, the highly hybridized speech of the people who inhabit this area—who often move in and out of the border, receive television and radio signal from Brazil, and, currently, have access to Portuguese-Spanish bilingual education—has puzzled these studies. Marked by the mingling of Portuguese, Spanish, and other linguistic and semiotic resources, the mixed forms spoken by the border residents were first classified in structuralist studies as '*fronterizo*' [from the border] (Rona, 1959). In lay discourses, they have been variously called 'dialect, Brazilian, Bahian or Portuñol' (Bortolini et al., 2015, p. 166). In the 1980s, Elizaincín and Behares (1981) coined the term Dialectos Portugueses del Uruguay (DPU) to distinguish this set of heterogeneous practices from the 'relatively abstract codification' called Standard Portuguese (Bortolini, Garcez, & Schlatter, 2013, p. 181). The moniker DPU—a classification that simultaneously confined translingual forms into the box of 'dialects' and made them distinct from an idealized standard norm—was soon adopted by linguists, educators, and policymakers.

Although the transidiomatic practices in the region are ordinary, they came to be described in sociolinguistic studies, and legislated in educational politics, as an extraordinary and intermediary stage between homogenous and bounded languages. Graciela Barrios (2001), for instance, hierarchically describes the situation of linguistic diversity on the border comprising:

a   Two **standard languages**:

   1. **Spanish**—the majority standard (…) acquired by many local citizens through schooling, required in legal and public procedures and associated with the language used in the capital city. (…)

   2. **Portuguese**—the minority standard, occupying a small niche in the repertories of the communities of northern Uruguay, mostly in passive use (…)

b   **Dialectal varieties of Portuguese, the DPU**: the highly stigmatized (…) primary language of many economically disadvantaged families, mostly confined to social practices within the household (summarized by Bortolini, Garcez, & Schlatter, 2015, pp. 167–168).

Derrida (1992) argued that dichotomies are not equal pairings of different terms but violent hierarchies 'where one term governs the other'. Thus, Barrios' concise description ranks seemingly opposite terms in the form of two main dichotomies: one that hierarchically elevates standard languages over dialects and, nested in the latter, another that opposes a higher-ranking standard to a less-prestigious standard. Standard Spanish figures as the 'majority standard', that is, a superordinate extract of language that is both distinct and superior to standard Portuguese and to Portuñol. The latter is classified as a dialect. Even though a standard variety may be seen as a specific social dialect of a language (Agha, 2007, pp. 134–142), the labeling of Portuñol as DPU seems to echo the traditional connotation of dialects as subordinate, disorderly scales of language. Ultimately, the DPUs will never acquire the full status of a 'language', as Elizaincín and Behares (1981, p. 404) predicted in the very article that invents the term: these translingual communicative practices, according to them, will never be endowed with 'a future stabilization (normalization), [...] much less [will] constitute a new language'.

Other dichotomies are couched in Barrios's description, such as languages that belong in the public/private domain, and languages of active/passive use. However, bounded classifications such as these, when contrasted to empirical situations of language use, fail to provide a more nuanced account of the sociolinguistic life on the border. For instance, the ethnography of Bortolini, Garcez, and Schlatter and the writing of Fabian Severo are shreds of evidence that the classification of standard languages as being the default of public interactions and the DPU or Portuñol as being restricted to the household does not account for the complexity of everyday linguistic practices in the region. Bortolini, Garcez, and Schlatter (2015, p. 179) argue that, despite the public educational programs' conceiving of bilingualism as parallel monolingualisms, students in bilingual schools 'used their full repertoire knowledge [i.e. their translanguaging] to solve classroom [i.e. public] tasks'. Fabian Severo, in turn, not only publishes (i.e. makes public) his poetry and novels in Portuñol but has also been awarded literary and educational prizes from Brazilian and Uruguayan *public* institutions for his writing.

The culture of monoglot standard in Uruguay and Brazil

In our encounter with Severo, the poet challenged the main terms of the 'culture of monoglot Standard' (Silverstein, 1996). For Silverstein, even though 'plurilingualism is everywhere about us, on urban public transportation, in classrooms, wherever service-sector personnel are encountered', one of the 'strongest lines of demarcation' of nation-states that continuously attempt to claim for themselves a uniform public culture is precisely the notion of standard language (p. 284). Based on Benjamin Whorf's analysis of the patterns of objectification of categories such as 'time' articulated in users' fashions of speaking about the world, Silverstein argues that there are metacommunicative patterns of objectification—or ideologies of language—which offer 'metaphoric models of interpretation' (Silverstein, 1996, p. 287) for a given sociolinguistic situation.

In the metacommunicative patterns of the culture of monoglot standard in the United States, two fashions of speaking about language seem to anchor the ideological work that legitimizes the Standard as the optimal dialect to perform things in the world. In short, these socially widespread fashions of speaking are predicated in the ideas that (1) the main function of language is to denote (i.e. represent or describe) entities 'out there' and that (2) the best accuracy in denotation will position the successful speakers—that is, those who are able to accurately use the Standard to single out the world—in the most elevated extracts of a unequal and commodified linguistic market.

Fabian Severo's metapragmatic discourse challenges both the foundations of the culture of monoglot standard. His discomfort with a primary referential function of language, which would be best achieved by the Standard, was most clearly articulated in the interview when we asked him to elaborate on his often cited remark that, since the womb, he listened to a mixed language.

> I am father, right? [...] And since Julieta, my daughter, was in the womb, my wife and I talked to Julieta, in addition to playing songs. Many songs, for instance 'At first sight' by Chico César [...] She always listened to it in the womb. When she was very agitated ... I would play this song to her. And then she would immediately quiet herself. She listened to it until she learnt to how to sing it [...] We don't even know, I can't even put a name on what we speak. We speak as we speak. In the university, people need to study what they study. Let them place names on it. [...] Because we ourselves don't have to even know what we do, much less how we do it. We have to do it. We do it naturally, like breathing, right? So I recently realized that things were sorted out at school. I just realized [that] there were words from here or from there at school, when they started correcting me. 'No, here you can't speak like this'. All my life I have been corrected.

In this excerpt, Severo's discomfort with the referentialist ideology, which sorts out words as belonging in 'here' and 'there', is best evidenced in his claim that those from the border 'can't even put a name on what we speak. We speak as we speak'. Naming the referent is less relevant than performing it through language practices that are fluid, mobile, and dynamic. As he articulates in the narration of his playing a Brazilian song to his daughter in the womb, translanguaging is less a question of pursuing 'referential accuracy' than accomplishing 'interactional efficiency'. Following Agha (2007), Jacquemet (2016, p. 80) explains that:

> A referential act is interactionally efficient, regardless of its denotational accuracy, if interactants have a relatively symmetrical grasp of what the referent is, that is, if they can be said to be 'mutually coordinated' to the referent based on their relative behavior during an interaction.

In addition to involving distinct modes of interaction, accuracy and effectiveness invoke different philosophical aspirations. In a tradition that begins in Plato, philosophers have explained that the best way of cognizing the world is by using language referentially—that is, by accurately singling out entities, states, and relations in the world. In this view, propositions would only have (reliable) meaning if they aim at describing reality. Yet, for Severo, the forms of cognition involved in his playing a song in Portuguese to his daughter who was just beginning her process of language socialization is not logico-propositional but performative: even before learning the meaning of words, she would be affected by the verses sung in another language, thus calming herself when listening to them. Rather than being predicated in the denotational accuracy of the lyrics, the playing of a song and the effects it produced in his baby daughter are lodged in the interactional and affective efficacy involved in their mutual calibration of affects through the medium of music.

Later, Severo seems to scale this experience up to the communicative practices on the border. Just after recalling this story, he then generalizes that 'We speak neither Portuguese nor Spanish. We don't even know [what we speak]... We just speak as we speak'. Thus, for him, on the Northern Uruguayan border, speakers of Portuñol orient themselves in the world by mutually coordinating themselves to a referent—their hybrid communicative forms—that they don't even know how to name. They just ordinarily blend Portuguese and Spanish as they move in and out of the border daily.

Severo critiques the second foundation of the culture of monoglot standard—namely, the view that the Standard is the highest commodified form because it provides the best modes of denotation—especially by challenging its mode of legitimacy. In his account, the monolingual Standard is misrecognized as having magical powers of best denotation. In addition to this misrecognition, its legitimacy is grounded in the social reiteration of power-laden acts of border de-marcation, which circumscribe the boundaries of the authoritative social dialect by delegitimizing linguistic forms that index other types of social membership.

Contrary to the view that non-standard translingual forms are denotationally poor, Severo argues in various moments of the interview that Portuñol has a highly expressive potential. For instance, in recalling his first attempts to write fiction, he explains why he failed to do it in standard Spanish:

> So I would like to say myself, I want to say many things that were going on and could not find how. Then, once the words all came mixed, and I let them all come mixed. And this word was another, and the other was a verse, and a book, and the other book was many books and thousands of pages.

Poetically, the parallelism in the last utterance, in which he articulates his writing tokens (words, verses, pages, books) and gradually enlarges them, gestures to the productivity of the translingual resources in Portuñol. Later, he elaborates on the grammatical singularity of the blended forms that are typical of the border:

> Someone who has never been corrected, who has never been told to change one's way with words, may have never felt what I felt. This fear, which affects one's subjectivity. Obviously, I conjugate verbs in a distinct way. I use plural forms in a distinct way, right? [...] I repeat the direct and indirect objects, I do things that are typical in the border. For you it is natural. Because it's like your mother speak, right? My mother speaks well. For me. So I consider maternal the language of my mother.

Note that the grammatical distinctiveness of the translanguaging in Artigas is discussed in line with the boundary-work that frames these forms as wrong. Although these grammatical constructions are, for him, 'typical', 'natural', and 'maternal', they are positioned as odd and incorrect. There is thus a boundary-work that makes people realize their linguistic difference: 'When they start correcting you ... that is when you focus on what's going on'. Acts of border demarcation like these are performative in the sense that they 'affect one's subjectivity' by imparting fear.

Essentially, for Severo, the delegimation of Portuñol as subordinate or inaccurate is not to be explained on the grounds of language; he provides examples of the naturalness, generativity, and expressiveness of these communicative forms. Like a lay linguist, Severo explains that Portuñol is as grammatical and expressive as any language. Instead, for him, the delegetimation of translanguaging and its bodily effects ought to be located in politics. It is only by gauging the boundary-work of the culture of monoglot standard, its performative gatekeeping, and its exclusionary effects that one may come to terms with the political delegetimation of translanguaging as incorrect and non-ordinary.

Conclusion

Severo's twofold critique of the naturalizations of the culture of monoglot Standard in Uruguay and Brazil may also be seen as scaling of communicative practices and language ideologies down to the ordinary. His view of the 'ordinary' seems to encompass two directions of ordinariness. First, pragmatically, the ordinariness of translanguaging is expressed in his reiterative comments that people in the northern border of Uruguay both ordinarily engage in translingual communicative practices and attempt to fix some of the political problems accrued from the demarcation of borders by trying to 'cross the bridge', that is, by ordinarily being mobile subjects. He says:

> For me, it is not a problem to cross the bridge. It is natural. That someone all of a sudden decides that Brazil is located there and that here something else ought to be done is not a problem of mine ... all this happening two blocks away from my house. We fix this naturally. (...) [Yet] the border is there for the poor. The rich have no borders.

Thus, in this direction, the ordinariness of language and border crossing ought not to be seen as a pacific or sovereign act of resistance (the poor may just naturally try to cross the bridge and mingle, but the border may be impassable for them). As the poor are those who feel the material consequences of the borders—such as their translingual repertoires being framed in monolingual discourses as exceptional and marginal—the ordinariness predicated in their translanguaging and in their attempt to jump the symbolic walls is regarded by Severo vis-à-vis the Standard idealizations about the 'non-ordinariness' of their practices and the exclusionary effects of these rationalizations. As displayed in Severo's habitus, some of these effects include silence and fear.

Second, philosophically, Severo handles the ordinariness of translinguistic practices in ways that echo the 'descent to the ordinary' (Das, 2007) in Ordinary Linguistic Philosophy. In this philosophical movement, led by J.L. Austin and Ludwig Wittgenstein, the analytic concern moved away from 'the purified metaphysical voice' and toward that of the 'ordinary' communicative practices (Das, 2007, p. 6). Austin and Wittgenstein's critique of metaphysics coincided in the argument that philosophers—in their insistence on privileging armchair linguistic examples, transcendental categories, and hidden mental processes—lost sight of the fact that we primarily use language socially. In discussing the differences between constative and performative utterances, Austin (1962, p. 143) points that our everyday using of language—in contradistinction with armchair sentences—precludes us from providing clear cut delimitations between a true or false utterance (i.e. constative) from a felicitous or infelicitous one (i.e. performative): 'In real life, as opposed to the simple situations envisaged in logical theory, one cannot answer in a simple manner whether it is true or false'. The adequate handling of philosophical problems is to be found in real, ordinary life situations. Wittgenstein (1953), in turn, used the metaphor of sublimation—that is, the chemical transformation of a substance from solid to gas—to problematize this philosophical scaling of an utterance from its bodily, everyday predicaments up to the spiritual, occult processes involved in comprehending it. His argument is that a 'queer conception' of language 'springs from a tendency to sublime the logic of our language' (§ 38). As the famous saying in this passage goes, 'the philosophical problems' embedded in this metaphysical stance 'arise when language *goes on holiday*'.

As if following Wittgenstein, Severo brings translingual practices back from their alleged vacations into ordinary, everyday life; he dismisses the allegations of these practices as being odd or exceptional by pointing to the productivity and creativity of his writing in Portuñol and of his fellow Artigas residents. We are stressing that this is a movement *down* to the ordinary because, as ordinary language philosophers did with the aspirations of metaphysics, Severo places a tenacious language-ideological effort in positioning Portuñol in contradistinction with the culture of monoglot standard, whose many aspirations include legitimizing the Standard as *the* ordinary. As if thinking with Austin, he claims that translingual practices—like his daughters' sensing rather than understanding a song, or that people in the border region speak translingual forms without knowing what they are speaking—are better understood not in the constative register of connotation or description of a pre-existing, independent world but in the performative register of affection, practice, and co-engagement in a world that is being continually reinvented.

The descent into the translinguistic ordinary amounts to looking at languages and language users alike as continuously mutating, recombining, and flowing in the chain of semiosis. As Severo reminds us, the people on the border may not be able to easily define themselves as 'Brazilian or Uruguayan'. They might performatively escape from the monoglot constative boundary making by eschewing questions such as 'who are you'? and rather choosing to be asked: 'whom are you being'?

Note

1 The differences between the two countries' projects of white nationality are a bit more nuanced. In Brazil, a historic narrative of *mestiçagem*, that is, the ideological construction that people from different colors and social classes would engage in non-violent social relations and form mestizo families, has always interdicted black and indigenous identities. It has also hidden the racial conflict while projecting the country as occupied by individuals seen as mestizos yet felt as whites or whitened. The main proponent of this ideology, now discredited as the 'myth of racial democracy', was Gilberto Freyre, a Brazilian social historian and anthropologist trained with Franz Boas at Columbia. His famous oeuvre, *The masters and slaves*, attempts to depict the singularity of racial relations in Brazil—especially *vis-à-vis* those in the United States—as the outcome of the pacific sexualized relation between Iberian male colonizers and indigenous and African women. As discussed by Sztainbok (2010, p. 175), Uruguay, differently from other Latin American countries, has nearly entirely 'reject[ed the idea] of *mestizaje* (…) as a national marker', following the 'almost complete erasure of indigenous presence' and the cultivation of narratives that hid the African and indigenous presence in the population. Uruguay has, thus, been portrayed as a white nation, whose citizens are 'mostly the descendants of Europeans' (Sztainbok, 2010, p. 175).

References

Agha, A. (2007). *Language and social relations*. Cambridge, UK: Cambridge University Press.

Austin, J. (1962). *How to do things with words*. Oxford, UK: Oxford University Press.

Bakhtin, M. (1981). *The dialogic imagination*. Austin: University of Texas Press.

Barrios, G. (2001). Políticas lingüísticas en el Uruguay: estándares vs. dialectos en la región fronteriza uruguayo-brasileña. *Boletim da ABRALIN, 24*: 65–82.

Behares, L., & Brovetto, C. (2008). Políticas Lingüísticas en Uruguay: Análisis de sus modos de establecimiento. In C. Brovetto (Ed.), *Primer Foro Nacional de Lenguas de A.N.E.P* (pp. 143–174). Montevideo, Uruguay: ANEP.

Bortolini, L., Garcez, P. M., & Schlatter, M. (2013). Práticas linguísticas e identidades em trânsito: espanhol e português em um cotidiano comunitário escolar uruguaio na fronteira com o Brasil. In L. P. Moita Lopes (Ed.), *Português no século XXI: Ideologias linguísticas* (pp. 249–273). São Paulo, Brazil: Parábola.

Bortolini, L., Garcez, P. M., & Schlatter, M. (2015). Language practices and identities in transit: Spanish and Portuguese in everyday life in a Uruguayan school community near the border with Brazil. In L. P. Moita Lopes (Ed.), *Global Portuguese: Linguistic ideologies in late modernity* (pp. 163–184). London, UK: Routledge.

Canale, G. (2015). Mapping conceptual change: The ideological struggle for the meaning of EFL in Uruguayan education. *L2 Journal, 7*(3), 15–39.

Carr, S., & Lempert, M. (Eds.) (2016). *Scale: Discourse and dimensions of social life*. Berkeley: University of California Press.

Cavalcanti, M., & Maher, T. (Eds.) (2018). *Multilingual Brazil: Language resources, identities and ideologies in a globalized world.* London, UK: Routledge.

Das, V. (2007). *Violence and the descent into the ordinary.* Berkeley: University of California Press.

Derrida, J. (1992). *Positions.* Chicago, IL: The University of Chicago Press.

Dovchin, S. (2017). The ordinariness of youth linguascapes in Mongolia. *International Journal of Multilingualism, 14*(2), 144–159.

Elizaincín, A., & Behares, L. (1981). Variabilidad morfosintáctica de los dialectos portugueses del Uruguay. *Boletín de Filología de la Universidad de Chile, 3,* 401–417.

Hamel, R. (2004). Regional blocs against English hegemony? The language policy of the Mercorsur in Latin America. In J. Maurais & M. Morris (Eds.) *Languages in a globalizing world* (pp. 111–142). Cambridge, UK: Cambridge University Press.

Jacquemet, M. (2016). Asylum and superdiversity: The search for denotational accuracy during asylum hearings. *Language & Communication, 44,* 72–81.

Lee, J., & Jenks, C. (2016). Doing translingual dispositions. *College Composition and Communication, 68*(2), 317–344.

Lopes, A. & Silva, D. (2018). Todos nós semos de frontera: ideologias linguísticas e a construção de uma pedagogia translíngue. *Linguagem em (Dis)curso, 18*(3), 695–713.

Rona, J. (1959) *El dialecto 'fronterizo' del norte del Uruguay.* Montevideo, Uruguay: Universidad de la República.

Severo, F. (2010). *Noite Nu Norte: poesía de la frontera.* Montevideo, Uruguay: Rumbo.

Severo, F. (2013). *Viento de nadie.* Montevideo, Uruguay: Rumbo.

Severo, F. (2015). *Viralata.* Montevideo, Uruguay: Rumbo.

Silverstein, M. (1996). Monoglot 'standard' in America: Standardization and metaphors of linguistic hegemony. In D. Brenneis & R. Macaulay (Eds.) *The matrix of language* (pp. 284–306). Boulder, CO: Westview.

Sztainbok, V. (2010). From Salsispuedes to *Tabaré*: Race, space, and the Uruguayan subject. *Thamyris/Intersecting, 20,* 175–192.

Wittgenstein, L. (1953) *Philosophical inverstigations.* Malden, MA: Blackwell.

9

TRANSLANGUAGING AS A PEDAGOGICAL RESOURCE IN ITALIAN PRIMARY SCHOOLS

Making visible the ordinariness of multilingualism

Andrea Scibetta and Valentina Carbonara[1]

Introduction

This chapter introduces data and results of a project named 'L'AltRoparlante', which aims at encouraging and promoting individual and collective multilingual repertoires for inclusive instruction in Italian primary schools. The project, which has been recently awarded the European Language Label 2018, embraces *translanguaging* as a pedagogical resource (García & Li Wei, 2014) and has been carried out in five multilingual superdiverse primary schools located in central and northern Italy since 2016. In this chapter, we analyze interviews with teachers of three schools involved, focusing on their attitudes toward pupils' linguistic repertoires, on their usual strategies for multilingual class management, and on their evaluation of the newly implemented translanguaging activities in relation to their ordinary teaching praxes. The analysis reveals that the majority of the participating teachers had already been adopting occasional multilingual practices before the project on the basis of the traits of inclusivity of the Italian educational system. However, as a result of the implementation of the project, all agreed on the necessity of constructing a more structured translanguaging-based pedagogical framework in their ordinary activity.

The need for an 'ordinary' translanguaging pedagogy in superdiverse educational contexts[2]

In the current age of global mobility, school contexts have to be understood through the concept of superdiversity, namely, the 'diversification of diversity' (Vertovec, 2007, p. 1025). We argue that through the use of a translanguaging-based pedagogy, which fosters the legitimation of language and semiotic repertoires (García & Li Wei, 2014), in schools it is possible to encourage mutual interaction and more dynamic translinguistic practices, contributing to a better 'local and situational production of sense' (Quassoli, 2006).

As far as the concept of 'translanguaging' is concerned, we approach it from two perspectives. The first is a sociolinguistic one, which foregrounds the fluidity and dynamicity of language practices in an era of post-multilingualism (García, Flores, & Spotti, 2017; Li Wei, 2017). The second is an applied linguistics-based one, which views translanguaging as a precious resource for conceiving an innovative, inclusive pedagogical framework (Cenoz, 2017; Creese & Blackledge, 2015), able to give voice to language plurality and to acknowledge 'difference as the norm' (Pennycook, 2010, p. 50). Further, drawing on the interdependent key concepts of 'language as a local practice' (Pennycook, 2010) and 'ordinariness of diversity' (Dovchin, 2016), we argue that language plurality can be integrated in the daily teaching process, taking inspiration from the ordinary multimodal and multilingual communicative practices that already take place among pupils.

Therefore, to promote this model of inclusive instruction, it is crucial not only to try to apply a translanguaging-based pedagogy occasionally but also to adopt it in the ordinary teaching praxis. Several studies, in fact, show that translanguaging-based pedagogy is effective both in terms of students' positive attitude toward collective language repertoires and in terms of development of metalinguistic awareness (Carbonara & Scibetta, 2018; Duarte & Günther-van der Meij, 2018; Mazzaferro, 2018; Paulsrud et al., 2017). The key question is whether it is possible to switch from the use of occasional inclusive practices to a more structured and ordinary framework of translanguaging-based pedagogy in the Italian school context.

The promotion of inclusive multilingual education in the Italian school system[3]

The latest national survey shows that today more than 826,000 foreign students attend Italian schools (from kindergartens to secondary schools), representing 9.4% of the total number (MIUR, 2018a).[4] Among those, more than 61% were born in Italy. Although the presence of pupils with different nationalities has rapidly risen in the past 15 years, the plurality of language repertoires have been a structural feature of many different Italian school contexts since the end of the 1980s. In terms of bottom-up language policy, since the 1970s, associations of teachers and scholars have focused on the necessity of encouraging the use of the entirety of linguistic repertoires, including dialects in particular, even in formal curricular activities, claiming a more democratic linguistic pedagogical framework (cf. the 'Ten theses for a democratic linguistic education', published in 1975 by a group of teachers guided by the linguist Tullio De Mauro). From a top-down point of view, however, institutions have neglected the importance of language diversity for decades, promoting a distorted image of Italian schools as monolingual environments. By doing so, on the one side, the vitality and the importance of dialects were underestimated (cf. De Mauro, 2014), while, on the other side, the idea of multilingualism initially prioritized the formal teaching of European languages and, in the past few years, also prestigious extra-European ones (Chinese, Arabic and Russian) in a growing number of secondary schools.

Nevertheless, institutional interventions in terms of promotion of bi- and multilingualism in Italian school contexts have visibly increased over the last 10 years, showing a rising attention toward an effective inclusion of minority language students. In 2007, the National Observatory for the Integration of Foreign Students and for Intercultural Education released the document *La via Italiana per la scuola interculturale e l'integrazione degli alunni stranieri* (The Italian way for an intercultural school and for the integration of foreign students, MIUR, 2007), which highlights the key role played by interculturality and fosters the promotion of a 'responsible multilingualism' through a specific Italian pedagogical model. In addition, the *Linee Guida per l'accoglienza e l'integrazione degli alunni stranieri* (Guidelines for welcoming and integrating foreign students, MIUR, 2014), provide recommendations related to the teaching of Italian as an L2 and to the advantages of bilingualism, including specific actions to effectively include foreign students (especially newly arrived ones) in the Italian school system. The document explicitly underlines for the first time the importance of the cognitive and affective development of foreign students' linguistic repertoires. Finally, the *Indicazioni nazionali e nuovi scenari* (National indications and new scenarios, MIUR, 2018b), attribute particular importance to the concept of development of global citizenship, including a more democratic language use in class.

Therefore, the Italian school system appears to be involved in a process of transformation toward more inclusive pedagogical praxes in terms of promoting multilingualism (Zanazzi, 2018). This process is connected with a wider inclusive teaching approach central to Italian education thanks to the contributions of influential pedagogists like Maria Montessori or Lorenzo Milani. Nevertheless, public and political discourse on inclusivity has especially increased in the last 30 years, with the purpose of providing normative instruments to develop inclusive and equitable education for all, regardless of any linguistic, cultural, physical, or cognitive differences (Ventriglia, Storace, & Capuano, 2015). Taking into specific consideration multilingualism as a trait of inclusive education, the publication and distribution (yet still not widespread enough) of documents of language and education policy elaborated in the European context (like the FREPA/ CARAP-Council of Europe, 2010, and the 'PlurCur', Council of Europe, 2018) have contributed to legitimating and strengthening top-down policies.

However, from a practical point of view, most of the initiatives in Italian schools are still based on a two-pronged approach, in which a prevalent role is still played by interculturality (mainly from an ethno-methodological perspective, cf. Demetrio & Favaro, 2002), while multilingual practices are still occasional and often adopted in non-curricular activities (Firpo & Sanfelici, 2016). The main challenge for Italian multilingual schools is trying to make those inclusive practices continuous, well-structured, and embedded in the ordinary teaching praxis.

The study[5]

Although considerable research in Italy has been devoted to the sociolinguistic aspects of multilingualism (Machetti, Barni, & Bagna, 2018), less attention has been paid to the educational perspective, mainly due to the limited number of schools, which adopt multilingual education practices extensively and with intent (Favaro, 2018). In this chapter, we focus on the project L'AltRoparlante, aiming at implementing a translanguaging-based approach in primary schools. The project L'AltRoparlante is a Transformative Action Research (García & Kleyn, 2016) in which all the actors involved—researchers, teachers, parents, and students—contributed to redefine educational practices through a process of expertise sharing, joint planning, negotiation of activities, and collective reflection to challenge monolingual instruction. The project has been conducted since 2016 in three primary schools and since 2018 in two further schools in northern and central Italy with a rate of immigrant minority students between 30% and 70%, distributed by different heterogeneity degrees. In this chapter, we take into account data collected in three of the five schools involved in the project: School 1, located in the medium-size town of Serravalle Scrivia (Piedmont); School 2, settled in the small village of Stabbia (Tuscany); and School 3, placed in the city of Prato (Tuscany). Table 9.1 provides information regarding schools' collective linguistic repertoires.

After an initial period of teacher training, adopting the concept of Critical Multilingual Awareness (García, 2016), and ethno-linguistic investigations (Blommaert & Dong Jie, 2010), we designed and implemented teaching activities based on translanguaging pedagogy (García & Li Wei, 2014). We engaged teachers and children to construct a more ecological linguistic schoolscape (Menken,

TABLE 9.1 Schools information

Schools	No. of students involved in L'AltRoparlante	Languages and dialects
S1	151 (69 with immigrant background)	Italian, Arabic dialects, Modern Standard Arabic, French, Albanian, Romanian, Polish, Russian, Spanish, Bini, Swahili, Punjabi, Italian regional dialects.
S2	48 (16 with immigrant background)	Italian, standard Chinese (Putonghua), other local varieties of Chinese (mainly Wenzhouhua), Albanian, Romanian, German, Italian regional dialects.
S3	118 (76 with immigrant background)	Italian, standard Chinese (Putonghua), other local varieties of Chinese (mainly Wenzhouhua), Arabic dialects, Modern Standard Arabic, Albanian, Romanian, Spanish, Georgian, Punjabi, Urdu, Bengali, Igbo, Italian regional dialects.

Rosario, & Valerio, 2018), in language portraits activities (Busch, 2012), in systematic bilingual storytelling with parents and in the reception and production of different types of multilingual texts (Cummins & Early, 2011), including narratives, argumentative, and content-based ones, using a variety of cooperative strategies. All the activities were planned in consonance with the regular teachers' program, during daily curricular classes, applying a translanguaging lens to usual teaching practices. The implementation was monitored through fieldnotes, observational schemes, and classroom video-recordings in addition to interviews and focus groups conducted with teachers and pupils.

The purpose of this study was to investigate the potential presence of educational actions with respect to multilingualism in class prior to the introduction of L'AltRoparlante project according to teachers' experience. Moreover, our main research questions concern teachers' evaluation of the translanguaging activities implemented, with regard to their functional use in achieving the curricular goals and the possible strategies for an ordinary employment of translinguistic practices in continuity with Italian inclusive pedagogy. To answer our research questions, we interrogated a corpus of in-depth, semi-structured interviews collected during 2017 and 2018 and conducted in multiple sessions (Charmaz & Belgrave, 2012) with 18 teachers of Schools 1, 2, and 3 for a total of 12 hours of video-recordings.

The interviews were transcribed and processed with Nvivo 11, following a Grounded Theory-based approach (*ivi.*). The analysis followed a cyclic procedure of open and focused coding to identify recurring patterns and retrieve interconnections or hierarchical relations between the thematic nodes that emerged (Hadley, 2017). The result is a map of 62 thematic nodes, partially presented in other works (Carbonara & Scibetta, 2018). In the following paragraphs, we will examine, in particular, the nodes related to our research questions, namely, concerning teaching approaches adopted over the years to manage multilingualism in terms of deployment of translinguistic practices, as well as the evaluation of translanguaging pedagogy in connection with the ordinary educational praxis.

Analysis and implications

Is there any continuum between the inclusive practices that were already widespread before the project and translanguaging-based pedagogy?[6]

The nodes and the references introduced below show teachers' attitudes toward the increasing presence of emergent bilingual students in their classes in the past few years/decades, as well as the strategies they adopted to welcome newly arrived pupils, as regards both the teaching praxis and the extra-curricular supports. The nodes 'First welcoming actions' and 'Initial difficulties' (Table 9.2) include interviewees' considerations about what used to be done to welcome emergent bilingual students before the implementation of the project, as well as the difficulties the school staff encountered in this process.

TABLE 9.2 References and sources of the nodes 'First welcoming actions' and 'Initial difficulties'

Node	References	Sources
First welcoming actions	31	12
Initial difficulties	27	15

The nodes in Table 9.2 partially overlap since in the opinion of several interviewees the inclusion of non-Italian speaking students used to be initially conceived as an obstacle to classroom cohesion. Various references, in fact, show that some years ago the initial procedures for 'foreign' pupils' inclusion at school were rather arbitrary and did not follow precise guidelines. More recently, on the contrary, in line with national documents and with the spread of specific literature, all three schools instituted *ad hoc* 'welcoming committees' for students with an immigrant background and to set up and maintain stable contacts with their families, following well-structured indications (*protocolli di accoglienza* in Italian).

Nevertheless, most teachers note that they continued to consider the presence of emergent bilingual students primarily in terms of 'communicative difficulties' for several years. According to such a perspective, the inclusion of such pupils was considered as a monodirectional effort, the main goal of which was linguistic assimilation. At the same time, however, besides the 'communicative difficulties' encountered, teachers used to focus on the relational and intersubjective aspect of pupils' inclusion. In this way, the empowerment of learners' subjectivities and the promotion of a favorable and welcoming environment were considered necessary conditions to further develop deeper work on pupils' development of language and disciplinary skills (cf. the statement of T5[7] below).

> T5: The first months were difficult; you started with basic literacy, from the attempts to recognise the environment. We used to work on relationships because the first children who arrived were withdrawn, you had to carry out an action of support and to give confidence to those children, because they were destabilized. Activities were interrelated but difficult, because you had to work on relationships, learning and on individual learners all at the same time.[8]

The three schools involved in the project have been characterized by increasingly heterogeneous multilingual repertoires in the past few years (cf. the 16 references of the node 'Composition of multilingual classes' in Table 9.3, which mainly regard teachers' awareness about the increasing language diversity in their classrooms). Taking into account this crucial aspect as well as the inclusive tendency of the Italian curriculum, most of the participants talked about specific actions to facilitate emergent bilinguals' inclusion in the ordinary teaching praxis.

TABLE 9.3 References and sources of the nodes 'Cultural mediation',
'L2 Italian teaching', 'Interculturality', and 'Composition
of multilingual classes'

Node	References	Sources
Cultural mediation	18	10
L2 Italian teaching	27	13
Interculturality	10	8
Composition of multilingual classes	16	9

One key instrument that allowed a better mutual understanding about emergent bilinguals' educational and familiar background, as well as their learning and communicative needs, is the use of cultural mediation. This kind of service has been offered for more than a decade through the regular presence of experts in several languages (mainly Mandarin Chinese, Arabic, and Albanian) at Schools 2 and 3 and for a period of time also at School 1. Nowadays, cultural mediation seems to be considered a crucial resource by all the teachers, not only as a source of communicative support but also to facilitate multilingual education. However, as T11 emphasizes, several teachers noted that, for years, little importance was given to this instrument.

> T11: Now there is more of a habit of turning to a mediator. Before, only two of us teachers used to think that we needed a mediator; now every teacher calls him/her.

Another structural action implemented in the past decade in the three schools consists of L2 Italian teaching addressed to immigrant minority pupils, usually conceived of as a key element to enhance their inclusion in the school context. Such support, however, was usually organized through language courses outside the class during the curricular teaching time, sometimes delegated to linguistic facilitators, and sometimes carried out by teachers of Italian language and humanities (regardless of their knowledge of L2 teaching methodologies). T6, in fact, confirms the priority attributed to the dimension of L2 Italian (often associated with the concept of 'literacy'):

> T6: Once, the learning pathway was mainly focused on the comprehension of Italian. Now, foreign children were born here, so their needs are different. Initially, we used to work on literacy from scratch, while now, sometimes they just need lexical support.

As far as the teaching routine is concerned, ten out of eighteen interviewees underlined that they had implemented activities based on interculturality for several years, drawing on the growing heterogeneity of cultural backgrounds in their classes. Such actions were mainly promoted through periodic workshops carried out during regular class time, sometimes in collaboration with experts. In other cases, teachers themselves took the initiative to include intercultural contents in their ordinary activities, as explained by T12:

> T12: Teaching English, for example when we talked about New Year's Eve, several times I found myself making a comparison to what happens in China, their holidays and the foods they eat on those occasions.

Although the perspective of interculturality often provided support in favor of a better visibility of cultural diversity as a resource, as explained earlier, some typologies of intercultural activities, if not well planned and not well structured, could lead to misunderstandings and stereotypical representations, amplifying differences instead of bringing into light a common ground between classmates. Taking into account the fertile environment represented by the inclusive practices mentioned above, as well as the increasing presence (in some cases, as in School 3, the prevalence) of emergent bilingual students, most participants underlined the necessity of taking further steps in the direction of multilingual education, going beyond the sole use of interculturality.

Table 9.4, in fact, summarizes the number of sources and references related to the nodes 'Adjustments in the teaching praxis' and 'Perception of changes in the teaching praxis'. The first node contains references related to teachers' pre-project attempts to adapt their teaching approach to facilitate pupils' inclusion mainly through processes of textual simplification and taking advantage of cooperative work and cooperative language learning. However, teachers' attempts to adjust their teaching praxis to better include emergent bilinguals were adopted sporadically, often not in line with the disciplinary programs. This dimension of tentative, occasional actions is represented by T5:

> T5: We carried on through different attempts and strategies. Experimenting little by little, we adopted corrective actions.

The node 'Perception of changes in the teaching praxis', instead, concerns interviewees' awareness about the means through which the school system (from both micro- and macro-perspectives) has changed and is changing toward better

TABLE 9.4 References and sources of the nodes 'Adjustments in the teaching praxis' and 'Perception of changes in the teaching praxis'

Node	References	Sources
Adjustments in the teaching praxis	31	12
Perception of changes in the teaching praxis	17	7

inclusivity in terms of promotion of multilingual repertoires. As regards the teaching praxis, several interviewees highlighted the need to focus on the attention to the subjective, inner dimension, with respect to students' linguistic diversity.

This raising awareness of the need for better inclusivity and for more effective and continuous promotion of multilingual repertoires in the teaching praxis could represent a fundamental preliminary condition to include translanguaging pedagogy to accommodate ordinariness. Therefore, we can notice a continuum between the inclusive strategies that were already in effect before the project and the translanguaging-based pedagogy promoted by L'AltRoparlante project.

Did translanguaging practices exist in teachers' approaches prior to the L'AltRoparlante project?[9]

As described above, the valuable measures adopted by teachers to ensure a successful learning process for emergent bilingual children are rooted in the Italian tradition of inclusiveness in education (Zanazzi, 2018). Since in the last 20 years the predominant approach of intercultural pedagogy has focused on cultural aspects, immigrant languages had a limited space in school: the linguistic dimension of minority children has usually only been considered in relation to the development of Italian language competence. However, over the years, teachers have made some attempts to draw upon the multilingual repertoires of their classes. This aspect also emerged in our investigation in the node 'Pre-project translinguistic practices' (Table 9.5).

Analyzing teachers' narratives, the majority of references reflect an occasional, unsystematic, and limited engagement of emergent bilingual children's languages. In fact, most of the teachers were accustomed to asking for translations of terms related to school life or subject contents, as T7 explains:

> T7: Coming from a situation in which we have always had many foreign pupils at school, as a teacher it comes spontaneous to you to ask a foreign child 'how do you say this thing in your language?' On the one hand, this is out of personal curiosity; on the other hand, as time went by we realized that it is important for foreign children to maintain their own languages.

The previous excerpt introduces how, over time, teachers reconsidered the educational purpose of immigrant languages in terms of instrumental reasons (i.e. achieving a better comprehension in Italian, translating a word from the

TABLE 9.5 References and sources of the node 'Pre-project translinguistic practices'

Node	References	Sources
Pre-project translinguistic practices	31	12

child's so-called 'mother tongue'), bilingualism maintenance, and finally as an inclusive tool.

In fact, T11 affirmed the need to adopt a 'trial and error approach' and to continually 'invent' new strategies of accommodation:

> T11: My experience has always been a kind of trial and error approach. In order to include Chinese-speaking children I had to use strategies I did not use regularly in a class where all of the children speak the same language. So I had to invent these things.

The tentative strategies mentioned by T11 counted, in addition to the one described earlier, as well as multilingual labeling of school objects and places (T4), creation of classroom multilingual dictionaries and phrasebooks (T15), multilingual singing of 'Happy Birthday' at children's parties at school (T8), involvement of parents in sporadic mother-tongue story telling (T18), celebration of the International Mother Language Day on 21st February (T16), and other circumscribed activities. Nonetheless, these positive ideologically oriented actions, derived from the inclusive trait of Italian school system, had rarely led to an ordinary and methodical adoption of translinguistic practices in teaching activities, mostly because of the delayed translation of national policy indications about multilingualism into practical strategies.

How can translinguistic practices become ordinary in education in view of teachers' evaluation of the project L'AltRoparlante?[10]

After the implementation of the translanguaging pedagogy in the three schools, the teachers were asked to express their opinions regarding how the project L'AltRoparlante had affected their teaching approach, as well as children's learning processes and attitudes. Table 9.6 reports the number of references and sources of the nodes 'Project evaluation' and 'Impact on children'.

We did not detect any negative comment from teachers regarding L'Alt-Roparlante: rather, all teachers involved judged it favorably in terms of personal professional development, educational effectiveness, and increase in students' motivation. Some teachers reflected specifically on the translinguistic interaction occurring in class, considering it not only as merely translating but as a dynamic

TABLE 9.6 References and sources of the nodes 'Project evaluation' and 'Impact on children'

Node	References	Sources
Project evaluation	44	16
Impact on children	38	15

meaning-making process revealing different cultural and cognitive paths in verbal communication across the different languages and in the contact between them. This idea is described, for instance, by T14:

> T14: This work made me reflect, I had neglected this aspect. For me the mother tongue was something worthy of respect...but instead you need to include it in your teaching and start from what they know already. When I asked them to translate something...I mean in Italian you deal with a sentence in a certain way, but I realised that when they also employed their languages, they would formulate the sentence in a different way [...]. And this shapes you in terms of mental rigidity and forma mentis.

Teachers interpreted the impact of the project on children as positive, both for first- and second-generation immigrant minority pupils and for Italian-born children. The former ones felt empowered by the possibility of using their whole linguistic repertoire in class as a resource for affirming their identity. Moreover, for first-generation students, translanguaging turned to be a linguistic tool to shift from a silenced condition—due to limited competences in Italian language—to a more participatory status. Italian children had the opportunity to be exposed to other languages, increasing language awareness, meta-linguistic skills, and cultural relativism. T11 summarizes children's responses as such:

> T11: With the experience of L'AltRoparlante, we noticed that many children who were not able to come out of their shells were finally able to show that they know many things which we did not know they knew. They acquired a bit more self-confidence, then they got stronger, they started to speak up. And also the other children looked at them through different eyes.

From a functional point of view, teachers recognized the versatility of a translanguaging-based pedagogy, which can support daily teaching activities even in various different school subjects. See, for instance, T9's statement:

> T9: I think that an important thing is the flexibility of these activities. When I teach math, actually I teach also Italian language at the same time and I combine my activities with hers [of the Italian teacher]. But it is not an effort, it is very spontaneous. And this type of work on languages can easily be embedded in every task we do.

The reflection implies a relevant feature of the Italian primary educational system, namely, interdisciplinarity. In addition, the extract explains the awareness of a linguistic dimension underlying every type of content instruction, which can be associated with the concept of 'languaging' (Swain, 2009). Interdisciplinarity

TABLE 9.7 References and sources of the node 'Post-project ordinariness of translinguistic practice'

Node	References	Sources
Post-project ordinariness of translinguistic practice	54	16

and 'languaging', along with inclusivity, are the key characteristics of the Italian school system, which can prompt the ordinariness of multilingual education in class. Regarding this topic, the node 'Post-Project ordinariness of translinguistic practices' (Table 9.7) collects those references in which the interviewees explore in details and in practical terms why and how a translanguaging pedagogy could be integrated in the usual teaching approach, taking their experience in L'AltRoparlante project into consideration.

Many teachers mentioned the principle of 'academic and teaching freedom', introduced in the Constitution of Italian Republic (article 33) and confirmed in several subsequent regulations over the years, as a guarantee and a vehicle of the potential implementation of translinguistic practices in ordinary teaching. Indeed, the more recent law 107/2015 underlines that schools can resort to any methodological strategies to pursue students' development of competences and to contrast socio-cultural inequality. With respect to the adoptable procedures to foster translanguaging in class, teachers' argumentation is rooted on the ideas of 'verticality', another cardinal issue in Italian educational discourse. The response by T4 is instructive:

> T4: You start from the first grade, you set some learning goals, maybe with the participation of the English language teacher, showing them how to name certain things in English -- and how about in the children's languages? Little vertical goals. If you let them get used to that from the very beginning, when you get to the fifth grade, you are able to reach more articulated and complex goals, because it becomes normal, as if it were your own methodology.

Teachers believe that the linguistic repertoires of the students with an immigrant background can be acknowledged as a useful resource by everyone only with a full incorporation of the translanguaging pedagogy into the regular learning goals and with careful longitudinal planning.

Expressions like 'tied to the program', 'anchored to the competences', 'interlaced with what I do in class' were very common in the interviews. Teachers identify this synthesis as the more effective and advisable path for the ordinary exercise of translanguaging, disregarding the occasionality of the previous activities, which, on the contrary, were not able to produce a profound contribution to the learning process and a real transformation of power relations in the class.

Other references remark that through translinguistic practices, the school reflects the increasingly multicultural and multilingual Italian society properly, providing students with those strategic competencies needed to operate successfully in the contemporary world, as described by the 'pluralistic approaches' of CARAP (Council of Europe, 2010).

Conclusions

In this chapter, we presented a research study conducted within the L'AltRoparlante project based on the introduction of translinguistic practices in Italian schools. We identified a continuum of several typologies of inclusive practices addressing immigrant minority children, which were already widespread before the project. We found that such preliminary practices partly consisted of occasional multilingual actions, even if confined to specific limited experiences, often based on teachers' individual initiatives. Taking into consideration the positive feedback expressed by the interviewees about the impact of the L'AltRoparlante project, teachers reflected on strategies through which they could turn the sporadic inclusive measures which they had adopted before into an ordinary translanguaging-based pedagogical framework.

As it stands, we believe that the only way to establish the ordinariness of translanguaging pedagogy in Italian schools is to embed it within the inclusive approach of Italian educational system. Such an approach acts as a springboard to move from the sole use of compensatory instruments to more democratic and transformative ones (Jaspers, 2018) with emergent bilingual children, differently from other educational contexts in Europe (Agirdag, 2010). According to this perspective, Table 9.8 shows what we see as the continuum of inclusive initiatives for multilingual management in Italian schools, put into practice over the years, up to the more recent and hopefully spreading introduction of translanguaging.

TABLE 9.8 Continuum of inclusive initiatives for multilingual management

Inclusive instruments	*Educational purpose*
Italian as an L2 support	Compensatory
Intercultural education	Welcoming/Incremental
Teaching adjustments (cooperative work, simplification, etc…)	Complementary/Adaptative
Preliminary multilingual initiatives (basic multilingual schoolscape, occasional storytelling, 'Mother language Day' celebration, class languages dictionaries, etc…)	Instrumental/Languages promotion
Ordinary translanguaging pedagogy	Democratic/Transformative

Acknowledgements

We would like to thank Prof. Massimiliano Spotti for his precious and continuous academic support, which allowed us to improve the quality of our research. In addition, we would like to express our gratitude to the headmasters and all the teachers of the schools involved in the L'AltRoparlante project.

Notes

1 This chapter is a result of a research project managed collaboratively by both authors. Data collection in School 1 was conducted by Valentina Carbonara. Data collection in School 2 was conducted by Andrea Scibetta. Data collection in School 3 was conducted by both authors.
2 Paragraph written by Andrea Scibetta.
3 Paragraph written by Andrea Scibetta.
4 The adjective 'foreign' is here considered from its juridical perspective. The current law concerning citizenship in Italy refers to the so called *jus sanguinis*, and considers children born and raised in Italy to be foreigners.
5 Paragraph written by Valentina Carbonara.
6 Section written by Andrea Scibetta.
7 The labels from T1 to T10 refer to teachers working in School 1; T11, T12, and T13 work in School 2; the labels from T14 to T18 refer to teachers working in School 3.
8 All the excerpts presented were translated from Italian.
9 Section written by Valentina Carbonara.
10 Section written by Valentina Carbonara.

References

Agirdag, O. (2010). Exploring bilingualism in a monolingual school system: Insights from Turkish and native students from Belgian schools. *British Journal of Sociology of Education, 31*(3), 307–321.

Blommaert, J., & Dong Jie (2010). *Ethnographic fieldwork: A beginner's guide.* Bristol, UK: Multilingual Matters.

Busch, B. (2012). The linguistic repertoire revisited. *Applied Linguistics, 33*(5), 503–523.

Carbonara, V., & A. Scibetta (2018). Il translanguaging come strumento efficace per la gestione delle classi plurilingui: il progetto 'L'AltRoparlante. *Rassegna Italiana di Linguistica Applicata (RILA), 1*(2018), 65–83.

Cenoz, J. (2017). Translanguaging in school contexts: International perspectives. *Journal of Language, Identity & Education, 16*(4), 193–198.

Charmaz, K., & Belgrave, L. L. (2012). Qualitative interviewing and grounded theory analysis. In *The SAGE Handbook of Interview Research: The Complexity of the Craft* (pp. 347–366). Thousand Oaks, CA: SAGE.

Council of Europe (2010). *A framework of reference for pluralistic approaches to languages and cultures* (CARAP/FREPA).

Council of Europe (2018). *PlurCur - Research and practice regarding plurilingual whole school curricula.*

Creese, A., & Blackledge, A. (2015). Translanguaging and identity in educational settings. *Annual Review of Applied Linguistics, 35*, 20–35.

Cummins, J., & Early, M. (2011). *Identity texts the collaborative creation of power in multilingual schools.* Stoke on Trent, UK: Trentham Books.

De Mauro, T. (2014). *Storia linguistica dell'Italia repubblicana.* Roma, Italy: Laterza.

Demetrio, D., & Favaro, G. (2002). *Didattica interculturale.* Milano, Italy: Franco Angeli.

Dovchin, S. (2016). The ordinariness of youth linguascapes in Mongolia. *International Journal of Multilingualism, 14*(2), 144–159.

Duarte, J., & Günther-van der Meij, M. (2018). A holistic model for multilingualism in education. *E-JournALL, 5*(2), 24–43.

Favaro, G. (2018). Le lingue, le norme, le pratiche. Il contesto, i dati, i riferimenti della scuola multiculturale e plurilingue. *Italiano LinguaDue 10*(1), 9–51.

Firpo, E., & Sanfelici, L. (2016). *La visione eteroglossica del bilinguismo: spagnolo lingua d'origine e Italstudio.* Milano, Italy: Edizioni Universitarie di Lettere Economia Diritto.

García, O. (2016). Critical multilingual language awareness and teacher education. In J. Cenoz, D. Gorter, & S. May (Eds.), *Language awareness and multilingualism* (pp. 1–17). Cham, Switzerland: Springer International Publishing.

García, O., Flores, N., & Spotti, M. (Eds.) (2017), *The Oxford handbook of language and society.* Oxford, UK: Oxford University Press.

García, O., & Kleyn, T. (2016). *Translanguaging with multilingual students: Learning from classroom moments.* New York, NY: Routledge.

García, O., & Li Wei (2014). *Translanguaging: Language, bilingualism and education.* Basingstoke, UK: Palgrave Macmillan.

Hadley, G. (2017). *Grounded theory in applied linguistics research: A practical guide.* Milton Park, Abingdon, Oxon: Routledge.

Jaspers, J. (2018). The transformative limits of translanguaging. *Language & Communication, 58*, 1–10.

Li Wei. (2017). Translanguaging as a practical theory of language. *Applied Linguistics, 39*(2), 261.

Machetti, S., Barni, M., & Bagna, C. (2018). Language policies for migrants in Italy: The tension between democracy, decision-making, and linguistic diversity. In M. Gazzola, T. Templin, B. A. Wickström (Eds.), *Language policy and linguistic justice.* Cham, Switzerland: Springer.

Mazzaferro, G. (Eds.) (2018). *Translanguaging as everyday practice.* Cham, Switzerland: Springer.

Menken, K., Rosario, V. P., & Valerio, L. A. (2018). Increasing multilingualism in schoolscapes. *Linguistic Landscape, 4*(2), 101–127.

MIUR (Italian Ministry of Education) (2007). *La via Italiana per la scuola interculturale e l'integrazione degli alunni stranieri.*

MIUR (Italian Ministry of Education) (2014). *Linee guida per l'accoglienza e l'integrazione degli alunni stranieri.*

MIUR (Italian Ministry of Education) (2018a). *Gli alunni con cittadinanza non italiana. Ufficio Statistica e Studi.*

MIUR (Italian Ministry of Education). (2018b). *Indicazioni Nazionali e Nuovi Scenari.*

Paulsrud, B., Rosén, J., Straszer, B., & Wedin, Å. (2017). *New perspectives on translanguaging and education.* Bristol, UK and Blue Ridge Summit, PA: Multilingual Matters.

Pennycook, A. (2010). *Language as a local practice.* London, UK: Routledge.

Quassoli, F. (2006). *Riconoscersi: differenze culturali e pratiche comunicative.* Milano, Italy: Raffaello Cortina Editore.

Swain, M. (2009). Languaging, agency and collaboration in advanced second language proficiency. *Advanced language learning: The contribution of Halliday and Vygotsky.* London, UK: Bloomsbury.

Ventriglia, L., Storace, F., & Capuano, A. (2015). *La didattica inclusiva. Proposte metodologiche e didattiche per l'apprendimento. Quaderni della Ricerca, 25.* Torino, Italy: Loescher.

Vertovec, S. (2007). Superdiversity and its implications. *Journal of Ethnic and Racial Studies, 30*(6), 1024–1054.

Zanazzi, S. (2018). *Inclusive education. A critical view on Italian policies.* Roma, Italy: Edizioni Nuova Cultura.

10

REIMAGINING BILINGUALISM IN LATE MODERN PUERTO RICO

The 'ordinariness' of English language use among Latino adolescents

Katherine Morales Lugo

Introduction

This chapter contributes to studies of translingualism in colonial contexts, motivated by insufficient literature regarding the phenomenon in non-European and non-cosmopolitan global contexts. The sustainability of translingualism as a theory of practice is tested on two ethnographic case studies of schools in Puerto Rico (PR). PR serves as a unique setting for a study of bilingualism and identity, particularly because of its unique status as a previous Spanish colony (1493–1898) and current 'unincorporated territory' of the United States of America (1898–present). The sample populations discussed here reflect the linguistic, educational, and class disparities found on the island; they were selected through the course of a 6-month participant-observation and informal interactions with participants. Through semiotically grounded discourse analysis of translanguaging practices, I offer an alternative lens by which speech styles may be observed as the outcome of: (1) languages histories, (2) educational opportunities, (3) social circumstances, and (4) peer-group engagements. The analysis reveals differences in the way adolescents make use of translingual styles, which may be interpreted as the outcome of their different access to the English language, orientations to local and non-local culture, and peer group engagements.

Toward a middle ground in the ordinariness and creativity debate

Critics of translingualism claim that *language boundaries*, though problematic, are an important piece to the overall picture of describing language in society. In the United States, for instance, the concept of a unitary 'language' has served as a discriminatory tool by conservative ideologues to promote an 'English-only' agenda (see Rosa, 2016). Some have suggested that adopting a framework that takes unhinged 'mobility' and 'mixing' (Blommaert, 2010, p. 12) as starting points glosses over the historical trajectories of language varieties, the social ine-qualities that shape our day-to-day practices, the ideologies of language mainte-nance and nationalism, and the controversial politics and cultural hegemony that may be found in situations of multilingualism and language contact (cf. Flores & Lewis, 2016). And, lastly, it has been suggested that such accounts assume *a pri-ori* mobility and globalization for all, and do not address circumstances facing underprivileged members of society (ibid).

Li Wei (2017) notes that while these criticisms exist, translingual approaches such as translanguaging do not discard the historical trajectories of different ways of speaking; rather, they create a *third space* (cf. Soja, 1996), by which new possibilities exist for language use and meaning making. In this languaging third space, there is 'a place of critical exchange where the geographic imagination can be expanded to encompass a multiplicity of perspectives' previously thought of as 'incompatible and uncombinable' (Li Wei, 2017, pp. 23–24). Even in García and Li Wei's (2014) earlier work, the importance of language as an ideological construct is not dis-carded, viewing bilingualism as 'one linguistic repertoire *with features that have been societally constructed as belonging to two separate languages*' (García & Li Wei, 2014, p. 2).

At its core translanguaging is a social movement. One that acknowledges 'the origin of current language ideologies' as importantly starting with the invention of the printing press and encouraged by 'the emerging capitalistic economic system' of the time (Flores & García, 2013, p. 244). Consequently, in these standardiza-tion practices, languages were codified and 'linguistically heterogenous speakers had to be molded into a homogenous linguistic group' (ibid). Translanguaging problematizes standardization practices while acknowledging hybrid linguistic realities. Cognitively, it understands bilingual speech as part of a spectrum, rather than two separate cognitive entities. While there are certain tendencies in this spectrum due to societal practices, or *habitus* (Bourdieu, 1994), there is also the opportunity to take from what is available in our 'repertoire' and produce mixed and semiotically rich utterances. It is a call to include multiplicity of use and meaning in our understanding of bilingual speech. It makes room for fuzziness and hybridity in language boundaries, and the variation within ideologically and cognitively perceived two-speech utterances.

Puerto Rico

In PR, a predominantly Spanish-speaking US territory, perceptions of distinct language boundaries, and the semiotic values to those boundaries, have formed the basis of standardization and educational practices, political debates, language ideologies, and group and identity formations. Spanish has historically taken up the role of the emblem of belonging and national identity; meanwhile, English has inherited a set of contradictory values and roles. English is often times perceived as an 'outsider's code' in that the successful acquisition of it may lead to better career opportunities and life experiences abroad, or, in this case, in mainland United

States, where Puerto Ricans have had the legal right to reside and work as citizens since 1917. At the same time, English is seen as the language of upward mobility on the island, as many professional jobs require functional command of English. It plays a pivotal role in higher education as many schools function bilingually or require intermediate knowledge of English to succeed (see Mazak & Carroll, 2017).

While PR is subject to more English influence than its other Latin American counterparts (see Lipski, 2008), most communicative practices on the island take place in Spanish. Pousada (2000) describes the dominant type of bilingualism on the island as 'receptive' or 'passive' bilingualism such that most islanders are able to understand basic English writing and speech but struggle to produce English-only discourse and writing. US Census findings provide a picture whereby most islanders claim to not speak English 'very well', and the upper-class *elite* have the upper hand in that they are those most likely to have access to private-school, English-only education, after-school tutoring, and other advantages (cf. Pousada, 2000). In light of these ideologies and reported uses of language, this chapter examines the extent to which young Puerto Ricans use and orient to Englishes and incorporate them in their mixed utterances.

Methods

To probe previous findings of Englishes on the island, data collection was conducted through participant-observations in two high schools on the island: one private school and one public school. Strategic note taking and documentation of natural language use, alongside focus group and individual interviews, formed the foundation of this study. The ethnographies were conducted during September 2015 to March 2016. A total of 20 volunteer participants were observed in a private high school (out of 136), each representative of different *communities of practice* (see Eckert, 2000), or friendship groups, in the 12th grade. A total of 30 students (out of 291) were observed in the 12th grade class of the public school, following the same peer sampling method, as well as accounting for differences in socioeconomic and linguistic practices.

Translanguaging in the private school

One of the fieldwork locations was a private school on the west side of the island that offered bilingual education, where they taught half of the day in Spanish and the other half in English. The school was affiliated with a local 7th Day Adventist Church, and they marketed themselves as purveyors of bilingual education in 'a safe and spiritual environment' (fieldnotes, November 2015). Subjects such as World Religions were offered alongside core subjects such as Science and Mathematics. Classroom materials (e.g. textbooks, handouts, and slides) were offered in English, regardless of the language spoken in the classroom. School activities were conducted in Puerto Rican Spanish.

Instructional strategies were highly mixed and translingual activities were common in the school. Despite practices that encouraged the mixing of languages, these co-existed with ideologies of discreteness of codes. For instance, in an interview with the World Religions teacher, he voiced his concern with students' mixing of languages outside of the classroom:

> I think the person is not fluent in either language, because they are passing from one to the other and that, well, I don't think should be done, in order to maintain the integrity of that language.
>
> *(Interview Translation, February 2016)*

The quote above demonstrates purist ideologies of keeping languages separate and the traditionalist perspective that mixing languages is indicative of an underlying language problem. His beliefs are in accordance with his role as a language model. His attitudes are also demonstrative of an underlying fear of endangerment of local culture and Spanish by encouraging a bilingual agenda.

The role of popular culture

Youth speech in the private school tended toward Puerto Rican Spanish conversational turns, or an underlying Spanish-dominant structure. In initial classification stages, it was found that conversational styles were complemented by frequent translanguaging activities, drawing on non-local repertoire features at both lexical and phrasal levels. Take, for instance, some of the examples in Table 10.1 from members across different communities of practices incorporating

TABLE 10.1 The role of popular culture and target language investments, Pt. 1

Disney enthusiasts		
1	Tatiana	Yo veo a lot of TV series, como
		*(I watch **a lot of TV series**, like)*
2		que, o Británico tambié:n (.) o
		(or British as well (.) or)
3		American polque yo lo veo todo
		*(**American** because I watch everything)*
4		pol Netflix, so, no sé loh canaleⱺ.
		*(through **Netflix,** so, I don't know the channels)*
5		Lah series que yo veo: (.) mucho
		*(The series **that I watch (.) a lot**)*
6		eh Once Upon a Ti:me, veo:,
		*(are **Once Upon a Time, I watch**)*
7		ehte the Walking Dead, veo:...
		*(umm **the Walking Dead**, I watch...)*

Note: Regular font = PR Spanish; Bold = Standard-like English.

TABLE 10.2 The role of popular culture and target language investments, Pt. 2

Choir girls		
1	Fiorela	**Umm, okay, Reign,**
2		**let's see—Pretty Little Liars, Reign**
3		**American Horror Story, umm (.)**
4		**oh my God, there's so much.**
5		Cuando so:n: episodio nuevo,
		(When they are new episodes)
6		loh veo pol Intelnet,
		(I watch them through the Internet)
7		porque I don't have cable
		*(because **I don't have cable**).*
8		**But I still use my**
9		**ex-boyfriend's Netflix.**

Note: Regular font = Spanish; **Bold** = Standard-like English.

Englishes in their discussions of television shows. Under a traditional classification of code-mixing, this phenomenon could be considered an insertion of a 'foreign' item (see Muysken, 2000).

The interaction in Table 10.2 further indicates that presuming a separate two-system practice would gloss over underlying sociolinguistic issues at play. For instance, the fact that the theme of television generates translingual styles is perhaps to be expected in a community like PR. That is, it is indicative of the soft power—or economic and cultural power—mainland US industries exercise over the island, such that there are few competing local PR Spanish shows and movies and an overwhelming presence and representation of mainland culture through different media including global influences, such as subscription-based Netflix cited above. As Joan Fayer and others (1998) noted 'there is a wide availability of cable TV either through a cable television company or a satellite dish' (p. 39). Arlene Clachar (1997) further corroborates this sentiment by citing the fact that US companies and investors that 'own and control a disproportionate share of the manufacturing economy in a predominantly Spanish-mother-tongue labor force have conferred prestige and status on the English language in the eyes of Puerto Ricans' (pp. 462–463).

It is hardly exceptional to find acts of translingualism in the discussion of popular media; there are a number of radio stations that cater to a bilingual public. Through different technological platforms—televisions, computers, online streaming services—the island youth become exposed to particular language practices that may then form part of their daily repertoires. The same can be said about the language of food and restaurants, as a large number of entities have taken over the island by storm and food Englishes have been documented as part of PR Spanish (see Cortés et al., 2005). The presence of English use in these domains is the inevitable outcome of mainland cultural imperialism exercised over local culture, and the colonial socioeconomic relationship between the United States and PR. The overwhelming environmental presence of English ultimately contributes to indexical notions of English as unique, desirable, and prestigious, as opposed to ordinary and limiting Puerto Rican Spanish. It is perhaps more the case that within contexts of food and popular culture translingual practices are *ordinary*, rather than *extraordinary*. Furthermore, it is also possible that within elite settings the island youth feel encouraged to draw on non-local youth subculture and entertainment trends, following the ideological status quo of immersion-style English as desirable.

The role of ethnic identities

Within elite settings, the dominance of English transcended topics of popular culture over to negotiations of ethnic identity. This particular deployment of English could be considered extraordinary outside Spanish-dominant contexts, which typically shun the use of English in the construction of a collective Puerto Rican identity. In Table 10.3, for instance, a private school student discusses her sense of national pride and ethnic identity by adopting translingual styles. She makes use of binary collocates 'nice' and 'evil' to define the culture of friendliness on the island, and the welcoming demeanor of most islanders toward strangers and tourists (Line 2). At the same time, she draws on translanguaging practices to express her sentiments toward the interview question—describing

TABLE 10.3 Tatiana's acts of ethnic identity

1	Tatiana	Well, damn. Bueno, no sé,
		(Well, damn. Well, I don't know,)
2		maybe (le) ehplicaría máh o menoØ
		(maybe I would explain more or less)
3		como somoØ nosotro: Ø y que: (.)
		(how we are and how (.))
4		**we are nice, we're not**
5		that evil, y que: no ehtamoØ
		(that evil, and well we are not)
6		como loh indígenaØ que pueh…
		(like the indigenous that well…)
7		que tenemoØ technology: y
		*(we have **technology** and)*
8		que: they should visit us.
		*(that **they should visit us.**)*

Note: Regular font = Spanish; Bold = Standard-like English.

TABLE 10.4 Tatiana's acts of ethnic identity, Pt. 2

1	Tatiana	I feel proud, en velda∅. Aunque sea,
		(I feel proud, truly. Even though,)
2		como que, casi nadie sepa de nosotro∅
		(like, almost nobody knows of us)
3		e∅ mejol polque así tu pone∅ el
		(it's better because that way you put our)
4		nombre en alto. Anyway, hay
		(name up high. **Anyway,** there's)
5		mucha gente que ha puehto
6		nuehtro nombre en alto, like J. Lo y
		(our name up high, **like** J.Lo and)
7		Bruno Mars.

Note: Regular font = Spanish; Bold = Standard-like English.

Puerto Rican culture to the outsider—through use of expletive 'Well, damn' (Line 1) followed by a Spanish-dominant utterance peppered with occasional English words and phrases 'no sé, *maybe* (le) ehplicaría…' (Lines 1–4). In addition to using translanguaging styles to describe her evaluation of island culture, it is also possible to interpret this speech sample as a simultaneous accommodation to outsiders in English, the indexical outsider code; this is certainly suggested in '*they should visit us*' (Line 4), as well as in the sociocultural reference to the misconception of a Puerto Rican uncivilized and 'indigenous' culture. She assures the outsider in Line 4 through translanguaging that PR has 'technology' and is, therefore, just as developed and competent as other cultures, constructing PR's identity in relation to mainland cultural expectations.

In the second part of her response, in Table 10.4, Tatiana talks about her Puerto Rican pride once again in translanguaging styles. At this stage, it becomes clear that English, just as Spanish, is an integral part of her self-conception and ethnic identity. She draws on cultural figures that personify the union of two ideologically separated cultures—the Anglo and the Hispanic—*J. Lo* and *Bruno Mars* (Line 3). Once again, Tatiana tests the ideological boundaries of ethnic we/they descriptions that suggest Spanish as the 'we' insider code, and 'they' as the US outsider code, by constructing a fluid and mixed vision of the island. In this way, this example fits García and Li Wei's (2014) understanding of translanguaging as an integrated system of ways of speaking with a simultaneous multiplicity of social meaning, such that there is no one-to-one relationship between displaying Puerto Rican identity and language, as suggested by traditional notions of bilingualism.

At the same time, while adolescents used Englishes toward their definitions of Puerto Rican culture, there were still some who believed in a limit of Englishes or translingual activities. For example, Dave from the Gamer CofP believed that

TABLE 10.5 Ideological limit for translanguaging in private school

Dave, Gamer CofP		
1	Dave	'There are people that that
2		**they get cocky**—Tiffany! Tiffany!
3		Well, and **they** get cocky and they believe they
4		are gringo every now and then and they
5		speak English all of the time.
6		(Interview Translation, October 2015).

Note: Regular font = Spanish; Bold = Standard-like English.

there was a fine line between incorporating certain English styles and acting like a *gringo* and thus *snobby* as demonstrated in his depiction of a mutual friend in Table 10.5.

Dave's response to English-only speech reminds us of certain indexical ties of English on the island as something foreign or belonging to *the gringos*, therefore, not owned by Puerto Ricans and not authentically Puerto Rican. At the same time, his assessment also draws on other local island discourses that paint the English-dominant speaker as a member of an 'elite' community, flaunting a non-local language and their unique understanding of it, consequently, a 'snobby' act of identity or superiority. It is also particularly noteworthy that, despite elite contexts which encourage bilingual practices, Dave condemns practices that exercise sociolinguistic dominance over the island vernacular.

Defining social identity through translanguaging

In private school settings, Englishes are used in negotiations of social identities. Because of the presence of English in students' academic formation, it is not particularly extraordinary to encounter bilingual practices in this sense. What is noteworthy, however, is the *multivalent* nature of such bilingual practices, as well as how bilingualism is not exhibited in a uniform way across subjects, rather, subjects move beyond traditionally established domains of bilingualism (e.g. popular culture, food, etc.) and take up locally specific roles, such as the construction of self and others. In the example below, adolescents from the Gamers community strategically draw on Netspeak repertoire features in the construction of their own social positionalities.

The exchange in Table 10.6 demonstrates the different translanguaging styles that are found in the negotiations of social identities in a group of boys. The *semiotic assemblages* (Pennycook, 2017) or stylizations may not be reduced to simple explanations of Spanishes or Englishes in interaction but rather warrant an in-depth look at what it means to use specific language or labeling strategies in interaction. At the beginning of the question, Dave resorts to PR

TABLE 10.6 'Hashtag Kawaii' and other acts of social identity

Gamers		
1	Dave	SON LOH NENEØ MÁH *(THEY ARE THE BOYS)*
2		<[*KʰUL*]> DE LA EHCUELA. *(COOLEST IN THE SCHOOL.)*
3	Miguel	{**Ou, n*****z, n*****z, I'm**
4		**fucking with these bitches and you**
5		**know it**} *((under breath))*.
6	Dave	**Hashtag KAWAII, hashtag EMO,**
7		**hashtag hot-topic-best-store-**
8		**ever, hashtag Pacsun, hashtag**
9		**coo:l kids.**
10	Daniel	**Emo.** Igual a él *((points to Dave))*. **(*Emo.** Same as him.)*
11	Dave	**Hashtag rebels.**
12	Roberto	PueØ, hay algunoØ que son *(Well, there are some that are)*
13		medio χaro, ehte= *(sort of weird, umm=)*
14	Dave	I am. Hay unos sport connoisseurs = **(*I am.** There are some **sport connoisseurs=**)*
15	Roberto	Ehtan tuh "average joe:s" *(There are your "**average joes**")*
16		ehta Miguel que eh u::n= *(there is Miguel who is a=)*
17	Daniel	Un cripple jujitsu master
18		*((referring to Miguel's crutches))*. *(A **cripple jujitsu master**)*
19	Miguel	No soy un master= I am not a **master=**
20	Dave	**Ninety nine red balloons…**

Note: Regular font = PR Spanish; Bold = Standard-like English.

Spanish labeling to talk about his group of friends in an exaggerated manner, that is, the *coolest* boys in school (Line 3); note that 'cool' in this case represents an Anglicism incorporated into PR Spanish phonology, thus reflective of a fluid translingual history. His friend Miguel notably draws on his own styles as a transnational returnee migrant, and uses expletive and ethnic slur 'n*****z' (Line 6) and other expletives such as 'fucking' and 'bitches' in playful banter to indicate friendly solidarity and comfort among friends, suggesting his friends are 'his bitches' and his 'n*****z', a style of speech tied to mainland

African American communities in their displays of minority solidarity and pride (Rahman, 2012).

Dave speaks over Miguel's suggestion and resorts to more *global* youth practices by drawing on trends prevalent in Netspeak, such as 'hashtag' (Lines 8–9, Line 12). Alongside the iconic 'hashtag', showcasing his Netizenship (Crystal, 2011) as youth engaged in online technological practices, he uses this item as a *contextualization cue* (Gumperz, 1982), or discourse strategy, to communicate to his audience defining qualities of his community of practice, in this case, visual elements of the alternative rock subculture: 'emo', 'hot-topic-best-store-ever', and 'Pacsun'. The latter two are clothing stores at the nearby mall that adolescents from a particular demographic or community of interest invest in, particularly those that follow surfing, alternative rock, or gaming trends. Other less obvious qualities of these shops are that they can be seen as *class* barometers within the local landscape, as their prices are mid-end or high-end, considerably more expensive than neighboring alternatives. Off-beat labels such as 'emo' (Lines 6, 8) and 'rebels' (Line 9) are used alongside PR Spanish discourse. Other labels are offered to suggest an element of distinction in their group: 'sport connoisseurs' (Line 11) and 'average joes' (Line 12). Dave dazes off in song by citing the lyrics of '99 Red Balloons', a lesser known English translation of the 1983 song '99 Luftballons' by the German band Nena, further cementing the importance of international music in his construction of an alternative persona by resorting to non-local intertextual citations. Thus, by drawing on different semiotic resources at their disposal, the gamers construct their uniqueness and social identity in relation to others.

Translingual practices in a public school

The public school on the island follows Spanish-only education for all subjects with the exception of English class. It was one of the two main public educational institutions within the region and the largest one. It counted on a population of over 858 students, of which 53% fell under 'the poverty line' according to the Department of Education PR statistics (ELADEPR, 2015). Few, if any, translingual practices occurred on the instructional level, and the core textbooks in *Spanish* were supplied by the Department of Education to students, rather than privately purchased.

The majority of signages and brochures distributed in public school settings were in PR Spanish, in accordance to a largely Spanish-speaking population. However, when it came to bulletin board signs and banners, few were in English, such as those that advertised days of the month or holidays (e.g. Valentine's Day). Vocational programs such as those affiliated to DECA, or *Distributive Education Clubs of America*, used decorative banners, posters, and flyers in English (Figure 10.1). Thus, within Spanish-dominant linguistic landscapes of the public school, English still played a role behind the scenes as the language of scholastic organizations and programs.

FIGURE 10.1 'Be epic' banners outside of DECA classroom celebrating marketing month.

The role of circumstance

In contrast to private school findings, there was a significant language gap in the practices of public school students, where a majority produced PR Spanishes and few times resorted to translingual styles.

In an interaction with a student that I call Penelope, a female 12th grader from a lower working-class family, she expresses her frustrations at the lack of continuity and development in public school English language education. Penelope was enrolled in the Intermediate English alternative offered in the public school, which regularly assigned short readings and vocabulary lists to be studied and completed in class. She often required additional help in completing her work, and at times was unable to complete her assignments. Penelope claimed that her difficulties were not adequately addressed by her English teacher, who assumed competence in English literacy when assigning material (Interview, March 2016). Her translingual practices were kept at minimum, with a few lexical items, such as discourse markers like *so*, as storytelling techniques. This particular item may 'signal relationship across utterances' (Flores-Ferrán, 2014, p. 57). Lipski (2005) notes that the insertion of *so* into Spanish-dominant discourse is not noteworthy, rather, visible across subjects of different bilingual competences, and, so, perhaps linguistically *ordinary*, and the outcome of similar grammatical structures.

The role of identities

In an informal interaction with the school principal, she suggested that I observe the Advanced English classroom, of which only 30 out of 291 students of the 12th grade were enrolled. Upon speaking to an English teacher in the school whom I call Ms. Cruz, she further directed me to students who self-identified as 'Rockers', who hung out outside of a school candy shop and often dressed in black (fieldnotes, October 2015). Out of the 30 participants of the 12th grade I interviewed, 8 of were self-identified 'Rockers', and coincidentally some of the most salient bilingual speakers in my data.

Table 10.7 below demonstrates an exchange between students when discussing their positive evaluations of fellow peer, Federico, and his outward demeanor as 'socially awkward' and shameless. Students turn to Englishes to discuss their evaluation and consequent approval of deviating practices.

Both Luis and Angélica celebrate their friend's socially awkward and deviating demeanor by engaging in translingual practices of admiration. In Line 4, Angélica introduces the label 'bae' when admitting to her admiration of him. And, in Lines 7–8, when asked to clarify what she meant through this unusual language use, Angélica demonstrates her knowledge of appropriacy and social meaning of innovative labels that have come into use through social media practices, also cementing her status as an adolescent in the 21st century and *leader of language change* (see Eckert, 2000). Luis adopts the role of the language analyst and offers an explanation about the way words come to acquire meaning, suggesting an abstract nature of language and sound in 'when things begin, they

TABLE 10.7 'El es bae': Translanguaging in the public school

Rockers		
1	Federico	Yo no tengo velguenza. *(I do not have any shame.)*
2 3	Luis	**You can do whatever you want. I admire you** ((*to Federico*)).
4	Angélica	El e' bae. *(He is **bae**.)*
5	Katherine	¿Cómo que bae? *(What do you mean **bae**?)*
6	Angélica	**Before anyone else.**
7	Katherine	¿En serio? *(Seriously?)*
8	Angélica	Cuando yo digo bae no e' <u>como que</u> *(When I say **bae** it is not like)*
9		they're babe', no, e que they're ***(they're babe**, no, it's that **they're**)*
10		**before anyone else.**
11 12 13	Luis	**The thing is when things begin they just are, and then someone gives it a meaning.**

Note: Regular font = PR Spanish; Bold = Standard-like English; Underline = Discourse marker.

TABLE 10.8 Urban solidarity through translanguaging

Rockers		
1	Federico	Sí, lah de pública son máh outgoing.
		*(Yes, in the public schools they are more **outgoing**.)*
2	Angélica	You're all my bitches.
		(You're all my bitches.)
3	Loli	Acho no, yo ehtuve en una privada hahta
		(Man no, I was in a private (school) until)
4		noveno y cuando me movieron yo
		(ninth (grade) and when I moved I)
5		ehtuve, como que, "let it go:, let it go:"
		*(was like **"let it go, let it go"**.)*

Note: Regular font = PR Spanish; Bold = Standard-like English.

just are', and then the role of human beings to attaching meaning to already existing items 'then someone gives it meaning' (Lines 9–10). This latter comment showcases Luis' metalinguistic awareness of the fast-pace rate at which languages change over time and may acquire additional interpretations; it also places him in a position of expert of innovative language and insider to English teen talk. Cognitively, it also showcases his ability to rationalize on the instability of language in a second language, something that would not be accounted for in a traditional approach to bilingualism.

In Table 10.8, members of the Advanced English group engage in acts of solidarity by 'ganging up' on or 'Othering' those from prestigious elite schools on the island, who they perceive as a threat to their own identity. They boastfully uptake public school membership in translingual speech: by using adjectives such as 'outgoing' (Line 1), and explicit declaration of solidarity 'you're all my bitches' (Line 2). In this sense, we see Englishes being deployed by public school students in the construction of social identities and definition of 'in group' urban status. Therefore, problematizing the notion of English belonging solely to the island elite, while simultaneously showcasing their ability to engage in expressive explicit language in an ideologically conceived 'foreign language'. In Line 3, we notice Loli playfully drawing on popular culture, or intertextual references of Disney's (2013) *Frozen*, to describe the moment in her life in which she switched from private to public school and the sense of relief it brought her in performance of the iconic song 'let it go, let it go' (Line 4). Further embracing her status as an urban Spanish-speaking student and challenging the idea that private schooling—emblematic of the US education system—is desirable and somehow 'superior' to the local Spanish-dominant education.

Discussion: translanguaging in Puerto Rico

In Li Wei's (2017) latest case for translanguaging, he describes it as a 'space where… (people) can go between and beyond socially construct language and educational systems, structures and practices, to engage diverse multiple meaning-making systems and subjectivities' (p. 24). As I have shown in this chapter, translanguaging on the island inhabits 'multiple meaning-making systems' in that it is not merely the outcome of a linear relationship between language and (ethnic or national) identity (Tables 10.3 and 10.4), neither is it the ability to communicate in two languages separately; rather, individuals have variable *access* to semiotic systems, which is both the outcome of agentive factors (identities, ideologies) and inherited societal circumstances (English language education, in this chapter). In reimagining bilingualism as a less binary construct and toward a more fluid constellation of signs, we are able to detect differences in the way signs are deployed. In the first example, English is used to discuss popular culture in elite settings at times through Spanish-dominant structures and smaller English units, and others through English-dominant structures. We see differences in ideologies of language and culture (Tatiana in Tables 10.3 and 10.4), in elite settings islanders defend English social uses as legitimate parts of ethnic identity, while others reject it (Dave in Table 10.5). In Tables 10.6 (elite) and 10.8 (non-elite) we see a joint ability of being able to make use of repertoire features and symbols toward the construction of solidarity and in-group social identities, regardless of inherited circumstances.

The presence of translanguaging in elite settings is not surprising but ordinary, yet this ability to move beyond sociocultural-established domains of English—popular culture and education and toward the construction of social identity—is particularly extraordinary and not in accordance with previous literature which conceives of PR as a 'two-speech' community determined by class (see Hermina, 2014). Thus, while we see that for some cases personal educational and social circumstances play a role in determining the extent to which a person engages in translanguaging, ultimately, all students engage in translanguaging as Spanish-speaking US citizens and youths of late modernity. *Ordinariness* is also dependent on access: while translanguaging is the norm in elite settings, the same cannot be said for non-elite general settings. In non-elite contexts, adopting a communities of practice approach enables the detection of language practices that are not made available to everyone. We see evidence of 'rocker' youth going 'beyond' socially constructed language and educational systems in the construction of their identities; thus, in the case of colonial settings such as PR, we must remember to put context and identities at center stage and privilege the local over universal theories of hybridity or static depictions of languages.

References

Blommaert, J. (2010). *The sociolinguistics of globalization.* Cambridge, UK: Cambridge University Press.

Bourdieu, P. (1994). Structures, habitus, power: Basis for a theory for symbolic power. In N. B. Dirks, G. Eley, & S. B. Ortner (Eds.), *Culture/power/history: A reader in contemporary social theory* (pp. 155–199). Princeton, NJ: Princeton University Press.

Clachar, A. (1997). Resistance to the English language in Puerto Rico: Toward a theory of language and intergroup distinctiveness. *Linguistics and Education, 9,* 69–98.

Cortés, I., Ramírez, J., Rivera, M., & Viada, M. (2005). Dame un hamburger plain con ketchup y papitas. *English Today, 21*(2), 35–42.

Crystal, D. (2011). *Internet linguistics: A student guide.* London, UK: Routledge.

Eckert, P. (2000). *Language variation as social practice: The linguistic construction of identity in Belten high.* Oxford, UK: Wiley-Blackwell.

Estado Libre Asociado de Departmento de Educación de Puerto Rico. (2015). *Estudio Socioeconómico 2015–2016.* Mayagüez, Puerto Rico: Departmento de Educación de Puerto Rico.

Fayer, J. M., Castro, J., Díaz, M., & Plata, M. (1998). English in Puerto Rico. *English Today, 14n*(1), 39–44.

Flores, N., & Lewis, M. (2016). From truncated to sociopolitical emergence: A critique of super-diversity in sociolinguistics. *International Journal of Sociology of Language, 241,* 97–124.

Flores, N., & García, O. (2013). Linguistic third spaces in education: Teachers' translanguaging across the bilingual continuum. In D. Little, C. Leung, & P. Van Avermaet (Eds.), *Managing diversity in education: Languages, policies, pedagogies* (pp. 243–256). Bristol, UK: Multilingual Matters.

Flores-Ferrán, N. (2014). So pues entonces: An examination of bilingual discourse markers in Spanish oral narratives of personal experience of New York City-born Puerto Ricans. *Sociolinguistic Studies, 8*(1), 57–83.

García, O., & Li Wei (2014). *Translanguaging: Language, bilingualism, and education.* London, UK: Palgrave Macmillan.

Gumperz, J. J. (11982). *Discourse strategies* (Vol. 1). Cambridge, UK: Cambridge University Press.

Hermina, J. (2014). Two different speech communities in Puerto Rico (Doctoral dissertation). The University of New Mexico, New Mexico.

Li Wei. (2017). Translanguaging as a practical theory of language. *Applied Linguistics, 39*(1), 9–30.

Lipski, J. M. (2005). Code-switching or borrowing? No sé so no puedo decir, you know. *Proceedings of the Second Workshop on Spanish Sociolinguistics,* 1–15. Somerville, MA: Cascadilla Proceedings Project.

Lipski, J. M. (2008). "Puerto Rican Spanish in the United States". In *Varieties of Spanish in the United States.* Washington, DC: Georgetown University Press.

Mazak, C., & Carroll, K. (2017). Language policy in Puerto Rico's higher education: Opening the door for translanguaging practices. *Anthropology & Education Quarterly, 48*(1), 4–22.

Muysken, P. (2000). *Bilingual speech: A typology of code-mixing.* Cambridge, UK: Cambridge University Press.

Pennycook, A. (2017). Translanguaging and semiotic assemblages. *International Journal of Multilingualism, 14*(3), 269–282.

Pousada, A. (2000). The competent bilingual in Puerto Rico. *International Journal of Sociology of Language, 142*(1), 103–118.

Rahman, J. (2012). The N word: Its history and use in the African American community. *Journal of English Linguistics, 40*(2), 137–171.

Rosa, J. (2016). Standardization, racialization, languagelessness: Raciolinguistic ideologies across communicative contexts. *Journal of Linguistic Anthropology, 26*(2), 162–183.

Soja, E. (1996). *Thirdspace: Journeys to Los Angeles and other real-and-imagined places.* Oxford, UK: Blackwell.

11

THE ORDINARINESS OF DIALECT TRANSLINGUISTICS IN AN INTERNALLY DIVERSE GLOBAL-CITY DIASPORIC COMMUNITY

Amelia Tseng

Introduction

This chapter offers insights into the ordinariness of difference via sociolinguistic and ethnographic investigation of dialect contact and translinguistics in the Latino community of Washington, DC, a population characterized by internal diversity and a unique Salvadoran/Central American majority. It describes Spanish dialect diversity in DC and identifies participant attitudes toward dialect diversity and transdialecting. Findings demonstrate that normalization of transdialecting and dialect diversity coexists with ideologies of identity difference within the pan-ethnocultural identity 'Latino', in which dialect variation is a salient marker of subgroup identities. This ordinariness of linguistic diversity and translanguaging behavior relates directly to the local DC social context, where Spanish encompasses many varieties and national origins and diversity is normalized and celebrated. This study contributes to the re-theorization of the notion of ordinariness within diversity and its implications for sociolinguistic inquiry. The chapter begins with a brief review of key background information, followed by presentation and discussion of findings, and concludes with implications for future research directions.

Background

Translanguaging refers to bilinguals' 'accessing different linguistic features or various modes of what are described as autonomous languages, in order to maximize communicative potential' (García, 2009, p. 140), or 'the deployment of a speaker's full linguistic repertoire without regard for watchful adherence to the socially and politically defined boundaries of named (and usually national and state) languages' (Otheguy, García, & Reid, 2015, p. 218). Translingualism, thus, not only respects diversity but takes plurality and fluidity as the norm (Lee, 2017). Much research addresses the role of translanguaging in social identity: different languages can index ethnocultural membership or enact interactional roles (Auer, 2005, 2013; Myers-Scotton, 1995), and code-mixing itself can be stigmatized and/or an identity marker (Auer, 2005; Zentella, 1997). In this, ideology is a key analytic dimension that reveals social beliefs about languages and linguistic behavior. However, normalization of translanguaging is less well understood.[1] Further, dialects are relatively understudied within the current translanguaging paradigm[2] despite the potential for comparison with previous code-switching and dialect- and style-shifting research (Bell, 1984; Coupland, 2000; Labov, 1963; Schilling, 2004).

The highly diverse DC metropolitan area, where Latinos make up the third-largest racial/ethnic group, is home to the twelfth-largest US Latino population (Pew Research Center, 2016).[3] The DC Latino community largely grew post World War II; community identity[4] solidified in the 1960s and 1970s via activism and institutions such as the Latino Festival and Office of Latino Affairs (Cadaval, 1998; Sprehn-Malagón, Hernández-Fujigaki, & Robinson, 2014), and the population increased exponentially with large-scale Central American migration in the 1980s, establishing Salvadorans as the largest regional group (Singer, 2007). As of 2013, 32% of Latinos were of Salvadoran origin; the next largest group is of Mexican origin (16%), and the majority of respondents (52%) report 'other' Latino origins (Brown & López, 2013), including all Latin American countries and Spain (Pessar, 1995). Roughly 30% of the foreign-born population in DC and the metropolitan area are Latino, though percentages vary by county (US Census, 2015).

Data and methodology

Data are a subset of questions from sociolinguistic surveys/interviews with 63 first- and second-generation adult immigrants collected by the researcher and team[5] over a one-year period. Surveys were conducted in conversational settings via community-based organizations. Participant responses were grounded in the local social context using large-scale demographic information, additional data collected by Cadaval (1998),[6] existing literature, and ethnographic observation.

Participants were asked whether they preferred to conduct the interviews in English or Spanish; most chose Spanish. Fifty-three (84%) of interviewees were first-generation; 10 (15%) were second-generation. Participants were from 10 countries; the largest number was from Central America (El Salvador). All second-generation participants were born in the metropolitan area (Table 11.1). All participants spoke Spanish; 77% reported feeling more comfortable speaking Spanish

TABLE 11.1 National origins

Country/region	N	%
Central America	39	61.9
El Salvador	33	52.38
Guatemala	2	3.17
Honduras	6	9.52
United States	10	15.87
DC metro	10	15.87
Mexico	5	7.93
South America	5	7.93
Argentina	1	1.58
Colombia	1	1.58
Peru	3	4.76
Caribbean	2	3.17
Puerto Rico	1	1.58
Dominican Republic	1	1.58
Total	63	100

than English, and 10% reported speaking only Spanish. The majority reported employment in industries such as the service sector.

This study examined the normalization of dialect diversity and transdialecting via metalinguistic commentary and self-reported language behavior. I focus on a subset of survey questions that elicited accent-related responses. Participants were asked questions such as:

¿Cómo describiría su acento en español? ¿Habla usted algún dialecto del español? ¿Es su español igual o diferente al de otras personas que conoce? ¿Cómo describiría el español que se habla en esta zona?

(How would you describe your accent in Spanish?[7] Do you speak a particular dialect of Spanish? Is your Spanish the same or different from other people that you know? How would you describe the Spanish spoken in this area?)

To specifically address dialect shifting, participants were asked:

A veces la gente usa diferentes tipos de español dependiendo de con quién o dónde están hablando. ¿Me puede decir si usted usa diferentes tipos español y darme un ejemplo?

(Sometimes people use different types of Spanish according to whom or where they are speaking. Can you tell me if you use different kinds of Spanish and give me an example?)

This question was asked, for example, as a means of clarifying participant responses and to potentially elicit performativity, which provides insight into language beliefs and stereotypes.

Analysis and discussion

Spanish dialects

Spanish has long been a unifying factor and a marker of group identity and solidarity for the DC Latino community, providing a common language of communication and an important means of creating community (Cadaval, 1998). Both dialect diversity and a strong Central American presence were represented in survey results. Forty-eight percent of study participants reported that DC Spanish is Salvadoran or Central American. Of these, 39 (62%) respondents were Salvadoran and 24 (38%) non-Salvadoran. Thirty-one percent reported DC Spanish was varied, and 22% gave responses that did not fit either category (i.e. 'bien') (Table 11.2). Sample responses were: '[Es centroamericano] como lo mayoría somos de Centroamérica. Salvadoreño creo que mucho mas'. ('[It's Central American] as the majority we are from Central America. Salvadoran I think much more') and 'Acá diferentes paises tienen diferentes españoles' ('Here different countries have different Spanishes').

Dialects were associated with national identity. A representative comment is:

> Cada país tiene su modo de hablar. Honduras, Nicaragua, El Salvador hablan casi igual. Los de Argentina y España hablan diferente. Los de Centroamérica hablan casi igual.
>
> (Every country has its way of speaking. Honduras, Nicaragua, El Salvador speak almost the same. Those from Argentina and Spain speak differently. Those from Central America speak almost the same.)

This quote not only demonstrates the salience of national boundaries in dialect differentiation but also a perception of certain pan-regional (Central American) similarities. When asked to describe their own Spanish, participants specified countries ('el acento salvadoreño') or simply responded, 'de mi país' ('of my country').

TABLE 11.2 DC Spanish

Salvadoran/Central American	Varied	Other response	Total
48% (*n* = 30)	31% (*n* = 19)	22% (*n* = 14)	100% (*n* = 63)

Participants gave examples of lexical, phonetic, and morphosyntactic variation. For example, a Salvadoran participant commented:

> Los salvadoreños se conocen por el acento de hablar, como 'ey vos, e vos', o la forma de llamar a un niño, 'cipote', sí, en México es 'chamaco', nosotros le decimos 'cipote', y en Honduras les dicen 'guiros'.
>
> (Salvadorans know each other by their accent in speaking, like 'hey you, hey you', or the form of calling a child, 'cipote', yes, in Mexico it is 'chamaco', we call them 'cipote' and in Honduras they call them 'guiros'.)

This quote uses the example of non-standard, second-personal, singular pronoun use ('vos') in typical Salvadoran usage (Lipski, 2008) and contrasts Salvadoran vocabulary with that of other countries. Another Salvadoran referred to dialectal pronunciation: 'Por ejemplo, en México chocan con la zeta, pero nosotros no' ('For example, in Mexico, they emphasize the "z", but we don't'). This quote refers to Salvadoran sibilant weakening when comparing Mexican and Salvadoran Spanish. Participants of different backgrounds also gave examples of regional vocabulary and referred to 'accent', 'sound', and speech rate (e.g. commenting that Dominicans talk fast).

Dialects were associated not only with national origin but with local communities and social networks. One participant drew attention to family networks, commenting, '[La gente habla con] el acento de su mamá' ('[People speak with] their mother's accent'). Another participant, a second-generation immigrant of South American origin, commented, 'Well from the people I hear at my church, I go to Spanish Mass, they all talk in their own ways I guess their own slang, people will get into a group, from what I see, their own country and they make their own group and they talk, they all speak in their own slangs, from where you're coming from, where your roots are'. While dialects had strong national-identity associations, these social meanings also related to particularities in the local social environment.

Dialect contact

The majority of participants reported dialect shifting. Of 49 responses to the question, 55% ($N = 27$)[8] of participants reported 'using different kinds of Spanish depending on who or where they are speaking'. Lack of evaluative comments indicated a normalization of this dialect translanguaging.

Participants reported dialect shifting when speaking with non-conationals and the use of more 'general' Spanish to facilitate communication. To give two representative examples, one participant commented:

> Hay de todo un poco … Depende también con quién uno esté platicando porque a veces hay cosas que uno las conoce por un nombre verdad y hay persona las conoce por otro pero refiriendo a lo mismo.

(There is a little of everything … It also depends on whom you are talking to because sometimes there are things which one knows by one name right and there is a person who knows them by another [name] but referring to the same [thing].)

Another gave an extended example of mutual accommodation to reduce dialectal differences that impede communication with friends:

Tenemos unos amigos que son de la República Dominicana. Ellos hablan español pero totalmente diferente al de nosotros … El mismo español si estamos hablando del español. Pero no entendí nada. Tiene que cambiar un poquito porque ellos hablan como diferente, el o sea el acento de ellos diferente de nosotros. … Y a veces me dejan a mí. … Entonces ahora cuando tratan de hablar conmigo tratan de hacerlo como hablamos nosotros [los hondureños] decimos. Y el mismo les pasa a ellos. '[Nombre], ¿qué tú dijiste?' 'Esto y esto', 'Ah ya, te lo agarré'.

(Yes, we have certain friends from the Dominican Republic. They speak Spanish but totally different from ours … The same Spanish if we are talking about Spanish. But I don't understand anything. [It] has to change a little because they speak differently, their accent [is] different from ours. … And sometimes they leave me behind [in the conversation]. … So now when they talk with me they try to do it the way we [Hondurans] do you could say. And the same thing happens to them. '[Name], what did you say?' 'This and this', 'Oh ok, I got it for you'.)

Participants also described shifting based on register, formality, and humor, where style and dialect perceptions overlapped in that regional usage was avoided in formal settings.

Some participants reported dialect acquisition, which they attributed to diverse Latino social networks: 'A veces cuando uno pasa más pegado con una persona, se le pega el acento. Quizás algunas palabras que uno mezcla del mexicano, o de Guatemala'. ('Sometimes when you are closer to a person their accent affects you. Maybe some words that you mix from the Mexican [Spanish], or from Guatemala'). For example, one participant mentioned that she has acquired a Guatemalan accent and can dialect-shift between this and Mexican Spanish:

Yo antes había trabajado con [gente] de Guatemala, entonces, yo creo que me ha pegado su acento. Porque yo sí vivía en Maryland casi por dos años. Cuando me regresé a DC, yo llegué aquí y alguien me preguntó o sea '¿De dónde eres'? 'De México'. 'No, tú hablas como chapina', me dijo, 'de Guatemala'. Entonces le dije tal vez porque estuve trabajando con guatemaltecas.

(I worked with [people] from Guatemala, so I think that I picked up their accent. Because I lived in Maryland for almost two years. When I returned to DC, I arrived here and someone asked me 'Where are you from'? 'From Mexico'. 'No, you talk like a chapina [Guatemalan]', s/he told me, 'from Guatemala'. So I told them maybe because I was working with Guatemalans.)

However, other participants (31%, $N = 15$) reported that their Spanish did not change depending on whom they were talking to. For example, a Salvadoran participant commented that she categorically uses Salvadoran Spanish. In another example, a South American participant commented that he does not shift due to perceptions of home-dialect formality/correctness, which he positively evaluates in comparison with Central American Spanish:

> Hablo el español que yo sé, no lo cambio, me gusta más mi español en comparación de los centroamericanos. Yo siento que mi español es más formal.

> (I speak the Spanish that I know, I don't change it, I like my Spanish more in comparison with that of Central Americans. I feel that my Spanish is more formal).

Normalization of transdialecting and diversity

Based on findings, the ordinariness of dialect translanguaging in the DC area relates to several factors: (1) mutual intelligibility and awareness of dialect diversity in the Spanish-speaking world; (2) ideologies of named languages as unified entities; and (3) the normalization and celebration of diversity in the local environment.

Mutual intelligibility between varieties of Spanish may reduce the noticeability of dialect shifting, as evinced by numerous comments to the effect of 'it's all Spanish, it's understandable':

> [El español aquí es] normal ... Todas las personas que hablan español, yo entiendo

> ([The Spanish here is] normal ... All the people that speak Spanish, I understand).

The belief in named languages as unified entities has a strong sociohistorical footprint, and Spanish is well-established as a marker of pan-Latino identity (Urciuoli, 2008; Zentella, 1997). Another participant commented, '[El español aquí es] él que habla nosotros los latinos'('[The Spanish here is] that which we Latinos speak'.) Perception of Spanish dialects as 'all part of the same language' may make their separation or accommodation less noticeable than that of named languages (see Trudgill, 1986).

The DC social context supports normalization of dialect diversity and the normalcy of dialect shifting. In the absence of an overwhelming dialect majority, assimilatory pressure to conform to a local 'norm' may be reduced, and the existence of local national communities with transnational ties to their countries of origin may support dialect maintenance. Further, diversity within the Latino community is normalized and celebrated. Discourses of diversity and tolerance have circulated in the Latino community since its inception (Cadaval, 1998). Foundational leader Carlos Rosario specifically celebrated inter-Latino socialization in a 1981 interview with Olivia Cadaval:

> Tenían que tener un sitio seguro aquí, yo les ayudaba y esto así fue como empezó a promulgarse la comunidad y de la noche a la mañana creció. La comunidad hispana que más pronto ha crecido, esta comunidad en Washington fue la base de la comunidad de Virginia y Maryland porque nosotros nos organizamos aquí y después … organizamos al comité de Virginia y después seguramente el comité de Maryland … Esa era era un proceso de entendimiento, de progreso, se conocía la gente. … Muy lindo se casaban, los ecuatorianos con los peruanos se casaban. Los salvadoreños con los hondureños son países que tú sabes no se hablan uno con los otros, colombianas con venezolanos. Los países se tiran entre ellos pero no, un colombiano, venezolano. Siempre buscaba esta clase de comunidad, entendimiento entre todos los grupos … yo buscaba merge.

> (But [Latinos] had to have a safe place here, I helped them and this was how the community began to promote itself and from night to day [it] grew. The Hispanic community that quickly grew, this community in DC was the base of the community in Virginia and Maryland because we organized ourselves here and after … we organized the Virginia committee and afterward surely the Maryland committee … This era was a process of understanding, of progress, people got to know each other. … Very beautifully they married each other, Ecuadorians with Peruvians married each other. Salvadorans with Hondurans are countries which you know don't speak to each other, Colombians with Venezuelans. The countries fight amongst themselves but no, a Colombian, Venezuelan. I always sought this kind of community, understanding between all the groups … I looked for merge.)

Beyond normalization, this local community discourse may contribute to the celebration of linguistic diversity as part of cultural diversity, as evinced by participant comments such as 'Pues bien, como los paises son diferentes nosotros tenemos nuestra cultura cada país tiene su cultura' ('It's good, as countries are different we have our culture each country has its culture'). Another participant commented favorably that 'uno aprende de otras culturas' ('You learn from other cultures') through speaking with Latinos of different backgrounds. The normalization of diversity in the Latino community is consistent with the normalization of multilingualism and multiculturalism in the metropolitan area more broadly. A recent large-scale study in the DC area demonstrated that exposure to diversity significantly increases its acceptance (Bader & Warkentien, 2016), and discourses of diversity and tolerance are salient parts of DC's identity as a place (Modan, 2008a, 2008b). The normalization and celebration of diversity and social mingling may render dialect translanguaging unremarkable even as dialects maintain their associations with different Latino subgroups.

Other language attitudes

Normalization of dialect diversity and shifting coexisted with national dialects as markers of identity and a sense of Salvadoran Spanish as the most prominent local variety. However, dialect attitudes that negatively evaluate Salvadoran Spanish were also present, expressed through comments such as, 'In Peru, we speak a more formal Spanish. My friends from Central America seem to speak a more informal Spanish'. Another commented that DC Spanish is 'muy vulgar'. These attitudes are consistent with previous research on Washington, DC, where, in keeping with US and Latin American dialect hierarchies (Lipski, 1985, 2008; Parodi, 2003), Salvadoran Spanish is seen as less correct than other varieties (Hart-Gonzalez, 1985), making it a site of identity tension and covert pride (Tseng, 2018).

Summary and implications

Normalization of dialect diversity and transdialecting are related to the particularities of the local environment such as exposure to and discourses of diversity. Mutual intelligibility and the unifying notion that 'it's all Spanish', related to a pan-Latino ethnocultural identity, also played a role. However, dialects retained their social meaning as an index of national identity and in relation to broader prescriptive ideologies.

The study demonstrates that normalization of diversity and diversity as a unifying aspect of identity ('sameness of difference' and 'ordinariness of diversity' (Pennycook, 2007, 2010)) can coexist with dialect variation as a salient marker of different group identities. Findings challenge assumptions that the differences encoded in language diversity are necessarily foregrounded in translinguistic behavior, demonstrating that, in highly diverse communities, speakers may perceive these encounters as unremarkable. This challenges the premise that, as markedness is predicated upon difference (Irvine, 2001; Labov, 1972), unnoticeability is predicated upon homogeneity: while dialect distinctions were perceived and socially salient, transdialecting went unremarked in the data. The finding underscores the importance of social context in linguistics and resonates with Milroy's (1982) observation that linguistic diversity can be normalized when small, dense, diverse speaker-groups coexist and multilingualism is valued.

The study opens directions for much future research on dialect within a translanguaging paradigm and in highly diverse contexts. Lack of an overwhelmingly dominant/majority DC Latino group may contribute to the ordinariness of transdialecting, supporting participants' framing of dialect shifting as a feature of communicative expedience rather than 'crossing' (Rampton, 1998). The lack of an overwhelming local Latino majority and locally dominant variety may also reduce accommodation pressure (as opposed to the typical case of Central American accommodation to Mexican Spanish in much of the United States (Lavadenz, 2005; Parodi, 2008; Raymond, 2012)) and contribute to the normalization of transdialecting. Milroy's (1982) observation that the lack of dominant/majority groups can reduce prestige, and stigma evaluations might be relevant to the coexistence of Spanish dialect normalization, pride, and stigma in the DC metropolitan area. Further, the transdialecting participants described did not always involve shifting between dialects but rather neutralizing marked features, or *dialect downgrading*. This difference may make shifting less socially salient, being seen as neutralizing features rather than taking on a different dialect and its identity associations or even be supported as a more neutral 'standard', which tends to be seen as more correct and prestigious (Milroy, 2001).

The question of varietal boundaries versus fluid notions of feature grading within linguistic repertoires is another area where dialects can contribute to the translanguaging conversation as it seeks to expand understandings of the boundedness and dynamism of language systems. Similarly, while excluded due to space constraints, it would be interesting to explore speaker perceptions of 'non-native' accents versus varietal features in linguistic repertoires that contain multiple languages and, potentially, contact-influenced varieties such as Latino English.

In this study, I used participants' self-reported data to examine their attitudes and ideologies about transdialecting. This approach revealed that transdialecting's normalization coexisted with subgroup identity associations. Future research could productively compare findings with naturalistic recordings, as data collected under different conditions might reveal different patterns and identity work. Self-reported data may over- or underreport transdialecting, where naturalistic data might reveal (mis)matches between expressed sociolinguistic beliefs and behavior. Further, different aspects of identity construction, pride, and contestation may be highlighted in other contexts, leading to dialect shifting being 'noticeable' for interactional goals (the importance of dialects in local identity negotiation in performative contexts can be seen in Salvadoran artist Quique Avilés's *Los Treinta* (2010), among other pieces).

Future research could productively address later generations' linguistic repertoires, attitudes, and translanguaging behavior to determine whether transdialecting itself is an aspect of DC Latino identity. As conversational accommodation is a dialect-mixing mechanism (Trudgill, 2008), future research could also investigate longitudinal mixing and potential varietal emergence, a theme which has been explored locally in terms of Latino English (Tseng, 2015). The consequences of dialect downgrading and mixing for the trajectory of local Spanish would offer new insight into the emergence of US Spanishes, which tend to reflect both locally dominant varieties and leveling and diffusion based on local social relations (Zentella, 1990), and contribute to the knowledge of varietal emergence more generally. Identity-wise, transdialecting may inspire stronger reactions if younger generations are losing 'their' dialect features or acquiring Salvadoran Spanish. It would also be interesting to explore dialect translanguaging in different social classes as the present study skews working-class due to recruitment through community-based organizations, despite the diversity of socioeconomic statuses in DC's global-city environment.

Conclusions

Spanish dialects retain their social salience as identity markers in the Washington, DC metropolitan area at the same time that dialect diversity and translanguaging are normalized. This challenges the assumptions that the differences encoded in language diversity are necessarily foregrounded in translinguistic behavior in quotidian interactions, demonstrating that, in highly diverse communities, speakers may perceive these encounters as unremarkable. The study contributes new insight into the ordinariness of translinguistics (Blommaert, 2013; Pennycook & Otsuji, 2015) as a product of sociolinguistic diversity, contact, and identity grounded in the local environment. By demonstrating that difference and sameness of difference can operate simultaneously at different scalar identity levels, it raises new directions for translanguaging research and for research in global cities and other contexts that unsettle traditional sociolinguistic paradigms and complicate the relationship between language and society.

Notes

1 Though see Dovchin (2017) on urban Mongolian youth normalization of translanguaging.
2 Despite significant work in education (Martínez, Hikida, & Durán 2014; Sotiroula, 2015), transnational/online literacy (Androutsopoulos & Jufferman, 2014; Schreiber, 2015), and certain languages, such as Chinese (Li Wei, 2010; Liang, 2015).
3 The largest groups in DC are African Americans (47%), Whites (36%), and Latinos (11%); according to the DMV, Whites (46%), African Americans (25%), and Latinos (15%).
4 I understand 'community' to mean groups of people with shared senses of identity, norms, and beliefs. In DC, a sense of shared Latino identity coexists with other Latino communities, as can be seen in Fiesta DC, a pan-Latino festival, and events celebrating different national groups.
5 Data were collected in collaboration with Noemí Enchautegui-de-Jesús and student research assistants on Bilingualism and Latin@s in DC 2015–2016 with support from the American University Metropolitan Policy Center and Center for Latin American and Latino Studies.
6 Olivia Cadaval generously shared her data with me for this chapter, which were additionally supported by the Smithsonian Center for Folklife and Cultural Heritage.
7 Some participants took 'accent' to mean English influence on their Spanish and vice versa. This is interesting in itself as it indicates an understanding of 'accent' as either varietal or non-native, despite emergent ethnolectal varieties such as Latino English (Fought, 2003; Tseng, 2015). As this discussion is beyond the scope of this chapter, these responses were excluded.
8 55% (N = 27) reported shifting, 31% (N = 15) reported not shifting, 14% (N = 7) responded with Spanish dialect comparisons rather than descriptions of their own language behavior.

References

Androutsopoulos, J., & Juffermans, K. (2014). Digital language practices in superdiversity: Introduction. *Discourse, Context & Media, 3*(4–5), 1–6.

Auer, P. ([1998] 2013). The 'why' and 'how' questions in the analysis of conversational code-switching. In P. Auer (Ed.), *Code-switching in conversation* (pp. 164–187). London, UK: Routledge.

Auer, P. (2005). A postscript: Code-switching and social identity. *Journal of Pragmatics, 37*(3), 403–410.

Avilés, E. (2010). *Los treinta*. Washington, DC: GALA Hispanic Theater.

Bader, M. D., & Warkentien, S. (2016). The fragmented evolution of racial integration since the civil rights movement. *Sociological Science, 3*, 135–166.

Bell, A. (1984). Language style as audience design. *Language in Society, 13*(2), 145–204.

Blommaert, J. (2013). *Ethnography, superdiversity and linguistic landscapes: Chronicles of complexity*. Bristol, UK: Multilingual Matters.

Brown, M. H., & López, A. (2013, August 29). Mapping the Latino population, by state, county and city. *Pew Research Center*. Retrieved December 24, 2018, from http://www.pewhispanic.org/2013/08/29/mapping-the-latino-population-by-state-county-and-city/

Cadaval, O. (1998). *Creating a Latino identity in the nation's capital: The Latino festival*. Abingdon, UK: Routledge.

Coupland, N. (2000). Language, situation and the relational self: Theorizing dialect-style in sociolinguistics. In P. Eckert & J. Rickford (Eds.), *Style and sociolinguistic variation* (pp. 185–210). Cambridge, UK: Cambridge University Press.

Dovchin, S. (2017). The ordinariness of youth linguascapes in Mongolia. *International Journal of Multilingualism, 14*(2), 144–159.

Fought, C. (2003). *Chicano English in context*. London, UK: Palgrave MacMillan.

García, O. (2009). Education, multilingualism and translanguaging in the 21st century. In A. Mohanty, M. Panda, R. Phillipson, & T. Skutnabb-Kangas (Eds.), *Multilingual education for social justice: Globalising the local* (pp. 128–145). New Delhi, India: Orient Blackswan.

Hart-Gonzalez, L. (1985). Pan Hispanism and sub-community in Washington, DC. In L. Elías-Olivares, E. Leone, R. Cisneros, & J. Gutiérrez (Eds.), *Spanish language use and public life in the United States* (pp. 73–89). Berlin, Germany: Mouton de Gruyter.

Irvine, J. T. (2001). 'Style' as distinctiveness: The culture and ideology of linguistic differentiation. In P. Eckert & J. Rickford (Eds.), *Style and sociolinguistic variation* (pp. 21–43). Cambridge, UK: Cambridge University Press.

Labov, W. (1963). The social motivation of a sound change. *Word, 19*(3), 273–309.

Labov, W. (1972). *Sociolinguistic patterns* (No. 4). Philadelphia: University of Pennsylvania Press.

Lavadenz, M. (2005). Como hablar en silencio (like speaking in silence): Issues of language, culture, and identity of Central Americans in Los Angeles. In A. C. Zentella & C. Genishi (Eds.), *Building on strength: Language and literacy in Latino families and communities* (pp. 93–109). New York, NY: Teachers University Press, and Covina: California Association for Bilingual Education.

Lee, J. W. (2017). *The politics of translingualism: After Englishes*. London, UK: Routledge.

Li Wei (2010). Moment analysis and translanguaging space: Discursive construction of identities by multilingual Chinese youth in Britain. *Journal of Pragmatics, 43*(5), 1222–1235.

Liang, S. (2015). *Language attitudes and identities in multilingual China: A linguistic ethnography*. New York, NY: Springer.

Lipski, J. (1985). /s/in Central American Spanish. *Hispania, 68*(1), 143–149.

Lipski, J. (2008). *Varieties of Spanish in the United States.* Washington, DC: Georgetown University Press.

Martínez, R. A., Hikida, M., & Durán, L. (2014). Unpacking ideologies of linguistic purism: How dual language teachers make sense of everyday translanguaging. *International Multilingual Research Journal, 9*(1), 26–42.

Milroy, J. (2001). Language ideologies and the consequences of standardization. *Journal of Sociolinguistics, 5*(4), 530–555.

Milroy, L. (1982). Language and group identity. *Journal of Multilingual and Multiculutral Development, 3*(3), 207–216.

Modan, G. (2008a). *Turf wars: Discourse, diversity, and the politics of place.* Malden, MA: Blackwell Publishing.

Modan, G. (2008b). Mango fufu kimchi yucca: The depoliticization of 'diversity' in Washington, DC discourse. *City & Society, 20*(2), 188–221.

Myers-Scotton, C. (1995). *Social motivations for codeswitching: Evidence from Africa.* Oxford, UK: Oxford University Press.

Otheguy, R., García, O., & Reid, W. (2015). Clarifying translanguaging and deconstructing named languages: A perspective from linguistics. *Applied Linguistics Review, 6*(3), 281–307.

Parodi, C. (2003). Contacto de dialectos del español en Los Ángeles. In G. Perissinotto (Ed.), *Ensayos de lengua y pedagogía* (pp. 23–38). Santa Barbara: University of California Linguistic Minority Research Institute.

Parodi, C. (2008). Stigmatized Spanish inside the classroom and out. In D. Brinton, O. Kagan, & S. Bauckas (Eds.), *Heritage language education: A new field emerging* (pp. 199–214). London, UK: Routledge.

Pennycook, A. (2007). *Global Englishes and transcultural flows.* London, UK: Routledge.

Pennycook, A. (2010). *Language as a local practice.* London, UK: Routledge.

Pennycook, A., & Otsuji, E. (2015). *Metrolingualism: Language in the city.* Abingdon, UK and New York, NY: Routledge.

Pessar, P. (1995). The elusive enclave: Ethnicity, class, and nationality among Latino entrepreneurs in Greater Washington, DC. *Human Organization, 54*(4), 383–392.

Pew Research Center. (2014, September 6). Hispanic population and origin in select US metropolitan areas, 2014. Retrieved December 24, 2018 from http://www.pewhispanic.org/interactives/hispanic-population-in-select-u-s-metropolitan-areas/

Rampton, B. (1998). Language crossing and the redefinition of reality. In P. Auer (Ed.), *Code-switching in conversation: Language, interaction and identity* (pp. 290–317). London, UK: Routledge.

Raymond, C. (2012). Reallocation of pronouns through contact: In-the-moment identity construction amongst Southern California Salvadorans. *Journal of Sociolinguistics, 16*(5), 669–690.

Schilling-Estes, N. (2004). Constructing ethnicity in interaction. *Journal of Sociolinguistics, 8*(2), 163–195.

Schreiber, B. R. (2015). 'I am what I am': multilingual identity and digital translanguaging. *Language Learning & Technology, 19*(3), 69–87.

Singer, A. (2007). *Latin American immigrants in the Washington, DC metropolitan area.* Woodrow Wilson International Center for Scholars. Washington, DC.

Sotiroula, S. (2015). *Learning through translanguaging in an educational setting in Cyprus* (Doctoral dissertation, University of Birmingham).

Sprehn-Malagón, M., Hernández-Fujigaki, J., & Robinson, L. (2014). *Latinos in the Washington Metro Area.* Mount Pleasant, SC: Arcadia Publishing.

Trudgill, P. (1986). *Dialects in contact.* New York, NY: Basil Blackwell.

Trudgill, P. (2008). Colonial dialect contact in the history of European languages: On the irrelevance of identity to new-dialect formation. *Language in Society, 37*(2), 241–254.

Tseng, A. (2015). *Vowel variation, style, and identity construction in the English of Latinos in Washington, DC* (Doctoral dissertation, Georgetown University).

Tseng, A. (2018). Bilingualism, ideological recentering, and new Latinx identity construction in the global city. Latina/o Studies Association 3rd Biennial Conference, Latinx Studies Now: DC 2018+. Washington, DC July 12–14.

Urciuoli, B. (2008). Whose Spanish?: The tension between linguistic correctness. In M. Niño-Murcia & J. Rothman (Eds.), *Bilingualism and identity: Spanish at the crossroads with other languages* (pp. 257–278). Amsterdam: John Benjamins.

US Census. (2015). *American Community Survey.* Retrieved December 24, 2018 from https://factfinder.census.gov/faces/nav/jsf/pages/community_facts.xhtml

Zentella, A. C. (1990). Lexical leveling in four New York City Spanish dialects: Linguistic and social factors. *Hispania, 73*(4), 1094–1105.

Zentella, A. C. (1997). *Growing up bilingual: Puerto Rican children in New York.* Malden, MA and Oxford, UK: Blackwell Publishers.

PART III

Translinguistics for whom?

12

THE EVERYDAY POLITICS OF TRANSLINGUALISM AS TRANSGRESSIVE PRACTICE

Sender Dovchin and Suresh Canagarajah

The analytic potential of the translingual tradition can be enhanced through a stronger focus on 'political implications'—a way to understand the ordinariness of everyday resistance. That is, when people engage in linguistic resistance in everyday life, it might have mixed motivations; it might not be theoretically informed; it might draw from their cultures of resistance in their community history; and it might need ideological analysis by scholars so that we can create more awareness among ordinary people. Scholars might also have to appreciate and theorize these everyday forms of resistance without overlooking them. Though translingual scholars have always been aware of the political implications of their work, they have not articulated them in relation to diverse geopolitical considerations. To a large extent, they have been concerned about articulating the implications for monolingual ideologies of modernity (Canagarajah, 2013; Pennycook & Otsuji, 2015) and of European colonization (see Canagarajah, 1999; Makoni & Pennycook, 2007). They have overlooked relating translingualism to ongoing ideological conflicts and geopolitical developments.

In this chapter, we consider the translingual practices of young people in different geographical contexts and these practices' transgressive implications. We are mindful of several cautions. First, as these practices are intuitive and/or habituated, the interlocutors do not always have a theorized position on the politics of their communication. As critical scholars, we are interpreting the possible politics of their acts without necessarily imputing our interpretations as their intentions. Second, because of its unreflective nature, this everyday politics may feature a mix of resistant and accommodative tendencies. Critical sociolinguists have to interpret the mix of motivations and implications in a balanced way. Third, such an analysis should lead to raising awareness among our research participants on the ideological limitations and strengths of their communicative practices so that their transgressive potential can be further developed. Such an activity calls for engaged scholarship. Finally, the nature of this study calls for sociolinguists to act as organic intellectuals. That is, they should not assume that, because there is an ideological lack of clarity among their research participants, they can impose their own agendas and meanings onto everyday language practices. They have to think along with the motivations and practices of their participants to develop their own theorization in resonance.

Though theoretical discourses can facilitate interpretation, translingual scholars should base their data on socially situated practices. Further, translingual scholarship can be expanded not only through resisting essentialization but also reconfiguring theories and policies in sensitivity to different politics and linguistics of communication in diverse contexts and communities. Translingual practice is thereby not a model that is universally applicable to all contexts (Canagarajah, 2017). It should be defined as a situationally changing practice, rather than as a static theory or body of knowledge open to appropriation, institutionalization, and marketization. If we treat translingualism as a practice, sociolinguists will be open to the changing implications of this practice in different contexts and historical conditions. If there are attempts to appropriate translingualism by powerful institutions for their ulterior purposes, we can consider how this practice can shift to resist those tendencies. Translingualism then would be treated as an emergent grassroots-level practice that gets reconfigured according to changing social, historical, and geographical conditions (Lee, 2017).

Along these lines, we present practices from two different geographical contexts. The first set of data relates to the language politics of Kazakh and dominant Mongolian. In using this data, we address a criticism raised by Piller (2016) regarding sociolinguistic scholarship on multilingualism. Piller (2016) has argued that scholars in multilingual studies have largely focused on local languages in relation to English. We have much less knowledge about the contact of languages without reference to English as the dominant other. In fact, much of the analysis on issues of linguistic creativity in late modernity is developed around the extensive discussion of English as a dominant language, while much less attention has been paid to non-English linguistic resources. Thus, we see the need for translingual studies outside English-dominant settings, with relevance to the dynamics of diverse local languages and semiotic repertoires. Though our second dataset does involve English in Japanese university English as a foreign language (EFL) classrooms, it addresses a setting outside the powerful English-dominant center communities. It particularly focuses on Japanese students in English classes negotiating diverse genres and languages.

Codeswitching as a resistance strategy: Mongolian-Kazakh youths

While the majority of the Mongolian population are Khalkh Mongols, Kazakhs constitute 5% of the population, mostly residing in the far west of the country. They started migrating to Mongolia in the 1860s, mainly from the Xinjiang region of China. The majority of Khalkh Mongolians are Tibetan Buddhists, while

Islam is the dominant religion among ethnic Kazakhs in Mongolia. Today, 90% of Mongolian-Kazakhs live in Bayan-Ulgii province, which was established in 1939 as a semi-autonomous homeland for Kazakhs living in Mongolia. Bayan-Ulgii has a distinct Kazakh culture, and Kazakh is the language of everyday communication, with Mongolian used for inter-ethnic interactions and official communication. The relationship between Mongolians and Kazakhs in Mongolia has been largely amicable and harmonious (Soni, 2008), but it has not always been straightforward. While the Mongolian Constitution guarantees the rights of ethnic minorities and recognizes their rights to language, religion, and customs, it is no secret that Mongolian-Kazakhs still face problems on a daily basis in Mongolia. One main challenge is the dominance of the Mongolian language. Very few Mongolians speak Kazakh or engage with Kazakh linguistic and cultural practices. The Mongolian legal system, as well as large educational establishments, professional institutions, and even medium and small private sectors, require the Mongolian language. Most of the secondary and high schools in Bayan-Ulgii encounter difficulty finding Mongolian language teachers, and a majority of classes are taught in Kazakh or a combination of Mongol-Kazakh languages. As a result, many young Mongolian-Kazakhs are not competitive enough to enter the best Mongolian universities or find good jobs in urban settings.

Nevertheless, a small number of young Mongolian-Kazakh people from Bayan-Ulgii who move to Ulaanbaatar to study at universities or to look for jobs start interacting with Khalkh-Mongols on professional and personal levels. The data used in this section, thereby, derive from a larger 'linguistic (n)ethnographic' study, exploring specifically the online interactions of ethnic minority Kazakh youths in Mongolia. 'Linguistic (n)ethnography' is the outcome of the combination of two methods—'netnography' and 'linguistic ethnography' (Dovchin, 2018)—which considers the fact that translingual practices may occur both in offline and online environments. Virtual ethnographic analytic frameworks such as 'netnography' (Kozinets, 2002, 2015) and 'Internet/online ethnography' (Androutsopoulos, 2011; Stæhr, 2015) were primarily employed to look at the online linguistic behaviors of young Mongolian-Kazakh Facebook users (conducted between July and November 2010 and between April and June 2011). Facebook was chosen as the main research site due to its widespread popularity in recent years; it plays a significant role in the daily linguistic repertoires of people around the world (de Bres, 2015), involving semiotic, heteroglossic, and linguistic creativity. Under Facebook netnography, overall 40 students from various sociocultural backgrounds between the ages of 17 and 29 from the National University of Mongolia (NUM) volunteered to participate in the research. Their socioeconomic and regional backgrounds were diverse, varying from affluent to poor and from rural to urban, before they gained admission to university and came to live in Ulaanbaatar. Out of the 40 students, 4 research participants were Mongolian-Kazakh background students who came to Ulaanbaatar to study at NUM. Their daily Facebook interactions were monitored from the moment Facebook friendship was established.

The data gained from Facebook were further validated by the research participants using the methods of 'linguistic ethnography'. Recent studies have found that the methodological framework of 'linguistic ethnography' may constitute seeds of profound understanding about the sociolinguistic realities of language users (Blommaert & Dong, 2010; Dovchin, Pennycook, & Sultana, 2018). The study, thus, adopted a 'linguistic ethnographic' qualitative design in understanding young people's everyday sociolinguistic experiences and realities. The participants were interviewed on a one-to-one basis about their metalinguistic Facebook practices. Their direct voices and first-person perspectives were captured in relation to their translingual practices, as well as their everyday linguistic contests and resistances. These participants were interviewed face-to-face or through Skype to understand what everyday politics of translingualism would look like to them, documenting the events they deemed critical, including issues such as what exactly led to an incident and why it was significant or critical.

As the research progressed, some representatives of the Mongolian-Kazakh group said that they have to conform to the dominant linguistic norms and policies at educational institutions and workplaces in Mongolia, especially in Ulaanbaatar. That is, they have to uphold the standard language requirements of speaking and writing fluent Mongolian. Possessing 'broken Mongolian' often becomes a cause for discrimination. As Fatima, (a Mongolian-Kazakh student at NUM) says:

> To be honest, it is very hard to study with Mongolians. They never want to make friends with us. They mock us when we speak Mongolian. They never make any efforts to make friends with us. They laugh at us. They bully us. It is extremely difficult to integrate with Mongolians. Even some of our lecturers [referring to Mongolian lecturers] tend to discriminate us and give preference to fellow Mongolians because we are not Mongolians. Some lecturers do not understand why I cannot write good essays in Mongolian. They never try to help us. They only tell us to learn Mongolian properly. Very ignorant. As a result, we have this reputation that Kazakh women never marry Mongolian men. They never make friends with Mongolians.
> *(Interview, September 25, 2010, Ulaanbaatar, Mongolia;*
> *Mongolian-English translation by the researcher)*

Because of this daily experience of discrimination, many Mongolian-Kazakhs have to implement one of the three observed resistance strategies. First, many Mongolian-Kazakhs tend to bond with each other. Mongolian-Kazakh groups maintain strong relationships, as they create a group bond around their shared daily struggles and make their daily experiences more harmonious and bearable. Fatima explains:

> We just hang out with each other and share our problems, feelings and thoughts. We can speak Kazakh to each other without any restrictions or

judgements. We help each other how to improve our essays or presentations in Mongolian. We feel at ease when we are together.

(Interview, September 25, 2010, Ulaanbaatar, Mongolia)

Similarly, Mongolian-Kazakhs use hidden sites for using uninhibited Kazakh. These sites serve to preserve Mongolian-Kazakhs' heritage language in an oppressive environment, develop fluency in the language, and foster in-group networks. However, these language users switch to dominant Mongolian in public and formal sites. This shuttling activity requires translingual competence and skills.

While the safe houses above are physical, sometimes language users also construct safe digital spaces (as we see next). These digital spaces are socially constructed and require more creative agency. Though other friends from diverse language groups are present in social media spaces, Kazakh youth decide on appropriate contexts to use Kazakh, and they define certain interactions as in-group by switching to their heritage language. Different from language use in physical safe houses, use of Kazakh in digital spaces is performed in front of other language groups. It is a safe form of resistance as it allows them to use Kazakh and celebrate their Kazakh identity right under the noses of dominant communities, without being threatening, as they define these interactions as in-group.

For example, many young Mongolian-Kazakh informants view social media space as their 'safe houses', as their engagement with Facebook is very personal and private. It is obvious in their everyday Facebook updates and interactions with their Facebook friends that their preferred linguistic choice is Kazakh. Many Mongolian-Kazakh Facebook users praise and glorify the beauty of Kazakh language and culture, in addition to the longevity and prosperity of Kazakh tradition and custom. They use various multimodal features, such as images, song lyrics, music videos, photographs, links to news and movies, tag lines, and characters from popular cultural resources using extended Kazakh orthography. Consider the examples in Figures 12.1 and 12.2, where the standard Kazakh orthography (not Romanized) is commonly used for daily Facebook interactions.

Fatima explains that using her native language, Kazakh, on Facebook provides a sense of language ownership:

> When I go to job interviews and start using Kazakh, I would be in big trouble. When I start speaking Kazakh during my presentation at university, I would be mocked. I need to speak perfect Mongolian. When I'm out of my comfort zone, I don't usually use Kazakh unfortunately. So, using Kazakh is very personal to me. I use Kazakh within my friend's level, who obviously understand Kazakh.
>
> *(Interview, September 25, 2010, Ulaanbaatar, Mongolia)*

In other words, she may not 'use language in the same way with community outsiders as [she does] with insiders' (Bucholtz, 2003, p. 406). She has the linguistic competence to switch from one language norm to another in different

FIGURE 12.1   A Mongolian-Kazakh girl posts a music video of a Kazakh song with an extract of its lyrics. One of her ordinary, everyday linguistic practices on her Facebook is to use as much Kazakh as possible.

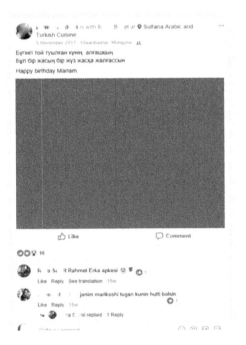

FIGURE 12.2   A Mongolian-Kazakh girl wishes a happy first birthday to her friend's child using Kazakh orthography, accompanied by English. Note that her Facebook respondents are also interacting with one another using Kazakh.

contexts for her desired linguistic performances (Kramsch & Whiteside, 2008). For Fatima, therefore, using Kazakh and Mongolian is both exclusive and inclusive. Pre-planned institutional discourses, which reach dominant Mongolian audiences, need to be executed through standard Mongolian. In contrast, her daily language practice within her peers' circle can be in Kazakh. From this perspective, Fatima's in-group Kazakh language usage is a form of 'strategic resistance'. She strategically adopts a language within her in-group interactions that is perceived as undesirable by the dominant society. Her use of Kazakh is exclusive to inside audiences, strengthening her sense of language ownership and distancing the language from outsiders.

Lastly, many Mongolian-Kazakh youths integrate English into their daily online and offline linguistic practices. In fact, Mongolian is the language that they use least, while English is a popular language choice. Some Mongolian-Kazakh informants say that they feel 'empowered' to use English because they want to show Mongolians that Kazakh people can speak good English. As Fatima suggests:

> English is very important language in Mongolia. If you speak good English, you are more likely to get a good job. You get a lot of respect from Mongolians if you speak good English. I think Kazakh people are naturally talented in learning foreign languages because we are inclined to learn Mongolian from very young age. So, sometimes we speak better English than Mongolians.
>
> *(Interview, September 25, 2010, Ulaanbaatar, Mongolia)*

We might label this strategy as 'playing competing linguistic markets against each other'. That is, different languages have value in different markets—Mongolian in the nation-state and English globally. Because Kazakhs are excluded from the Mongolian market, they lay claim to the global market through their use of English. In contexts of multilingualism, we have to realize that markets and languages are layered (see Park & Wee, 2012).

From this view, Fatima feels more empowered than some Mongolians because she can speak English fluently. In fact, a majority of Mongolian-Kazakh young people opt for English as the main linguistic choice for their Facebook interactions. Consider the examples below where they appropriate English in varied ways:

> User: Like this place, so simple yet very comfortable, and has tasty food. French taste [posted along with a photo of a meal that she is having at French café in Ulaanbaatar]

> User: International Kazakh miss in Mongolia [showing support for a Kazakh participant in a beauty pageant in Mongolia]

> User: This is me: 'I am happiest when doing something useful for somebody else, whether it be a friend, family member, colleagu or even a stranger. When I've done something valuable for them, they are happy which makes me happy'!

In another case, a Mongolian-Kazakh girl, whom I call EJ, stands firm in using English instead of Mongolian even though she is interacting with her former Mongolian classmate, BB (see Figure 12.3). This girl speaks fluent Mongolian and finished her undergraduate degree at NUM. However, she prefers using English while interacting with her Mongolian friend. The Facebook interaction starts when she updates her Facebook wall in Kazakh. The use of English here indexes global youth culture, which might be considered more desirable than local youth culture in some cases.

In line 1, EJ updates her Facebook wall exclusively using Kazakh orthography: 'Өлгейдегі достарым мені қымызханаға бір ертіп барыңдаршы' [Dear friends in Ulgii, Please take me out to the 'Airag' house.]. In response to this Facebook post, her Mongolian friend, BB (line 2) asks EJ what she has just written because he is not able to read Kazakh. This shows that a majority of Mongolians

FIGURE 12.3 Facebook conversation in Kazakh, Mongolian, and English.

are not able to understand the Kazakh language. Although Cyrillic Mongolian is the standard orthographic system in Mongolia, BB uses Romanized Cyrillic Mongolian here, a common orthographic choice for many Mongolian online users because of its convenience (e.g. some computers in Mongolia have no Cyrillic keyboards). In line 3, EJ's first choice is English to translate her Kazakh Facebook post for her Mongolian friend: 'Dear friends in Ulgii, Please take take me out to the "Airag" house'. Then, she provides a translation of the Cyrillic Standard Mongolian orthography in line 4. In line 5, using Romanized Mongolian, BB expresses his wish to join her to drink 'airag' [fermented mare's milk, a traditional beverage of Mongolia, that contains a small amount of carbon dioxide and up to 2% alcohol]. In line 6, EJ responds to him in English again: 'in Ulgii' [abbreviation for Bayan-Ulgii, where the 'airag' drinking place is located]. In line 7, BB again expresses his wish to visit Bayan-Ulgii and talks about a fond memory from when they were classmates. EJ's response, line 8, is again in English: 'Worth coming once in a life', reminding him that visiting Bayan-Ulgii would be a once-in-a-lifetime experience. In this Facebook interaction, we can see how EJ insists on using English instead of Mongolian even though she is interacting with a Mongolian person, who is continually using Mongolian. English gives EJ an alternative space to feel empowered.

Codemeshing as a resistance strategy: Japanese EFL university students

According to McMillan and Rivers (2011), 'an English-only approach in the classroom' appears to EFL educators, students, and other stakeholders in Japan 'to be a cure for all that ails the English education system' (p. 252). In fact, much EFL activity in Japanese university contexts is determined by English textbooks and the restricted language policy of 'Standard English-only' (Saito & Ebsworth, 2004). 'Standard English-only policy' continues to enjoy hegemonic status in most Japanese EFL university contexts, with students and instructors mainly prevented from using any types of 'unstandardized English' (Mishima, 2016). EFL students at the Centre for Language Research, University of Aizu, Japan are no exception. Their main exposure to English is the 'good-old English textbooks'. This approach also lends itself to normative learning and usage of the English language (McMillan & Rivers, 2011).

Meanwhile, current translingual trends in applied linguistics, informed by pedagogical and sociolinguistic research, acknowledge that 'Standard English-only', that is, 'textbook English' policy, in EFL classrooms weakens the overall role of English in the language classroom to 'a language used and taught only in its own presence' (Pennycook, 2008, pp. 4–5). Some scholars recognize the paradigm shift occurring with regard to sensible 'translingual English' (or codemeshing) application in the classroom as having great potential to enhance the effectiveness of English language learning and teaching processes (Canagarajah, 2013). Introducing 'translingual English' in the classroom could 'make links for classroom participants between the social, cultural, community, and linguistic domains of their lives' (Creese & Blackledge, 2010, p. 112). It may help language educators understand multiple desires, identities, and aspirations embedded within their students' 'multiple ways of speaking, being and learning' (Pennycook, 2007, p. 157).

Following these lines of thought, a classroom ethnographic research, funded by Japan Society for the Promotion of Science—KAKENHI—was conducted at the University of Aizu, Japan between October 2016 and April 2018 in English courses, such as 'English and Globalization', 'English and Cyber Culture', and 'English for Active Communication', focusing on improving students' English reading, writing, and speaking skills, as well as critical thinking and social media awareness. These courses were open to undergraduate students of computer science studying at the University of Aizu. A favorable pedagogical space was sought by the researchers to help students explore English beyond textbooks and give them an opportunity to see English through alternative eyes. A learning environment was developed through texts and interactions on Facebook, in which the readings and writings emerged out of English texts that were commonly presented on Facebook. Students were asked to critically analyze texts and interactions on Facebook, which concerned some critical and urgent local and global issues. The main topic was the Tohoku earthquake of 2011 and its devastating aftermath of the Fukushima nuclear disaster. This topic was particularly important for students at the University of Aizu because these students live in Fukushima—the epicenter of the disaster. Many students had also personally experienced the disaster in 2011.

Surprisingly, a majority of the students claimed that they had never read the ongoing arguments, issues, and disputes about the Fukushima nuclear disaster in English, and their critical awareness of how the rest of the world perceived this disaster was incredibly ambiguous. Students, therefore, started reading various opinions, articles, and reviews on the given topic that circulated on Facebook and their accompanying comments written by Facebook users. Upon the completion of this Facebook text analysis, students were asked to write a critical essay, deliver critical presentations on the topic of the Fukushima nuclear disaster and the area's revitalization, and their experience with English on Facebook. Overall, 140 students were involved in this project. Upon completion of the Facebook analysis, students were asked to participate in a face-to-face interview with an instructor to share their experiences with Facebook and English.

After the completion of this project, a majority of students reported that social media English—'translingual English'—has opened up a whole other world to them. Translingual English provided access to different information sources and ideological discourses from those in Japanese. Many students contested the dominant textbook English and English classroom norms, favoring 'real-life English' on Facebook. Translingual English helped them establish facility with social media and explore the critical subject of the Fukushima nuclear disaster with greater critical awareness, involvement, and relevance. In one activity, students found an article on Facebook, 'Radioactive boars roam area near Fukushima in Japan', written by the Australian media outlet, *Sydney Morning Herald*. After analyzing this article on Facebook, many students highlighted that they had learned 'completely new information' regarding the Fukushima nuclear disaster, which they had never seen on Japanese media. They were not aware of the 'radioactive boars' roaming in Fukushima, only a few kilometers away from where they live. From this perspective, Yuto, for example, highlighted the importance of English social media because he felt he finally had access to 'authentic information' about the disaster. He explained:

> I do not have a chance to read the authentic information about the nuclear disaster in Fukushima because the Japanese media does not report much on these issues. As soon as I started browsing Facebook, I was so surprised to find out so many information that I have never heard before.
>
> *(Interview, January 19, 2018, Aizu-Wakamatsu, Japan)*

Another student, Yoshida, expressed his critical views on learning English from textbooks and showed his preference for Facebook English:

> I have always thought English textbook was so boring. I learned about this 'worm composter' from my textbook, which is really useless and outdated. Who needs to learn about 'worm composter'? I definitely prefer engaging with Facebook now because I have learned a lot of updated and useful information about what is really happening in terms of Fukushima nuclear disaster.
>
> *(Interview, January 19, 2018, Aizu-Wakamatsu, Japan)*

Students were further asked to analyze the comments left by Facebook users. Many students highlighted the fun and engaging process of learning English on Facebook from 'real people'. See, for example below, where Facebook 'real people' start playing with English based on the main topic of the article:

> User 1: Who else looked at this and saw bebop from tmnt [Face with Tears of Joy Emoji]
> User 2: Is this how boarzilla created??
> User 3: Pigoons?
> User 4 (Replying to User 3): Spiderpig
> User 5: i don't even have to comment
> [3 Replies]
> User 6: Shoot them
> User 7: Boarzilla..
> User 8: Great film. Zombie boars
> User 9: Hotham
> User 10: Nuekiller
> User 11: …well stop eating them

As we see here, the language examples produced by Facebook users can be defined as 'translingual English' or 'codemeshing', where the online users twist, mix, and bend the standardized form of English. In some cases, it involves appropriation of English grammatical resources in relation to Japanese grammar and lexicology in an effort to Japanize English. As soon as the standardized form of English comes into contact with other linguistic resources, the idealization of the standard system makes no clear sense. Hence, English becomes 'translingual English'. For example, the English word 'boar' is combined with the Japanese word 'Godzilla'—a famous Japanese movie monster that was, ironically, formed from exposure to nuclear radioactivity. This combination creates the unconventional phrase 'Boarzilla', referring, perhaps, to the 'Godzilla-like boars from Japan'.

Note also other eccentric translingual phrases such as 'Spiderpig'—the blending of movie title 'Spiderman' and 'pig'; 'nuekiller'—the fusion of 'nuclear' and 'killer'; 'The rise of Xboars'—the transformation of 'The rise of Renegada X', a popular teen fantasy fiction. In these cases, English is meshed with semiotic resources of global youth culture. English is understood not so much through fixed grammar but rather its use shows how individuals can creatively mobilize and transcend different linguistic resources at their disposal and adopt different negotiation strategies to make meanings. A Japanese EFL student, Saito, says:

> I found the words such as Boarzilla, Spiderpig etc. hilarious and engaging. It was fun and engaging how English can be mixed with the famous Japanese movie characters. It made me laugh. It was much better than textbook. That is for sure.
>
> *(Interview, January 19, 2018, Aizu-Wakamatsu, Japan)*

In a similar vein, Kimura explains:

> I thought it was real. They were written by real English speakers. Not textbook authors. So I felt much more alive. Of course, learning English from textbook is important but I think we should also have more opportunity to see 'real life English' because we have no real life English environment in Japan anyway.
>
> *(Interview, January 19, 2018, Aizu-Wakamatsu, Japan)*

From this view, 'translingual English' (involving types of codemeshing) provided Kimura with a good chance of recognizing the dominant codes such as textbook English, while also of acknowledging the criticality and dynamics of English beyond the textbook—that is, 'real-life English'. Becoming acquainted with codemeshing on Facebook increased Kimura's critical thinking and stimulated his resistance strategy to differentiate the current and conventional expectations for English writing/reading from the real and authentic voices constructed by Facebook users.

Discussion

When we consider the translingual practices in these two communities, we see different resistant practices. We might label the strategy of Kazakh youths as 'codeswitching' and that of the Japanese youths as 'codemeshing'. Note that we are using codeswitching as a metaphor for reserving different languages for different contexts, following Heath (1983). We identify the term 'codeswitching' in this context toward a more flexible account of how people deploy different linguistic codes in their everyday practice to negotiate their resistance and difference (Pennycook, 2017). This is different from the use of the term in sociolinguistics for code alternation within the same utterance. What the Kazakh youth do to find spaces for using their own language in isolation from Mongolian is an example of codeswitching. Similarly, EJ's insistence on using English without adopting Mongolian or mixing Mongolian with English or Kazakh might be considered codeswitching. The Japanese youth, by contrast, engage in a more fluid and hybrid practice of meshing English with their own local and in-group semiotic resources, which resembles codemeshing.

Translingual scholars have debated the value of codemeshing over codeswitching in previous scholarship (e.g. Young, 2004). However, we have to approach this question situationally in relation to the histories and geopolitics of different communities. It is unwise to adopt a generalized position that codemeshing is always more resistant or critically informed than codeswitching. It appears that codeswitching performs an important political function for Kazakh youth. In a context where they are physically interacting with the Mongolian community, surrounded by that majority community in the Mongolian nation-state, a strategy of separation serves them well. They construct safe spaces to use only Kazakh, thus finding spaces to use their heritage language, to preserve its continuity, and to foster its identities. Minority communities in such contexts of domination have argued against codemeshing, stating that they prefer to preserve their language from mixing (see Lyons, 2009). However, for Japanese youths, when they do not face immediate and direct threats from 'textbook English' policy, a type of codemeshing on Facebook offers them resistant possibilities. We have to, therefore, acknowledge that the ideological implications of language choices are different based on different histories and geopolitical communities.

We have to also analyze the different politics of using English by youth from both communities. In one sense, scholars might argue that using English in multilingual contexts or in codemeshing eventually plays into the global power of English (see Skutnabb-Kangas, 2002). Codemeshing is two-edged. While it is a form of appropriating English and making it impure with values and influences from local languages, it can still introduce English and its values to local interlocutors and give English more life. However, we have to consider social domains as layered, with different potential for resistance at different scales of consideration. The use of English in Mongolia by Kazakh youths is resistant to the language ideologies in the nation-state of Mongolia. As the market for these languages is layered (Kazakh's ethnic value within the in-group; Mongolian's value in the nation-state; English's value transnationally), the adoption of English is strategic. Kazakhs are unable to compete for rewards from Mongolian, as they are deemed not proficient or are discriminated against. Therefore, the choice of English is a better alternative for them. Note that such a strategy has also been observed in Malaysia, where the Chinese minority is learning English and obtaining rewards from a different market, when the local Malays are promoting their language for nation-state rewards and dominating the local market. As for the Japanese students, their attitude toward codemeshing and 'unstandard English' is resistant in the local scales of EFL classroom relations. In a context where language purity, standard English, normativity, and native-speaker authority is valued, their co-demeshing is transgressive. It also enables them to appropriate English according to their own values and identities for their own national interests.

Despite these transgressive possibilities in their local contexts of use, we must acknowledge that the translingualism of these youths is complicit with neoliberal ideologies and markets at a more translocal scale of consideration. Though these research participants are adopting a translingual orientation to English, meshing it with their other semiotic resources and shuttling between diverse languages, the very practices of flexibilization, hybridity, and repertoire building are part of the human capital valued for neoliberal marketization (see Canagarajah, 2017). Kazakh and Japanese youths are developing neoliberal dispositions and practices even as they are resisting and negotiating English at a local level for their own strategic purposes.

Furthermore, the strategy of safe house resistance also comes with mixed ideological implications. As it has been well studied under the metaphor of 'weapons of the weak' (Scott, 1985), such spaces allow for marginalized communities' hidden forms of resistance. In a contemporary twist on this notion, both youth groups find social media a potent space for safe house discourses, which were not available to the feudal communities studied by Scott in the past. However, we have to acknowledge that safe houses still leave the public and visible social spaces unchallenged. Dominant languages and ideologies continue to hold sway in those spaces. Scott does argue that keeping subversive discourses alive in the safe houses is valuable, as such discourses find expression and implementation when the time is ripe for direct confrontation. However, direct resistance should be facilitated.

All this is not to argue that the strategies of our participants are useless. They do have value in their local contexts. However, such untheorized, spontaneous, and intuitive everyday resistance has to be interrogated to lead to structural change at translocal scales of consideration. From this point of view, a scalar approach is useful for sociolinguists (see Canagarajah & De Costa, 2016). Too often, sociolinguists adopt a monolithic orientation to social life, which leads them to deterministic orientations to translingual politics. They do not allow for a layered approach, where resistance in local spaces might have value, develop challenge structures from the ground up, or have different positive values and diverse spaces.

However, to develop the incipient politics of everyday translingual practice, it will require the engagement of critical sociolinguists as organic intellectuals. They will have to look closely at everyday communicative practices to tease out transgressive from collusive implications, develop critical thinking among lay participants, and foster proficiencies that are ideologically informed. Dingo (2013), for example, has developed what she terms a 'networking pedagogy' to connect classroom practices to more expansive scales of geopolitical consideration so that students will not mistake their local resistance for structural change. Educators can help students see the varying implications of their practices in relation to the relative scales of consideration. The research of translingual scholars can also facilitate such an approach, especially in more public contexts of dissemination, to create critical awareness among non-scholars to understand the transgressive nature of their practices, critically analyze dominant language ideologies, and develop their communicative practices for radical change.

Acknowledgements

This research is funded by Japan Society for the Promotion of Science KAKENHI Grant Number JP17K13504.

https://kaken.nii.ac.jp/ja/grant/KAKENHI-PROJECT-17K13504

References

Androutsopoulos, J. (2011). From variation to heteroglossia in the study of computerme-diated discourse. In C. Thurlow & K. Mroczek (Eds.), *Digital discourse: Language in the new media* (pp. 277–298). Oxford, UK: Oxford University Press.

Blommaert, J., & Dong, J. (2010). *Ethnographic fieldwork: A beginner's guide.* Clevedon, UK: Multilingual Matters.

Bucholtz, M. (2003). Sociolinguistic nostalgia and the authentication of identity. *Journal of Sociolinguistics, 7*(4), 398–416.

Canagarajah, S. (1999). *Resisting linguistic imperialism in English teaching.* Oxford, UK: Oxford University Press.

Canagarajah, S. (2013). *Translingual practice: Global Englishes and cosmopolitan relations.* New York, NY: Routledge.

Canagarajah, S. (2017). *Translingual practices and neoliberal policies: Attitudes and strategies of African skilled migrants in Anglophone workplaces.* Cham, Switzerland: Springer.

Canagarajah, S., & De Costa, P. (2016). Introduction: Scales analysis, and its uses and prospects in educational linguistics. *Linguistics and Education, 34*, 1–10.

Creese, A., & Blackledge, A. (2010). Translanguaging in the bilingual classroom: A pedagogy for learning and teaching? *The Modern Language Journal, 94*(1), 103–115.

Dingo, R. (2013). Networking the macro and micro: Toward transnational literacy practices. *Journal of Advanced Composition, 33*(3–4), 529–552.

de Bres, J. (2015). Introduction: Language policies on social network sites. *Language Policy, 14*(4), 309–314.

Dovchin, S. (2018). *Language, media and globalization in the periphery: The linguascapes of popular music in Mongolia.* New York, NY: Routledge.

Dovchin, S., Pennycook, A., & Sultana, S. (2018). *Popular culture, voice and linguistic diversity: Young adults on- and offline.* Cham, Switzerland: Palgrave MacMillan.

Heath, S. B. (1983). *Ways with words.* Cambridge, UK: Cambridge University Press.

Kozinets, R. (2002). The field behind the screen: Using netnography for marketing research in online communities. *Journal of Marketing Research, 39*(1), 61–72.

Kozinets, R. (2015). *Netnography: Redefined.* London, UK: Sage.

Kramsch, C., & Whiteside, A. (2008). Language ecology in multilingual settings: Towards a theory of symbolic competence. *Applied Linguistics, 29*(4), 645–671.

Lee, J. W. (2017). *The politics of translingualism: After Englishes.* New York, NY: Routledge.

Lyons, S. (2009). The fine art of fencing: Nationalism, hybridity, and the search for a Native American writing pedagogy. *Journal of Advanced Composition, 29,* 77–106.

Makoni, S., & Pennycook, A. (2007) *Disinventing and reconstituting languages.* Bristol, UK: Multilingual Matters.

McMillan, B. A., & Rivers, D. J. (2011). The practice of policy: Teacher attitudes toward 'English only'. *System, 39*(2), 251–263.

Mishima, M. (2016). Searching for the best medium of instruction: Japanese university students' views on English-only instruction in EAP courses. *The Journal of Rikkyo University Language Center, 36,* 15–27.

Park, J., & Wee, L. (2012). *Markets of English.* Abingdon, UK: Routledge.

Pennycook, A. (2007). *Global Englishes and transcultural flows.* London, UK: Routledge.

Pennycook, A. (2008). Translingual English. *Australian Review of Applied Linguistics, 31*(3), 30.31–30.39.

Pennycook, A. (2017). *Posthumanist applied linguistics.* London, UK: Routledge.

Pennycook, A., & Otsuji, E. (2015). *Metrolingualism: Language in the city.* London, UK: Routledge.

Piller, I. (2016). *Linguistic diversity and social justice: An introduction to applied sociolinguistics.* Oxford, UK: Oxford University Press.

Saito, H., & Ebsworth, M. E. (2004). Seeing English language teaching and learning through the eyes of Japanese EFL and ESL students. *Foreign Language Annals, 37*(1), 111–124.

Scott, J. C. (1985). *Weapons of the weak: Everyday forms of peasant resistance.* New Haven, CT: Yale University Press.

Skutnabb-Kangas, T. (2002). *Why should linguistic diversity be maintained and supported in Europe?: Some arguments.* Strasbourg, France: Council of Europe.

Soni, S. K. (2008). Mongolian Kazakh diaspora: Study of largest ethnic minority in Mongolia. *Bimonthly Journal of Mongolian and Tibetan Current Situation (Taipei, Taiwan), 17*(3), 31–49.

Stæhr, A. (2015). Reflexivity in Facebook interaction–enregisterment across written and spoken language practices. *Discourse, Context and Media, 8,* 30–45.

Young, V. A. (2004). Your average Nigga. *College Composition and Communication, 55,* 693–715.

13

TRANßCRIPTING

Playful subversion with Chinese characters

Li Wei and Zhu Hua

On 28 August 2012, a group of over 100 language enthusiasts, public figures, and academics in China wrote an open letter to the State Administration of Press and Publication and the State Language Commission to protest the inclusion of 239 so-called alphabetic words in the latest, 6th edition of the popular dictionary *A Dictionary of Modern Chinese*. The letter writers claimed that the inclusion of words such as NBA, CPI, and $PM_{2.5}$ violated laws protecting the Chinese writing system because the Chinese script is logographic, not alphabetic. A national debate ensued, with unprecedented media coverage. The vast majority seemed to be on the side of the complainants who felt that the Chinese language was under threat from foreign influence. Those who argued for the acceptance of alphabetic words were in the minority and seen as rebels. The dictionary compilers, many of whom were senior academics in public office, had to issue lengthy explanations. They argued that the dictionary was not intended to dictate what was acceptable but to record words in common usage.

This incident is only one example of how strongly the Chinese feel about their writing system. They believe that the Chinese script is one of the oldest continually used writing systems in the world; that it has had a major influence on other East Asian languages and beyond; and that all attempts in history to change the system have failed. Nonetheless, new writing inventions appear all the time in China, and most of them are intrinsically tied to social, cultural, political, and economic changes. This chapter focuses on the emerging phenomenon scripts that defy the writing conventions of Chinese by incorporating elements that are deemed 'foreign' or by manipulating the structural norms of Chinese written characters, including their traditional sound-meaning mapping process and visual representation. We call this phenomenon 'tranßcripting'. While we want to highlight the creative processes of tranßcripting, our main purpose is to explore its sociopolitical dimensions, in particular, its playful subversiveness.

Understood from the analytical perspective of translanguaging, we emphasize how such subversion occurs through the usage of 'non-Chinese' language resources and how such practices are 'ordinary' linguistic phenomena created and circulated by ordinary people in everyday, digitally mediated social interaction (Dovchin, 2017). They are examples of how the 'ordinary' can be both linguistically 'playful' and 'subversive', commonly practiced despite official efforts to censor their usage and minimize their sociocultural impact.

The Chinese script and the Chinese uni-scriptal ideology

The Chinese writing system is roughly logosyllabic: a character generally represents a syllable in spoken Chinese, and it may be a word on its own or part of a di- or polysyllabic word. Some characters are pictographs or ideographs, depicting objects or abstract notions; others are either logical aggregates in which two or more parts are used to yield a composite meaning, or phonetic complexes, where one part indicates the general semantic category of the character and the other part the phonetic value, which are known as semantic and phonetic radicals, respectively. Many Chinese characters in use today can be traced back to the late Shang Dynasty, about 1200–1050 BCE, though the creation of the characters is thought to have begun some centuries earlier. Chinese characters have been used throughout East Asia: they spread to Korea during the 2nd century BCE; they were adopted for writing Japanese during the 5th century CE; and they were first used in Vietnam in 111 BCE. This spread gave rise to the notion of the Sinosphere or Sinophone World. Several languages of south and southwest China, including Zhuang, Miao, and Yao, were formerly written in Chinese characters or in writing systems based on Chinese characters. All these factors have contributed to the popular belief among Chinese language users that their writing system is unique and virtuous, as it is intrinsically linked with Confucianism, Taoism, and Buddhism, and has mystical power to bind people together culturally and spiritually.

The belief in the uniqueness of the Chinese writing system manifests in a number of contradictory views. Many Chinese believe that there is only one writing system for the Chinese language, and that the First Emperor of China, Zheng of Qin (259–210 BCE), unified the writing system so that speakers of mutually unintelligible regional varieties of Chinese could all use the same script in written communication. In fact, there is a very long tradition of regional written Chinese. Written Cantonese has been used since the Ming Dynasty, 1368–1644 CE (Bauer, 2018; Snow & Chen, 2015). Other regional varieties such as Wu, which includes Shanghainese and Suzhounese, developed writing systems at similar times (Snow, Shen, & Zhou, 2018; Snow, Zhou, & Shen 2018). Admittedly, these writing systems are based broadly on Chinese characters. But they would not be comprehensible to a reader fluent in Mandarin. Other well-documented cases include Nüshu, literally 'women's script', a phonetic system that was used among 13th-century women in the Hunan province. Dungan, used by the Dungan people in Central Asia, especially those who are Muslims of Chinese descent in Kazakhstan, Kyrgyzstan, and Russia, was previously written in Arabic script and is now written in Cyrillic. Moreover, there are at least two main transliteration systems for Chinese: *pinyin* and *bopomofo*. The former is based on the Latin alphabet. The latter, also known as Zhùyīn fúhào, derives its symbols from ancient Chinese writing, and was used in China before the 1950s and is still used in Taiwan. There is also Jyut6jyu5 for transcribing Cantonese. Historically, a number of transliteration systems, including the Wade-Giles for Mandarin, and the Morrison, Yale, and Lau systems for Cantonese, were used. In mainland China, there have been a number of attempts to simplify the characters, resulting in the current system that is so different from the traditional characters that remain in use in Taiwan, Hong Kong, and other Chinese-speaking communities.

The relationship between the written characters and pronunciation in Chinese is a complex and controversial one. Unlike the Latin alphabet, the Chinese characters do not represent pronunciation in general terms. If a character has a phonetic component, and many characters do not, then that component may give only a clue to the pronunciation of the character. The phonetic component itself is usually a character when used independently; however, its pronunciation when acting as a phonetic component may or may not affect its pronunciation as an independent character. Modern Chinese has many homophones, so the same spoken syllable may be represented by different characters. Cognates are characters with similar meanings represented by similar semantic components but different pronunciations. While children in China are taught that characters are visual representations of meanings, with a fixed template and strict stroke order, the pronunciation of the characters must be learned separately. Children are also taught that there is a standard way of pronouncing each written character, the Putonghua pronunciation, irrespective of how the meaning may be expressed in the spoken form of regional languages and dialects. An essential part of primary education in China is to learn how to write and pronounce written characters in a standardized way. The ability to do so indicates one's educational level. This puts speakers of regional varieties at an immediate disadvantage, as the standard pronunciation is based broadly on Mandarin, though many Mandarin speakers have accents that are quite different from Putonghua.

Many Chinese think that their writing system is exclusive in that it can and has influence(d) other non-Chinese languages, but it cannot and must not be influenced by others. Indeed, there is huge popular resistance to 'foreign invasion' despite the indisputable fact that Chinese, like all other world languages, is a contact language and has always borrowed from other languages. The impact of Manchu, a Tungusic language, on Chinese is well documented (e.g. Hidehiro, 1992; Wadley, 1996), so is the impact of Sanskrit through the translation of Buddhist classics (e.g. Zhu, 1994). The non-Han imperial dynasties that ruled northern China between the 10th and 13th centuries CE—Han being the dominant ethnic group in China—developed scripts including Khitan, Tangut, and Jurchen, and used them alongside Chinese characters. Opponents to foreign influence on Chinese point out that even 'borrowings' must adapt phonologically and morphologically into Chinese norms.

The Chinese take pride in believing that their script is the most complex writing system in the world. Laboratory evidence suggesting that processing Chinese characters involves neural networks that are not normally activated in processing the Latin alphabet (e.g. Tan et al., 2001) is often cited as an indication of Chinese literates' higher intelligence or cognitive advantage. Proponents of the superiority of Chinese also point to the fact that few foreigners, even those who have mastered the spoken form, write the characters fluently or in shapes that would be expected of a Chinese person with a reasonable level of education. The shape of each Chinese character conforms roughly to a square frame, each standing on its own. The components of the characters are further subdivided into strokes, which in turn fall into eight main categories. Children are taught the stroke order in schools in a fairly rigid way, and if an adult is seen to write a Chinese character following the wrong stroke order, they may be ridiculed or dismissed as uneducated.

These and other popular beliefs about the superiority of the Chinese writing system help to elevate its status to something almost sacred in the Chinese people's regard. In our survey of language attitudes and ideologies in various Chinese diasporic communities (Li Wei & Zhu Hua, 2010), many of our interviewees expressed a view that knowledge of the Chinese writing system was essential to Chinese cultural identity, and that overseas-born children of Chinese heritage could not be regarded as 'authentic' or 'proper' Chinese unless they knew how to read and write Chinese characters. In Chinese heritage language schools all over the world, the principal objective seems to be teaching the standard form of Chinese characters.

Sociocultural changes in China and the need for new writing

The last three decades have witnessed unprecedented development in China, with its economy becoming the second largest in the world. The Chinese government is more willing than ever to exercise its economic, political, and military power on the world stage. The promotion of the Chinese language internationally is a crucial part of China's geopolitical strategy. Hundreds of Confucius Institutes and Classrooms, which teach Chinese language and culture, have sprung up. There is a realization that language could play a key role in the relationship between mainland China and Taiwan as well as in strengthening ties with Chinese diasporic communities worldwide. *A Global Chinese Dictionary* (2010) and *A Comprehensive Global Chinese Dictionary* (2016) received unprecedented political support from mainland China, Taiwan, and Singapore, as did the *A Cross-Strait Dictionary of Commonly Used Words* (2012). While the intention of publishing these references was to facilitate communication between people in different Chinese-speaking regions, it also highlights the significant differences between the varieties of Chinese, spoken and written, across different regions and communities.

The government's policies on protecting local cultures, including regional languages and dialects, appear to be at odds with the policy of promoting a uniform standard national language. The Ministry of Culture is investing heavily in art forms that require the use of regional languages and dialects and traditional unsimplified characters. Creating written records of folk operas, songs, and poetry entails the revival of old characters that had been abandoned and the invention of new characters to transcribe regional expressions and dialectal words. This has led to complaints from many teachers, who, under the governance of the Ministry of Education, are tasked to teach only Putonghua and the standard script.

The Chinese government is acutely aware of the fast expansion of social media and the impact of new linguistic creations on the promotion of standard speech and script. The Xinhua News Agency, a ministry-level institution directly reporting to the Communist Party's Central Committee, has been issuing lists of banned words and expressions for the official media annually since 2015. Some banned words are politically sensitive expressions and euphemisms, but most are new creations by social media users that deliberately violate the conventions of standard Chinese characters and mix foreign elements. Such official mandates have had little effect; in fact, they may have pushed social media users to be more creative and critical, as new creations keep emerging and are more inventive than ever. These new linguistic creations pose challenges to authority, to central control, and to cultural and political hegemony.

The use of foreign words and expressions has been considered a particularly rebellious act. Although a written vernacular based on Mandarin Chinese was used in novels in the Ming and Qing dynasties, print literature and official documents were all written in classical Chinese before the early 20th century. After the last emperor was overthrown by the republicans in 1912, a group of intellectuals based at Peking University called for the creation of a new Chinese culture based on what they understood as Western standards. They charged classical Chinese as a barrier to social progress and promoted a new written vernacular known as *Baihuawen*, literally 'plain language writing'. Linguists began to adopt Western theories and models, and vernacular literature blossomed, with many works including transliterations of foreign terms. On 4 May 1919, students in Beijing protested the Paris Peace Conference, which transferred German territorial rights over the Shangdong peninsula to Japan. The New Culture Movement, especially the May the Fourth Movement, is now memorialized as an anti-foreign hegemony movement. Such memorialization glosses over the Movement's original objectives of developing vernacular literature for the common people, putting an end to the patriarchal family and supporting individual freedom and women's liberation, and promoting democratic and egalitarian values and an orientation to the future rather than the past. May the Fourth is now Youth Day in China. Ironically, the Movement saw the beginning of a massive importation of foreign words, expressions, and concepts, including communism, democracy, parliament, etc. Most Movement leaders were fluent in foreign languages and deliberately mixed foreign words and expressions in their speech and writing as a demonstration of their open-mindedness and global outlook.

We see parallels in China today, where people embrace certain aspects of globalization, such as free trade, mass open online technologies, and international tourism and consumption, but also express national pride and anti-foreign sentiments, especially against the United States and Japan. Public discourses concerning language practices are full of contradictions: protecting Chinese against borrowings from foreign languages and promoting it as a global language while investing heavily in foreign language education. For Chinese characters though, the dominant discourse is that they must be kept authentic and standard; foreign borrowings should be minimized and must conform to the shape and form of the Chinese script; and new concepts should be expressed through existing characters rather than through the creation of new ones.

It is against this sociocultural backdrop in China that a new translingual script is emerging. Technological advancement, especially the availability of social media, provides new affordances for tranßcripting. eMarketer estimated in 2017 that over 600 million people in China are regular social media users and usually over 200 million users are online simultaneously: these are the main tranßcripters. Practical challenges facing social media users include the following:

- How can Chinese characters be used to reflect the actual pronunciation/ accent of the language users in social interactions?
- Should social media users choose characters to match their pronunciation/ accent instead of using the standard characters that do not reflect their actual pronunciation/accent?
- How can they create new characters for new concepts, objects, and expressions?
- What are the implications for choosing existing characters?

Chinese linguists and language planners have struggled with these issues for generations. Before examining the solutions of some ordinary Chinese social media users, we will define tranßcripting and explain our analytical approach.

Tranßcripting from a translanguaging perspective

Tranßcripting refers to the linguistic practice of creating a script with elements from different writing systems, such as Chinese and English, or by mixing conventional language scripts with other symbols and signs. The *trans-* part of the term is about transcending, that is, going beyond the conventional scriptal systems, and *-ing* emphasizes the temporal nature, the instantaneity, of the practice. Together, these two parts of the term highlight the simultaneous and continuous engagement with two or more entities. They constrain the normative force of conventional scripts and simultaneously bring out the scripts' creative potential. The *-ing* aspect also gives agency to the scripter while accentuating the process of scripting. Behind each script, there is a person or a community and their life stories that motivate the process of writing the script in a particular way.

We approach tranßcripting from a translanguaging perspective. Translanguaging is a dynamic process whereby multilinguals use multiple linguistic and semiotic resources, including scriptal, digital, and visual resources, as an integrated communication system to mediate complex social and cognitive activities—to act, to know, and to be (Garcia & Li Wei, 2014; Li Wei, 2018). Tranßcripting, then, is a creative and critical act that pushes and breaks the boundaries between the old and the new, the conventional and the novel, and the acceptable and the unacceptable, and challenges received wisdom. Tranßcripting tells the stories of the scripters' social experiences and attitudes.

All the examples below are taken from WeChat, the most popular multipurpose messaging, social media, and mobile payment app in China, which is increasingly used outside China, too. These examples can be found on the Internet, freely accessible to everyone in China. We have selected those that mix elements from different scriptal systems, or language scripts, and other semiotic symbols. The analysis below centers on three types of tranßcripting: Chinese + English, Chinese characters + alphabetic letters, and Chinese characters + numerals.

Chinese + English

Figure 13.1 is a poster that has circulated widely on WeChat. This is a good illustration of the type of tranßcripting that gives common Chinese catchphrases and sayings new twists.

The formula is to use a similar-sounding English word to replace parts of the phrase or saying in Chinese. In the first example from the poster, 无fuck说 (*wu* **fuck** *shuo*), results from deliberately segmenting 无话可说 (*wu* **hua ke** *shuo*, or

FIGURE 13.1 Popular poster with Chinese + English tranßcript.

'have nothing to say') in a non-sensical way: 话可 (huake) = 'speech+can' does not make sense. But this kind of Chinese + English tranßcripting is the most productive formula, with hundreds of phrases appearing online all the time.

Generally, popular, common phrases are tranßcripted, with certain elements replaced by quasi-homophonic words in English. Some of the English words are vulgar, while others are linked to new media technologies. They bring out additional meanings that distort the meanings of the original phrases, giving them a humorous or satirical tone. But there is no apparent pattern as to which element in a phrase will be tranßcripted. And it is precisely this unpredictability of the tranßcripted elements that makes such constructions fun to read. Each expression becomes a story.

It is also difficult to ascertain how stable these phrases become and whether they are used in these forms consistently by the same people. The ones in the poster are widely circulated on social media. But there are many more created spontaneously by multilingual Chinese netizens, including the following:

关你peace (*guan ni* **peace**) = 关你屁事 (*guan ni **pi shi*** 'it's none of your business')
黄焖jimmy饭 (*huang men* **jimmy** *fan*) = 黄焖鸡米饭 (*huang men **ji mi** fan* 'braised chicken with rice')
笑到昏gucci (*xiao dao hun* **gucci**) = 笑到昏过去 (*xiao dao hun **guo qu*** 'laughing too much that one almost faints')
哈哈怎么都coach不清 (*ha ha zen me dou* **coach** *bu qing*) = 哈哈怎么都口齿不清 (*ha ha zen me dou **kou chi** bu qing* '[laughing] why are you speaking with a speech impediment')

Chinese characters + numerals

Another form of tranßcripting is combining traditional characters with numerals. One such example is 老老77 (*laolao qiqi* 'old old seven seven'), which is derived from 老老实实 (*laolao shishi* 'honest' or 'simple-minded'). The numeral 7 is used here to stand for the character实. Their pronunciations are similar, but in southern dialects and accented Mandarin—not standard Putonghua—they rhyme.

There are several other examples in common circulation, including those depicted in Figure 13.2. The first example, 森7 (*senqi*), literally 'forest seven', is 生气 (*shengqi*) or 'angry' tranßcripted. The Chinese character 森 (*sen*) is more complicated than 生 (*sheng*). But its pronunciation is closer to the accent of southern dialect speakers of Mandarin. The second example 亻3表 is shorthand for 三个代表 (The Three Represents), a guiding political theory credited to the former Chinese President, Jiang Zemin. In his speech at the 16th National Congress of the Chinese Communist Party in 2002, Jiang urged the Party to represent 'advanced social productive forces', 'the progressive course of China's advanced culture', and 'the fundamental interests of the majority'. The new character combines the two characters 代表 (*represent*), by having the亻radical on the left, the 表 character on the right, and the numeral 3 in the middle. Finally, 4言,

FIGURE 13.2 Examples of character + numeral invention.

comes from the current Chinese President Xi Jinping's call for more confidence in the Party's continuing legitimacy to govern China against criticism from foreign governments and pressures for political reform. It became known as 四个自信 (four types of self-confidence): 'confidence in our chosen path', 'confidence in our political system', 'confidence in our guiding theories', and 'confidence in our culture'. The character uses the numeral 4 to replace 亻in 信 (belief/confidence), the character and numeral look graphically similar. The pronunciation of 4 is *si*. The semantic radical on the right, 言, has an independent meaning of 'speech' when used alone and is pronounced *yan*. 4 + speech is homophonic to 食言 (*shiyan*) *'eat one's words'*. As we can see, tranßcripting that involves numerals can be used not only for frivolous purposes but also to reflect various 'serious' concepts, such as the critique of ubiquitous political ideologies.

Chinese characters + alphabetic letters

Another form of tranßcripting that involves replacing Chinese characters with alphabetic letters in two-character expressions shows even greater potential for playful language as well as political subversion. For example, P民 (*pì mín*) stands for 屁民 (*pi min*), literally fart people, meaning 'hoi polloi' and often used ironically, to reflect how ordinary people feel about their position in society. Kai子 (*kai zi* 'kai person') or K子, meaning an 'idiot', is a transliteration of a Teochew

FIGURE 13.3 (1) Niubi – awesome; (2) Ta – gender neutral third person singular pronoun.

term, popular in Taiwan and Hong Kong. The first syllable has no standard character and is sometimes written with 凯 or 开, whose Putonghua pronunciation is *kai*. These combinations, and the Chinese-English mixed phrases above, do not challenge the internal organizational principles of Chinese characters themselves—instead, Chinese characters and English words and letters are put side by side.

Other instances are arguably more creative because they combine a Chinese radical and a Latin letter in a single character. One such example is 牛B, which follows the semantic radical plus phonetic radical convention (see first image of Figure 13.3). The left part of the character is an animal radical, derived from the character 牛 (*niu* 'cow'). The right part is the letter B, standing for the Chinese taboo word for female genitalia. The pronunciation of the combined character is *niubi*, which is the pronunciation of the Chinese phrase meaning 'awesome'. While the new Chinese character has its own meaning, it does not have an independent, single-syllable pronunciation. The pronunciation as *niubi*, which is the only way to read it, violates the convention of the pronunciation of Chinese characters insofar as it has two syllables instead of the typical single syllable in a simple consonant-plus-vowel combination.

In another example, 亻A, the left part of this character is the semantic radical for human (see second image of Figure 13.3). The right part is a stylized letter A, and the pronunciation of this character is *ta*, for the third-person singular pronoun 'she', 'he', or 'it'. Standard Chinese characters for the third-person pronoun differentiate between genders, 她 (she) and 他 (he), and between human and non-human, 它 (it), as in English, but they are all pronounced as *ta*. 亻A, is the new, translingual gender-neutral, third-person pronoun in Chinese invented by multilingual Chinese social media users, manipulating the pinyin Romanization of the syllable sound and the character.

While the above example relies on manipulation of pinyin conventions, the first image of Figure 13.4 demonstrates how Chinese scriptal conventions can be unexpectedly adhered to through alphabetic letters. In the case of 尸Y, the character is a combination of 尸 (*shi*, 'corpse') and Y. Y stands for the character

FIGURE 13.4 (1) Shiwai – 'deadly person', euphemistically referring to CY Leung, the former Chief Executive of Hong Kong; (2) Oppose China, Destabilize Hong Kong; (3) Thief/Seller of Hong Kong; (4) Hong Kong independence.

歪 (pronounced *wai*, meaning 'crooked/devious/underhand'). The two-character word 尸歪 is sometimes used by Cantonese and Hokkien speakers to mean a deadly person who is full of intentions to hurt other people. Putting the letter Y underneath the character 尸 conforms to the semantic radical-plus-phonetic-radical formation rule, and it acts as a shorthand for the two-character/syllable word.

Tranßcripting is not merely about frivolous manipulation of language but at times emerges in direct response to serious contemporary sociopolitical issues. During and after the 2014 Umbrella Movement in Hong Kong, a protest triggered by the decision of the Standing Committee of China's National People's Congress to rescind universal suffrage in the 2017 election of Hong Kong's Chief Executive, a number of tranßcripted characters emerged with the English letters HK in them. The second example in Figure 13.4 stands for the phrase, 反中亂港, or 'Oppose China, Destabilize Hong Kong', a phrase that the pro-Beijing camp used to characterize the actions of the protesters. Here, the character 亂 has been tranßcripted with the character 反 (oppose) in the middle of the left-hand radical, the character 中 (middle/Middle Kingdom/China) is on the top right-hand side, and HK is below it.

Conversely, the third example in Figure 13.4 results from an adaptation of 賣港賊, which comes from the Chinese phrase 賣国賊, for traitor, literally 'sell + country + thief', with the middle character 国 (country) being replaced with港 (short for Hong Kong). 賣港賊 thus refers to someone who betrays Hong Kong. The tranßcripted character uses the character for sell (賣) as a radical on the left-hand side and incorporates the letters HK on top of the right-hand radical. The lower part of 賣 (sell) is the same as the left part of 賊 (thief). So the lower part of the tranßcripted character is 賊 (thief). This new character is used in signs targeted at people who are believed to have sold Hong Kong's interests to the Beijing government.

One of the most controversial examples of tranßcripting from the Umbrella Movement derives from 港獨, or 'Hong Kong independence' (see fourth image in Figure 13.4). In the tranßcripted version, the middle part of the right-hand radical 獨 (independence) is replaced by the letters HK. The tranßcripted 'Hong Kong independence' is widely associated with the anti-China political movement.

Playful subversion

The tranßcripted writing we have discussed disrupts the normative patterns and standards of the Chinese writing system, causing turbulence in the Chinese linguistic landscape. Ordinary Chinese netizens are acutely aware of and sensitive to how language has been used to support intensified nationalism, which is occurring in the context of new geopolitics—China's emergence as a new politico-economic world power has been met with hostility from both the United States and neighboring countries in East and Southeast Asia. There is a *de-han*, or de-Sinification, movement in Southeast Asia, particularly in Vietnam. Domestically, there is growing dissatisfaction with the rampant corruption at all levels of governance, resulting in abuse of power and social problems, such as pollution and food insecurity. This is a highly paradoxical situation, not uncommon in postmodern societies, where ordinary citizens are unhappy with what the state provides for them individually, yet are ideologically united in national pride. The tranßcripting phenomenon that emerges in this context is, thus, a running commentary on what is happening in China and provides insight into Chinese people's views of the world.

We can understand the tranßcripted characters as a form of 'playful subversion'. They manipulate the Chinese character formation template, visual representation and iconicity, sound, font, and scriptal system as a source of enjoyment (Crystal, 1998) to do things that conventional writing does not normally do, and to create an 'alternative reality' (Cook, 2000) by bending and breaking prescribed rules. The alternative reality is afforded by new media technologies, such as WeChat.

What results are resistance and subversion that are simultaneously tacit and overt, intimate, and public. They are tacit and intimate because manipulation of the linguistic norm is usually very subtle, and the motivations behind it may be quite personal; each invention tells a specific story and has an author behind the script. But these instances of tranßcripting are also overt and public, as they are shared via social media, and their connotations are usually fairly obvious. Further, they are subversive because they defy distinct and often long-held conventions. We see them as part of what Raessens (2006) describes as the 'ludification of culture', the mocking of authorities, the creation of alternative meanings and realities, the subversion and deception of roles, and the breaking of boundaries through play.

Most of the tranßcripted innovations involve rude or taboo words, pejorative or negative expressions, and euphemisms for politically sensitive issues. For these reasons, the Chinese authorities continue to be watchful. The 2018 list of banned words and expressions issued by the Xinhua News Agency contains tranßcriptal phrases such as 齐B短裙 (short shirt at the length/height of female genitals) and 装13 (showing off pompously and stupidly). Thirteen has a double meaning: it can stand for B referring to female genitalia, or it can be read as a Shanghai slang term referring to someone who thinks there are 13 hours on a clock face (implying stupidity). The official effort to censor tranßcripting seems to affirm its subversive potential. Further, tranßcripting represents the translinguistic resourcefulness of ordinary people in their everyday social interactions, which in turn challenges top-down control over language use.

Conclusion

The tranßcripting discussed in this chapter is only part of a larger translanguaging movement in China, including new Chinglish, net Chinese, regionalism, meme, the use of emoji, etc. (e.g. Lee, 2015a, 2015b; Li Wei, 2016; Wong, Tsang, & Lok, 2017). More innovations are appearing all the time. As we conclude this chapter, we consider an interesting recent case of tranßcripting. Kris Wu, a Chinese hip hop artist, actor, and model, born in the Cantonese-speaking city of Guangzhou, educated partly in Canada, and a former member of the South Korean pop band EXO, became the producer and a celebrity judge of the Rap of China TV show in 2017. His mixing of English words and phrases with Chinese became his trademark, and many memes were created online with one of the questions he asked the contestants: '你有freestyle吗? '(Do you have freestyle?). At the launch of the 2018 season of the show, Wu was asked to predict what would become the new buzzword. He said, 'Skr skr skr skr skr skr skr skrrrr', a sound that rappers often make in their performances. According to various online sources, *skr* represents the sound a car makes when it skids and has come to mean 'get off quickly'. It is also used as a reaction to bad ideas and suggestions, loosely an alternative to a facepalm emoji. Wu went on to use *skr* frequently during the show to refer to someone he regarded as talented or skillful, as in: 'His flow is *skr*! His break between the bars is *skr skr*!' In addition to adopting *skr* in their own daily interactions, Chinese social media users began mixing it with Chinese characters in common phrases, similar to the examples discussed earlier in the chapter, and splitting it into two syllables, and thereby manipulating the sound to make it homophonic with certain Chinese words:

skr 杀book辱 = 士可杀不可辱 (**shike** sha **buke** ru 'a scholar prefers death to humiliation')

笑skr人 = 笑死个人 (xiao **sige** ren 'deadly funny')

你s不skr以点个赞? = 你是不是可以点个赞? (ni **shibushi ke**yi diange zan? 'Are you able to "like" it?'—as in clicking on the 'like' icon)

In July 2018, someone posted a video to the popular sports website Hupu of an allegedly un-autotuned recording of Wu's singing. His female fans launched an online attack against the website, which in turn led to strongly worded responses from the predominantly male sports-loving followers of Hupu. A huge number of posts were circulated within a short period of time, with all sorts of rumors about Wu's private life. Another meme made fun of the scenario with a picture of Wu coming out of an airport. The caption says, 让我看看s哪skr在制造谣言 (rang wo kankan **s na skr** zai zhizao yaoyan 'Let me see who's making rumours'), in which 是哪个儿 (*shi nager* 'is who') has been tranßcripted as s哪skr (*s na skr*). As one comment underneath the meme on the website says, 'This is so funny. I bet it's true'. But telling the truth is not the point; subverting the truth on multiple levels and in multiple directions is. That is what playful subversion is all about, and it is the essence of tranßcripting.

Acknowledgements

We acknowledge the support from Arts and Humanities Research Council (AHRC) of UK for the grant AH/L007096/1 'Translation and translanguaging' which enabled us to undertake the analysis that is presented in this chapter. We are extremely grateful for the insightful comments by Jerry Won Lee and Sender Dovchin, which helped to improve the quality of the chapter significantly. The writing of the chapter benefited enormously from exchanges with Gao Yihong and Tong King Lee; the latter encouraged us to create the term tranßcripting. We are also grateful to Alfred Tsang, Zhu Tianqi and Chen Tiancheng for providing some of the examples that are discussed in this chapter.

References

Bauer, R. (2018). Cantonese as written language in Hong Kong. *Global Chinese*, *4*(1), 103–142.

Cook, G. (2000). *Language play, language learning.* Oxford, UK: Oxford University Press.

Crystal, D. (1998). *Language play.* London, UK: Penguin.

Dovchin, S. (2017). The ordinariness of youth linguascapes in Mongolia. *International Journal of Multilingualism*, *14*(2), 144–159.

García, O., & Li Wei. (2014). *Translanguaging: Language, bilingualism and education.* Basingstoke, UK: Palgrave.

Hidehiro, O. (1992). Mandarin, a language of the Manchus: How Altaic? *Aetas Manjurica*, *3*(2), 165–187.

Lee, T. K. (2015a). *Experimental Chinese literature.* Boston, MA: Brill.

Lee, T. K. (2015b). Translanguaging and visuality. *Applied Linguistics Review*, *6*(4), 441–465.

Li Wei. (2016). New Chinglish and the post-multilingualism challenge. *Journal of English as a Lingua Franca*, *5*(1), 1–25.

Li Wei. (2018). Translanguaging as a practical theory of language. *Applied Linguistics*, *39*(1), 9–30.

Li Wei & Zhu Hua. (2010). Voices from the diaspora: Changing hierarchies and dynamics of Chinese multilingualism. *International Journal of the Sociology of Language*, *205*, 155–171.

Raessens, J. (2006). Playful identities or the ludification of culture. *Games and Culture*, *1*, 52–57.

Snow, D., & Chen, N. (2015). Missionaries and written Chaoshanese. *Global Chinese*, *1*(1), 5–26.Snow, D., Shen, S., & Zhou, X. (2018). A short history of written Wu, Part II: Written Shanghainese. *Global Chinese*, *4*(2), 217–246.

Snow, D., Zhou, X., & Shen, S. (2018). A short history of written Wu, Part I. *Global Chinese*, *4*(1), 143–166.

Tan, L. H., Liu, H. L., Perfetti, C. A., Spinks, J. A., Fox, P. T., & Gao, J. H. (2001). The neural system underlying Chinese logograph reading. *Neuroimage, 13*(5), 836–846.

Wadley, S. A. (1996). Altaic influences on Beijing dialect: The Manchu case. *Journal of the American Oriental Society, 116*(1), 99–104.

Wong, N., Tsang, A., & Lok, P. (2017). *KONGISH DAILY: Laugh L Die. Old news is still exciting, and perhaps educative.* Hong Kong, China: Siu Ming Creation.

Zhu, Q. (1994). Some linguistic evidence for early cultural exchange between China and India. *Sino-Platonic Papers*, no. 66, University of Pennsylvania.

14

TRANSMULTILINGUALISM

A remix on translingual communication

Shanleigh Roux and Quentin Williams

Introduction

This chapter introduces the notion of transmultilingualism to expand the rhetorics and remit of translingual communication research. Our concern will be to discuss some of the central ideas in translinguistics (Part II) to account for the extraordinary ordinariness of multilingual forms and functions that are creatively *remixed* (Williams, 2017) by multilingual speakers in online and offline contexts; in particular, we consider how multilingual speakers embody transmultilingual communication. To illustrate what we mean by transmultilingualism, we report (in Part III) on a virtual ethnographic case study (following Hine, 2000) conducted by the first author of an online health and body campaign aimed at young South African women. We analyze how transmultilingual performance and interaction are accomplished through the remixing of multilingual resources, forms, and functions. We conclude with some suggested avenues for further research on transmultilingual communication.

Wicky, wicky, remix! Translingual communication as transmultilingualism

Recent research into the sociolinguistics of globalization has expanded its theoretical vocabulary and methodologies, as we have come to account more accurately for the messy dynamics of multilingual communication, local translingual communicative practices and intersections with popular culture, the performance of agency and voice, and linguistic diversity (Blommaert, 2010; Pennycook, 2007; Williams, 2017). Today there exists an array of concepts, nomenclatures, and meta-theoretical riffs. As it is now well known, the world we live in is normatively defined by global linguistic flows and unequal multilingual frictions (Alim, Ibrahim, & Pennycook, 2009; Appadurai 1996; Tsing, 2005);

this is a world that reveals not only the mundane and creative linguistic strategies of multilingual speakers but also the unequal ways multilingual speakers access linguistic and non-linguistic resources in online and offline spaces. But this is also a world defined by translingualism, those mundane and creative communications linked to the (re)imagination of identities, personae, and voice.

For some time now, translinguistics research has advanced our understanding of the problematics of named languages; the variability in linguistic repertoires and styles; the significance of new forms of communication; and the importance of place, space, and scale as tied to identity politics (building on Coupland, 2010). In Pennycook (2010), for example, an emphasis on the local practice of language shows that individuals rely not necessarily on named languages to navigate local objectives, but on the combined use of linguistic resources to perform communication. Further, studies on metrolingualism illustrate that where multilingual speakers anticipate embodied interactions, they rely heavily on their linguistic and spatial resources to successfully communicate (Pennycook & Otsuji, 2015). This is the unique linguistic algorithm of translingual communication.

As Dovchin, Pennycook, and Sultana (2018) suggest, translingual communication practices are not static nor can they be stratified; such practices have histories that continue to be defined by colonialism, global technologies, capitalism, and the nativism of nation-states. At the same time, as Dovchin (2019) recently implied, multilingual speakers with a translingual repertoire are continuously engaged in communication defined by 'complex linguistic practices that move beyond their cultural boundaries to form manifold communicative aims, agencies, identities, desires and lexes' (2019, p. 86; see also Lee, 2017, 2019).

In this chapter, our contribution to expanding research on translingual communication is to suggest a closer study of the 'remixing'[1] of multilingual communication practices across online and offline contexts (e.g., Williams, 2016, 2017), captured in the notion of transmultilingualism. Williams (2016) demonstrates this particular transcendence in the communication of young multilingual speakers engaged in the insertion of speech forms created in an offline context and brought to Facebook as a communicative resource. Williams illustrates not only the speed at which multilingual contact takes place in the online world but also the novelty in translinguistic variation that results from multilingual speakers creatively using forms and functions across contexts.

By transmultilingualism we mean to highlight the manifold ways in which multilingual speakers stylize their translingual communication through the mixture of embodied regimes, popular cultural discourses, and translinguistic resources. Transmultilingualism suggests a sociocultural approach to communication as the most relevant route to take if we are to go beyond language, the injurious effects of colonial language classifications, and the top-down assigning of functions to language. As such, transmultilingualism goes beyond the horizontal and vertical stratifications of multilingualism and focuses on the embodiment of multilingualism as a resource remixed in everyday communication and as a performance stylized in public and private spatial interactions, encounters, and behaviors.

The metaphor of remixing, we argue, contributes powerfully to the rhetorics of translinguistics; it helps us understand how the blurring between what is local and global (linguistically) brings us close to rethinking a new sociolinguistics that will standardize the vocabulary to describe the qualitative norms of multilingual communication today (Aronin & Singleton, 2008, p. 4). On the one hand, a remixed approach considers the stretching of global genres to hitherto unexplored localities in the global South (and ignored contexts in the global North) as well as how multilingual speakers revisit and reinvent local meanings and values of multilingual communication. As Williams (2017) puts it, to remix multilingualism 'is to engage in the linguistic act of using, combining and manipulating multilingual forms and functions tied to histories, cultural acts and identities to create new ways of doing multilingualism' (2017, p. 1; see also Alim, 2009, p. 115; Alim, Ibrahim, & Pennycook, 2009).

On the other hand, a remixing approach helps us to highlight further, and more specifically, the embodiment of multilingualism. First, the remixing of multilingualism as embodied is important because it brings into focus the scale and variability of various regimes of embodiment. Young multilingual speakers draw on embodied practices as a resource feature in their multilingual communication, and they do so from both online and offline contexts (and often at the same time in a given stretch of communication). Second, the embodiment of multilingualism, coupled with the use of speech forms from popular cultural practices such as Hip Hop, holds significant implications for how we understand and study multilingual contact situations and the expansion (or shrinkage) of multilingual repertoires in translingual ecologies (Canagarajah, 2013). Considered this way, remixing, the central defining tenet of transmultilingualism, is an approach to translingual communication that allows us to analyze multilingual speakers' creative efforts to embody their multilingual communication.

In the following, the data analyzed will illustrate how transmultilingualism emerges through the multilingual creativity of speakers as they stylize transmultilingual forms and function from their multilingual repertoires, picked up as a result of the embodied flows of multilingualism, cultures, and mixtures (Pennycook, 2007, p. 122; see also Alim, 2009, p. 7). The notion of stylization is useful here in that it allows us to demonstrate how multilingual speakers who perform transmultilingual communication do so in 'highly stylized' (Coupland, 2009) ways, and these performances 'tend to be among the most memorable, repeatable, reflexively accessible forms of discourse' (Bauman, 2005, p. 149). As such, our stylization analysis will reveal the dynamics of embodied practices and the scripts multilingual speakers follow when they use targeted speech forms and functions to manage and organize performances and interactions.

Vagina Varsity: a case study in transmultilingualism

In October 2016, Libresse, an international feminine hygiene brand, launched the Vagina Varsity campaign in South Africa as part of an effort to educate women about their bodies, with a specific focus on teaching about the vagina and menstruation.[2] The campaign aimed to counteract the marginalization of women's bodies by spreading a positive message of empowerment. The online campaign, developed by a psychosexual consultant and a well-known film-maker, was introduced like a university course. Professional marketers and educators designed the campaign for the larger South African public as well as for private participation where women could learn about everyday vaginal care (Makhele, 2016).

Like a typical university course, participants are introduced to the course content, outline, the specific lessons to watch, the various levels of difficulty in the assessment (from basic to advanced), and levels of sensitivity to the topic. The course begins with the conveners, Nwabisa and Thembe (well-known South African YouTube personalities) teaching the basic terminology of female genitalia, such as 'labia' and 'vulva', and it then advances toward more specific scientific topics, such as how to talk about different types of sexually transmitted infections (STIs) and different contraceptives. To fully participate in the campaign, online users sign up for a 4-week course, which is set up on a Monday-to-Friday schedule. For 4 days, users receive lessons via email, and on the 5th day, a quiz (see Table 14.1 for a breakdown of all 16 lessons).

The first author collected the data as part of her dissertation project, following the tenets and principles of virtual ethnographic research. She registered and logged on to the website to participate in the Vagina Varsity course, officially joining the course on 17 October 2016. She accessed the website regularly and for a period of 28 days received five emails per week, four of which contained video links. The links took her to a YouTube webpage, and there she watched the lesson received for the day and participated in an assessment at the end of

TABLE 14.1 Vagina Varsity timetable titles and video titles

Lesson	Timetable title (public)	Video title (private subscribers only)
1	Meet your vulva	Say hey to your va-jay
2	The outside bits	My bits, my bits, my lovely lady bits
3	The inside bits	Step inside my crib
4	Periods & pads	That time of the month
5	Hygiene	Let's keep it clean
6	Discharge	Honourable discharge
7	When to see the doctor	Call a doctor!
8	Underwear & cameltoe	Be careful of the camel
9	The gynae	Going to the gynae
10	The hymen	All that hymen hype
11	Growing a baby	Where do babies actually come from
12	Contraception	Preventing pregnancy
13	Sexually transmitted infections	Better safe than sorry
14	Decorating down there	What to wear, down there
15	Sexy time	Sexy time
16	All vaginas are amazing	All vaginas are amazing

the lesson. She archived and transcribed all the videos and proceeded to code transmultilingual practices.

Table 14.1 provides a contrasting, transmultilingual portrait of the various audiences the Libresse company targets through the course. The lesson titles that are promoted to the public differ significantly from the video titles given to subscribers in private. The lesson titles for the public are scientifically direct and descriptive, and they rely on scientific literacy and a named language, such as English, to be interpreted correctly. In contrast, the video titles given to subscribers in private suggest a transition from standard scientific jargon to a stylization of transmultilingualism via popular cultural discourses, multilingual practices, and Hip Hop music. For example, the video title 'My bits, my bits, my lovely lady bits' (Lesson 2) references the pop song 'My humps' by the Black Eyed Peas; the title 'Step inside my crib' (Lesson 3), to the American MTV show 'Cribs'; and the title 'Sexy time' (Lesson 15) alludes to the popularized sayings of the comically awkward character Borat Sagdiyev, played by Sacha Baron Cohen. Although all the lessons, on the surface, are in a variety of English, this use of English demonstrates the complex process through which transmultilingual communication is embodied.

Stylizing the transmultilingual female body

Nwabisa and Thembe teach the Vagina Varsity content. Both speak a variety of South African English, and throughout the course, they stylize their multilingualism at the phonological, lexical, and grammatical levels. They remix English accents, exaggerate Black South African English accents to challenge racial myths, and add for good measure African American English and Hip Hop language. All of these target styles are in their linguistic repertoires. For example, in Lesson 2, Thembe and Nwabisa use the word *labia*, which they pronounce as [labɪa] in a South African English accent. Though the standard pronunciation of labia is [leɪbɪə] or [læbɪə], the use of the /a/ vowel sound instead of /eɪ/ or /æ/ shows that not only are they aware of the variation in African Englishes, such as South African English, but that they pronounce words in a locally distinctive African English. Other examples show the stylization of linguistic forms from African American English, such as copula deletion (Nwabisa: 'Tomorrow **we** Ø **taking** a tour of my crib', Lesson 1) and contractions (Thembe: 'Also called the taint, because **it ain't** your anus and **it ain't** your vagina').

The presenters also stylize certain words and sentences away from an exaggerated Black South African English accent as a way to challenge (implicitly) racist language used often in South Africa by speakers to mock the accent of Black South African English speakers. For example, in Lesson 2, Thembe pronounces the word *girl*, typically pronounced by both White South African English (WSAE) speakers and aspirant WSAE speakers as [gɜːl], as *gal* [gæl] by inserting the open low (unrounded) front short vowel /æ/ between the velar voiced plosive /g/ and the lateral liquid /l/. Her use of *gal* as opposed to *girl* is a non-racial linguistic strategy that indicates her effort to perform a local form of black South Africa English as the target style instead of WSAE.

Another instance of the exaggerated Black South African accent occurs in Lesson 12, which deals with pregnancy prevention. Thembe lists abstinence as one method of preventing pregnancy. Interestingly, she pronounces the word /abstɪnəns/ as /abstɪneːns/. Here the length (apart from tone) of the pronunciation is very prominent because the use of the non-existent English phoneme */eː/ is the result of the influence of Nguni languages, such as isiXhosa and isiZulu, where length usually plays a major role. Length affects accuracy in pronunciation so that some syllables are lengthened almost naturally by the speaker in polysyllabic words. For this reason, a non-existent */eː/ is lengthened even though it does not exist in English. In Nguni languages, length is sometimes used for emphasis and exaggeration.

Throughout the course, the presenters refer to Hip Hop culture and often stylize their performance through African American English or Hip Hop language. For example, in Lesson 2, Nwabisa and Thembe describe the different parts of the vagina. As they take turns to explain, Nwabisa, struggling to express the scientific word perineum that describes a vaginal opening, subsequently performs a Hip Hop gesture when she remembered how to pronounce the word. This gesture, 'brush your shoulders off', was popularized in 2003 by African American rapper Jay Z with his song 'Dirt off your shoulder'. The presenters stylize their transmultilingual communication by embodying a Hip Hop gesture, which aired multimodally on television, developed as a multimodal genre and on-stage performance text (or genre), and became a transmodal cultural phenomenon. With the increase in technology and social media usage today, the transmodal and transtexutal fusion of the embodied Hip Hop gestures are now regularly observable and used normatively by speakers like Nwabisa and Thembe.

These remixes of language forms and accents at the lexico-syntactic level provide a translinguistic window onto the micro-level stylization of transmultilingual communication. An analysis of the video transcripts suggests that the enmeshing of historically marginalized speech forms (Black South African English, Nguni language lexemes) and the stylization of popular cultural speech forms, such as African American English and Hip Hop language, reveal not only the sociocultural structure of transmultilingual communication but the rich multilingual repertoires of the presenters.

Participants who sign up for the Vagina Varsity course are taken through a journey, from not having much knowledge about the female anatomy to becoming unofficial 'experts'. The Vagina Varsity slogan, 'The more you know, the less you fear', demonstrates that the producers of the course believe that acquiring knowledge will increase women's social power. Thus, the presenters take their participants through a journey toward becoming comfortable with the topic of vaginas, and they achieve this not only through the embodiment of transmultilingualism but through known, gendered references.

What follows is an analysis of the first two lessons of the Vagina Varsity course: 'Say hey to your va jay-jay' and 'My bits, my bits, my lovely lady bits'. Both these videos focus specifically on the popular description and stylization of the female anatomy, expressed first through euphemisms and then followed by the correct term(s). In the first lesson, Nwabisa and Thembe introduce themselves and what the course is about.

In Table 14.2, from turn 5, Nwabisa is unable or unwilling to say the word vagina. She states, 'We can definitely be using the words Vag Minaj, Va jay-jay, Down There', reassuring the viewers, and her co-presenter (in on the script), that they can use those popularized euphemisms. From a transmodal perspective, she is resemiotizing (Iedema, 2003) the name of the female African American rapper, Nicki Minaj, remixed with the popular euphemism Va Jay-Jay and the words Down There to outline what those euphemisms are. From a transmultilingual structural perspective, Nwabisa pronounces the African American English 'there' as [ðer]), which consists of the dental voiced fricative /ð/, the close mid-front short vowel /e/, and the alveolar approximant /ɹ/. This pronunciation contrasts with the standard American English pronunciation [ðɛː], which consists of the dental voiced fricative /ð/ and the open mid-front unrounded vowel /ɛː/.

Throughout the interaction, Thembe is the presenter who stylizes her words employing the rhotic /r/, which is typically found in American English, instead

TABLE 14.2 Lesson 1 – 'Say hey to your va-jay'

1.	Nwabisa:	Hi guys, my name is Nwabisa.
2.	Thembe:	And I'm Thembe.
3.	Nwabisa:	With the help of experts, we're here to host you at Vagina Varsity.
4.	Thembe:	Did you know that more than half of women lack the basic understanding of their female genitalia? But don't worry. That's why we're here. The next four weeks, we're going to be talking everything vagina-related.
5.	Nwabisa:	We can definitely be using the words Vag Minaj, Va jay-jay, Down There.
6.	Thembe:	Uh, no. We're going use the correct terms, because things like euphemisms: cookie, flower, enough. We need to know the correct terms so we know what we talk about.
7.	Nwabisa:	That's fine for you, but I can guarantee you that there are ladies out there, even men, even me, who are uncomfortable talking about this stuff.
8.	Thembe:	We're gonna get to a place where we can talk about our vaginas same way we talk about our hands, our feet, and do you know what's great? We're gonna get to a point where we're empowered. We get to talk health and pleasure.
9.	Nwabisa:	Tomorrow, we taking a tour of my crib, so you might wanna take a mirror, get familiar with your lady parts.
10.	Thembe:	When she says 'a tour of her crib', she means a tour of the vulva. We're gonna be talking vulva and vagina kind of interchangeably. We're at your cervix.

of the non-rhotic /r/, which is common in South African and African American English. She does this to correct her mispronunciation of the scientific terms under discussion but also to put forward a less popularized and more scientific persona. For example, in line 6, she reassures the viewers that she disagrees with Nwabisa's popular euphemisms and that instead, 'We're going use the correct terms, because things like euphemisms: cookie, flower, enough. We need to know the correct terms so we know what we talk about'. A transmodal link is made with the appearance of images of a cookie and a flower when Thembe mentions those words. The images add to the ridiculousness of describing a vagina with those words.

The interactions between Nwabisa and Thembe mimic typical interactions between young multilingual speakers today, with opposing personalities, values, and tastes in popular culture music. This becomes apparent when Thembe corrects Nwabisa for her use of euphemisms. It also becomes clear that the aim of the course is not only to learn the correct terms but also to become comfortable with using them. In this particular lesson, Nwabisa and Thembe play two different roles: one who is embarrassed about talking about the vagina (Nwabisa) and one who is unashamed (Thembe). The characters are, therefore, relatable to a larger audience with varying levels of knowledge and comfort about the topic.

Toward the end of Lesson 1, Nwabisa informs viewers what they can expect in the following lesson. She states, 'Tomorrow, we taking a tour of my crib, so you might wanna take a mirror, get familiar with your lady parts' (turn 9). Nwabisa says 'we Ø taking a tour of my crib' instead of 'we are taking…', stylizing copula deletion, a feature of African American English. Thembe shakes her head, which shows that she does not agree with what Nwabisa is saying. Nwabisa uses the word 'crib' (meaning house) as a euphemism for the word 'vagina'. The word 'crib', while a reference to MTV's Cribs, Thembe explains that Nwabisa is actually referring to the 'vulva' (turn 10). Another very common euphemism used here is 'lady parts', which is considered a playful euphemism. Interestingly, 'lady parts' is not recognized by Thembe as a euphemism. She only focuses on the euphemism 'crib'.

In Lesson 2, Nwabisa and Thembe go through the different parts of the vagina and what they are called (Table 14.3). Nwabisa is once again relying on euphemisms while Thembe gives the correct words. As they reference the parts of the vagina, a cartoon illustration pops into the video as an extra layer of representation, helping the participants to learn the content transmodally.

In this extract, the first body part the presenters refer to and define is the mons venus, which Nwabisa describes as the 'space at the top there, which has the pubic hairs' (Lesson 2, turn 2). They proceed to talk about the labia. Nwabisa calls the labia the 'entrance gates' (Lesson 2, turn 6) because she sees it as the entrance of the vagina. After that, she refers to it by a different euphemism, 'the lips' (Lesson 2, turn 6), another common female body part. In fact, Thembe uses this euphemism to teach the participant the correct term.

When they move on to discuss the internal clitoris, Nwabisa uses euphemisms such as 'doorknob' and 'Peeping Tom' (Lesson 2, turn 8). Her use of these

TABLE 14.3 Lesson 2 – 'My bits, my bits, my lovely lady bits'

1.	Thembe:	So, remember in the last episode, she said that she would use a mirror to 'visit her crib'? Did you do it?
2.	Nwabisa:	I did. I hope you guys did too. Because I mean, I saw some stuff. There's a space at the top there, which has the pubic hairs. Uhm it's called the =
3.	Thembe & Nwabisa:	mons venus
4.	Nwabisa:	I knew that.
5.	Thembe:	So that's a mound of skin that's above the pubic bone.
6.	Nwabisa:	What about the entrance gates? The—the lips?
7.	Thembe:	So those are separated into two parts. You have the external lips, the labia majora and then you have the internal lips which are called the labia minora.
8.	Nwabisa:	Your labia isn't supposed to be symmetrical. Uneven, pink, or brown, wrinkly, or smooth, tucked in, poked out. I mean, your labia is beautiful, so stop stressing. Then I know that there's like the doorknob, the B and the P, you know? The peeping Tom.
9.	Thembe:	Please, again. This is the internal clitoris. The internal clitoris is shaped like a wishbone. And get this, it approximately has 8000 nerve endings, which is twice as many as the head of a penis, and its sole purpose is pleasure.
10.	Nwabisa:	Then we move further down. Uh, the urethra opening. It's pretty much where we pee from, right?
11.	Thembe:	Right.
12.	Nwabisa:	Then below that is the vagina opening.
13.	Thembe:	Okay! Okay gal.
14.	Nwabisa:	I know this one. Uhm, the perineum. That's the skin between, or the space between the vaginal opening and you anus. I mean.
15.	Thembe:	Also called the taint, 'cause it ain't your anus and it ain't your vagina.
16.	Nwabisa:	You have got to stop.
17.	Thembe:	Okay. The next other thing is the fourchette. The part where your vulva ends.
18.	Nwabisa:	Fourchette.
19.	Thembe:	It's fine.
20.	Nwabisa:	Wow.
21.	Thembe:	Those are the most important things you need to know about your vagina, vulva, you know. So stay tuned for more Vagina =
22.	Nwabisa:	Varsity.

demonstrates that people use many euphemisms for this particular body part. A doorknob is a round door handle which opens the door once it is turned, while Peeping Tom is a nickname for a male voyeur, based on the legend of a man named Tom who was struck blind after peeping through a hole in his shutters to see a woman, Lady Godiva, riding naked on a horse through the streets of Coventry, England. Similar to her African American English pronunciation of the word 'there' in Lesson 1, Nwabisa stylizes the words *doorknob* and *Tom* in a similar

English accent. In WSAE, the word *doorknob* is typically pronounced as [dɔːnɒb], with a non-rhotic /r/ and the open back rounded vowel /ɒ/, but in this lesson, Nwabisa pronounces this word as [dɔːrnɒːb], with a rhotic /r/ and open back unrounded long vowel /ɑː/. While perhaps not as significant, the name Tom, typically pronounced in South Africa as [tɒm] with the open back rounded vowel /ɒ/, is pronounced by Nwabisa as [tɑːm], with the open back unrounded long vowel /ɑː/. This provides further evidence of the remixing of local forms and functions and an indication that the presenters' linguistic repertoires have developed a local form of transmultilingualism that are not only defined by translocal accents (e.g. African American English) but by phonological and lexico-grammatical forms remixed with South African Englishes, Nguni languages (found throughout the data), and popular culture such as Hip Hop.

Conclusion

We have attempted to introduce and apply the notion of transmultilingualism as our contribution to translinguistics. Our case study analysis elaborates on a Southern concept of multilingualism, on the one hand, and illustrates the notion as an embodied form, on the other hand. This embodiment of multilingualism, as we have illustrated, remixes multilingual resources, forms, and functions. Inspired by work on translingual communication, our notion of remix builds on a definition of multilingualism as non-static and stratified to develop a conception of transmultilingualism as fluid and messy, and as having an inherent structure despite superficial indications otherwise.

The stylized multilingualism by Nwabisa and Thembe during the Vagina Varsity campaign is a case of transmultilingual communication. Our analysis demonstrates that, although most of the content delivered by the conveners of the course is in English, it is not necessarily achieved in a strict binary sense. The remixing of popular speech forms, non-standard English, and various accents characterize the type of transmultilingual communication stylized throughout the Vagina Varsity course. By stylizing multilingualism in this way, the conveners appeal to young multilingual speakers in the country who, one could safely assume these days, are almost always involved in one or another type of popular cultural discourse and transmultilingual practice.

Apart from the linguistics and stylization of multilingualism, our analysis also indicates that the embodiment of transmultilingualism is achieved through, in this online context, transmodal and transtextual engagement (what Dovchin, Pennycook, & Sultana, 2018 would refer to as transglossia). In the videos, the presenters use particular gestures (as in the case of 'Dirt off your shoulder') to teach and reinforce different terms and concepts (see, for example, Lesson 2); this instruction is remixed with overlays of visual modes, such as cartoon images, writing styles, colors, and the strategic use of sounds and music.

But why should we care about this type of remixing? And why is the type of embodied multilingualism described here important? The immediate and perhaps long-term effects of the type of embodiment described above suggest the importance of not only feminist discourses that feed into the remixing of multilingualism but also our attempt as researchers to attend to the subtle and explicit ways in which the agency and voices of women remain unequally distributed across place and space. Remixing as a perspective on translingual communication is useful because it provides the rhetoric for a deeper analysis and argument of multilingual communication in our globalized world today.

The analysis, then, implies the need for further research on transmultilingual communication. We briefly point out three foci that could be central to advancing this notion for translinguistics:

1. We have explicitly defined transmultilingual communication as an embodied practice. As such, if we are to develop the focus on the body (as the data analysis has also illustrated), we need to pay attention to corporeal regimes and the intersection of such regimes across contexts. In other words, we have to pay attention to how transmultilingual practices highlight those social, political structures of power that box in the body;
2. The potential of transmultilingual communication brings attention to the difficulty of racialized agency and voice experienced by multilingual speakers in an increasingly unequal world (see Dovchin, 2019); and
3. To continue to capture the creative predilections of multilingual speakers, it is important that we pay attention to the logics of transmultilinguistic practice to further understand how what is created becomes an enduring feature of translinguistic communicative behavior.

Acknowledgements

We would like thank VLIR-UOS for providing the funding towards the research collected and analyzed, and the National Research Foundation (NRF) for providing funding towards the authoring of this chapter.

Notes

1   Our notion of remix finds inspiration in the work of Pennycook (2007) and Alim (2004).
2   The campaign can be accessed here: www.vaginavarsity.co.za.

References

Alim, H. S. (2004). *You know my Steez: An ethnographic and sociolinguistic study of styleshifting in a Black American speech community.* Durham, NC: Duke University Press.

Alim, H. S. (2009). Translocal style communities: Hip Hop youth as cultural theorists of style, language, and globalization. *Pragmatics, 19*(1): 103–127.

Alim, H.S., Ibrahim, A., & Pennycook, A. (Eds.) (2009). *Global linguistic flows: Hip Hop cultures, youth identities, and the politics of language.* London, UK: Routledge.

Appadurai, A. (1996). *Modernity at large: Cultural dimensions of globalization*. Minneapolis: University of Minnesota Press.

Aronin, L., & Singleton, D. (2008). Multilingualism as a new linguistic dispensation. *International Journal of Multilingualism, 5*(1): 1–16.

Bauman, R. (2005). Commentary: Indirect indexicality, identity, performance, dialogic observations. *Journal of Linguistic Anthropology, 15*(1): 145–150.

Blommaert, J. (2010). *A sociolinguistics of globalization*. Cambridge, UK: Cambridge University Press.

Canagarajah, S. (2013). *Translingual practice: Global Englishes and cosmopolitan relations*. New York, NY: Routledge.

Coupland, M. (2009). *Style: Language variation and identity*. Cambridge, UK: Cambridge University Press.

Coupland, N. (Ed.) (2010). *The handbook of language and globalization*. Oxford, NJ: Wiley-Blackwell.

Dovchin, S. (2019). The politics of injustice in translingualism: Linguistic discrimination. In T. Barrett & S. Dovchin (Eds.), *Critical inquiries in the sociolinguistics of globaliztion* (pp. 84–101). Clevedon, UK: Multilingual Matters.

Dovchin, S., Pennycook, A., & Sultana, S. (2018). *Popular culture, voice and linguistic diversity: Young adults on- and offline*. Basingstoke, UK: Palgrave MacMillan.

Hine, C. (2000). *Virtual ethnography*. London, UK: Sage.

Iedema, R. (2003). Multimodality, resemiotization: Extending the analysis of discourse as multi-semiotic practice. *Visual Communication, 2*(1), 29–57.

Lee, J. W. (2017). *The politics of translingualism: After Englishes*. New York, NY: Routledge.

Lee, J. W. (2019). Translingualism as resistance against what and for whom? In T. Barrett & S. Dovchin (Eds.), *Critical inquiries in the sociolinguistics of globaliztion* (pp. 102–118). Clevedon, UK: Multilingual Matters.

Makhele, T. (2016). *SA launches world's first Vagina Varsity*. Retrieved November 30, 2016, from https://citizen.co.za/lifestyle/fitness-and-health-your-life-your-life/1328824/sa-launches-worlds-first-vagina-varsity/

Pennycook, A. (2007). *Global Englishes and transcultural flows*. London, UK: Routledge.

Pennycook, A. (2010). *Language as a local practice*. London, UK: Routledge.

Pennycook, A , & Otsuji, E. (2015). *Metrolingualism*. London, UK: Routledge.

Tsing, A. L. (2005). *Friction: An ethnography of global connection*. Princeton, NJ: Princeton University Press.

Williams, Q. (2016). Youth multilingualism in South Africa's Hip-Hop culture: A metapragmatic analysis. *Sociolinguistic Studies, 10*(1): 109–133.

Williams, Q. (2017). *Remix multilingualism: Hip Hop, ethnography and the performance of marginalized voice*. London, UK: Bloomsbury Press.

15

'BAD HOMBRES', 'ALOHA SNACKBAR', AND 'LE CUCK'

Mock translanguaging and the production of whiteness

Catherine Tebaldi

During the 2016 US presidential campaign Donald Trump combined multiple linguistic registers and repertoires, from Mock Spanish (Hill, 1998) to dog whistles, and blank verse to Twitter (Blommaert, 2017). His speeches describe 'bad hombres', while his Twitter asserts he 'loves Hispanics'—purportedly a self-evident truth because 'The best taco bowls are made in Trump Tower Grill'. In his indexical chains (Hanks, 1992; in Hill, 2009), 'bad hombres' stood in for descriptions of migrants as rapists, behind a discussion of tacos echoed in Iowa Congressman Steve King's description of Mexicans as drug dealers with 'calves the size of cantaloupes'. Each of these tropes became part of a use of Spanish that is not fluent, but fluidly used to construct images of the migrant-as-servant and migrant-as-threat. Soon afterwards, 'bad hombres' began to stand in for the whole 'tough on immigration' discourse; it became a tag on white nationalist[1] forums, highlighting scare stories on immigration. 'Bad hombres' multiplied on the nastier corners of the Internet.

Although Trump is known for his use of Mock Spanish, in this chapter, I explore how a right wing pro-Trump online forum uses Mock Spanish, French, and Arabic. In keeping with this volume's focus on ordinary translanguaging, I explore how the use of multiple linguistic repertoires and semiotic resources are so ordinary that they even appear on the xenophobic US far right. Bringing together Mock Spanish (Hill, 1998) and transglossia (Dovchin, Pennycook, & Sultana, 2018), I ask how multiple and transgressive linguistic repertoires are used by the right to construct whiteness as ordinariness. I argue that translanguaging can be used in norm-enforcing, as well as norm-challenging, ways, depending less on which languages are spoken than on which differences, histories, or ideologies are given voice. Here, I look at the role of translanguage in right populist discourses, an 'everyday language of white nationalism'.

I ask what we can learn by applying the idea of language crossing borders to those in the US in favor of 'building a wall' between the US and Mexico border to curtail migration. White nationalists do translanguage; they use multiple linguistic repertoires, fluid and shifting linguistic meanings, not to construct fluid, transnational identities, but in a populist language that naturalizes nationalistic whiteness. Right populism frequently uses the language of the left with the goals of the right, discursively mobilizing fear to construct a pure people in opposition to a hated Other and a corrupt elite (Judis, 2016; Wodak, 2015). Online, far-right affective discourses proliferate (Simpson & Druxes, 2015; Wodak, 2015). The languages of ethnocultural Others are transformed into Mock speech and used to demonize migrants, satirize multilingual global elites, and produce popular whiteness as both desirable and ordinary.

In this chapter, I apply a transglossic lens not to migrants and other language minoritized populations in the United States but to those who want to keep them out. Translanguaging is emerging as a way for white nationalists to produce a white English, less a language of border crossing than for reinforcing the borders of language and culture. Bringing together literature on translanguaging and Mock Language, I explore how translingual practices are mobilized in examples from an online forum for American white nationalists. I argue that everyday white nationalists use multiple semiotic resources to construct a populist discourse of American whiteness. I end with implications for future research in the hope that, with a fuller understanding of the language of the right, we may be able to counter their ideological positions.

Translanguaging and Mock language

Translanguaging, the fluid use of multiple linguistic and semiotic resources, is described as a border crossing, deterritorializing use of language (Jacquemet, 2005). Often focused on multilingual and migrant speakers, especially in education (García, 2009), research explores how translanguaging blurs borders between languages and creates a transnational identity (Tetreault, 2015) through linguistic hybridity and carnivalesque, sometimes transgressive, word play (Martínez & Morales, 2014; Sultana, 2015). Such practices have been understood as challenging standard language ideologies and nationalism (Heller, 2008) and ultimately the idea of language itself (Makoni & Pennycook, 2005). All share an idea of a deterritorializing language, building nomadic identities along lines of flight (Deleuze & Guattari, 1988).

Deleuze and Parnet (1977) note that extraordinary words should be put to ordinary use. Likewise, translanguaging can be found in small, everyday practices. Recent work challenges the necessity of multiple official languages, exploring how varied and truncated repertoires (Blommaert, 2010) are used for community, play, and identity building (Tetreault, 2015). Dovchin (2015) extends this to youth online and argues that translanguaging incorporates popular culture and subtextual ideology as well as official language. Sultana (2015) highlights the transgressive potential of these multiple voices. Transglossia (Dovchin, Pennycook, & Sultana, 2018) brings translanguaging's linguistic fluidity together with heteroglossia's historicity and mulivocality. Transglossia foregrounds the ideological, political, and transgressive aspects of translanguaging, which I draw on to understand how white nationalists voice the Other.

While translanguaging has generally been promoted as a positive development in sociolinguistics, in voicing alterity, translanguage itself is also reterritorializing speech that reifies norms and hierarchies. Hill's work on Mock Spanish (1998) and *The Everyday Language of White Racism* (2009) demonstrates how dominant groups use stigmatized language varieties to directly index their own casual superiority and indirectly index demeaning stereotypes. Users create Mock Spanish to convey a casual cosmopolitan identity, while through hyperanglicization, semantic pejoration, and intertextual consistency portray Spanish and its speakers as comical, lazy, and dirty. Additional research has explored how Mock Ebonics (Ronkin & Karn, 1999) and slang or transgressive speech reproduces vertical racialized and gendered ideologies (Bucholtz, 1999, 2011).

Mock language can be understood as a form of translanguaging because, despite categorical distinctions such as 'Mock Spanish' or 'Mock Arabic', they blur the distinction between English and other languages. This is evident, for instance, in examples such as 'bad hombres' not only because of the mixing of English ('bad') and Spanish ('hombres') but, more significantly, because the expression has become fully enregistered as a derogatory term in the US national imaginary that one need not know Spanish to deploy it. As such, 'bad hombres', as a form of Mock Spanish, is neither English nor Spanish (on the challenges to categorizing fluid language practice, see Pennycook, 2010). In this sense, Mock language is reterritorializing, showing how multiple languages can create white space (Hill, 1998) and repeat white racial hierarchies (Barrett, 2006; Bucholtz, 2011) using language to create demeaning figures of alterity (Hastings & Manning, 2004). The online right is using multiple codes as part of a broader transgressive, transglossic creation of white normative ordinariness.

Methods

White nationalism thrives on social media (Nagle, 2017). In this chapter, I focus on the use of translanguaging in an online discussion forum devoted to supporters of Trump. It is recognized as a key intersection of rightist discourses: a forum where multiple far right communities, from white supremacists to men's rights activists, come together in white nationalism. The forum uses transglossia and transgression, combining the subtext ideologies of white and male supremacy. Posts can be tagged to indicate their topic; posts about criminals, for instance, are tagged 'bad hombres'.

Beginning with 'Bad Hombres', recursive searches of these posts were used to obtain linguistic data. Following an initial keyword search for 'Bad Hombres', it was noticed that it was a clickable tag or 'flair' on many posts about immigrant criminality. Upon using this to search for every post where 'bad hombres' was tagged, several instances of Mock French were also discovered. Tracing the use of French to look up each of the keywords that were discovered, terms such as 'le cuck' and 'bon jour' were found. This led to a subsequent discovery of Mock Arabic: 'aloha snackbar', 'Mohammed', and 'kebab'. The most recent or most liked posts appear first. Posts are archived and searchable.

'Bad hombres' say 'aloha snackbar'

The contributors to the forum use Mock language to name dangerous Others; Mock Arabic and Mock Spanish, along with sexual humor, construct figures of alterity. Two key terms dominated: 'Aloha Snackbar' and 'Bad Hombres'. 'Bad Hombres' is Mock Spanish, the consistently pejorative use of Spanish to denigrate its speakers. Here, in headlines and in tags, echoes of Trump's 'Spanish' index a multitude of imagined dangerous Others: immigrants, criminals, and terrorists. 'Bad Hombres' is used in both user posts and the forum's tags to refer to posts about migrants, terrorists, and criminal Others. Spanish indirectly indexes migrants, and in context is always linked to discussions of criminality. Multiple 'bad hombre' posts, available by search or a simple click on the tag 'Bad Hombres', creates an unofficial list of crimes committed by migrants, consistently linking the two. 'Bad Hombre' is used to title a post that linked to a news article about an immigrant who committed multiple murders. Other uses of 'bad hombre' escalate the threat, for instance, in posts about terrorist infiltrating migrant caravans: 'BAD HOMBRE! Eureka Univision Exposes Terrorist infiltrator in Migrant Caravan'. Occasionally, 'bad hombres' no longer indirectly indexes immigrants, but does so directly. One user posted 'a wall will keep bad hombre voters out', revealing that in this group all migrants are bad hombres.

'Aloha snackbar' is Mock Arabic, a hyperanglicization of 'Allah Akbar'. It indexes terrorism, either as a Mock version of 'Allah Akbar', as a noun referring to terrorist attacks, and as an adjective referring to terrorists; 'Aloha snackbar' has become enregistered to indirectly refer not only to terrorist attacks as in the noun 'an aloha snackbar' but an adjective to describe Muslims as terrorists and barbarians with childish language (and kebabs). Aloha snackbar is the keyword for Islamophobia. It was linked not only to terrorist attacks but to rape, violence against women, and child marriage: criminal images of the Muslim Other (Tiktin, 2011). One post highlights the connection between terrorism, multiple attacks on women, and Muslim immigrants using 'aloha snackbar' to refer to a migrant presumed to be Muslim and violent. It also accompanies caricatures of Muslim men as hypersexual, bestial, with child brides (see Puar, 2007). These discussions also refer to longstanding rape myths about white womanhood under threat and current uses of women to reinforce nationalism and Islamophobia (Farris, 2017).

That this term does not simply refer to terrorism but serves as a link to terrorism is shown in dubious jokes about the former US President Barack Obama. In one such instance, 'Aloha snackbar' is used to refer to the myths that Obama was a Muslim, a key element of the Othering that accompanied negative reactions on the far-right to a black president. In addition to 'aloha snackbar', Mock language on the forum uses several images of food to suggest the endangerment of cultural purity. Britain's multicultural cities are described as the 'Kebab Archipelago'. Posts titled 'kebab shop' are linked to piles of trash. Mock Spanish is used to describe Mexican food as dirty or nauseating as in: 'No quiero taco bell. Taco bell es muy nauseabundo'. In another post, a US website calls on British media to bring a scare story about a presumably Muslim killer serving up the women of the working class in a kebab shop. A food associated with Muslims becomes dangerous and impure while Muslims are imagined as killing women, enabled by politicians who ignore the forgotten white working class.

Users do not restrict themselves to one code but use multiple forms of Mock language and figures of alterity. 'Bad hombre' titles and tags accompany images of violence and articles about 'Aloha snackbar' and terrorism. These form indexical chains linking Mexicans to Moroccans, migrants to terrorists, and difference to corruption. The populist right voices an imagined Other as social pollution and sexual perversion. Mixing multiple repertoires to create Mock speech, their wordplay echoes populist discourses of fear and exclusion (Wodak, 2015).

'Le cuck' says 'bonjour'

Central to the language of right populism or white nationalism online is the construction of the voice of the global elite. Mock French frequently borrows French morphology like 'le', anglicized misrepresentation of French pronunciation, and the use of token French words. In many instances, 'le' indexes Frenchness, similar to the addition of '-o' in Mock Spanish. The most common example is 'Le cuck', which is the Mock French version of cuck (fr. *cocu*), the common alt right apocope for cuckold. According to the white nationalists and right populists of this site, social changes such as multiculturalism and immigration are the result of a nefarious global elite who are destroying white culture: too weak, too evil, or too deluded to stop the flow of immigration. On the forum, Mock French is habitually used to ironically voice 'le cuck', the upper class, globalist, effeminate, racially conscious man who lets his country be invaded by Mohammed the migrant terrorist. In one instance, 'Cuck' refers to French president Emmanuel Macron, whose victory over Marine Le Pen (less than his actual immigration policy) has made him a figure of contempt on the US far-right.

One image on the forum shows bot, or automated, use of Mock French, and visual signifiers of French nationalism: Le Pen is liberty leading the people. This was one of several images that brought Pepe, the green anthropomorphic frog and symbol of the alt right, and Trump together with images of the French Revolution or resistance. In this instance, Pepe, with Trump's trademark hairstyle, is shown as part of the French resistance, or at the center of the French flag, resulting in a visual transglossia.

Contributors use token French words such as 'bonjour', as in 'Do They Really Want Paristan? BON JOUR, MOHAMMED... PLEASE INVADE AND DESTROY OUR COUNTRY. WTF????' and phrases, especially 'vive le' and as used in 'vive le pen,' but also to voice the 'cuck' globalist Macron. Many call him 'Macaroon', which is both French and effeminizing. One poster called him 'Macaroni': 'vive le caliphate'! A longer example of the voice of Macron made the gendering of this language and elite more explicit; the poster states that perhaps we should just let Paris become 'Paristan', while declaring in the voice of Macron, 'Oh, bonjour! Je suis petite de fille. Au revior!' Accompanied by a visual of Macron on a bicycle, Mock French is used to show him saying he is a little girl who is incapable of combating terrorism and immigration. In all of these examples, Mock language is used to depict a leader who is ceding to invading migrants, linking to cultural representations of the French as effeminate cultural elites, weak and prone to let Paris become 'Paristan'.

A longer exchange illustrates more clearly how multiple Mock languages are used on the right to represent global elites, nefarious Others, and whiteness under threat. In this exchange, the poster makes a translingual joke that 'Allah Akbar' is a French phrase that means 'refugees welcome'. This wordplay uses both translation and previous community repertoires of Mock French and Mock Arabic. It implies that France has already been taken over by Islam by using Mock Arabic as interchangeable with Mock French to show this takeover. The multiple levels of Mock language are more sophisticated than the racial ideology it is showing. This Mock translation is reflective of what the right perceives as elite leftist failure to understand the link between immigration and terrorism.

Commenters respond below the original post with more translingual practices, including Mock Arabic, such as 'Aloha Snackbar', referring to terrorism as murder in the name of food trucks. Others use a similar Mock translation to suggest that the translation of 'Allah Akbar' is 'Satanism'. Other posters in their fake translations suggest terrorists would use Mock French ('we in ze pants monsieur'), suggesting that French is terminally linked to weakness in the form of incontinence. They blend not only Mock French, Arabic, and English but combine translanguage with transgression, voicing the terrorist with 'my knife is in thy ass', which has elements of religious registers in 'thy' as well as homophobic vulgarities about anal penetration that also index effeminate weakness. While the ideas are retrograde, the mix of registers and languages is complex, moving from sex to religion, snacks to Satanism.

Translanguaging patriots

In addition to voicing the racialized Other through Mock Spanish or Arabic, and voicing the global elite as effeminate and weak, the forum's participants use multiple registers to construct their own identities. They employ a normative ideology in posts about English Only that constructs them as the cultural center, as well as hagiographic language about themselves; their president is the GEOTUS, or God Emperor of the United States, and their posts are tagged 'America First' and 'super elite'. The forum is a hypermasculine space characterized by images of trucks, soldiers, and, of course, the president. This forum cultivates an image of white masculinity and strength considered flexibly superior to both racial Other and global elite.

Multiple semiotic resources are used to show users' authentic, earthy masculinity. Forum participants produce a normative, unfiltered, masculinity through vernacular speech like 'y'all', along with embodied metaphors, coding posts as 'salty tears' referring to liberals as quick to cry over political issues, and 'spicy' to refer to shocking truths or transgressive humor. The uptake of visual symbols of masculinity is shown in the front page results, which users have upvoted. They frequently include glamorous shots of Trump, and large photos of soldiers or of guns tagged 'Sunday Gunday'. One post uses image play, references to Normandy, and 'Sunday Gunday' to position users as World War II soldiers.

Male dominance is also produced by mocking women, liberals, and 'cucks'. Binder and Wood (2012) note that, in the provocative political style, discourses of gender difference are also used to show the insanity of the left. Besides images of Melania Trump, the only photos of women to be featured on the front page are gross caricatures of female politicians, trans women in jokes about gender debinarization, or unflattering images of women in 'this is what a Feminist looks like' shirts. Many of the posts take a stand as the tellers of truth and tellers of jokes against politically correct liberals too weak to take either.

Despite the language play and multiple forms of Mock speech, image play, and transgressive humor, the explicit language ideology of the forum is, of course, English Only. Many link English Only with Trump's policy of America First (itself an echo of earlier KKK slogans, a particularly ghoulish transglossia). In other posts, 'English Only' is accompanied either by images of Trump or tagged with his slogan, 'MAGA', or 'Make America Great Again'. In some posts, multiple users laud Trump and suggest that promoting English is self-evident. In one post, an image references the recent deletion of the Spanish-language webpage for the White House, complemented by a Mock Spanish inversion of Obama's slogan, '¡No, No Puede'! instead of 'Yes, We Can'! in a translingual and multimodal statement of why English Only is connected to political participation and power.

One post perhaps best represents the language ideologies of the forum's participants. They use 'FUCKING CUCKS', sexual, and transgressive language to complain about a loss of traditional values as indicated by a popular US chain steakhouse not offering 'merry Christmas' gift cards in English but only in 'Mexican'. This post blends two right culture war discourses, the purported 'war' on Christmas and English Only, mixing xenophobia with resentment politics. The poster refers to 'Merry Christmas gift cards' rather than 'holiday gift cards', explicitly asserting the right to say 'merry Christmas' while counteracting the alternative of 'happy holidays'. For white nationalists, the popularization of the religiously inclusive 'happy holidays' epitomizes what they perceive to be an emerging anti-Christian agenda in the United States. Indeed, by pairing 'Merry Christmas' with 'cuck', the user suggests the liberal media and mediocre steak restaurants see these as equivalent slurs. Finally, the author says 'Mexican' instead of 'Spanish', a semantic pejoration whose vivid (and deliberate) ignorance positions him as a 'real American' mobilizing resentment politics to suggest he is experiencing, not calling for, cultural exclusion. On the front page of the forum they advocate one language, but use multiple semiotic resources calling for Pepe and GEOTUS Trump to storm the beaches with racism, culture wars, resentment politics, and transgressive language.

Discussion

Linguistic fluidity, while generally characterized in the scholarship as representative of the language practices of marginalized speech communities, is so ordinary and ubiquitous that even white nationalists do it. Applying a transglossic framework to the users of the forum shows how their Mock language, as a form of translanguaging, circulates in the social and ideological subtext of populist discourse. In this case, multiple and multimodal forms of Mock language are used to move between racism and sexism, and between affective populist discourses (Wodak, 2015); these represent discourses of fearful exclusion and discourses of transgressive enjoyment.

More than Mock language, this is Mock translanguaging. It blends multiple forms of Mock language—French, Spanish, and Arabic—with openly racist and sexist expression. While Hill's (1998, 2009) work focuses on indirect racism, these groups perform overt racism with more transgressive speech. Further, while Hill focuses on Mock Spanish, here multiple registers form a Mock translanguage that fluidly blends with other kinds of transgressive, racist, sexualized speech, and images to construct populist identities and joyously violent affects. The conservative so-called 'silent majority' actually uses multiple languages at the service of creating populist identities and discourses. Similar to the dialectical premises that a pure American can only be made through opposition to an impure Other, that the American soldier needs an enemy, or that the forgotten individual only makes sense with an evil elite, Mock language practices perform the exclusionary ethos of the US far-right. Mock Spanish and Mock Arabic are blended together to create a language of the dangerous, dirty, and hypersexual Other through discourses that suggest both fear and transgressive pleasure. Mock French voices the elite as a feminine 'cuck' who has ceded to globalization, mocking the opposition with carnivalesque enjoyment. Mock language defines through exclusion, and brings humor and play into discourses of resentment and fear.

The use of multiple forms of Mock language allows the users of this forum to position themselves as both 'winners' above the migrant Other and as 'patriots' more authentic and purer than the global elite. In this way, the multiple discourses follow Judis's (2016) discussion of right populism as tripartite, a middle class (or marginal part of the elite) defining itself as the true people, against both the corrupt elites and the corrupting Others. Mock language, with its multiple, ostensibly humorously deployed codes, also represents the Others' transgression and corruption, Spanish infecting and Arabic attacking. Mock French shows elites who are not more intellectual, but who have ceded nationalistic interests to the forces of globalization.

In this forum translanguage reterritorializes. Deleuze and Guattari (1988) describe reterritorialization as the renewal of a familiar refrain, a simple melody, and one that reinforces the known rather than challenging strata, binaries, hierarchies. Here, creative language also reproduces traditional values and white identities. Language like 'cuck' does not challenge any boundaries but is used at the service of traditional ideas of white masculinity and white male dominance. Fluid language does not challenge borders, but reproduces them—and calls for figurative and literal walls.

Mock Spanish produces white space (Hill, 1998); online this is repeated hundreds of times over in calls for a white nation. In this space, world languages index not transnational identities but weak elites who oppose the common people, or dangerous Others who have come to corrupt them. The racial indexicality is no longer indirect, and other languages become slurs: 'le cuck', 'bad hombre', 'aloha snackbar'. Because translanguage is frequently associated with racial Others or elites, it simultaneously reinforces the idea that English Only indexes whites only. Fluid language is used to draw boundaries around Americanness, building a wall that suggests authenticity and ordinariness are synonymous with whiteness.

Conclusion

If populism is the language of the left for the purposes of the right, future research could explore more closely how the language of superdiversity, hybridity, and globalization is being used by those who oppose it. We might ask how nationalist ideals circulate online across borders, or how complexity and diversity are mobilized as harbingers of social decline, and what chronotopes are evoked with 'Make America Great Again'. In particular, more research is needed that applies transglossic frameworks that see popular culture within their social, political, and ideological contexts to better understand how individuals engage with rightist ideas online. The right uses popular culture, affect, and carnivalesque play; understanding the language of the online right is a step toward imagining a future that is more linguistically and socially inclusive.

Note

1 Terms for online white supremacist groups are varied; I refer to the ideology as white nationalism and their discourse as right populism.

References

Barrett, R. (2006). Language ideology and racial inequality: Competing functions of Spanish in an Anglo-owned Mexican restaurant. *Language in Society, 35*(2), 163–204.

Binder, A. J., & Wood, K. (2012). *Becoming right: How campuses shape young conservatives.* Princeton, NJ: Princeton University Press.

Blommaert, J. (2010). *The sociolinguistics of globalization.* Cambridge, UK: Cambridge University Press.

Blommaert, J. (2017). Society through the lens of language: A new look at social groups and integration. *Tilburg Papers in Cultural Studies, 178,* 1–26.

Bucholtz, M. (1999). You da man: Narrating the racial other in the production of white masculinity. *Journal of Sociolinguistics, 3*(4), 443–460.

Bucholtz, M. (2011). 'It's different for guys': Gendered narratives of racial conflict among white California youth. *Discourse & Society, 22*(4), 385–402.

Deleuze, G., & Guattari, F. (1988). *A thousand plateaus: Capitalism and schizophrenia.* London, UK: Bloomsbury.

Deleuze, G., & Parnet, C. (1977). *Dialogues.* Paris, France: Flammarion, 49.

Dovchin, S. (2015). Language, multiple authenticities and social media: The online language practices of university students in Mongolia. *Journal of Sociolinguistics, 19*(4), 437–459.

Dovchin, S., Pennycook, A., & Sultana, S. (2018). *Popular culture, voice and linguistic diversity.* Cham, Switzerland: Palgrave Macmillan.

Farris, S. R. (2017). *In the name of women's rights: The rise of femonationalism.* Durham, NC: Duke University Press.

García, O. (2009). *Bilingual education the 21st century.* Oxford, UK: Blackwell.

Hanks, W. F. (1992). The indexical ground of deictic reference. In A. Duranti & C. Goodwin (Eds.), *Rethinking context: Language as an interactive phenomenon* (pp. 43–76). Cambridge, UK: Cambridge University Press.

Hastings, A., & Manning, P. (2004). Introduction: Acts of alterity. *Language & Communication, 24*(4), 291–311.

Heller, M. (2008). Language and the nation-state: Challenges to sociolinguistic theory and practice. *Journal of Sociolinguistics, 12*(4), 504–524.

Hill, J. H. (1998). Language, race, and white public space. *American Anthropologist, 100*(3), 680–689.

Hill, J. H. (2009). *The everyday language of white racism.* Oxford, UK: Wiley.

Jacquemet, M. (2005). Transidiomatic practices: Language and power in the age of globalization. *Language & Communication, 25*(3), 257–277.

Judis, J. B. (2016). *The populist explosion: How the great recession transformed American and European politics.* New York, NY: Columbia Global Reports.

Makoni, S., & Pennycook, A. (2005). Disinventing and (re) constituting languages. *Critical Inquiry in Language Studies: An International Journal, 2*(3), 137–156.

Martínez, R. A., & Morales, P. Z. (2014). ¿Puras groserías?: Rethinking the role of profanity and graphic humor in Latin@ students' bilingual wordplay. *Anthropology & Education Quarterly, 45*(4), 337–354.

Nagle, A. (2017). *Kill all normies: Online culture wars from 4chan and Tumblr to Trump and the alt-right.* Alresford, UK: Zero Books.

Pennycook, A. (2010). *Language as a local practice.* London, UK: Routledge.

Puar, J. (2007). *Terrorist assemblages: Homonationalism in queer times.* Durham, NC: Duke University Press.

Ronkin, M., & Karn, H. E. (1999). Mock Ebonics: Linguistic racism in parodies of Ebonics on the Internet. *Journal of Sociolinguistics*, *3*(3), 360–380.

Simpson, P. A., & Druxes, H. (2015). *Digital media strategies of the far right in Europe and the United States*. Lanham, MD: Lexington Books.

Sultana, S. (2015). Transglossic language practices: Young adults transgressing language and identity in Bangladesh. *Translation and Translanguaging in Multilingual Contexts*, *1*(2), 202–232.

Tetreault, C. (2015). *Transcultural teens: Performing youth identities in French cités*. Oxford, UK: Wiley.

Tiktin, M. (2011). *Casualties of care: Immigration and the politics of humanitarianism in France*. Berkeley: University of California Press.

Wodak, R. (2015). *The politics of fear: What right-wing populist discourses mean*. Newbury Park, CA: Sage.

16

INVISIBLE AND UBIQUITOUS

Translinguistic practices in metapragmatic discussions in an online English learning community

Rayoung Song

Introduction

Linguistic practices entailing the fluid movement among different semiotic resources have been explored through concepts such as translanguaging (García & Li, 2013), translingualism (Canagarajah, 2013), metrolingualism (Pennycook & Otsuji, 2015), transglossia (Dovchin, Pennycook, & Sultana, 2018; Sultana, Dovchin, & Pennycook, 2015), and linguascape (Dovchin, 2017). In a world that is highly connected through transnational digital networks, online spaces have diversified linguistic codes in communication and have fueled translinguistic practices (e.g. Internet language, emoticons, videos, and memes). Following this reality, researchers have explored language use and linguistic practices in online spaces, with research following two strands: (1) detailing linguistic practices and (2) examining metapragmatic discourse, or explicit comments about language. The research detailing linguistic practices has illustrated the ways that multilinguals employ linguistic and semiotic codes in online spaces (Alimi & Matiki, 2017; Androutsopoulos, 2015; Kulavuz-Onal & Vásquez, 2018; Vazquez-Calvo, 2018) and has investigated how translinguistic practices are employed by multilinguals to perform their transnational, global, and multilingual identities (Black, 2009; Dovchin, 2015; Kim, 2016; McGinnis, Goodstein-Stolzenberg, & Saliani, 2007; Schreiber, 2015).

The research investigating metapragmatic discourse has revealed language ideologies circulating in online spaces (Karimzad & Sibgatullina, 2018; Phyak, 2015; Song, 2019). Such research confirms that emphasizing creative linguistic innovation in online spaces may underplay the fact that this same place can also be constrained by existing linguistic norms and language ideologies (e.g. linguistic purism, monolingual ideologies). In fact, Phyak (2015) reveals how Facebook language policing reproduces homogenous language ideologies rather than embraces fluidity, contrary to previous research. Similarly, Karimzad and Sibgatullina (2018) examine the metapragmatic discourse of practicing 'pure' Tatar and Azerbaijani on social media. They reveal how social media becomes a site for formal language, unlike previous research that found informal language use to be more prevalent in such spaces. Combining these two research trends, I argue that examining language use *within* metapragmatic discourse will offer a more nuanced understanding of translinguistic practices as a form of 'meaningful symbolic behavior' (Blommaert, 2005, p. 2) employed to express one's meaning, identity, positions, and emotions. Examining translinguistic practices within metapragmatic discourse is instructive for two reasons: (1) metacommentary reveals the users' beliefs about *appropriate* language use and (2) the linguistic practices that align with or contradict their beliefs can provide insights into where and why such contradictions arise. In turn, such an examination can unveil users' language ideologies and how they impact their linguistic practices.

The current study examines metacommentary on language in an online English learning community of Korean bloggers. Relying on virtual ethnographic methods, the findings reveal the mundanity of translinguistics despite the Korean bloggers' subscription to monolingual ideologies. Furthermore, the findings suggest why certain practices are acceptable while others are not. The juxtaposition between the metapragmatic discussions of their linguistic use and their actual linguistic practices will not only foreground the normality of translinguistic practices but also reveal the users' reasons for engaging in certain translinguistic practices but not in others.

Exploring language ideologies: practices versus metacommentary

Language ideologies can be broadly defined as shared beliefs, notions, and attitudes about language structure and use through experiences of members of society (Irvine, 1989; Rumsey, 1990; Silverstein, 1992; Woolard, 1992; Woolard & Schieffelin, 1994). There are two main stances on how language ideologies should be observed. Some argue that explicit metalinguistic discussions on language are the most accurate examples of language ideologies, while others maintain that actual linguistic behaviors and practices are more reflective of language ideologies (McGroaty, 2010; Woolard & Schieffelin, 1994). Hence, exploring both sides would allow a more balanced understanding of language ideologies in a given context. I further argue that detailing the linguistic practices *within* metapragmatic discourse will be especially useful in highlighting contradictions and investigating the reasons for such contradictions. A dual-faceted approach will be especially useful for understanding the realities of language ideology in contemporary Korea as they relate to the English language.

Background: English language ideologies in Korea

Park (2009) investigates the English language ideologies in Korean society in the context of Korean media's representation of English and the TOEFL (Test of English as a Foreign Language). He identifies three English language ideologies: necessitation (i.e. viewing English as imperative for economic and political survival in the global era), self-deprecation (i.e. regarding themselves as incompetent speakers of English), and externalization, in which Koreans recognize English as 'a language of an Other' and thus representing a potential betrayal of Korean identity (Park, 2009, p. 26). Other scholars reveal how English is associated with 'middle-class credentials' (Lee, 2016; J. Song, 2010) or a class marker through which some parents can pass on their high socioeconomic status (Lee, 2016). As hinted at in Park's three ideologies, English seems to occupy a contradictory ideological space. Koreans see English as a necessity but simultaneously consider it a threat to the Korean identity. In this light, translinguistic practices employing English are understandably seen as marked behaviors even when translinguistics itself is nothing but ordinary in communication (Dovchin, 2017). Thus, I will examine the metapragmatic discourse on how Korean bloggers in an online English learning community believe language should be used and will reveal how different translinguistic practices are treated in this community.

Methods

This study is the first part of a virtual ethnography that started in 2015. Virtual ethnography embraces the notion of culture being bounded by human relations rather than a geographical location (Hine, 2000). Starting from this approach, I explored the relationships and culture built around an English learning blog initiated by a Korean blogger, Yejin

The site and participants

Yejin is a Korean woman residing in the United States and is a fluent speaker of Korean, English, and Spanish. Yejin began her blog in 2014 on a popular Korean blogging website. She has shared language learning ideas, study tips or materials, and some opinions about her language use and learning. Since 2015, she began organizing virtual study groups with her followers, and her blog became a vibrant English learning community attracting more than 4,500 people by the end of 2017.

Because Yejin hangs her blog on a popular Korean blogging website, which is published almost exclusively in Korean, it is safe to assume that a majority of Yejin's followers are Korean or at least are fluent in Korean. Although most of Yejin's followers live in Korea, there are some who live outside Korea, mostly in one of the English-speaking countries, such as Australia, Canada, and the United States. Even the followers who live in Korea or in non-English-speaking countries often work in an environment where English is frequently used. Lastly, many of the followers seem to have lived in an English-speaking country for a study abroad or have aspirations to live overseas.

Data collection and analysis

This chapter includes the analysis of Yejin's blog data from 2014 to 2017. While explaining discourse-centered online ethnography (DCOE), Androutsopoulos (2008) states that the systematic observation of online sites becomes a basis for a more focused linguistic analysis. Taking this approach, I began observing Yejin's blog site in 2014. At first, this observation started organically, as I was a fellow blogger and language learner myself. Later, I became interested in her blog as a researcher and began my systematic observation in 2015 when she first launched study groups. I visited Yejin's blog whenever there was a new post and visited on subsequent occasions to examine comments from her followers. I took notes of striking posts and interactions as I followed her blog activities. As I started the analysis, I revisited all the striking posts and comments to follow additional comments.

My deep engagement in the community allowed me to notice some patterns of communication by and beliefs of the bloggers. For instance, I noticed that the blog communications often revolved around metapragmatic discussions (Silverstein, 1992) of how language, specifically English and Korean, should be used. I focused on these metacommentary posts, analyzing them by exploring pre-textual history, contextual relations, subtextual meaning, and intertextual echoes (Dovchin, Pennycook, & Sultana, 2018; Pennycook, 2007). For this chapter, I selected three blog posts accentuating the discrepancy between the Korean bloggers' beliefs and their actual linguistic practices. It should be noted that all the posts and comments are written in Korean unless noted otherwise. I translate the Korean texts to English and avoid providing the original Korean posts to protect her identity and respect her participation in my study. The presentation of texts in their original form are limited to instances in which it is necessary for the purposes of presenting visual representation of translinguistic practices.

Findings and discussion

In this section, I will first show the juxtaposition between the Korean bloggers' metacommentary on translinguistics and their actual practices. The contradictions between their beliefs and practices reveal what types of translinguistic practices are considered acceptable and why. In the latter part, I will focus on the reasons for such contradictions.

Acceptable versus unacceptable translinguistic practices

Yejin and her followers often discuss the need to use Korean and English separately to develop both languages in a more balanced manner. In her post titled

'Be Good at Your Own Mother Tongue', Yejin shared her beliefs on language separation and that she tries to avoid mixing English words when speaking or writing Korean. Many followers agreed with Yejin although they also admitted to the practice of translanguaging in their bilingual work environments. Moreover, while agreeing with Yejin, they simultaneously engaged in translinguistic practices themselves. In (1), Commenter 1 writes about mixing English and Korean in her bilingual workplace and offers a commitment to no longer engage in such languaging:

> (1) Commenter: I am commenting because it struck a chord with me ^^; I work at a trading firm, and a majority of my co-workers mix English [when speaking Korean]. [...] I see that it is to show off, so I feel appalled, but I end up imitating them ㅠ because I don't want to lose;; But after reading your post, I made up my mind. I'm not going to mix Korean and English ㅎㅎ[1]

The commenter used emoticons and a cyber onomatopoeia here to be more expressive with her emotions and positions. The first emoticon '^^;' is a face sweating and the second 'ㅠ' is a Korean character sounding *yu*, which is often used to illustrate an eye with tears, reflective of her regret over following her co-workers' language-mixing practices despite her objections. The third emoticon ';;' denotes drops of sweat, which is generally used to express awkwardness or embarrassment. This suggests her embarrassment over her reasoning for mixing English words when speaking Korean, that is, so as '[not] to lose'. The last two letters 'ㅎㅎ' have an *h* sound in Korean and are a short-hand, cyber version of the onomatopoeia to describe sounds of laughs, such as *ha ha* or *he he*. This type of onomatopoeia was popularized as Koreans started using text messages and Internet messengers in their daily lives. This is a very informal way of communication, which can be used to lighten up the mood of the entire message.

Example (1) reflects the belief that mixing cyber language is acceptable while mixing English with Korean is not. The first possible reason for this may be that emoticons and cyber onomatopoeias are regarded as being in the same nationalistically defined linguistic boundary (i.e. Korean). The second reason may be due to the status of these practices. Commenter 1 said she is opposed to English mixing because she believes it is done to 'show off', and this idea is echoed by Yejin in (2). Because English has been regarded as a marker of one's high socioeconomic status in Korea (Lee, 2016), it is considered a linguistic resource to 'show off' one's distinctiveness whereas cyber onomatopoeias and emoticons are available to everyone.

In the post titled 'Complete Rambling', Yejin wrote that she wondered why people mix English words when speaking Korean. After formulating some possible guesses, as shown in (2), she tried mixing Korean and English to understand. Her mixing of Korean and English seems exaggerated, which was pointed out by one of the commenters. This may be an effort to mock Korean speakers who mix

English and Korean. In the subsequent paragraph, Yejin gives up mixing English words and provides an explanation as to why:

> (2) Suddenly, I was curious about the thoughts/intentions/feelings of those who mix Korean and English. Do they want to show off that they know such a difficult word in English? Are they just giving up on thinking about the word in Korean? Or is using an [English] word in their daily life a strategy for remembering a new word they've learned? Because I am curious, I'm going to write the rest of this post mixing Korean and English
> [...]
> I feel I sound obnoxious while writing this. If I speak like this, I might get slapped on the mouth. Let's just not mix languages. Let's speak one language at a time.

This post, which again stresses her strong opposition to translinguistic practices, generated varied responses from other bloggers. Many of them acknowledged again that they do mix English and Korean in their bilingual work environments but admitted regret over this, stating that they should be more careful not to mix. However, Commenter 2 appears ambivalent:

> (3) Commenter 2: In fact, I mix Korean and English when I'm working... Of course all are easy(?) words but I guess this is how it looks... A ㅏ

With her frequent use of ellipses, she seems to be reticent about what she thinks. Moreover, at the end of the comment, she uses a cyber onomatopoeia 'A ㅏ', which is a mixture of English and Korean alphabets. The English 'A' represents the sound *ah*, as does the Korean letter 'ㅏ'. Hence, she wrote 'Ah', which is an onomatopoeia for realization. This is an ambivalent way to express her realization in response to Yejin criticizing the mixing of English and Korean in the original post.

Although Yejin seems highly averse to translinguistic practices, especially mixing Korean and English, she does engage in translinguistic practices quite seamlessly. For example, Yejin always uses a photo to match the content of her post. The picture in Figure 16.1 was used as the background for 'Complete Rambling', where Yejin mocked the translinguistic practices of mixing English and Korean. The photo includes the English words 'SO MANY THOUGHTS YET SO LITTLE WORDS', which matches the title of her post. However, English words in the photo did not seem to be problematic for her despite her objections shown in the post.

Examples (2) and (3) along with Figure 16.1 show the contradiction between the metacommentary that opposes mixing English in Korean and the actual practice of using English. In this case, English mixing seems acceptable because it is used as a visual representation. Though they are strongly opposed to mixing English words in Korean, English words in a photo did not even seem to

FIGURE 16.1 Complete Rambling.

catch their attention. Similarly, the cyber interjection of 'A ㅏ', which is a mixture of English and Korean orthography accentuating visual and sound aspects of language, did not seem to pose a problem.

I have shown that cyber onomatopoeias and emoticons are frequently employed to express the bloggers' emotions. The post titled 'Spelling' and comment (4) explicitly highlight this point:

> (4) I'm not confident in word spacing ㄷㄷㄷ […] I think it is a problem that I rely on it [the spell checker] too much nowㅠㅠ I cannot write without youㅠㅠ
>
> While I was writing about an intermediate level study group, I checked my spelling with the spell checker as usual(.) And it said there was no errors. Wow! I felt so 좌릿좌릿 so I am taxidermizing it as writing on this day of Samil Jeol. But now, the spell checker says that 좌릿좌릿 is not a correct wordㅋㅋㅋㅋ I know, but 짜릿짜릿 cannot fully express my emotion!

In the first line, Yejin uses a string of 'ㄷ', which has a *d* sound, to express her nervousness with word spacing, which is an important feature of the Korean language as two or more words can be combined into one cluster without spacing in between, and there are different rules for cluster spacing. When 'ㄷ' is used repeatedly in a string of two or three, as in (4), it is an informal version of the onomatopoeia '덜덜덜' *dul-dul-dul*, which describes the sound of chattering teeth. This onomatopoeia is often used to express a feeling of nervousness or awe. Furthermore, Yejin uses the emoticons for tears 'ㅠ' to lament her reliance on the spell checker. In the second paragraph, Yejin says that she was excited because she had not made any errors when writing her post. The word that she uses to express her excitement is '좌릿좌릿', which is a *deviated* version of the mimetic word '짜릿짜릿'. The word '짜릿짜릿' describes the sensation of excitement or thrill. While she indicates that the spell checker showed a red underline to signify that '좌릿좌릿' was wrong, Yejin argues that the conventional version, '짜 릿짜릿', could not fully express her emotion and that she had to use the deviated version instead.

Commenter 3 mentions that she also has the same habit:

> (5) Commenter 3: I also check my spelling out of habitㅠㅠㅠ to an extreme extent(☞_☜) […] I also use the [deviated] expressions reflecting my feelings in order to fully express the nuanceㅠㅠㅠㅠㅠㅠㅠ

While acknowledging that she checks her Korean spelling 'to an extreme extent', she further states that if it is an expression to describe her feelings, she would use deviated words even though she knows they are not correct. In this comment, she uses an onomatopoeia 'ㅠㅠㅠ' to signify the sound of a giggle or chuckle and an emoticon '(☞_☜)' to express a face covering its eyes.

The two metapragmatic examples from the post 'Spelling' describe the Korean bloggers' explicitly acknowledging their translinguistic practices despite their efforts to preserve the purity of Korean. On the one hand, both Yejin and Commenter 3 say they strive to use Korean correctly; on the other hand, they acknowledge that sometimes the *standard* Korean could not fully express their emotions. Within these metacommentaries that discuss the limitations of the standard Korean, they still employ onomatopoeias and emoticons to express a variety of emotions in a more enriched way.

The reasons for unacceptable translinguistic practices

The background photo Yejin uses for 'Spelling' may explain why certain translinguistic practices are considered unacceptable. This photo is a screenshot of a news segment featuring an event held on Korean Independence Day in 2016. The event was centered on the Korean national flag and was nationalistically motivated. The screenshot shows the speech of a third grader who argues the importance of knowing how to draw the Korean flag. The caption reads, 'Dear pretty women, isn't it a shame if you don't know how to draw the Korean flag when you can draw your eyelines well'? He is wearing a headband with a Korean national flag.

Her use of this screenshot shows her association with the Korean language, the Korean national flag, and patriotism. It should be noted that her post was written on the day of Samil Jeol, one of the Korean national holidays that commemorates the major resistance movement against colonial Japan that happened on March 1, 1919. Furthermore, Yejin writes that she was writing the post to celebrate that she did not make any spelling mistakes on Samil Jeol. Therefore, she consciously makes an association between writing Korean correctly and Korean nationalism. This is further accentuated through her use of the screenshot featuring the Korean national flag, because, at the end of the post, Yejin wonders why there were not cool designs of the Korean national flag, thus revealing her motive for using the photo of the Korean national flag as the background of the post.

In sum, while Korean bloggers are deeply invested in English language learning, they are equally compelled to use Korean in the correct manner by not mixing English and striving to use the right spelling and word spacing. The background photo for 'Spelling' suggests that this is because they associate the correct use of the Korean language with loyalty to the Korean nation-state. This belief may be explained by *externalization*, one of Park's (2009) English language ideologies, in which closely identifying with English may be seen as a possible betrayal of Korean identity. For Korean bloggers, striving to use Korean 'correctly' becomes more important as it is their way of reconciling the tension that arises from applying themselves to learn English. By striving to use Korean as well as English in the 'correct' manner, not only do they develop their Korean proficiency but they can also maintain allegiance to the Korean language and the nation-state.

Conclusions

The current study investigates translinguistic practices deployed in metapragmatic discussions and examines acceptable and unacceptable translinguistic practices using language ideologies. The seamless deployment of emoticons, cyber onomatopoeias, and photos, while bloggers contend for linguistic purism, reflects the ubiquitousness of translinguistic practices. Furthermore, the juxtaposition between their metacommentary on language and their actual linguistic practices provides a more nuanced understanding of why certain types of translinguistic practices are considered ordinary and acceptable yet others are unacceptable in the Korean context.

In light of the translinguistic practices employed by the Korean bloggers, translinguistics does not just include crossing boundaries among different languages but across different registers, varieties, and semiotic codes, especially in digital environments (Sultana, Dovchin, & Pennycook, 2015). My findings, in particular, foreground the prevalence of nationalistic language ideologies in such environments, despite the scholarly endeavor to break apart the link between nationalism and language. With the current political climate around the globe promoting isolationist and nationalist movements, we have observed aggressions against minority language practices. In South Korea, where its language has been used to claim its unique national identity in the midst of foreign invasions, the discussions on translinguistics have an even further way to go. The nationalistic discourse to promote the purity of Korean, along with the historical discourse that ties learning English to national and individual success, complicates the dynamics of language ideology and linguistic practices even further. In this environment, preserving the purity of the Korean language may have a different meaning with the monolingual ideology circulated in the United States and elsewhere. Hence, further studies need to be done to investigate language ideologies and their impact on linguistic practices in different contexts.

Note

1 Modified versions of (1) and (2) were published in R. Song (2019). Yejin's previously published post included her attempt at mixing.

References

Alimi, M. M., & Matiki, A. J. (2017). Translanguaging in Nigerian and Malawian online newspaper readers' comments. *International Journal of Multilingualism, 14*(2), 202–218.

Androutsopoulos, J. (2008). Potentials and limitations of discourse-centred online ethnography. *Language@Internet, 5*(8).

Androutsopoulos, J. (2015). Networked multilingualism: Some language practices on Facebook and their implications. *International Journal of Bilingualism, 19*(2), 185–205.

Black, R. W. (2009). Online fan fiction, global identities, and imagination. *Research in the Teaching of English, 43*(4), 397–425.

Blommaert, J. (2005). *Discourse: A critical introduction*. Cambridge, UK: Cambridge University Press.

Canagarajah, S. (2013). *Translingual practice: Global Englishes and cosmopolitan relations*. New York, NY: Routledge.

Dovchin, S. (2015). Language, multiple authenticities and social media: The online language practices of university students in Mongolia. *Journal of Sociolinguistics, 19*(4), 437–459.

Dovchin, S. (2017). The ordinariness of youth linguascapes in Mongolia. *International Journal of Multilingualism, 14*(2), 144–159.

Dovchin, S., Pennycook, A., & Sultana, S. (2018). *Popular culture, voice and linguistic diversity: Young adults on- and offline*. London, UK: Palgrave Macmillan.

García, O., & Li Wei. (2013). *Translanguaging: Language, bilingualism and education*. London, UK: Palgrave Macmillan.

Hine, C. (2000). *Virtual ethnography*. Thousand Oaks, CA: SAGE.

Irvine, J. T. (1989). When talk isn't cheap: Language and political economy. *American Ethnologist, 16*(2), 248–267.

Karimzad, F., & Sibgatullina, G. (2018). Replacing 'them' with 'us': Language ideologies and practices of 'purification' on Facebook. *International Multilingual Research Journal, 12*(2), 124–139.

Kim, G. M. (2016). Practicing multilingual identities: Online interactions in a Korean dramas forum. *International Multilingual Research Journal, 10*(4), 254–272.

Kulavuz-Onal, D., & Vásquez, C. (2018). 'Thanks, Shokran, Gracias': Translingual practices in a Facebook group. *Language Learning & Technology, 22*(1), 240–255.

Lee, M. W. (2016). 'Gangnam style' English ideologies: Neoliberalism, class and the parents of early study-abroad students. *International Journal of Bilingual Education and Bilingualism, 16*(1), 35–50.

McGinnis, T., Goodstein-Stolzenberg, A., & Saliani, E. C. (2007). 'indnpride': Online spaces of transnational youth as sites of creative and sophisticated literacy and identity work. *Linguistics and Education*, *18*(3–4), 283–304.

McGroaty, M. E. (2010). Language and ideologies. In N. H. Hornberger & S. L. McKay (Eds.), *Sociolinguistics and language education* (pp. 3–39). Bristol, UK: Multilingual Matters.

Park, J. S. (2009). *The local construction of a global language: Ideologies of English in South Korea*. Berlin, Germany: Walter de Gruyter.

Pennycook, A. (2007). *Global Englishes and transcultural flows*. London, UK: Routledge.

Pennycook, A., & Otsuji, E. (2015). *Metrolingualism: Language in the city*. London, UK: Routledge.

Phyak, P. (2015). (En)Countering language ideologies: Language policing in the ideospace of Facebook. *Language Policy*, *14*(4), 377–395.

Rumsey, A. (1990). Wording, meaning, and linguistic ideology. *American Anthropologist*, *92*(2), 346–361.

Schreiber, B. R. (2015). 'I am what I am': Multilingual identity and digital translanguaging. *Language Learning & Technology*, *19*(3), 69–87.

Silverstein, M. (1992). The uses and utility of ideology: Some reflections. *Pragmatics*, *2*(3), 311–323.

Song, J. (2010). Language ideology and identity in transnational space: Globalization, migration, and bilingualism among Korean families in the USA. *International Journal of Bilingual Education and Bilingualism*, *13*(1), 23–42.

Song, R. (2019). 'This may create a zero-lingual state': Critical examination of language ideologies in an English learning blog. *CALICO Journal*, *36*(1), 59–76.

Sultana, S., Dovchin, S., & Pennycook, A. (2015). Transglossic language practices of young adults in Bangladesh and Mongolia. *International Journal of Multilingualism*, *12*(1), 93–108.

Vazquez-Calvo, B. (2018). The online ecology of literacy and language practices of a gamer. *Educational Technology & Society*, *21*(3), 199–212.

Woolard, K. A. (1992). Language ideology: Issues and approaches. *Pragmatics*, *2*(3), 235–249.

Woolard, K. A., & Schieffelin, B. B. (1994). Language ideology. *Annual Review of Anthropology*, *23*(1), 55–82.

17

ON DOING 'BEING ORDINARY'

Everyday acts of speakers' rights in polylingual families in Ukraine

Alla V. Tovares

Introduction

Recent developments in sociolinguistics have brought to the fore the mobility and complexity of linguistic resources and led to the problematizing and re-examining of 'languages' as neatly classified and distinct phenomena in favor of a more dynamic understanding of speakers' repertoires. Drawing on such fluid, mixed repertoires is identified as 'translanguaging' (García & Li Wei, 2014), 'polylingual languaging' (Jørgensen, 2008), and 'metrolingualism' (Pennycook & Otsuji, 2015), among other terms.

While translingual practices are everyday, ordinary occurrences (Dovchin, 2017; Lee, 2017), monolingual ideologies are still prevalent in many European nation-states, especially in institutional settings (Unger, Kryzanowski, & Wodak, 2014). Such ideologies, with the concomitant notions of 'mother tongues' and 'native speakers', promote the view of language as a static, bounded entity. After the collapse of the Soviet Union, many of its successor states, including Ukraine, took 'a monolingual turn' (Pavlenko, 2008, 2013) and adopted 'one-nation, one-language' policies. As a result, the polylingual speakers in such countries are confronted with state-sponsored monolingual policies and ideologies. In Ukraine, for instance, Ukrainian is the official language of the country, yet many people draw on Russian and a set of stigmatized Russian/Ukrainian mixed varieties collectively known as *surzhyk* on a daily basis. Furthermore, not only Ukrainian but also its 'correct' version is privileged, promoting the state-sponsored monoglot 'standard' (Silverstein, 1996) ideology. While researchers, especially in the West, normalize the translingual practices of everyday speakers, such speakers often face what Dovchin (2018) describes as the 'dark side' of translingualism. Namely, they experience scorn and discrimination for not adhering to monolingual standards. Put differently, polylingual speakers are stigmatized for not being what is considered 'the norm' or 'the ordinary', as defined by the state. In her work on youth rights and identities in Ukraine, Fournier (2012) cites a Ukrainian teacher who reminds her students that they live in 'a normative state' and warns them against the perils of being 'a *bila vorona*, or a white crow among black crows' (p. 42). Thus, as Sacks (1984) suggests, 'being ordinary' requires work, and venturing outside ordinariness has its costs.

This chapter investigates how young adult Ukrainians negotiate their translingual family identities and practices as ordinary against the backdrop of the increasingly monoglot standard ideology in Ukraine. To show how ordinariness is metalinguistically (re)constructed, I mobilize the analytical lens of stance (Du Bois, 2007) in relation to research on the sociolinguistic situation in Ukraine (Ivanova, 2013; Masenko, 2004; Pavlenko, 2011, 2013), metalanguage (Jaworski, Coupland, & Galasínski, 2004), and family as a social category (Bourdieu, 1996). Drawing on a larger dataset that includes ethnographic observations and online data, I analyze four metalinguistic interviews with young Ukrainians who report practicing 'non-accommodating bilingualism' (Bilaniuk, 2005) at home, or when one family member speaks Russian and the other Ukrainian without accommodation. Additionally, all interviewees report using—and utilize during the interviews—*surzhyk*, and two of them—computer professionals—also use English at home and at work. Thus, all participants are steeped in heteroglossic polylanguaging. The analysis shows that because Russian/Ukrainian non-accommodation between family members is often perceived by those outside their families as unusual, the participants take up defensive stances to (re)claim the ordinariness of their families and their linguistic practices, and in so doing engage in private acts of speakers' rights. Furthermore, the monoglot standard ideology is contested by the participants' creative drawing on Russian, Ukrainian, *surzhyk*, and English. Finally, this study demonstrates how metalinguistic interviews can reveal competing linguistic ideologies that circulate in Ukraine.

The language situation in Ukraine: monoglot standard ideology and translingual practices

The language situation in Ukraine remains a thorny topic as it is inextricably linked to the country's sociopolitical history. At different times, Ukraine—or its parts—was under the rule of the Polish-Lithuanian Commonwealth, various imperial powers (Russian, Austro-Hungarian, and Ottoman), and the Soviet Union (Subtelny, 2005), with policies regarding the Ukrainian language ranging from prohibition to development (Pavlenko, 2013). The most recent, Soviet (1917–1991), period started with developing and promoting Ukrainian as part of *korenizatsiya* (nativization) but also witnessed the loss of Ukrainian among ethnic Ukrainians, expansion of Russian, and proliferation of *surzhyk* (Bilaniuk, 2005; Ivanova, 2013; Masenko, 2008). This can be explained that, although *de jure* the USSR guaranteed rights to all national languages, its politics of creating a new blended identity of 'a Soviet person', alongside the state-supported voluntary (for economic opportunities) or involuntary (deportations) migration of peoples, led to the dominance and development of Russian as the *lingua franca* of the Soviet Union and eventually as L1 among its multilingual population (Pavlenko, 2008, 2013). After the demise of the Soviet Union, in a reverse move, many successor states (including Ukraine) took 'a monolingual turn' (Pavlenko, 2008, 2013) and adopted 'one-nation, one-language' policies.

The post-Soviet language situation in Ukraine is often viewed through a post-colonial lens (Masenko, 2004, 2008); however, unlike many African, Asian, and Latin American countries that maintained ex-colonial languages, Ukraine followed a divergent path by disassociating itself from both Russia and the Russian language (Pavlenko, 2013). Yet, with Russians as the largest ethnic minority (17.3%) and about 30% of the population, including ethnic Ukrainians, as Russian speakers, Russian in Ukraine remains widespread, especially in the southeast (Ivanova, 2013). *Surzhyk* is also common but, in contrast to other non-standard hybrid varieties in post-colonial contexts, such as *Tsotsitaal* in South Africa and *Sheng* in Kenya (Nassenstein & Hollington, 2015), is devoid of covert prestige and urban trendiness and instead is linked to rural, unfashionable, and unsophisticated individuals, and, as a result, is stigmatized by all speakers, including those who themselves can be described as *surzhyk*-speaking (Bilaniuk, 2005).

In contrast to their Western counterparts who approach *surzhyk* with objectivity, if not sympathy (Bilaniuk, 2005; Del Gaudio, 2015; Hentschel & Taranenko, 2015), many prominent Ukrainian linguists (Farion, 2013; Masenko, 2008; Serbens'ka, 1994) act as 'agents of the state' (Pavlenko, 2011, p. 53) and promote not only monolingualism but also 'pure' Ukrainian as an attribute of a 'true' Ukrainian identity. For instance, Farion (2013, p. 289) asserts that Ukrainians cannot become free while using a Russified, 'distorted Soviet language' and dedicates a quarter of her book to the language 'norm' by dividing the pages into 'correct' and 'incorrect' columns. Del Gaudio and Tarasenko (2009, p. 327) observe that many Ukrainian academics 'advocate the use of highly normative, to a certain extent "artificial" Ukrainian language, distant from real language praxis'. Such 'purist' language attitudes contribute to linguistic insecurity among many speakers and, ironically, to Russian speakers' maintaining their language out of fear of 'corrupting Ukrainian', as one of my participants observed. Therefore, linguistic non-accommodation—'to speak either Russian or Ukrainian in most contexts, and to receive responses in either language, without the expectations of linguistic accommodation' (Bilaniuk, 2005, p. 35)—is frequent.

The events of the 2013 *Euromaidan Revolution*—when Ukrainian citizens of diverse ethnic and linguistic backgrounds, 'including Russian and Ukrainian speakers with standard and nonstandard speech' (Bilaniuk, 2017, p. 352) confronted the Russian-leaning President Yanukovich to demand European integration—challenged the view that the 'true' national identity is predicated on 'pure' Ukrainian or even Ukrainian *per se*. As one of Kulyk's (2016, p. 96) study participants stated, 'I am a Russian-speaking Ukrainian nationalist'. Furthermore, in the armed conflict in the east, Ukrainian soldiers—many of whom are Russian speakers—defend, and die for, Ukrainian national interests against the Russia-backed separatists. How do young Ukrainians navigate the complexity of the language situation in Ukraine, especially in families whose linguistic practices diverge from the prescriptive monolingual norm? In this regard, metalanguage, or metalinguistic reflexivity, can offer an insight.

Metalanguage and stance, metalanguage as stance

Prior studies (Jaffe, 1999; Jaworski, Coupland, & Galasínski, 2004) show that metalanguage both describes and evaluates languages. Because it offers a window into speakers' understanding 'how language works, what it is usually like, what certain ways of speaking connote and imply, what they *ought* to be like' (Jaworski, Coupland, & Galasínski, 2004, p. 3), metalanguage is of particular interest for researchers seeking to understand how language is perceived, valued, and used by groups and/or individuals. Put differently, 'the social "work" of language' (Jaworski, Coupland, & Galasínski, 2004, p. 3) takes place at the intersection of use and evaluation that includes regulating and breaking social norms. As Coupland and Jaworski (2004) observe, 'the "meta" dimension of language in use points precisely to an *interaction* between socially structured meanings and values for talk and their activation in local contexts under local contingencies' (p. 26). Thus, metalanguage reveals the interplay of larger ideologies and local practices.

The focus on the socially constructed meaning and evaluation connects meta-discourse with stance. In his three-part definition of stance, or stance triangle, Du Bois (2007) notes, 'social actors simultaneously evaluate objects, position subjects (themselves and others), and align with other subjects, with respect to any salient dimension of value in the sociocultural field' (p. 169). For Du Bois (2007), stance-taking is dialogic as it allows stance-takers to converge or diverge in their assessment of the stance object and in so doing create alignment with co-present—and I also suggest with absent—stance subject(s). Like metalanguage, stance is context dependent and can be fully understood only when analyzed in linguistic and sociocultural contexts. Metalanguage is a type of stance family members take when discussing their linguistic practices at the intersection of the public and private.

Family as a private unit of public origin

Bourdieu (1996) highlights the interpenetration of public and private spheres by arguing that public ideas and beliefs are inescapably present in private relationships, including family. Thus, for a family to be viewed as 'ordinary', family members must incorporate societal rules and expectations into their everyday practices, into how they 'do' family, and in this way family is shaped by public institutions.

However, as Holstein and Gubrium (1999) argue, family not only mirrors society, it also constructs it. Family 'is constantly under construction, obtaining its defining characteristics somewhere, somehow, in real time and place, past or present, through interpretive practice' (Holstein & Gubrium 1999, p. 4). Extant work on discourse in monolingual, bilingual, and polylingual families (e.g., King, 2013; Ochs & Taylor, 1992; Palviainen & Bergroth, 2018; Piller, 2002; Tannen, Kendall, & Gordon, 2007) shows how through a detailed linguistic analysis researchers can gain a better understanding of a moment-by-moment construction of individual and joint (linguistic) identities and ideologies. Elsewhere (Tovares, 2007, 2012), I demonstrate how in everyday talk family members draw on public texts as resources to create, reaffirm, and contest identities and ideologies. Therefore, while it is important to situate families in larger social contexts, it is also imperative to be attuned to how family members navigate such contexts and negotiate their identities, beliefs, and actions, including linguistic choices and practices.

Contextualizing the study, methods, and participants

Data for this work are drawn from a larger study that investigates language ideologies and identities among young (18–25 years old) Ukrainians who grew up in independent Ukraine with Ukrainian as its official language. As part of this study, I conducted 24 metalinguistic interviews in 2017 and 2018 in a western Ukrainian city where, according to the latest (2001) census, the overwhelming majority of respondents (97%) self-identified themselves as linguistically and ethnically Ukrainian. However, as prior studies (Bilaniuk, 2005, 2017; Kulyk, 2016; Onuch & Hale, 2018) demonstrate, overt identity claims do not always accurately reflect everyday (linguistic) practices; therefore, it is helpful to collect various types of data (Scollon & Scollon, 2004). A month-long visit to the site gave me the opportunity, in addition to conducting interviews, to interact with some of the participants, carry out ethnographic observations, and collect examples from digital (social) media.

The participants were recruited through a friend-of-a-friend approach. All of them were either enrolled in or had completed postsecondary education, majoring in diverse subjects such as music, political science, English, computer science, jurisprudence, engineering, physics, religious studies, etc. Depending on the interviewees' preferences, the interviews were conducted either mostly in Ukrainian or mostly in Russian with inevitable translanguaging. Thus, the linguistic labels I use in this study (Ukrainian, Russian, *surzhyk,* English) are provisional. The collected data are not representative of all Ukrainian youth or all Ukrainians; however, the analysis and findings of this work contribute to a discussion of the sociolinguistic situation in Ukraine.

In contrast to sociolinguistic interviews designed to mask researchers' interest in language (Schilling, 2013, p. 92), my questions focused specifically on language, and thus allowed the participants to express their metalinguistic observations about their families' and friends' linguistic practices. This way the participants were positioned as experts, or consultants, from whom I—taking up a learner's stance—was seeking information, thus minimizing the power asymmetry created by the question–answer interview format (Milroy, 1987). Additionally, in keeping with an open-ended design, participants were encouraged to speak at length, provide individual examples and stories, thus exercising some control over the content and course of the interview. In this chapter, I center my analysis on the interviews with four participants who report practicing Russian/Ukrainian non-accommodation at home. To protect their identities, I substituted the participants' names with pseudonyms.

Participants

Zhanna is 23 years old and lists Ukrainian, Russian, and (a beginner level) English as the languages she speaks. During the interview she spoke Ukrainian. She has a BA in religious studies and works as a manager at a local restaurant. Zhanna is married; at home she speaks Ukrainian while her husband speaks Russian.

Natalia is a single 20-year-old recent graduate with a degree in political science. At the time of the interview she was job searching. The interview was in Ukrainian. She lists Ukrainian, Russian, and English as the languages that she speaks. Natalia's mother, father, and older brother speak Russian, making Natalia the sole Ukrainian speaker in their family.

Kateryna is 23. While she identified Ukrainian, Russian, and English as her languages, Russian was the language of the interview and is the language that she speaks at home with her husband, Petro. Kateryna majored in computer science and works as a web designer.

Petro, a 22-year-old IT specialist with a bachelor's degree in computer engineering, is married to Kateryna with whom he communicates in Ukrainian. He identifies Ukrainian, Russian, and ('so-so') English as the languages that he speaks. During the interview he spoke Ukrainian. Petro and Kateryna also shared with me some of their text messages, which they describe as 'ordinary'.

All four participants received their postsecondary education and live in the city where the interviews were conducted. Natalia, Kateryna, and Petro were also born, raised, and educated (secondary school) in that city. Zhanna was born and raised in the neighboring town. Kateryna is the only participant who went to a Russian-language secondary school (the rest got their education in Ukrainian-language schools); hers and everyone else's postsecondary education was in Ukrainian. Although it appears that the language of the secondary school affects one's 'home' language, Zhanna's husband and Natalia's brother went to Ukrainian-language schools but speak Russian at home.

The 'ordinary' Russian/Ukrainian non-accommodation in family communication

All participants observe that Russian/Ukrainian non-accommodation in their families started naturally, indirectly indicating that their private language practices were not determined by external, public influences. In Zhanna's

TABLE 17.1 Sample 1 of text messages between Petro and Kateryna

Petro ((Ukrainian and English))	Kateryna ((Russian))
	пиццу заказал?
	did you order pizza?
	я сказала, что ты будешь в 12
	I told them that you will be there at 12
заказав	
ordered	
в 12 заберу	
will pick up at 12	напиши, что ты на англ не идешь
	write that you will not attend engl[ish] [class]
okay	

articulation, it happened '*плавно*/seamlessly', without any preliminary discussions. Only later, when being asked by others why she speaks Ukrainian and her husband Russian, she has developed the answer: '*У нас це принципова позиція*/ This is our principled position', but adds, '*нам це не заважає абсолютно*/this does not bother us at all'. Natalia, the only Ukrainian speaker in her family, expresses similar sentiments: '*У нас так з дитинства було*/it's been this way with us since childhood', and '*всі розуміють прекрасно один одного*/we all understand each other perfectly'. Similarly, Petro does not perceive non-accomodation as an obstacle: '*Мені це не мішає; їй це не мішає*/this does not bother me; this does not bother her' and confirms that he and Kateryna understand each other '*та нормально*/just fine'. As noted above, Petro and Kateryna shared with me their 'ordinary' text messages. As evident from an excerpt from their texting exchanges (Table 17.1), there appears to be no misunderstanding between the spouses who, to coordinate their daily activities, engage in Ukrainian/Russian non-accommodation and draw on polylingual resources, including English, a point to which I will return later.

By describing their Russian/Ukrainian non-accommodation as something they just 'do' and asserting that speaking different languages does not prevent mutual understanding, family members not only take up defensive stances to (re)-frame their families as 'normal' but they also display resistance stances against state-sanctioned ideologies of Ukrainian monolingualism. Additionally, if family is a unit of society, then the very existence of such families undermines the view of Ukrainian monolingualism as the key to the country's unity. Furthermore, the participants describe the external evaluative stances toward their familial non-accommodation not as hostile but rather as curious and/or humorous. For instance, Zhanna's friends' initial comments were '*це дуже дивно*/it is very strange'. In Natalia's circle of friends and extended family '*всі сміються, як так?*/everyone is laughing, how come?' Similarly, for Kateryna's friends, '*да, очень смешно*/yes, it [was] very funny', but with time '*все привыкли*/everybody got used to it', so it became the 'norm'. Such metalinguistic reactions, while indicating that linguistic non-accommodation among family members is viewed as unusual, also point to tolerance among Ukrainians toward linguistic diversity, corroborating findings from earlier studies (Del Gaudio & Tarasenko, 2009).

Non-accommodation as accommodation and speakers' rights

The state of political affairs between Russia and Ukraine is projected onto the relationship between the Russian and Ukrainian languages and between Russian and Ukrainian speakers (Pavlenko, 2011, p. 49). Not surprisingly, the geopolitical conflict between the two countries has led to valorizing Ukrainian and vilifying Russian, or as Zhanna describes Russian in Ukraine, '*від мови сусіда до мови ворога*/from the language of a neighbor to the language of an enemy'. At the same time, many Russian-speaking Ukrainians condemn Russia's actions, defend Ukrainian national interests, and strongly identify 'with the inclusive Ukrainian nation without abandoning their accustomed language' (Kulyk, 2016, p. 91). When asked to comment about the future of language in Ukraine, Petro noted, '*Не знаю, у нас кожний день щось міняється*/I do know, we experience changes every day'. Both Zhanna's and Petro's evaluative stances indicate that the participants have to maneuver between the country's fluctuating language policies and attitudes and their own everyday practices.

Pavlenko (2011, p. 53) argues that in independent Ukraine, under the umbrella of 'language rights', the promotion of Ukrainian 'was co-opted to justify what could be alternatively seen as coercive and illiberal monolingualizing policies' that diminish speakers' rights. While all participants—including Russian-speaking Kateryna who states, '*Я живу в Украине; мне необходимо знать украинский язык*/I live in Ukraine; I need to know Ukrainian'—concur that it is imperative to know Ukrainian in Ukraine, they do not passively accept or blindly follow the top-down monolingual ideologies. Instead, they take agentive stances to defend speakers' rights. For instance, Natalia notes that people should be able to speak '*кому як зручно; це вільна держава*/whatever is convenient for them; it's a free country', and observes that while her mother knows Ukrainian, it is simply easier for her to speak and write in Russian. Kateryna recalls that once, when she was caught off guard and automatically replied in Russian in class, her professor reprimanded her for speaking Russian, but her classmate—who personally refuses to speak Russian out of principle—defended her: '*она имеет право*/she has the right'. Kateryna notes that younger Ukrainians tend to be more tolerant toward Russian and Russian speakers. As Natalia notes, '*Я нічого не маю проти людей, які розмовляють російською*/I have nothing against people who speak Russian'. Additionally, because the events of *Euromaidan* marked Ukraine's decisive move toward European integration and the Western ideals of freedom and democracy, Ukraine's monolingual policies can be viewed as infringing on the speakers' rights of its citizens.

Thus, the participants, their friends, and families align in their defense of speakers' rights, and in so doing, challenge the monolingual policies that often masquerade as 'language rights' in Ukraine. Furthermore, it can be suggested that linguistic non-accommodation *is* a type of accommodation when speakers' rights are respected.

Translanguaging and monoglot 'standard' ideology

As noted earlier, while Ukrainian is the official language in Ukraine, people regularly draw on translingual resources that include Russian, *surzhyk*, and more recently English. *Surzhyk*, a fluid and contested phenomenon, is a fraught topic among academics and is generally viewed negatively outside academia because *surzhyk*-vilifying discourses have been circulating in the Ukrainian public sphere for some time. Not surprisingly, the participants in this study define *surzhyk* as '*смесь языков; неправильная речь*/a mixture of languages; incorrect speech' (Kateryna) and evaluate it '*негативно*/negatively' (Natalia). At the same time, all participants indicate that they do not treat people who speak *surzhyk* negatively and admit that they and most people they know use it daily. This incongruity reflects the clash between the abstract notion of a 'pure', 'correct' language and hybrid translingual practices. Of interest, Natalia—who describes her Ukrainian as '*далека від ідеалу*/far from the ideal'—strives for '*чиста*/pure' but not '*літературна*/literary (standard)' Ukrainian because she believes '*мене ніхто не зрозуміє*/nobody would understand me' should she use 'bookish' Ukrainian. Such metalinguistic reflexivity underscores that the state-sponsored and promoted by many Ukrainian academics as 'correct' or 'pure' linguistic norm remains outside the social life of language, as well as its speakers.

If Ukrainian, Russian, and *surzhyk* were not enough, globalization and new media technologies have contributed additional linguistic resources, such as English, to the repertoires of many Ukrainians. For Petro and Kateryna, who both work for international companies, using English at work and at home has become a daily occurrence. Kateryna notes that when she speaks Russian or Ukrainian, she does not translate work-related English terms (e.g. task, banner, preview, team leader) as her husband and co-workers understand them and views such translanguaging as shorthand. She and Petro also use English words and phrases as resources in their text messages, such as 'okay' (Table 17.1) or 'how are you?' (Table 17.2), further hybridizing their practices.

Finally, the participants' drawing on translingual hybrid resources, including *surzhyk*, undermines the belief that using non-standard varieties is reflective of one's intelligence. For instance, Serbens'ka (1994, pp. 6–7, my translation) describes *surzhyk* as 'a crippled language [that] makes a person stupid'. All participants are graduates of universities, and their education, coupled with their insightful metalinguistic discussion of their 'ordinary' linguistic practices, proves otherwise.

TABLE 17.2 Sample 2 of text messages between Petro and Kateryna

Petro ((English, Russian, and Ukrainian))	Kateryna ((Russian))
How are you?	
	нормик ((informal))
	fine
	ты помнишь, что надо быть на связи
да ((Russian))	do you remember that you have to stay connected
yes	
то ти прийдеш до ((NAME)) за	
ключами? ((Ukrainian))	
so will you come by ((NAME)) to pick up	
the keys?	
	да
	yes

Conclusion

The analysis of metalanguage shows that by asserting that Russian/Ukrainian non-accommodation does not inhibit their family 'ordinary' communication and expressing respect for family members' linguistic preferences, the participants defend speakers' rights against the backdrop of the state-promoted Ukrainian monolingualism. Metalanguage, thus, can be understood as a type of stance speakers take toward various linguistic practices and ideologies at the intersection of the public and private.

According to Kroskrity (2016), there are always multiple language ideologies; however, not all of them receive equal attention. In this regard, metalinguistic interviews, complemented by other types of data, can reveal everyday speaker beliefs vis-à-vis state-sponsored language ideologies. While the participants in this study subscribe to the symbolic ideal of 'pure' language, they are not only tolerant toward translanguaging but they also practice it by creatively drawing on Ukrainian, Russian, *surzhyk*, and English. This points to a discrepancy between state-supported monoglot standard ideology and local translingual practices. Additionally, because family both reflects and creates society, family members' metalinguistic comments reveal competing language ideologies that circulate in Ukraine.

In April 2019 Ukrainian parliament approved a law reinforcing a special status of Ukrainian as the sole official language by making its knowledge and use obligatory for all citizens, especially in the public sphere, and relegating all other language varieties to the private sector. It remains to be seen whether the legislation protecting the 'language rights' of Ukrainian would eventually influence ordinary translanguaging practices of many Ukrainians or whether their defense of speakers' rights would go beyond private conversations.

References

Bilaniuk, L. (2005). *Contested tongues: Language politics and cultural correction in Ukraine*. Ithaca, NY: Cornell University Press.

Bilaniuk, L. (2017). Purism and pluralism: Language use trends in popular culture in Ukraine since independence. In M. Flier & A. Graziosi (Eds.), *The battle for Ukrainian: A comparative perspective* (pp. 343–363). Cambridge, MA: Harvard University Press.

Bourdieu, P. (1996). On the family as a realized category. *Theory, Culture and Society, 13*(3), 19–26.

Coupland, N., & Jaworski, A. (2004). Sociolinguistic perspectives on metalanguage: Reflexivity, evaluation and ideology. In A. Jaworski, N. Coupland, & D. Galasínski (Eds.), *Metalanguage: Social and ideological perspectives* (pp. 15–51). Berlin, Germany: Mouton de Gruyter.

Del Gaudio, S. (2015). Украинско-русская смешанная речь 'суржик' в системе взаимодействия украинского и русского языков. [Ukrainian-Russian mixed speech 'surzhyk' in the system of interaction between Russian and Ukrainian languages]. *Slověne, 2*, 214–246.

Del Gaudio, S., & Tarasenko, B. (2009). Surzhyk: Topical questions and analysis of a concrete case. In J. Besters-Dilger (Ed.), *Language policy and language situation in Ukraine: Analysis and recommendations* (pp. 327–358). Frankfurt, Germany: Peter Lang.

Dovchin, S. (2017). The ordinariness of youth linguascapes in Mongolia. *International Journal of Multilingualism, 14*(2), 144–159.

Dovchin, S. (2018). *Dr. Sender Dovchin on translingualism and youth culture*. Retrieved from https://www.diggitmagazine.com/videos/dr-sender-dovchin-translingualism-and-youth-culture

Du Bois, J. (2007). The stance triangle. In R. Englebretson (Ed.), *Stancetaking in discourse: Subjectivity, evaluation, interaction* (pp. 139–182). Amsterdam, the Netherlands: Benjamins.

Farion, I. (2013). *Мовна норма: Знищення, пошук, віднова [Language norm: Destruction, search, revitalization]*, 3rd ed. Ivano-Frankivs'k, Ukraine: Misto HB.

Fournier, A. (2012). *Forging rights in a new democracy: Ukrainian students between freedom and justice*. Philadelphia: University of Pennsylvania Press.

García, O., & Li Wei. (2014). *Translanguaging, language, bilingualism and education*. New York, NY: Palgrave MacMillan.

Hentschel, G., & Taranenko, O. (2015). Мовний ландшафт Центральної України: Українська мова, російська мова, 'суржик' (уживання–мовна компетенція–національне позиціювання). [Language landscape of Central Ukraine: Ukrainian, Russian, 'surzhyk' (usage–language competency–national positioning]. Мовознавство, *4*, 3–25.

Holstein, J., & Gubrium, J. (1999). What is a family? Further thought on a social constructionist approach. *Marriage and Family Review, 28*(3/4), 3–20.

Ivanova, O. (2013). Bilingualism in Ukraine: Defining attitudes to Ukrainian and Russian through geographical and generational variations in language practices. *Sociolinguistic Studies, 7*(3), 249–272.

Jaffe, A. (1999). *Ideologies in action: Language politics on Corsica*. Berlin, Germany: Mouton de Gruyter.

Jaworski, A., Coupland, N., & Galasínski, D. (2004). Metalanguage: Why now? In A. Jaworski, N. Coupland, & D. Galasínski (Eds.), *Metalanguage: Social and ideological perspectives* (pp. 3–10). Berlin, Germany: Mouton de Gruyter.

Jørgensen, J. N. (2008). Poly-lingual languaging around and among children and adolescents. *International Journal of Multilingualism, 5*(3), 161–176.

King, K. A. (2013). A tale of three sisters: Language ideologies, identities, and negotiations in a bilingual, transnational family. *International Multilingual Research Journal, 7*(1), 49–65.

Kroskrity, P. V. (2016) Language ideologies: Emergence, elaboration, and application. In N. Bonvillain (Ed.), *The Routledge handbook of linguistic anthropology* (pp. 95–108). New York, NY: Routledge.

Kulyk, V. (2016). Language and identity in Ukraine after Euromaidan. *Thesis Eleven, 136*(1), 90–106.

Lee, J. W. (2017). *The politics of translingualism: After Englishes.* New York, NY: Routledge.

Masenko, L. (2004). *Мова і суспільство. [Language and society].* Kyiv, Ukraine: Akademiia.

Masenko, L. (2008). *(У)мовна (У)країна. [Provisional country/linguistic Ukraine].* Kyiv, Ukraine: Tempora.

Milroy, L. (1987). *Observing and analyzing natural language.* Oxford, UK: Blackwell Publishers.

Nassenstein, N., & Hollington, A. (Eds.). (2015). *Youth language practices in Africa and beyond.* Berlin, Germany: Mouton de Gruyter.

Ochs, E., & Taylor, C. (1992). Family narrative as political activity. *Discourse and Society, 3*(3), 303–340.

Onuch, O., & Hale, H. E. (2018). Capturing ethnicity: The case of Ukraine. *Post-Soviet Affairs, 34*(2–3), 84–106.

Palviainen, Å., & Bergroth, M. (2018). Parental discourse of language ideology and linguistic identity in multilingual Finland. *International Journal of Multilingualism, 15*(3), 262–275.

Pavlenko, A. (2011). Language rights versus speakers' rights: On the applicability of Western language rights approaches in Eastern European contexts. *Language Policy, 10*, 37–58.

Pavlenko, A. (2013). Multilingualism in post-Soviet successor states. *Language and Linguistics Compass, 7*(4), 262–271.

Pavlenko, A. (Ed.). (2008). *Multilingualism in post-Soviet countries.* Clevedon, UK: Multilingual Matters.

Pennycook, A., & Otsuji, E. (2015). *Metrolingualism: Language in the city.* Abingdon, UK: Routledge.

Piller, I. (2002). *Bilingual couples talk. The discursive construction of hybridity.* Amsterdam, the Netherlands: John Benjamins.

Sacks, H. (1984). On doing 'being ordinary'. In J. M. Atkinson & J. Heritage (Eds.), *Structures of social action* (pp. 413–429). Cambridge, UK: Cambridge University Press.

Schilling, N. (2013). *Sociolinguistic fieldwork.* Cambridge, UK: Cambridge University Press.

Scollon, R., & Scollon, S. W. (2004). *Nexus analysis: Discourse and the emerging Internet.* New York, NY: Routledge.

Serbens'ka, O. (Ed.). (1994). *Антисуржик. [Antisurzhyk].* L'viv, Ukraine: Svit.

Silverstein, M. (1996). Monoglot 'standard' in America: Standardization and metaphors of linguistic hegemony. In D. Brenneis & R. K. S. Macaulay (Eds.), *The matrix of language: Contemporary linguistic anthropology* (pp. 284–306). Boulder, CO: Westview Press.

Subtelny, O. (2005). *Ukraine: A history,* 3rd ed. Toronto, ON: University of Toronto Press.

Tannen, D., Kendall, S., & Gordon, C. (Eds.). (2007). *Family talk: Discourse and identity in four American families.* New York, NY: Oxford University Press.

Tovares, A. (2007). Family members interacting while watching television. In D. Tannen, S. Kendall, & C. Gordon (Eds.), *Family talk: Discourse and identity in four American families* (pp. 283–310). Oxford, UK: Oxford University Press.

Tovares, A. (2012). Watching out loud: A television quiz show as a resource in family interaction. In C. Gerhardt and R. Ayaß (Eds.), *The appropriation of media in everyday life: What people do with media* (pp. 107–130). Amsterdam, the Netherlands: John Benjamins Publishing.

Unger, J. W., Kryzanowski, M., & Wodak, R. (Eds.). (2014). *Multilingual encounters in Europe's institutional spaces.* London, UK: Bloomsbury.

18

ORDINARY ENGLISH AMONG MUSLIM COMMUNITIES IN SOUTH AND CENTRAL ASIA

Brook Bolander and Shaila Sultana

Introduction

Our chapter explores possible ways of rethinking the relationship between language and religion. Adopting a transglossic approach (Sultana, 2015; Sultana, Dovchin, & Pennycook, 2015), we present two case studies based on data collected during ethnographic fieldwork among Muslim communities in Hunza, northern Pakistan, and Khorog, eastern Tajikistan (Case study 1), and in Dhaka, Bangladesh (Case study 2). We thereby pay attention to the ordinariness of English, a choice which is motivated both by the ways our interlocutors variously imagine and use English for the construction of religious identity, as well as by the tendency in the literature to perceive English as somehow 'foreign' to Islam, given its associations with colonialism and the West (cf. e.g. Karmani, 2005).

Our transglossic approach highlights issues of ordinariness from the perspectives of voice and space, through a focus on varying degrees of contextual (physical location and participants), pretextual (historical trajectory of texts), subtextual (ideologies mobilized by the texts), intertextual (meanings that occur across texts), and post-textual interpretations (the ways texts are read, interpreted, resisted, and appropriated). As made manifest in Dovchin's (2017, 2018) research on the ordinariness of youth linguascapes in Mongolia, it is central to take these varied dynamics into account. Indeed, as Dovchin demonstrates, a firm analytical focus on the situatedness that engenders diversity is central to avoiding its exoticization and recognizing instead that diversity is more often viewed and imagined as ordinary. In writing about the ordinariness of English in connection with the construction and performance of our interlocutors' religious identity, we aim to encourage a move away from having to explicitly state that English is not necessarily foreign to Islam, and, by implication, that Arabic is not necessarily central.

We argue that the process by which English becomes ordinary for religious identity can only be studied if we adopt an understanding of religion as situated, discursive, and interactive. While sociolinguistics is firmly committed to the theoretical discussion of variables understood to be intersecting with or performed through language (e.g. gender, age, class), and while there has been a range of productive research on various facets of identity as emergent, relational, and intersubjective, rigorous research on religion is largely lacking. To begin to address this gap, our work with Muslim interlocutors in Pakistan, Tajikistan, and Bangladesh shows that the entanglement of language and religion constitutes both a context and a discourse for the negotiation of identity. Creative language practices that emerge in our face-to-face and online ethnographic data provide insight into this process of negotiation, which we argue offers grounds for a more general discussion of how we might reconceptualize the relationship between language and religion.[1] We show that religious identity for these youths is not so much an adherence to any particular religion; instead, religious identity is constituted by performances, realized in everyday conversations through the use of diverse linguistic and cultural resources, among which English is an ordinary and regular element.

Due to a relative lack of sociolinguistic research on South and Central Asia (exceptions include Bolander, 2016, 2017a, b; Bolander & Mostowlansky, 2017; Dovchin, 2017, 2018; Sultana, 2014, 2015, 2018), the data also contribute to an integration of these underresearched and underrepresented areas in the sociolinguistics of globalization. To provide the rationale for the two case studies presented in Sections 3 and 4, we first turn to the relationship between language and religion.

Rethinking language and religion

Within (socio)linguistics there has been sporadic interest in language and religion since the 1960s, with research becoming more systematic from the 2000s onwards. We find, for instance, the publication of the first encyclopedia on language and religion in 2001 (Sawyer & Simpson, 2001); the emergence of a new field devoted to 'The Sociology of Language and Religion' in the mid-2000s (e.g. Omoniyi, 2010; Omoniyi & Fishman, 2006); and an upsurge in special journal issues on religion (e.g. Darquennes & Vandenbussche, 2011; Karmani, 2005; Mukherjee, 2013). However, a review of the literature highlights that there are only rare instances where scholars explicitly theorize religion, make transparent their perspective and approach, introduce working definitions that could provide grounds for discussion and debate, and reflect upon how their conceptualizations of religion might be compatible with the understandings of language or communication adopted.

This tendency is, however, not unique to sociolinguistics. As stated by Masuzawa (2005, pp. 1–2), '[i]n the social sciences and humanities alike, "religion" as a category has been left largely unhistoricized, essentialized, and tacitly presumed immune or inherently resistant to critical analysis'. It has been regarded 'as a transhistorical and transcultural phenomenon', presumed to be fixed in time and across space (Asad, 1993, p. 28) and studied without recognition that its usage and very categorization are shaped by historical conditions, by perspective, and by power. Belief has, thereby, been favored as 'the guiding concept' leading to 'a concern with interiority, meaning and consciousness […] at the expense of issues of power, practice, and materiality' (Meyer & Houtman, 2012, p. 2). Whereas the challenges posed by the concept of religion have led some scholars to reject the validity of the concept and argue for its disbandment altogether (e.g. Fitzgerald, 2003; McCutcheon, 2003), others call for critical engagement with the notion and for recognition of the pertinence of history, ideology, and power.

Such critiques foreground the study of religion as social (Beckford, 2003), human (Jensen, 2016), and interactional (van der Veer, 2001), intricately connected to power (Asad, 1983, 1993), and as reflecting, and being shaped, by perspective and positioning (Mostowlansky & Rota, 2016). Thus, as stated by Beckford (2003, p. 2),

> whatever else religion is, it is a social phenomenon. Regardless of whether religious beliefs and experiences actually relate to supernatural, superempirical or noumenal realities, religion is expressed by means of human ideas, symbols, feelings, practices and organisations. These expressions are the products of social interactions, structures and processes and, in turn, they influence social life and cultural meanings to varying degrees.

From this perspective, research shifts away from an emphasis on 'models of cultural transmission focused on internalized cognitive systems […]' and hence toward practice (Verma, 2008, p. 9), involving discussions of meaning-making, contestation, and negotiation. Such critical viewpoints on religion encourage its study as spatially and temporally situated interaction, authentication, and knowledge, with scholars variously analyzing how the expression of religion in, and as, ideas, symbols, feelings, practices, and organizations is related to broader social interactions, structures, and processes. This entails working with empirical data in an attempt to study what religion can and might mean and be made to mean through social practice.

We argue that this understanding of religion is epistemologically compatible with the approach to language foregrounded in critical sociolinguistic research, and it offers a vantage point from which to explore how language becomes a possible resource for the negotiation, legitimation, and authentication of religious identity. In our chapter, we view language as transglossic and as an extension of Bakhtin's heteroglossia (cf. Dovchin, Pennycook, & Sultana, 2017; Sultana, 2015; Sultana, Dovchin, & Pennycook, 2015). This perspective allows us to push the exploration of the relationship between language and (religious) identity to include an exploration of voices and how these voices engender new meanings. For example, voices adopted through the use of various semiotic resources—spoken and written texts, images, videos, and photographs—allow individuals to flout the boundaries of modes; and those with borrowed intonation, stress, or paralinguistic features enrich language with new ideological, historical, local, discursive, and interpretive elements (cf. Bakhtin, 1981, 1986). Transglossia also directs attention to a consideration of where voices are borrowed from and how they are recontextualized with new meanings, and hence, become central to the process whereby space becomes (re)constituted. From this vantage point, language no longer remains attached to any specific location, culture, or, as we argue in our chapter, religion.

Ordinary English and religious identity among Ismaili Muslims

The first of our case studies reflects upon ordinary English and religious identity among Shia Ismaili Muslims in Hunza, Northern Pakistan and Khorog, Eastern Tajikistan. Ismailis in these locales belong to the larger transnational Ismaili community, which lives in over 25 countries around the world. Since 1957, it has been led by the Aga Khan IV. Conceived of as an 'intermediary between the divine and human realms', the Aga Khan is the sole individual who can, via his *ta'wil* or 'interpretation', 'reveal the true, inner meaning, *the batin*, of religion', while 'simultaneously [being] a social [and] political [...] leader to Isma'ilis' (Steinberg, 2011, p. 10). By virtue of the community's spread and diversity (e.g. with respect to ethnicity), strategies are needed to draw 'disparate and scattered communities into the Isma'ili complex, [to] bring [...] them into the fold of the imamate' (Steinberg, 2011, p. 15)—in other words, to create unity and a shared identity. This is largely achieved via the Aga Khan IV, who makes widespread use of nation-state symbols and structures, including a constitution and a flag, a cohesive 'development bureaucracy' (Devji, 2009, p. xii), a 'highly centralized [...] institutional infrastructure' (Steinberg, 2011, p. 1), and an official language—English (Bolander, 2016, 2017a, b).

The root of the current importance of English can be traced back to the beginning of the 'modern period in the history of the [...] Ismailis' (Daftary, 2007, p. 473), against the backdrop of the British Raj (1858–1947) (Bolander, 2016). Today, English is readily used in official Ismaili discourse and policy; it has been introduced in Aga Khan Schools and Academies around the world as one or the only language of instruction; its importance is stressed in the Aga Khan IV's speeches and farmans (*edicts*), which are themselves almost solely in English; and, in perhaps the most explicit reference, English is denoted the community's official 'second language', which was chosen as part of a 'language policy' designed to further the community's 'development potential' (Nano Wisdoms Blog).

It was with knowledge of the official importance of English that Brook set out to conduct ethnographic fieldwork among Ismailis in Hunza, Northern Pakistan and Khorog, Eastern Tajikistan. These locales were deemed particularly interesting for understanding the role of English in the integration of individual communities into the Ismaili complex, given that English typically only has third (after Burushaski and Urdu in Hunza) and fourth (after Shughni, Russian, and Tajik in Khorog) language status. In addition, Ismaili communities form a minority in both Pakistan and Tajikistan, which have majority Sunni Muslim populations; yet, Ismaili Muslims form a majority in Hunza and Khorog. Against this backdrop, Brook was intrigued to reflect upon how English might be made important for the construction of religious identity. In an attempt to follow her own understanding of religion as situated, discursive, and interactive, she was careful not to make links between English and Ismaili identity when talking with Ismailis, but to see if and how her interlocutors made English relevant to processes of identity construction.

During interviews and informal discussions, Brook's interlocutors readily suggested an important relationship between English and Ismaili identity, one which is formed and informed by the Aga Khan IV. She was told repeatedly how the Aga Khan's use of, and emphasis, on English inspired individual Ismailis to want to learn English. Ismailis in Hunza, for example, explained the local importance of English by referring to a *farman* ('edict') uttered by the Aga Khan IV during his first visit in 1960, where he ordered his followers to 'think in English, speak in English and dream in English'; and interlocutors from Khorog reported that many people in the region are trying to learn English in an attempt to gain 'direct access' to their spiritual leader, given his own use of English in speeches and farmans. Many interlocutors in Hunza and Khorog deem the Aga Khan's call to learn English as obvious given the perceived status of English as an 'international', 'global' language; at the same time, they claim that Ismaili attempts to learn English are compatible with their 'intellectual faith', which is described as one of 'process' and not 'product'. English, thus, metonymically comes to stand for a community that orients itself toward progress, and sees itself as 'up to date' in comparison to other Muslim communities in Pakistan and Tajikistan (Bolander, 2016, 2017a, b). An example reflecting these perceptions of English's importance is shown in Table 18.1, taken from an interview with two young men in a village in Hunza.

Returning to our argument that transglossia prompts a focus on both voice and space, we are encouraged here by Karim and Saeed to hear the voice of the Aga Khan, whose repeated emphasis on English (*on many platforms, on many forums, he has been saying this on his farmans*) is constructed as central to how Ismailis interpret English. At the same time, it is an emphasis that is tied to the particular geographical space of *these areas*, where *areas* metonymically come to stand for those living in these areas, and hence, given the majority Ismaili population, for Ismailis. Following Clifford (1994, p. 322), it is 'the connection (elsewhere) that makes a difference (here)', with the entanglement between English and Ismaili identity coming to stand for difference between these and other surrounding areas, where English is deemed to have a different status because the people are not Ismaili.

We see, in other words, how contextual parameters—the physical location and participants—are made to interact with textual ones—the Aga Khan's

TABLE 18.1 Interview with two young men in a village in Hunza, Northern Pakistan

Karim:	And specially in these areas people …[1] ah people are trying, people are trying to learn English. Like they want to have a good ah grip on English and that's because- ah only because the farman of Hazir Imam, Prince Karim Aga Khan, he has a- a strongly- like he strongly wants us to speak English, like on many platforms, on many forums, he has been saying this on his farmans, and you can see the schools here. You don-- ah you- you must have seen there is no government school here and there's not even primary school. Every set up is by ah the Aga Khan AKDN, you can see the Diamond Jubilee schools, and this system in the Hunza again.
	<two additional turns>
Karim:	So it's the influence of Hazir Imam.
Saeed:	Influence of religion.
	<interruption>
Saeed:	I think ah religion ah also has played a role a little. But, partly I- I think ah this new generation they're- they're not very religious. It's just the- the realization that they do need to understand it in order to, you know, succeed in life, for a job, for anything. Communicating with the world [because. I don't think these- this new generation is very religious. […] So, it's just the need. Ah the- the requirement. Ah the- the prerequisites, everywhere for a job, for anything.
Karim:	yes.] Exactly.
Saeed:	[So I think
Karim:	But- but] but the fundaments were- the fundaments were set by him.
Saeed:	Yes. [They were
Karim:	The basis.] The realization of th-- telling the people about [the importance of English
Saeed:	Parents- parents] stressing their children to ah s-- study English, learn it, so it could be useful.

1 The transcription of the data is broad, but includes indications of false starts and repetitions (marked using single or double hyphens), overlaps (marked using square brackets), and salient silences (relative to the speakers' pace of speaking; marked using ellipses), as well as instances where the speaker laughs or his/her voice quality is suggestive of laughter (marked with an explicit comment in diamond brackets).

farmans and their historical and spatial trajectory (pretextual), ideologies mobilized by the texts (subtextual), and post-textual interpretations and appropriation. Karim and Saeed invoke the physical locale, asking Brook, as their interactional partner, to look around and see for herself the absence of government schools compared to the presence of those funded by Aga Khan. The Aga Khan's voice is given permanency in his farmans, which are transformed from an oral call to his followers to learn English to written texts, which circulate among Ismaili communities around the world, for example, in the form of pamphlets or booklets. This historical traversal of his voice is essential to understanding how English is subtextually imagined as ordinary in the minds of these young people. Indeed, ideologies of English as central to Ismaili progress are mobilized through the farmans and subsequently appropriated (post-textual interpretation) to coexist with perceptions that English is an index of the community's modern and process-oriented thinking. It is in this way that Karim and Saaeed frame (*Influence of religion*), qualify (*I think ah religion ah also has played a role a little*), and then reframe (*but the fundaments were- the fundaments were set by him*) the Aga Khan as key to local exposure to and attempts to learn English, and hence for English's ordinariness in these areas. As indicated, they thereby simultaneously construct English as a language that has market value (*they do need to understand it in order to, you know, succeed in life, for a job, for anything*), and that, if learned, can facilitate not only a job but also general success in life (*succeed in life, for a job, for anything*).

English, in this example, thus, emerges as an index of religion and, at the same time, as an ideological necessity for economic advancement. Indeed, given the fact that the Aga Khan highlights the importance of economic development for his followers in his farmans, perhaps it does not make sense to treat English as an index of religion as separate from English as a tool for economic advancement. Writing about the former Aga Khan III's farmans in East Africa, Adatia and King (1969, p. 185), for instance, maintain that '[i]t is a constant refreshment in the firmans to find what westerners would call secular and religious inextricably intertwined'. This claim, if applied to language, suggests that neither religious (English for Ismaili identity as Ismaili) or secular (English for economic advancement) does justice to the role played by English. In Table 18.1, Karim and Saeed encourage us to rethink religion as discursive, situated, and interactive. Indeed, through their conversation about English, they construct and co-construct religion, situating it in relation to space and invoking polyvocality. In their appropriation and negotiation of the Aga Khan's farmans, Karim and Saeed, thus, prompt us to go beyond and transgress binaries like secular and religious, and to reflect instead upon how the relationship between language and religion is constructed and made variously meaningful. In this way, we can understand how English can become emblematic of an ordinariness predicated on a shared identity as Ismaili, without suggesting that this relationship between English and religious identity is or can be regarded as fixed.

Ordinary English and religious identity among Muslim youth in Dhaka

For our second case study, we reflect on ordinary English and religious identity among Muslim youth in Dhaka. We, thereby, explore the ways Bangladeshi youths engage with English, Bangla, and other linguistic and multimodal semiotic resources as ordinary practices of life. Building on the previous discussion, this section demonstrates that these resources are used by young adults to perform what are deemed desired Muslim identity attributes in the context of Bangladesh. As in Table 18.1 above, here we demonstrate that this is an identity that is co-constructed and emergent across interaction, and that should not be linked *a priori* to any particular language or semiotic resource.

Islam has played a significant role in the political history of Bangladesh (cf. Riyaz, 2003). In 1947, when the British monarchy ended its colonial rule in the Indian subcontinent, Bangladesh was separated from India and became a part of Pakistan based on religious identity. In 1971, Bangladesh fought against Pakistan for its freedom and won its independence based on a distinct Bengali nationalism and culture. Since then, it seems that Bangladeshis have become increasingly conflicted and divided ideologically with regards to their adherences to, and preferences for, ethnolinguistic Bengali nationalism, Islamic Bangladeshi nationalism, and Islamic religiosity (cf. Riyaz, 2003). On the one hand, Bangladeshi nationalism and 'bangali' culture have been associated with the spirit of independence and specifically promoted and preserved with a strong nationalistic fervour. On the other hand, Bangladesh was declared a Muslim country, and Islam has been used in various ways to ensure a 'nationalisation of Islamism', to fulfill political agendas by the ruling parties (Riyaz, 2003). While these dysfunctional politics have led to unrest and instability, Islamic radicalism has gained popularity among educated upper-class Bangladeshis (Kabir, 2016). There has also been a resurgence of Islamic fundamentalism (Hussain, 2010). Against the backdrop of the rise of radical Islam and extremist groups across the world (Fair & Shepherd, 2006), Bangladesh has also experienced several terrorist attacks (Hussain, 2010).

The following extract, taken from a Facebook (FB) conversation between Ria and Foara, shows how young adults in Bangladesh, within and across the complexity of relations of multiple modes, negotiate their Muslim identity with reference to radical Islamic discourses prevalent in the media. These young adults were participants of an ethnographic research project conducted in a university in Bangladesh (Sultana, 2015). Specifically, Shaila adopted the virtual ethnographic method of 'blended ethnography', which entails collecting both 'user-based' and 'screen-based' data (Androutsopoulos, 2008). She, thereby, observed participants' use of English, Bangla, and other languages; and their manipulation of signs, symbols, and multimodal materials, such as photos, links to newspaper articles, and blog entries and embedded videos. She also engaged in FB messenger conversations with the participants, eliciting participants' own opinions of their practices. This approach enabled her to get a more in-depth understanding of the young adults' language practices, and to thereby ensure the validity, reliability, and trustworthiness of both the research and the findings.

Language practices of young adults were then explored from the perspective of the transglossic framework delineated above. In Table 18.2, we demonstrate how religious identity attributes were negotiated through English and other semiotic resources, which are, in fact, part of the interlocuters' everyday routine language practices. Hence, for these young adults, religion emerges as a way of life demonstrated here through an amalgamation of linguistic and semiotic resources. In this extract, Ria begins by inserting a link to a newspaper article published in the *Daily Star* that focuses on Abu Bakr al-Baghdadi, the leader of the Islamic State. In the article, Baghdadi calls the *ummah* (or global Muslim community) to take up arms against the infidels, or non-believers of Islam.

TABLE 18.2 Facebook conversation between two young adults in Bangladesh

		Facebook conversation
1.	Ria:	lol ((laugh out loud)) **https://www.thedailystar.net/top-news/** **islam-religion-fighting-not-peace-leader-82432** **Islam is religion of fighting, not peace: IS leader** An image grab taken from a propaganda video released on July 5, 2014 by al-Furqan Media allegedly shows the leader of the Islamic State (IS) jihadist group, Abu Bakr al-Baghdadi, aka Caliph Ibrahim, addressing Muslim worshipers at a mosque. Photo: AFP
2.	Foara:	hahahaha. The only thing I ever wanna know about Isis ((Islamic State of Iraq and the Levant)) and this particular dude is what he's smoking.
3.	Ria:	He is on **bideshi** ((foreign)) yaba
4.	Foara:	My money is on acid. **Bideshi** ((foreign)) yaba still leaves you functional. **Er** ((his)) perception of reality is so warped, I am fairly sure he believes unicorns are real and his royal steed is Pegasus
5.	Ria:	**Aye** … i can't get over his rolex!
6.	Foara:	hahaha. I know. I am still laughing at that. Also, I have always wondered – do people just wake up and decide one day "Today onwards I am the leader of a new world!" I mean, if these guys weren't such zealous sociopaths, it would have been fascinating to just study their psychological make up after whatever army finally arrests them. I mean, all that faith, greed, bloodlust whatever might you aside ((said)) – the very idea of waking up one day thinking you are the leader of a new world order is something that makes less sense to me than a salad minus salad dressing.
7.	Ria:	Sociopaths with sycophants…
8.	Foara:	Sociopaths minus sycophants are just lonely serial killers **ar ki**. He decided to make a party out of the bloodlust.

Language guide: Bangla – **bold**; English – regular.

The news shared by Ria on her FB shows that Abu Bakr al-Baghdadi suggests that 'Islam is religion of fighting, not peace'. This invokes a neo-fundamentalist 'deterritorialized' form of Islam in the era of globalization, in which Islam is no longer ascribed to any specific region or territory (Bubalo & Fealy, 2005; Roy, 2007). People in different locations around the world can address Muslims on the basis of Islamic fraternity. With a post-textual reference to the title of the news, both Ria and Foara intend to show the ludicrousness of the statement, using lol/ ha ha ha in lines 1 and 2, that is, instances of what has become en-registered as Internet language (Squires, 2010). In line 2, Foara states that the only thing that interests her about ISIS and Abu Bakr al-Baghdadi is what he smokes. In reply, in line 3, Ria speculates that Baghdadi is addicted to for-eign/ 'bideshe' yaba. Yaba, a Thai word for 'crazy medicine', is a tablet form of methamphetamine, a powerful stimulant which has become popular among drug addicts in Bangladesh. With an intertextual reference to the side-effects of the chronic use of Yaba, which include irritabilities, aggressions, hallucinations, psychotic episodes, paranoid delusions, violent behaviors, mental confusion, memory loss, and psychosis similar to schizophrenia (Islam et al., 2012), Ria seems to mean that the authoritative claim made by Baghdadi is the outcome of a hallucinated brain and drug abuse, and that, consequently, the statement cannot be accepted as authoritative. Thus, subtextually, Ria and Foara are dismissive of Baghdadi's claim and dissociate themselves from his interpretation of Islam. In line 4, Foara states her preference for alcoholic drinks with acid content. She is sarcastic because a 'yaba'-addicted Baghdadi is still deemed functional and hence able to call up the *ummah* to *jihad* and to fight against the enemies of Islam. However, she uses allusions to 'unicorns' (a legendary horse- or a goat-like creature with a spiraling horn on its forehead) and 'pegasus' (a mythical winged white stallion from Greek mythology), and refers to the 'warp reality' visualized by Baghdadi's 'yaba-addicted' brain. In other words, she translocalizes the Greek mythological characters to reframe Baghdadi's claims as mere outcomes of his hallucination and distorted sense of reality; distancing herself further from his perspective on Islam.

In lines 5 and 6, Ria and Foara identify the Rolex around Baghdadi's wrist in the photo from the newspaper article. Here they seem to mock Baghdadi's comfortable socioeconomic status that allows him to wear a luxury watch. Ria uses the photo of the watch to identify the juxtaposition of his accessory and the lifestyle of Islam espoused and circulated in IS propaganda (e.g. simple codes of life and rejection of material pursuits). In line 6, Foara agrees adding, 'today onwards I am the leader of a new world'. She, thereby, separates her voice from the one in this quotation as it echoes the voices of terrorists who rise from nowhere and use social media from secret locations to send terrorist messages to the world. She, thus, uses genre-specific expressions found in the discourse of terrorists to distance herself from them. She also defines leaders like Baghdadi as 'a zealous sociopath' with 'faith, greed, and bloodlust'. This refers to the faith he shows in his understanding of Islam as a religion of fighting, his greed for power as a leader of a terrorist group, and his lust for blood in the form of killing of innocent people all around the world. She also refers to the preposterousness of his claim by referring to the 'salad' without the 'salad dressing' (another item prototypically associated with the Western world, going back to the Babylonian period). In line 7, Ria replies to Faora's question—why these people decide to become leaders of terrorist groups—by stating that they are sycophantic, that is, acting unctuously by using Muslims to their own advantage. They are sociopaths because they do not have a sense of right and wrong and they are involved in killing in the name of 'jihad' (cf., the reports in the newspaper).

With their references to the Rolex watch, unicorn, Pegasus, and salad and salad-dressing, Ria and Foara mark their distance from the terrorist group and its leader. They reflect on the grave and volatile religious order through the apparent lightness of mimicry and sarcasm. Through pre-textual, intertextual, and subtextual references, and manipulation of various kinds of modes—such as written forms of Bangla and English, references to Greek mythological and other legendary mythical characters, Internet language, images, and news links from the national media—they engage in transculturization. They unravel the malicious intentions of these discourses of terrorism, thereby showing their stance toward the type of Islam represented in the discourses and distancing themselves from it.

This extract depicts how young adults can transcend affordances of the written mode in virtual space. By inserting news links along with references to various linguistic and cultural resources, they manipulate various modes of communication. English, thereby, plays an ordinary but vital role in this interaction and hence in the construction of the relationship between language and religion. The interlocutors' English is heavily influenced by local religious and cultural ideologies and social factors. On the one hand, English works within the interface of the global and local and helps young adults' mobility in virtual space. They learn about the discourses of international terrorism in this language and share these discourses on FB for their own purposes (e.g. to adopt a distancing stance toward the type of Islam espoused by IS). On the other hand, the interlocutors question the ideological and value-laden interpretations of Islam with mockery, ridicule, and sarcasm in English while also drawing on other linguistic and cultural resources as part of their repertoire. Consequently, their positioning toward Islamic radicalism and the resurgence of Islamic fundamentalism is expressed at the intersection of both local and global contexts.

Conclusion

Drawing on two ethnographic case studies among Muslims in Pakistan, Tajikistan, and Bangladesh, this chapter takes an empirical, transglossic approach to rethinking the relationship between language and religion. We illustrate how an understanding of religion as discursive, situated, and interactive is compatible with critical sociolinguistic perspectives. We further highlight the need to explore questions of the ordinariness of diverse linguistic and cultural resources, specifically of English in youth language practices, and their role in youths' performances of religious identity. As the analysis of our extracts shows, an approach to religion that sees it as co-constructed and emergent in, across, and through language and other semiotic resources does justice to the entangling of religion's relationship to language. We thereby aim to avoid a paradoxical treatment of religion and language—where language is understood in terms of flows, movement, and process, while religion is rendered static. Religion and language need to be conceptualized in an epistemologically compatible way. This, we propose, is the basis upon which to study (English) language practices as ordinary.

To return then to the phrase in our title of 'Ordinary English', English is not per se ordinary. It is rather rendered ordinary by our interlocutors because it is employed and invoked to perform religious identity. Yet, in accordance with the epistemology adopted in this chapter, being ordinary does not mean it is, can, or should be mapped onto religion, or more specifically onto Islam or any particular orientation of Islam. Instead, English becomes a resource that our interlocutors draw on to engage in processes of positioning, a resource that is simultaneously translocal and polyvocal while also locally meaningful in the situated practices we set out to study.

Acknowledgements

We would like to express utmost thanks to our interlocutors for their time and insights.

For Brook: The research leading to these results has received funding from the People Programme (Marie Curie Actions) of the European Union's Seventh Framework Programme (FP7/2007–2013) under REA grant agreement n° [609305]; and from the University of Zurich's 'Forschungskredit'.

For Shaila: The research presented here has been a part of her doctoral study funded by International Research Scholarship (IRS) and UTS President Scholarship from the University of Technology, Sydney (UTS). Shaila is also indebted to UTS for the position of Associate, Adult Learning and Applied Linguistics Programme, Faculty of Arts and Social Sciences (FASS), UTS which allows her access to resources for conducting research.

Note

1 The two case studies explored in this paper are taken from larger research projects, which encompass both online and offline data. For the purposes of this paper we have chosen one vignette of face-to-face interactional data (Case study 1) and one of mediated interactional data (Case study 2). Both provide insight into young Muslims' engagement with language as a resource for religious identity construction.

References

Adatia, A. K., & King, N. Q. (1969). Some East African firmans of H. H. Aga Khan III. *Journal of Religion in Africa, 2*(2), 179–191.

Androutsopoulos, J. (2008). Potentials and limitations of discourse-centered online ethnography. *language@internet*, 5. Retrieved from http://www.languageatinternet.org/articles/2008/1610

Asad, T. (1983). Anthropological conceptions of religion: Reflections on Geertz. *Man, 18*, 237–259.

Asad, T. (1993). *Genealogies of religion: Discipline and reasons of power in Christianity and Islam.* Baltimore, MD: Johns Hopkins University Press.

Bakhtin, M. (1981). *The dialogic imagination: Four essays.* Trans. C. Emerson & M. Holquist. Austin: University of Texas Press.

Bakhtin, M. (1986). *Speech genres and other late essays.* Trans. V. McGee. Austin: University of Texas Press.

Beckford, J. A. (2003). *Social theory and religion.* Cambridge, UK: Cambridge University Press.

Bolander, B. (2016). English and the transnational Ismaili Muslim community: Identity, the Aga Khan, and infrastructure. *Language in Society, 45*(4), 583–604.

Bolander, B. (2017a). English, motility and Ismaili transnationalism. *International Journal of the Sociology of Language, 247,* 71–88.

Bolander, B. (2017b). Scaling value: Transnationalism and the Aga Khan's English as a 'second language' policy. *Language Policy, 17*(2), 179–197.

Bolander, B., & Mostowlansky, T. (2017). Introducing language and globalisation in South and Central Asian spaces. *International Journal of the Sociology of Language, 247,* 1–11.

Bubalo, A., & Fealy, G. (2005). *Between the global and the local: Islamism, the Middle East, and Indonesia.* Washington, DC: Saban Center for Middle East Policy at the Brookings Institution.

Clifford, J. (1994). Diasporas. *Cultural Anthropology, 9,* 302–328.

Daftary, F. (2007). *The Ismailis: Their history and doctrines.* Cambridge, UK: Cambridge University Press.

Darquennes, J., & Vandenbussche, W. (2011). Language and religion as a sociolinguistic field of study: Some introductory notes. *Sociolinguistica, 25,* 1–11.

Devji, F. (2009). Preface. In M. van Grondelle (Ed.), *The Ismailis in the colonial era: Modernity, empire and Islam, 1839–1969* (pp. ix–xvi). London, UK: Hurst & Company.

Dovchin, S. (2017). The ordinariness of youth linguascapes in Mongolia. *International Journal of Multilingualism, 14*(2), 144–159.

Dovchin, S. (2018). *Language, media and globalization in the periphery: The linguascapes of popular music in Mongolia.* New York, NY: Routledge.

Dovchin, S., Pennycook, A., & Sultana, S. (2017). *Popular culture, voice and linguistic diversity: Young adults on- and offline.* New York, NY: Palgrave Macmillan.

Fair, C. C., & Shepherd, B. (2006). Who supports terrorism? Evidence from fourteen Muslim countries. *Coastal Management, 29*(1), 51–74.

Fitzgerald, T. (2003). *The ideology of religious studies.* Oxford, UK: Oxford University Press.

Hussain, N. A. (2010). Religion and modernity: Gender and identity politics in Bangladesh. *Women's Studies International Forum, 33,* 325–333.

Islam, R. N., Tabassum, N. E., Shafiuzzaman, A. K. M., Umar, B. U., & Khanam, M. (2012). Methamphetamine (YABA) abuse: A case study in young male. *Faridpur Medical College Journal, 7*(2), 102–104.

Jensen, J. S. (2016). Closing the gaps: Some notes on the *making* of perspectives. *Method & Theory in the Study of Religion, 28,* 465–477.

Kabir, A. (2016). Terrorism is global, but its causes are not: Action points for Bangladesh following the Dhaka attack [Blog post]. Retrieved from: https://blogs.lse.ac.uk/southasia/2016/07/18/terrorism-is-global-but-its-causes-are-not-action-points-for-bangladesh-following-the-dhaka-attack/

Karmani, S. (2005). Islam and English in the post-9/11 era: Introduction. *Journal of Language, Identity & Education, 4*(2), 85–86.

Masuzawa, T. (2005). *The invention of world religions: Or, how European universalism was preserved in the language of pluralism.* Chicago, IL: The University of Chicago Press.

McCutcheon, R. T. (2003). *Manufacturing religion: The discourse on sui generis religion and the politics of nostalgia.* Oxford, UK: Oxford University Press.

Meyer, B., & Houtman, D. (2012). Introduction: Material religion—How things matter. In D. Houtman & B. Meyer (Eds.), *Things: Religion and the question of materiality* (pp. 1–23). New York, NY: Fordham.

Mostowlansky, T., & Rota, A. (2016). A matter of perspective? Disentangling the emic–etic debate in the scientific study of religion\s. *Method and Theory in the Study of Religion, 28*, 317–336.

Mukherjee, S. (2013). Reading language and religion together. *International Journal of the Sociology of Language, 220*, 1–6.

Nano Wisdoms Blog. Lebanese Broadcasting Corporation International Interview (Aleppo, Syria and Lebanon). Retrieved from http://www.nanowisdoms.org/nwblog/6073/

Omoniyi, T. (Ed.). (2010). *The sociology of language and religion: Change, conflict and accommodation.* London, UK: Palgrave Macmillan.

Omoniyi, T., & Fishman, J. A. (Eds.). (2006). *Explorations in the sociology of language and religion.* Philadelphia, PA: John Benjamins.

Riyaz, A. (2003). 'God willing': The politics and ideology of Islamism in Bangladesh. *Comparative Studies of South Asia, Africa and the Middle East, 23*(1), 301–320.

Roy, O. (2007). *Secularism confronts Islam.* New York, NY: Columbia University Press.

Sawyer, J. F. A., & Simpson, J. M. Y. (Eds.) (2001). *Concise encyclopedia of language and religion.* Amsterdam, The Netherlands: Elsevier.

Squires, L. (2010). Enregistering Internet language. *Language in Society, 39*, 457–492.

Steinberg, J. (2011). *Isma'ili modern: Globalization and identity in a modern community.* Chapel Hill: The University of North Carolina Press.

Sultana, S. (2014). Heteroglossia and identities of young adults in Bangladesh. *Linguistics and Education, 26*, 40–56.

Sultana, S. (2015). Transglossic language practices: Young adults transgressing language and identity in Bangladesh. *Translation and Translanguaging in Multilingual Contexts, 1*(2), 68–98.

Sultana, S. (2018). Gender performativity in virtual space: Transglossic language practices of young women in Bangladesh. In S. Kroon & J. Swanenberg (Eds.), *Language and culture on the margins: Global/local interactions* (pp. 69–90). New York, NY: Routledge Critical Studies in Multilingualism.

Sultana, S., Dovchin, S., & Pennycook, A. (2015). Transglossic language practices of young adults in Bangladesh and Mongolia. *International Journal of Multilingualism, 12*(1), 93–108.

van der Veer, P. (1996). Introduction. In P. van der Veer (Ed.), *Conversion to modernities* (pp. 1–23). New York, NY: Routledge.

INDEX

Note: *italic* page numbers refer to figures; page numbers followed by "n" denote endnotes.

Abbas, A. 2
Adatia, A. K. 247
Aga Khan IV 244–247
Agha, A. 109
Alim, H. S. 62–63
Androutsopoulos, J. 220
Arnhem Land (Australia): multilingual practices in 90–91, 93–94; translinguistic policing in 94, 99; translinguistic practices in 94–99
assemblages, semiotic 12, 18, 137
assimilation: and asset based pedagogy 62
Austin, J. L. 105–106, 112
Australia: language landscape of 93; *see also* Arnhem Land (Australia)
authenticity: and heteroglossic practices 46–47; and jajangmyeon 33; in Puerto Rico 137; and whiteness 214

Baghdadi, Abu Bakr al- 248–250
Bakhtin, M. M. 37, 106, 243
Bangladeshi youth: ordinary English among 247–251
Barrios, Graciela 107–108
Baudrillard, J. 31
Bauman, R. 25
Beckford, J. A. 243
Behares, L. 104, 108
Bell, G. 15
Bhabha, H. K. 26

Biel/Bienne, Switzerland: diglossia in 55; linguistic landscape of 53; linguistic ordinarization in 49, 53, 58; official bilingualism of 51, 54–58; ordinariness of language practice in 51–56, 57; signage in 52–53, 54
bilingual education: in Puerto Rico 132–138
bilingualism: of Biel/Bienne 51, 54–58; elite 40; fluidity of 143; immigrant 40; in Italian schools 119–124; non-accommodating 229, 230, 233–235, 237; and ordinariness 56; in Puerto Rico 130, 136, 141–142, 143; and translanguaging 146–147; and translingualism 131; in Ukraine 229–237
Binder, A. J. 212
Blommaert, J. 11, 29, 87n7
Blumer, H. 87n1
Boas, Franz 113n1
Bortolini, L. 106–107, 108
Bourdieu, P. 231; on habitus 11
Brazil: and *mestiçagem* 113n1; and monolingualism 106
Briggs, C. L. 25

Cadaval, O. 147, 153, 156n6
Canagarajah, A. S. 63, 91
Chakrabarty, D. 25
China: and globalization 183–184; translanguaging in 191

Chinatowns: in Korea 24–34; *paifangs* in 28; translingual excess of 33; *see also* Incheon Chinatown

Chinese language: banned words 190–191; foreign influences on 181; and globalization 182; governmental regulation of 183; in Korea 31–32; and nationalism 190; Putonghua 181, 183, 186, 188

Chinese script 179; *Baihuawen* 183; foreign borrowings in 184; history of 180–181; and identity 182; and pronunciation 181, 184; and translanguaging 180; *see also* tranßcripting

Chungking Express (film) 2

Cicourel, A. 85, 87

Clachar, Arlene 134

codemeshing 175–176

code-mixing: and identity 147; among Puerto Rican students **133**, **134**; stigmatization of 147

codeswitching 43–45; and codemeshing 175; on Facebook 174; among Mongolian-Kazakhs 167, 169, 175; as resistance 164; strategic 44–45

Cohen, Sacha Baron 198

Colombo, E. 10

Comozzi, I. 10

Comte, August 49

corner shops, Bangladeshi 12–20, *13, 15*; interactions in **16–17, 19**; ordinary diversity of 13–14

Coupland, N. 231

Coutinho, Bruno 105

cyber onomatopoeia: in Yejin blog 221, 222–224, 225

de Certeau, M. 31; on everyday practices 10

De Cock, B. 77–78

Deleuze, G. 207, 214; any-space-whatever 2–3

Del Gaudio, S. 230

De Mauro, Tullio 116

Derrida, J. 107

dialectic diversity: normalization of 146, 148–149, 152–155

dialectic translinguistics: in Washington, DC 146–155

Dialectos Portugueses del Uruguay (DPU) 104, 107–108

dialect translanguaging 150; normalization of 150–152, 156; ordinarization of 152, 154

diglossia: in Biel/Bienne 55; in Uruguay 106

Dingo, R. 177

discourse analysis 38–39, 85; of translanguaging practices 130

diversity: dialectic 146, 148, 152–155; everyday 12, 20; ordinariness of 9–10, 14, 49, 50–51, 91; superdiversity 90, 116, 214; translinguistic 49, 50–51

Dominguez, Marcus 105

Dovchin, S. 61, 91, 99, 207–208; on "dark side" of translingualism 229; on translingual communication practices 195; on youth linguascapes 241

Du Bois, J. 231

EFL (English as a foreign language) 164, 171–176

Elizaincín, A. 104, 108

emoticons: in Yejin blog 217, 221, 223–224, 225

emplacement 31, 32

Enchautegui-de-Jesús, Noemí 156n5

Enfield, N. 93

English language: and class 219, 221; and cosmopolitanism 32; as dominant 164; and Facebook 171–175; and Islam 241–242; and Ismailis 244–247, **246**; and Koreans 218, 219–226; Latino English 155; learning of 171–175, 217–225; market value of 247; and modernity 32; and Mongolian-Kasakhs 169–170, 171; ordinariness of 241–242, 244–252; in Puerto Rican schools 139–140; in Puerto Rico 131–132, 135–136; translingual English 171–172, 174

English-only politics 130; and America First policy 212–213; in white nationalist online forums 211–212; and whiteness 214

ESL (English as a Second Language) 67–68; discourse-centered online ethnography (DCOE) 220

ethnography: blended 248; linguistic ethnography 165, 166; netnography 165; virtual 219, 248

Eurocentrism: and communication 25

everydayness 12; and simultaneity 21; and worldliness 18

everyday practices 10–11

Facebook 165; codeswitching on 174; and English language learning 171–175; Kazakh language on 167, *168*, 170–171; language policing on 218; translingual English on 174

family 229, 231; and language 232
Farion I. 230
Fayer, Joan 134
Flores, N. 63, 68
Foucault, Michel: on *normalisation* 49, 50
Freyre, Gilberto 113n1
Frisina, A. 10
Fukushima nuclear disaster 172–173

Gallagher, C. 63
Galton, Francis 49
Garcez, P. M. 106–107, 108
García, O. 62, 63, 131, 136
Garfinkel, H. 76
geosemiotics 26–28, **27**, 33
globalization 11, 214; and China 183–184;
    and Chinese language 182; and French
    chauvinism 47n4; and language 236;
    sociolinguistics of 4, 61, 242; and
    translingualism 131; and translingual
    practices 99, 131; and translinguistics 92;
    and Ukraine 236
Goffman, E. 27, 85–86; "realms" of 78,
    80, 85
Gonzàlez, I. 37
Goodwin, C. 85, 86
Goodwin, H. 85, 86
Guatttari, F. 214
Gubrium, J. 231–232
Gulamuwu, James 99

habitus 11, 131; socialization of 37, 44
Hall, E. T. 26, 27
Hall, J. 62
Hangeul 32
hashtags: and contextualization 77, 79–80;
    as framing devices 76, 78, 80–85, 84,
    85; #*justsaying* 78–85, 87n3; and social
    interactions 86; as translinguistic 76–78,
    79, 86; on Twitter 76, 77, 78–85; unstable
    functions of 77–78
heteroglossia 243
heteroglossic practices 37–38; and
    authenticity 46–47; of immigrants 38,
    44–46; and translinguistic mudes 40, 44,
    45–46
Higgins, M. 9, 21n1
Hill, J. H. 208, 213
Hjorth, L. 15
Hobsbawm, E.: on invented
    traditions 28, 29
Holstein, J. 231
Horst, H. 15
Hymes, D. 87n2

identity: and Chinese script 182; and
    code-mixing 147; and language 232,
    245; Latino 152–153, 156n4; Puerto
    Rican 134–137; and Spanish 147, 149,
    152–153; and translanguaging 147, 207;
    transnational 207; and Ukrainian 230;
    and white nationalism 211–212
immigrants: heteroglossic practices of 38,
    44–46; language socialization of 38–39,
    40–47
Incheon Chinatown: Chineseness in 26, 31,
    34; Fairy Tale Town in 31; interaction
    orders in 32–33; invented tradition
    in 32–33; and nationness 26, 32, 34;
    paifangs in 28–31, *29–30*; place semiotics
    of 28–31; red, excessive use of 29, *30*,
    34; semiotic landscape of 25, 28–32;
    translingual landscape of 26; visual
    semiotics of 31–32; *see also* Chinatowns
interaction order 27–28, 32–33
interculturality: in Italian schools 122; and
    pedagogy 123
invented traditions 28, 29
Islam: in Bangladesh 248; and English
    241–242
Islamophobia 209–210
Ismailis: ordinary English among
    244–247, **246**

Jacquemet, M. 109
jajangmyeon 32–33
Jajangmyeon Museum 32–33
Japanese youth 171–176; codemeshing of
    175–176
Jaworski, A. 26, 231
Jay Z 199
Jiang Zemin 186
Judis, J. B. 214

Karimzad, F. 218
Kazakh language: on Facebook 167, *168*,
    170–171
Khubchandani, L. 11
King, N. Q. 247
King, Steve 206
knowledge: and power 50, 59n1
Korea: Chinese language in 31–32;
    Chinatowns in 24–34
Korean language 220–224; and English
    learning 218, 219–226; purity of 226
Koreanness 26; and jajangmyeon 33
Kramsch, C. 9
Kroskrity, P. V. 237
Kulyk, V. 230

L'AltRoparlante 115, 118–127
language: and communication 1;
    disinvention of 25; and family 232;
    and globalization 236; and identity
    232, 245; and land 93–94; language
    pluralism 61–64; and mobility 93;
    and performativity 149; and religion
    241, 242–252; and social space 25; as
    transglossic 243; *see also* Mock language
language ideology 218
language pluralism: and difference 62–64; of
    Queens College 61
language socialization 37–38; translinguistic
    45–46
Lee, E. 63
Lee, J. W. 61
Le Pen, Marine 210
linguascapes 1, 217, 241
Lipski, J. M. 140
Li Wei 18, 131, 136; on translanguaging
    space 25, 143
Lyons, A. 18

Macron, Emmanuel 210
Makoni, S.: and disinvention of language
    25; on multilingua franca 98
Masuzawa, T. 242–243
McMillan, B. A. 171
metalanguage 231, 237
metaphysics 112
metapragmatic discourse 217; and English
    learning 219–220; translinguistic
    practices within 218
metrolingualism 1, 195, 217, 228; mundane
    9, 12, 18, 20
Mignolo, W. D. 12
Milani, Lorenzo 117
Milroy, L. 154, 155
Minaj, Nicki 200
mobile devices: and everyday life 14, 20; as
    mediating devices 20; and simultaneity
    21; and space 15
Mock language 213; Mock Arabic 209;
    Mock French 209, 210; Mock Spanish
    206, 209, 213; and racialized Others
    209–211, 213–214; as reterritorialization
    208; as translanguaging 208; and white
    nationalism 208–211
Mohanty, A. 11
Mongolian-Kazakhs 164–165;
    codeswitching among 167, 169, 175;
    English use of 169–170, 171, 175–176;
    online interactions of 164–171; resistance
    strategies of 166–169, 175

Mongolian language 165, 166
monolingualism 104; and Brazil 106; in
    Ukraine 228, 230–231, 234–237; *see also*
    bilingualism
Montessori, Maria 117
Montréal, Canada: multilingual practices in
    42–45, 47n4
Mroczek, K. 20
mudes 37–38, 39; translinguistic 40, 44,
    45–46
multilingualism: embodiment of 195–196;
    everyday 11; and migration 51; in
    Montréal 42–45, 47n4; normalization
    of 153–154; ordinariness of 63, 68; and
    pedagogy 115–127; at Queens College
    68; and remixing 203–204; sociological
    scholarship in 91; and superdiversity 90,
    116; and transmultilingualism 195–196;
    truncated 1; and western/urban bias
    92, 99; and writing instruction 62, 64,
    67–69; *see also* transmultilingualism

nationalism: Bengali 248; and Chinese
    language 190; Islamic Bangladeshi 248;
    white nationalism 206–213
nationness 26; Chinese 34; and Incheon
    Chinatown 26, 32, 34; Korean 32, 34
neoliberalism: and translingualism 176
Nettheim, J. 15
Noble, G. 10
Noonan, M. 63
normalisation 49–50
normality 49–50
normalization: of dialectic diversity 146,
    148, 152–155; of multilingualism
    153–154; *normalisation* 49–50; of
    translanguaging 146–147, 150–152, 156;
    see also ordinarization
Nwabisa (YouTube personality) 197,
    198–203

Obama, Barack 209–210, 212
online English learning 218; and
    metapragmatic discourse 219–220
online-offline nexus 87; and translingualism
    75–76
ordinariness: and bilingualism 56; of
    difference 116, 146; of diversity 9–10,
    13–14, 49, 50–51, 91; of English language
    241–242, 247–252; of everyday resistance
    163; and homogeneity 105; of language
    practice 51–56, 57; and monolingualism
    105; of multilingual education 125–
    126; of multilingualism 63–68; and

normalisation 49; and ordinarization 49; of
Portuñol 106, 110–113; of translanguaging
pedagogy 127; of translingualism 25,
106, 146; of translingual practices 86–87,
112–113, 228; of translinguistic diversity
49, 50–51; of translinguistics 1–4, 58, 91,
156, 218; visibility of 3
ordinarization 49, 58–59; of dialectic
translanguaging 152, 154; of language
use 57; linguistic 39, 53, 58; and
normality 49, 57; and ordinariness 49; *see
also* normalization
Ordinary Language Philosophy 105, 112
Orientalism 1
Otsuji, E. 25

Paek, S. 2
Paris, D. 62–63
Park, J. S. 219, 225
Parkin, D. 87
Parmegiani, A. 61
Parnet, C. 207
Pavlenko, A. 235
pedagogy: asset-based 62; and
interculturality 123; and multilingualism
115–127; translanguaging as 115–116,
118–127
Pennycook, A.: and disinvention of
language 25; on language creativity 67;
on local practice of language 195; on
multilingua franca 98; on translingual
communication practices 195
Phyak, P. 217–218
Pillad, Manoël 2
Piller, I. 91, 164
Pink, S. 15
Pizarro Pedraza, A. 77
polylingualism 1
polylingual languaging 228
Portuñol 104, 105–108; delegitimation of
110–111; ordinariness of 106, 110–113
praxis: ethnographic 10
Puerto Rico: authenticity in 137;
bilingualism in 130, 136, 141–142,
143; code-mixing in **133**, **134**; English
language in 131–132, 135–136; ethnic
identity in 134–137; translingualism
in 130, 131–132; *see also* schools,
Puerto Rico
Pujolar, J. 37

Queens College: cultural and linguistic
pluralism of 61, 63–64; multilingualism
at 68; writing instruction at 66

Raessens, J. 190
religion: and language 241, 242–252; and
social practice 243; and transglossia
243–244, 245
remixing 194; and multilingualism 203–204;
and transmultilingualism 195–196, 199
representation: and actuality 3; and the
ordinary 2–3
resistance: and codemeshing 175; and
codeswitching 164; everyday forms of
163–164; and social media 176–177; and
translingual practices 164, 166–169, 175
reterritorialization: mock language as 208
Rivers, D. J. 171
Rosa, J. 63
Rosario, Carlos 153

Sacks, H. 229
Santos, B. de S. 12
Schatzki, T. R. 10–11
Schlatter, M. 106–107, 108
schools, Italian: academic freedom in
126; bilingual students in 119–124;
interculturality in 122; interdisciplinarity
in 125–126; multilingual instruction in
115, 116–127
schools, Puerto Rican 132–143; bilingual
education in 132–138; bilingualism in
130, 136, 141–142, 143; English language
in 139–140; translanguaging in 132–139;
translingual practices in 139–143; *see also*
Puerto Rico
Scollon, R. 26–28, 33
Scollon, S. W. 26–28, 33
Scott, J. C. 176
Semi, G. 10
semiotic landscapes: translinguistic analysis
of 26
semiotics: of Incheon Chinatown 25–32;
place semiotics 26–27, 28–31; visual 27,
31–32
Severo, Fabian 104, 105, 108–113
Sibgatullina, G. 218
Silverstein, M. 90, 105–106, 108
simultaneity 21
socialization: and discourse analysis 38–39;
of habitus 37, 44; of immigrants 38–39,
40–47
social media: and resistance 176–177; *see
also* Facebook; Twitter
sociolinguistics: ethnocentrism of 90; and
globalization 4, 61, 242; and online
interactions 69–70; representational
politics of 3; translinguistic turn in 2

Spanish language: dialectic hierarchy of 154; and identity 147, 149; Mock Spanish 206, 208; and pan-Latino identity 152–153; in Puerto Rico 131–143; in Washington, DC 149–156

stance 229, 231

stylization: of transmultilingualism 196, 198, 203–204

sublimation 112

Sultana, A. 208; on translingual communication practices 195

superdiversity 90, 116, 214

supervernacularization 77

surzhyk 228, 229, 236

Szabla, M. 87n7

Sztainbok, V. 113n1

Tarasenko, B. 230

Thembe (YouTube personality) 197, 198–203

Thurlow, C. 20, 36

tranßcripting: censoring of 190–191; Chinese characters + alphabetic letters 187–189, *188, 189*; Chinese characters + numerals 186–187; Chinese + English 185–186; defined 184; playful subversiveness of 179–180, 190, 192; and politics 189; and translanguaging 184; *see also* Chinese script

transdialectics: normalization of 146, 148, 152–155

transglossia 1, 206, 208, 217, 251; and religion 243–244, 245; and white nationalism 213

transidioma 1

translanguaging 1, 62, 206, 217, 228; and bilingualism 146–147; as border crossing 207; and Chinese script 180; delegitimation of 110–111; dialectic 150; and dialectic research 154; and fluidity 147; Mock language as 208, 213; normalization of 146–147, 150–152, 156; and online technology 87n2; as pedagogy 115–116, 118–127; ordinariness of 106–113; in Puerto Rican schools 132–139; and social identity 147; and space 25; and tranßcripting 184; and transnational identity 207; in Ukraine 236; in white nationalist online forums 207

translingualism 217; and bilingualism 131; critiques of 130–131; everyday practices of 166; and globalization 131; of global peripheries 91; as grassroots practice

164; and language difference 63; and multilingualism 63; and neoliberalism 176; and online communication 75; ordinariness of 25, 49, 50–51, 106, 146; and popular media 133–135; in Puerto Rico 130, **141, 142**; as social movement 131; and writing instruction 63; *see also* transmultilingualism

translingual practices 1; discourse analysis of 130; and excess 29, *30*, 33, 34; and globalization 99, 131; within metapragmatic discourse 218; online 217–226; ordinariness of 86–87, 112–113, 228; in Puerto Rican schools 139–143; and resistance 164, 166–169, 175; in Uruguay 104–113; in Yejin blog 221–222

translinguistics: fetishization of 2; and globalization 92; as "innovative" 2–4; in/visibility of 3; ordinariness of 1–4, 58, 91, 156, 218; and space 3; spatial orientation of 25–26; and time 3

transmultilingualism 194; as embodied practice 203, 204; and globalization 194–195; multilingual communication as 194; performance of 194; and remixing 195–196, 199; stylization of 196, 198, 203–204; and Vagina Varsity campaign 196–203; *see also* multilingualism; translingualism

Trump, Donald 206, 208–209

Trump, Melania 212

Twitter: hashtags, use of 76, 77, 78–85

Ukraine: bilingualism in 229; and globalization 236; state-promoted monolingualism in 228, 230–231, 234–237; translanguaging in 236

Ukrainian 228–231, 234–237; and identity 230

Umbrella Movement 189

Uruguay: diglossia in 106; and monolingualism 106; translingual practices in 104–113; and white nationality 105, 113n1

Vagina Varsity campaign 196–203; euphemism in **200**, 201–202, **202**; Hip Hop, incorporation of 198, 199; timetable of **197**; transmultilingual practices in 196–203

Varis, P. 12

Velayutham, S.: on everyday multiculturalism 11

Washington, DC: demographics of 147, 156n3; dialectic diversity in 148–149, 152–154; dialectic translinguistics in 146–155; dialect shifting in 150–152; Latino identity in 156n4; Spanish language in 149–156
WeChat 185, 190; tranßcripting on *185*
Wessendorf, S. 10
white nationalist online forums 206, 210; English Only politics in 211–212; and gender 212; and identity formation 211–212; and masculinity 212, 214; Mock language in 208–211; translanguaging in 207
whiteness: and authenticity 214; and English Only 214; naturalizing of 207; and ordinariness 206–207, 214
Whorf, Benjamin 108

Williams, Q. 195, 196
Wise, A. 11
Wittgenstein, L. 105–106, 112
Wood, K. 212
worldliness 9, 12; and everydayness 18
Wu, Kris 191–192

Xi Jinping 187

Yanukovich, V. 230
Yejin (English learning blog) 219–225, *223*; correct Korean on 224–225; cyber onomatopoeia in 221, 222–224, 225; emoticons in 217, 221, 223–224, 225; metacommentary in 220; on translinguistic practices 221–222

Zhu Hua 18

Made in the USA
Las Vegas, NV
04 April 2021

20734018R30155